The Complete Database Marketer

❏ ❏ ❏

SECOND-GENERATION STRATEGIES AND TECHNIQUES FOR TAPPING THE POWER OF YOUR CUSTOMER DATABASE

Revised Edition

Arthur M. Hughes

McGraw-Hill

New York San Francisco Washington, D.C. Auckland Bogotá Caracas Lisbon
London Madrid Mexico City Milan Montreal New Delhi San Juan Singapore
Sydney Tokyo Toronto

ISBN 1-55738-893-8

Printed in the United States of America

Library of Congress Cataloging-in-Publication Data

Hughes, Arthur Middleton.
    The complete database marketer : second-generation strategies and techniques for
tapping the power of your customer database / Arthur M. Hughes. -- 2nd ed.
        p.   cm.
    Includes index.
    ISBN 1-55738-893-8
    1. Database marketing. I. Title.
HF5415. 126.H84   1996
658.8'4--dc20   95–21714

2   3   4   5   6   7   8   9   0   BRB/BRB   9   0   2   1   0   9   8   7

Contents

Preface

Database marketing has come a long way since the first edition of this book appeared in 1991. At that time, not more than 5 percent of the Fortune 1,000 were doing any active database marketing. Since then, database marketing has arrived:

- almost every major corporation in the United States and Canada has appointed a Director of Database Marketing. There have been many very profitable databases built and maintained.

- every trade magazine has a department devoted to this subject; there are successful newsletters devoted to it.

- attendance at the National Center for Database Marketing's two annual conferences has grown to more than 1,000 per event. Many competitive conferences have sprung up.

Despite all of this activity, not all database marketing programs have been successful. There have been some notorious failures. The central problem which underlies most of the failures has been this: an inability to devise a profitable strategy for use of the database. Just compiling an accurate and clean list of customers is not enough. You have to do something profitable with that list, or all your money will be wasted.

What is the correct strategy? The answer is simple: a database will be profitable only if the customer sees some personal benefit for himself in being on it. When creating a database, say to yourself, "Why would I want to be on this database? What would be in it for me?" If you can't find a good answer to that question, don't build the database.

Success in database marketing does not involve discounts. Most successful database members pay full price. What they get as benefits are recognition, service, information, helpfulness, and other rewards which mean a great deal more to them than they cost the company which is providing them.

This edition keeps much of the material that made the first edition so popular. I have added much new material, reflecting the rapid pace of innovation in our industry. In particular, most of the material in chapters 6, 7, 10, 19-26 and 28 is entirely new.

Communication methods with customers are undergoing a revolution. E-mail, fax, interactive TV, and the Internet are fast overtaking coupons, shelf space, mail, telephone, and personal contacts as the way to carry on a successful dialog. Database marketing is in the midst of a terribly exciting revolution. These are great days to be alive.

Acknowledgments

I have interviewed and quoted scores of people in the process of writing this book. Most of them are quoted by name. But there are some others to whom I owe a special debt of gratitude for working with me, providing leadership, and helping me to understand this exciting new marketing method. Among these people are:

Paul Wang, Associate Professor of Database Marketing, Northwestern University. Paul taught me the essentials of lifetime value and customer migration. He is a dynamic, exciting lecturer, and a good friend.

Victor Hunter, President of Hunter Business Direct, Milwaukee, who taught me most of what I have learned about business to business database marketing.

Ben Spaisman, President of ACS, Inc., who started with a small direct mail service bureau and turned it into a major player in the modern database marketing world.

Arthur M. Hughes

Introduction

The Old Corner Grocer

Sally Warren was surprised. She was used to getting commercial messages in the mail, but this one was different. The St. Paul Luggage Company was writing her to congratulate her on her son David's upcoming graduation from Hobart. In the letter, they suggested that she and Dan consider giving David luggage as a graduation present. The letter included a small colorful catalog featuring St. Paul luggage. But the letter suggested that she could probably beat the listed prices through sales in the three stores in Rochester that carried the famous St. Paul brand. The store names were listed along with the direct dial number of the luggage departments. The topper was a $5 rebate check good at any of the three stores, or also good if she ordered the luggage direct using an 800 number.

Sally Warren's relationship with the St. Paul company went back more than a year, when she and Dan bought their first set of matched luggage for a trip to Florida. Included in the package was an owner registration form offering a $5 rebate from St. Paul's for filling it out and returning it. She did so, and received her check. Six weeks later she also received a nice telephone call from a customer service rep at St. Paul asking, "How did you like your trip to Disney World?" They had a nice talk about Disney World, her family and her job, but not much about luggage.

Six months after that first call, when Sally's daughter, June Baumgartner, gave birth to Sally's first granddaughter, Sally received another letter from St. Paul's congratulating her on becoming a grandmother and suggesting either a St. Paul's Stroller or Car Seat as a useful gift. St. Paul was becoming a household word for the Warrens!

What Sally doesn't know yet, because it is still in the future, is that before she and Dan take that long, planned vacation to Spain (which she told the St. Paul's customer service representative about), she will get another letter from St. Paul's wishing them well in Spain, suggesting that they both might want to take along two matching overnight bags specially designed to fit into an airplane overhead compartment.

Sally Warren was experiencing database marketing, the way that business will be conducted in the future. It is a system that sees in every customer an opportunity for a long-term relationship. In past years, marketing aimed at making a sale; database marketing begins with the sale and aims at establishing a lifetime friendship.

Our mythical St. Paul Luggage Company has established a Customer Marketing Database: an interrelated series of computer records about the Warren household that enables St. Paul to know and retain a hundred useful facts about this household and to bring them to bear at the right time.

This is what the corner grocer did in the old days. He knew that the Warren's daughter was having a baby and that their son was graduating from Hobart and, if he was successful, he used this information in his work. That was why his customers kept coming back to him, even though the supermarket down the street had lower prices. But the corner grocer is no more. The rising tide of mass markets and discounted prices did him in. Stores in the Seventies, Eighties, and Nineties became impersonal warehouses where no one knew anyone, and clerks were impossible to find.

Database marketing exists today because of one important development: every year, the price of storing and using information has become cheaper and cheaper. The constant improvement in microchips means that vital facts about 800 customers that the grocer used to keep in his head can now be maintained on 8 million St. Paul customers on a mainframe computer.

St. Paul's has set up an integrated system of software, direct mail, telemarketing, rebate checks, and intercompany data exchange which is coming closer and closer to recreating the marketing technique of the corner grocer.

Think about it: from what Sally told them on their first telephone call, they learned that Sally's daughter June was recently married to Jack Baumgartner and that the couple were living in Oswego. They stored that information in Sally Warren's file.

Figure I-1 The Old Corner Grocer's Store

Once a month, St. Paul's Stroller and Baby Car Seat Department gets a list of expectant mothers. They were able to link expectant mother June Baumgartner in Oswego with Sally Warren in Rochester and know that they had a proud grandmother who was in the market for the perfect gift. The corner grocer would have done this effortlessly. St. Paul required a lot of advance planning, organization, and software, but they did it. And what's more, if they hadn't done it, they wouldn't have been able to maintain market share in the face of modern competition!

That is what this book is about—database marketing, as defined by the National Center for Database Marketing:

> *Managing a computerized relational database system, in real time, of comprehensive, up-to-date, relevant data on customers, inquiries, prospects and suspects, to identify our most responsive customers for the purpose of developing a high quality, long-standing relationship of repeat business by developing predictive models which enable us to send desired messages at the right time in the right form to the right people— all with the result of pleasing our customers, increasing our response rate per marketing dollar, lowering our cost per order, building our business, and increasing our profits.*

SOME BASIC DEFINITIONS

We need to distinguish a number of terms: let's begin with direct marketing and distinguish it from general advertising.

Direct marketing is any marketing activity in which you attempt to reach the consumers directly, or have them reach you:

- A television or radio ad which features a telephone number to call for information or to order the product.

- A print ad with a coupon, an order solicitation, or a telephone number to call.

- Any direct mail piece or catalog sent to a household, designed to sell a product or service.

General advertising measures its success by whether possible customers are aware of or can recall your message. Direct marketing measures its success by whether the profits from direct sales exceed the cost of producing these sales. General advertising aims at projecting an image, positioning the product, and increasing general awareness; direct marketing aims at sales and generating leads.

Direct marketing has been around for a long time, but has been growing very fast in comparison with other forms of marketing. It has consistently grown at twice the rate of the United States' gross national product. It is and will continue to be the hottest growth area in advertising for the foreseeable future.

Database marketing is derived from direct marketing: the advertiser maintains an active list of customers and prospects which is updated on a regular basis with information about the customer's response to your message. It is the newest and fastest growing part of direct marketing. It has these features:

1. A list (database) of customers and prospects is maintained on a computer using software which permits ongoing revisions of information about each person.

2. The database is actively used by several different people at the same time to:

    — add names of customers and prospects to the database;

    — enhance these names with demographic and lifestyle information;

    — correct and clean the names and addresses;

    — plan marketing strategy using information from the database;

    — select names for mail or telephone contact, developing source codes for each different marketing package or message;

    — post each customer's record with his or her response to direct marketing with dates, amounts, and source codes, and new information specifically requested in the outgoing message;

    — prepare frequent reports on the results of marketing efforts and survey questionnaires; and

    — use the information in the database in a continuing, planned program which builds relationships with the customer and promotes sales.

INDIVIDUAL MARKETING

Direct marketing attempts to reach groups of potential customers. You screen media and mailing lists to concentrate on those most likely to reach groups of people who will respond and buy.

Database marketing attempts to talk one-on-one with people about whom you already know a lot. You want to make customers feel you have a product just for them. You build their loyalty to your product and service because you have demonstrated that you have taken the trouble to learn and remember their past purchases, past requests, past complaints, their lifestyles and interests. They feel that you know them and understand them.

I recently spent a night in a Hyatt Hotel in San Francisco. About 9:30 P.M., I pushed the button on the telephone marked "In-Room Dining" to order a hamburger. The operator said, "Hello, Mr. Hughes. What would you like to eat this evening?" I was surprised and pleased. It sounded as if she had been sitting by the phone all evening, hoping that I would call!

A week later, I stayed in another very new, very large, and very expensive hotel in San Francisco. I again pushed the button for room service. The operator did not know my name. He asked me what room I was in. I had to go to the dresser to look at my room key to be sure. He didn't know!

The Hyatt had a marketing database which permitted the operator to know my name as soon as I picked up the phone. I had only checked in one hour before the call, yet they already had my name on their system. A small matter, but enough to make me remember the Hyatt. I have forgotten the name of the other hotel.

THE IMPORTANCE OF COMPUTERS

Of necessity we will spend much time in this book talking about computers: what you can do with them, and what they will do for your business. There is no getting around it—database marketing owes its existence to the dramatic cost reductions and efficiencies made possible by what has happened to mainframe computers in the last ten years. Most of the techniques we will be discussing were possible, but not cost-effective, a few years ago. The way computers are developing, some techniques in this book may be obsolete ten years from now. We are on a very fast track. The race will go to the swiftest: the companies that learn these new techniques, and learn how to adapt their businesses to them.

If you are not computer literate, do not worry. There is nothing in this book that you can't understand or that will force you to consult some other book or expert. This is a book for marketing professionals, not for computer experts. As we introduce concepts that involve computers, we will explain what we mean in layman's language. Those who already know computers can skip these brief definitions.

THE CIRCLE OF PROFITS

If you took the time to study the old-fashioned, successful corner grocer you would have noticed his technique. He kept his eyes and ears open. He chatted with customers as they came in. I used to think that he was just wasting time: "Why doesn't he spend his time out in the warehouse working, instead of making small talk with the customers?" I thought to myself.

How wrong I was! Today's successful store manager is busy in the warehouse. He runs a clean, well-stocked, impersonal store where the customer never gets to know anyone and is loyal only until the competitor's ad appears in tomorrow's newspaper.

In the next few years all successful stores will begin to return to first principles, and treat their customers as the old-fashioned grocer did. They will be exploiting the circle of profits (Figure I-2).

Every contact with a customer will be used as an opportunity to collect more data about the customer. This data will be used to build knowledge about the customer. The knowledge will drive strategy leading to practical, directly personal, long-term relationships which produce sales. The sales, in turn, will yield more data, which will start the process all over again.

Figure I-2 The Circle of Profits

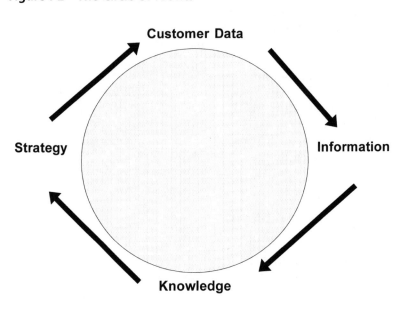

Overview

Marketing to Individuals

HOW A DATABASE AFFECTS MARKETING STRATEGY

In their stimulating book, *MaxiMarketing*, Stan Rapp and Tom Collins opened our eyes to the dramatic changes in marketing which began in the late 1980s:

> *The common wastefulness of the mass advertising of the past is giving way to the newly affordable ability to locate and communicate directly with a company's best prospects and customers. And this new-found ability can be equally rewarding to a manufacturer, a retailer, a service company, or a catalog merchant . . . Of all these changes, surely the most revolutionary is the ability to store in the computer information about your prime prospects and customers, and, in effect, create a database that becomes your private marketplace. As the cost of accumulating and accessing the data drops, the ability to talk directly to your prospects and customers—and to build one-to-one relationships with them—will continue to grow. A rising tide of technological change has brought this golden moment of opportunity. Almost everyone in advertising has heard their message and accepted it. In every major company, every agency, in every conference and convention, marketers are discussing ways of taking advantage of this golden moment and building a functioning marketing database for their company or client.*

Rapp and Collins cautioned: "*MaxiMarketing* is not a textbook or a how-to book. It is a "think" book that aims not to solve your advertising and marketing problems, but to stimulate you to think about them in a new way so that you can solve them yourself."

The book you now hold in your hands, *The Complete Database Marketer*, is a how-to book. We begin where Rapp and Collins left off in *MaxiMarketing* and their follow-up book, *The Great Marketing Turnaround*, to provide you with some of the background information necessary to create a functioning marketing database in your own situation.

The Complete Database Marketer is written for two audiences: the senior executive planning marketing strategy and the middle-level staffer who is actually building a database, setting up loyalty programs, developing marketing initiatives, and running a customer service program.

The Complete Database Marketer is state-of-the-art. Everything that you will read in these pages is either in existence or in the active planning stage somewhere. This book is for creative people who take ideas and run with them to make profits for their companies.

Database marketing has become a buzzword. Books and articles are written about it, and a National Center exists to bring professionals together. Every major and medium-sized corporation has appointed a Director of Database Marketing who is setting up or managing a customer database. If you are not sure exactly what it is, don't be embarrassed—many people still don't. (But then, they haven't read this book yet!)

Whether you are selling boots or boats, software or service, cars or computers, pharmaceuticals or financial services, to market effectively today you need a marketing database that links you to your loyal customers who are eager to be *the first to learn* about your new offerings. You will need to be linked to active prospects whom you will transform into loyal customers. You will need to use the information in the database to understand your customers and to communicate with them one-on-one.

A marketing database is not simply an "add-on" marketing technique which can be used to supplement your existing program. That is what it may be at first. But to make maximum use of database marketing, your entire *marketing strategy* must change. Your objective is no longer just to sell the product—*it is to build a lifetime relationship* with customers who will buy your products again and again and again. These may be your dealer's customers—but they are also yours.

This book will tell you how to build a marketing database and how to use it to establish and maintain profitable lifetime relationships with your customers.

We begin with a strategic overview which addresses the questions: How will database marketing affect your marketing strategy? How will it change the way that you run your business so as to create the maximum of loyal repeat business at the lowest possible cost?

THE CUSTOMER'S NEW ROLE

Mass marketing has generated a marketplace with some notable features:

- high quality products and services at reasonable prices;
- a sophisticated delivery system;
- a highly competitive sales environment; and
- affluent and informed customers.

But in the success of mass marketing, we have lost something valuable. In our drive to reach more and more people in a cost-effective way, we have lost contact with people as individuals. Instead of reaching out to them as valued repeat customers, working to maintain their loyalty, we treat them as if they were unknown masses. We barrage them with discount coupons, 15-second commercials, and junk mail. As providers, we have been acting as if price, product positioning, and image were the only important factors in sales.

The nature and desires of our customers are changing. These changes are having profound implications for marketing strategy. What are these changes?

- There are many more two-income families who have fewer children, more education, and less time for shopping. Their needs are no longer simple. They want a wider variety of choice and more personal services.

- It is no longer useful to categorize buyers into simple groups, such as manufacturing employees, government personnel, and service workers. Today customers spend their working days in thousands of occupational specialties which didn't exist twenty years ago. Many of them have very specialized needs.

- Customers are becoming skeptical and demanding. Most of them are very intelligent and knowledgeable and want more information about products than can be printed in ads or on packaging. They want a wider, more diverse group of products than they have encountered in stores as they exist today.

INDIVIDUAL MARKETING

There is a way in which the modern corporation can take advantage of these trends to develop a lifelong bond of loyalty with its customers. It is possible to develop individual marketing programs designed for each customer and prospect. We can build one-on-one relationships of recognition and service that will keep our current customers and win over users of competing brands.

The method is called database marketing. It consists of capturing quantities of information about current customers, and using that information to promote repeat sales and build an ongoing relationship. In a way, it is bringing back to us something that was lost in the development of mass marketing during the last thirty years. In much of retailing prior to mass marketing, we had truly personal service, recognition, and one-on-one relationships. In the average neighborhood, the grocer knew you and your family by sight. He knew what you wanted. He ordered things specially for you. He carried packages out to your car. He gave you credit. He talked to you as a friend. He established a two-way bond of communication that kept you as a loyal customer, made you feel appreciated, and built his business.

Mass marketing ended this relationship. Stores grew larger and more impersonal. Price, not loyalty, ruled shopper's decisions. Prices went down, quality went up, competition increased. But personal service went down; individual recognition and loyalty faded away.

Through database marketing, it is today possible to recapture some of that one-on-one communication, some of that recognition and service that was lost in mass marketing.

Building Customer Relationships

The corner grocer kept his customers coming back because he knew them personally, greeted them by name, remembered their special requests, and gave them personal, individual services. A modern customer database on a powerful computer allows a modern corporation to recreate many of these lost relationships and services. Find out who your customers are, and build a database that contains not only their names and addresses, but also individual information vital to maintaining a close relationship, such as:

- purchasing history;
- family makeup: age, education, children, pets;
- purchasing ability: income, home value, assets, credit cards;
- occupations of all family members;
- leisure-time interests: hobbies, travel propensity, sports, what kind of car they drive;
- responsiveness to direct mail, to telemarketing, to buyer's clubs;
- media interests: magazines, TV, radio, newspapers; and
- special requests, complaints, returns, refunds, mistakes.

This is basic information, the kind of data which the old corner grocer effortlessly kept in his head and recalled every time a customer walked into his store. Gathering this kind of information and storing it in a modern marketing database, through methods which are outlined in this book, is really not that difficult. Ten years ago it was too expensive to capture and use all this information effectively. But the price of computers and software has declined dramatically, and the cost per piece of information stored is a fraction of one percent of what it cost little more than a decade ago.

The difficult feat, however, is making creative and productive use of this information in ways that will help your company to create a one-on-one dialog with customers, to build loyalty and repeat sales. This part of database marketing, the creative part, cannot be described as in a cookbook; it will vary with each business situation. What you will find in this book are hundreds of examples and suggestions to stimulate your imagination so that you can develop your own marketing strategy.

BASIC STRATEGIES

Some basic strategies are common to virtually all marketing databases:

- Develop a method for exchanging information with your customers.

- Build a comprehensive customer service system.

- Determine who your preferred customers are, and work to build their loyalty.

- Compute the lifetime value of your customers to determine the economics of your marketing system.

- Develop a customer profile, and use it to clone your best customers.

- Test and count. Make every marketing initiative an experiment to improve your understanding.

- Change roles, attitudes, and compensation systems within your company to take maximum advantage of your new relationship with your customers.

- Set up a working team to manage your database effectively.

Let's explore these strategies.

Exchanging Information

One of the most valuable things that your company has to offer is something that is not even on your price list. It is information: information about what is available, how it works, what special features it has, how it compares with the competition, how to repair it, where to get it. In your ads, of course, you try to provide some of this data. But ads cluttered with information do not sell well—they must be kept simple.

Two groups are particularly eager for this information: your existing customers and your active prospects:

- I just bought a new van with all-wheel drive. It drives wonderfully, but I don't understand how the all-wheel transmission works. The salesman couldn't explain it to me. The manual was uninformative. I would love to know how it works.

- A new version of my accounting software has just been announced. Does it solve the problem I was having with accounts payable? Is it worth it for me to upgrade?

Somewhere in your company there are people who have the answers to questions like these. Your strategy should be to find a way, inexpensively, to give your customers and prospects this kind of technical information, and make them feel good about having asked for it.

At the same time, your customers have information that you want and need for your marketing program:

- Why did they select your product?
- What features really persuaded them?
- What other products that you sell are they likely to buy this year?
    Successful database marketing is a process of constantly exchanging information. Every contact with a customer (an owner registration form, a rebate coupon, an order form, a delivery receipt, a policy premium payment, a telephone call) becomes an occasion to ask a few more questions that provide more information for your database. At the same time,

as you learn more and more about your customers, you will begin to appreciate what they want to find out or buy from you. Use each occasion to give them specialized and pertinent information—a fair exchange is no robbery.

Developing Relationships

Somewhere in the fine print in the instructions that come with your product you have included an 800 number. Support consists of a few pleasant but harassed operators and a telephone system which puts the customers constantly on hold listening to music. Does this sound like your company?

With database marketing, that strategy has to change. Your image has to change. Your company has to appear to your customers like an old and valued friend: someone who is always there, ready and willing to listen; ready to provide advice, help, suggestions, ideas, service, information. General Electric has pioneered with this approach. With database marketing, customer service becomes your front line. Your ads say that you are caring and helpful, but your customer service has to be caring and helpful. You must change your whole approach to customer service:

- You will need to have enough Customer Service Representatives (CSRs) so that your customers are seldom kept on hold for very long. Your Call Center has to have modern call distribution equipment as described in Chapter 17.

- CSRs must be trained to know all of your products intimately: their good and bad features, how they work, how they differ from the competition. Their functions are described in Chapter 11.

- Backing up your CSRs are people in many different departments throughout your organization who have been trained when called on by your CSRs to help build customer relationships by providing helpful information. These are people in engineering, in product design, in the warehouse, in delivery, in billing.

- Your CSRs are constantly gathering information from your customers and entering it into your database. When customers call, they get the names and addresses, and information— about lifestyles, reasons for buying the product, how it is used, what they want in the way of new products or new features. This information is retrieved instantly whenever the customer calls again. It is used in follow-up thank you letters, and new product announcements.

- Finally, your CSRs are always selling. Not the hard sell; the very soft sell. "Our new Version 4.0 gets around that problem. As an existing customer, you can trade up for only $179.95. I could have it sent out to you this afternoon."

Selecting Preferred Customers

Not all customers are alike. Some will buy from you again and again. Some buy once, then disappear forever. Most companies treat them all alike. With database marketing, your strategy changes: you use the database to determine who your best customers are and then you lavish your services and attention on them. At the same time, you provide minimum service to your least profitable segment. Why discriminate? Because it is more profitable to discriminate. You want your best customers to feel they are in a privileged class. You want to pamper them. You design and provide super services that you could not afford to give to all your customers.

How do you determine who your preferred customers are? Recency, Frequency, Monetary (RFM) analysis, described in Chapter 7, provides a sophisticated analytical technique which can get you started. You will have to add your own ideas to it, based on your experience and your knowledge of your industry. The ranking system will rely on the information held in your marketing database. You will store your preference ranking in each customer's record. Then you will use that ranking to determine a whole range of benefits and services (described in Chapter 8) which will keep your best customers loyal and stimulate your second-best customers to buy more, so they also join the "preferred class."

As a part of your strategy, therefore, you must develop and install loyalty-building systems: preferred member clubs, newsletters, new product announcements, sneak previews, gold cards, "loyal member nights." You will find ways to let everyone recognize your preferred customers: your employees, your dealers, and the customers themselves.

Determining Lifetime Value

If it costs you $25 to acquire a new customer who buys a $50 item from you, you have probably lost money on that sale. But if that same customer, due to your marketing strategy, goes on to buy a $50 item from you several times a year for the next several years, your $25 was well spent.

Database marketing is based on the principle of lifetime value. When you acquire a customer, you try to determine what future sales you can expect from him or her. You can calculate contribution to profit and overhead for the customer's lifetime with your company. (This process is described in Chapter 10.) Once you know this, you can determine how much you can afford to spend to acquire the customer, and how much you should spend on your marketing database and follow-up activities to keep him or her happy, loyal, and buying.

Some executives fear that a marketing database is too expensive and doesn't pay for itself. This is a justified concern. But you needn't guess: you test, on a small scale, then you calculate lifetime value. You will soon find that it is possible to know exactly how much new business a marketing database will bring in, and whether you are making a profit or a loss from it.

Building a Customer Profile

Why do some people buy your product regularly, while others do not? This question has certainly been asked since the beginning of commerce. A marketing database can help to provide some answers. The strategy: get them to tell you the information you need to answer this question. The answer could be a combination of several factors:

- How you have presented your product as compared with the competition.

- The perceived worth and reliability of your product compared with its price.

- The service and support you provide: the loyalty you have been able to build.

- The lifestyles, affluence, education, age, media preferences, ethnic makeup, sex, and attitudes of your good customers, as compared with the people who are not buying your product.

The first three factors are within your power to change. The last factor can be investigated by *profiling your customers* (and non-customers). Profiling is a computer modeling process (described in Chapter 12) which enables you to use your database to choose, from the scores of facts known about customers and non-customers, those few attributes which seem to distinguish the buyers from the non-buyers. Once you have developed such a profile, you can use it in several ways:

- You can use it as a guide to change your marketing strategy to reach segments of the market that you have missed with your message.
- You can change your product, your pricing, your image.
- You can use it as a guide to seek out new prospects who have lifestyles that match your existing good customers. These prospects can be found reading the same media that your customers read, or you can rent their names on lists which have been coded according to the attributes you have deemed important.

Test and Count

Database strategy should always be tested. You think that something will work, but you can never be sure. The beauty of a marketing database is that you can build in response mechanisms that can prove in minute detail what happened (good and bad) to each of your marketing initiatives. Whenever you write to your customers, send them a fax, e-mail, or a product, you provide them with a response device coded with the source and a unique customer number, a postage paid business reply envelope or other rapid response mechanism, and, in most cases, a coupon, rebate offer, or some incentive which will get them to do what you want.

You may also include a survey form to acquire more information. When customers respond, the date, source code, and survey data are all entered into the database. You count how many were returned, how many inquired, how many purchased. Your counts are in detail, and verify every aspect of your initiative—i.e., they:

- determine what type of customer responded; what type did not;

- calculate the rate of return on your investment in the initiative;

- compare customer response of those who received one inducement with the response of those who received another (or no inducement).

You should spend as much time planning how to get response, and how to measure and count response, as you do in any other aspect of marketing strategy. Testing and counting is learning. Learning produces knowledge. Knowledge helps you improve your strategy and increase your profits.

Changing Roles within Your Organization

Once you begin database marketing, nothing will stay the same. Your marketing strategy will change in many ways. Consider your dealers, for example. Most organizations operate on the assumption that they pay for national advertising, and a portion of local cooperative ads, but beyond that it is the dealer's job to find the customers, rope them in, and sell them the product.

So where does the "lifetime value of a customer" fit into this scenario? Most dealers (automobile dealers, retail stores, hotels, travel agencies and so on) are too small to build a customer marketing database of their own. Most of them handle many products besides yours.

So if you build the marketing database, how do the dealers fit into your strategy?

The answer is that you build them in as a part of your organization. You furnish them leads, and track their handling of the leads. You keep track of the customer: when his car is four years old, you begin to direct him to a local dealer and you direct a local dealer to him. A marketing database tends to bring the independent dealer closer to your company; he becomes a working member of your marketing team.

In a business-to-business product situation, sales forces usually operate independently of the marketing or advertising staffs. But with a database, the database telemarketers will qualify leads for the salesman, enabling him to spend more time with prospects who are ready to buy. In time, salesmen become more and more a functioning part of your marketing strategy.

Customer service reps, of course, take on a central role—they are your primary link to your customers, building relationships, providing information, extracting data, promoting loyalty, and making sales. A marketing database always thrusts customer service into the forefront of marketing strategy.

Don't forget accounts receivable and delivery. Once you build a functioning marketing database, you will learn a great deal about your customers' feelings about the invoices they receive and their attitude towards the driver who comes to the door. Any service in your organization that touches the customer must be included in the database marketing system as a part of your total corporate image, as part of your one-on-one dialog with your customer.

You will soon find that the database is changing your company and its internal relationships.

Building a Database Team

A marketing database, by itself, will not bring you any of the benefits we have been discussing. It can only be profitable if it is a part of an integrated marketing strategy designed to extract data from customers, build loyalty, encourage repeat sales, include dealers and sales personnel in the loop, and promote customer service. To implement this strategy, you will have to build a broad marketing team within the company, under the direction of a forceful leader with the funds and delegated authority to make the database work.

The Database Administrator (DBA) probably should be someone from marketing or sales, depending on your company. Working as active members of this team should be staff from:

- an external direct creative advertising agency;

- a telemarketing firm (or inside staff) that handles customer service and direct marketing;

- an external service bureau which manages the database (see Chapter 5 on why the database should not be built in-house); and

- your sales organization (and, if appropriate, whoever handles dealer relations). After you organize your team, you will find that there are two types of people concerned with marketing databases:

  — *Constructors*—those who are interested in putting together a functioning database, designing reports, cleaning the names and addresses, adding information to it, acquiring names, and so on.

  — *Creators*—those who are interested in figuring out how your company can make a profit by *using the database*. They tend to be the marketing, sales, or advertising people. They will be the ones who come up with the exciting ideas for ways to cross-sell, to build continuity, to reduce attrition, and to create loyalty.

Your team must be staffed with both kinds of people. If you are lacking either one, your database project will never get off the ground.

A marketing database should be operational within one year from the time that a contract with a service bureau is signed.

To delay it for more than a year holds many dangers for your marketing strategy (see Chapter 5). At first, it should be tested with just a portion of your customer base. Gradually, as it proves itself, it should be expanded until it encompasses all of your repeat-business functions.

WHEN SHOULD YOU BEGIN TO BUILD A MARKETING DATABASE?

Because the learning curve and the return on investment begin after the database is operational, not during the planning phase, begin to build your database as soon as possible. You will begin to understand your customers, build loyalty and repeat sales only after the database is constructed and working to carry out your marketing strategy.

Many decades ago, Congress voted to begin shifting the American economy gradually to the metric system. There was to be an educational and planning process, followed by a full conversion at a future date. You know the results. What has come of the decades of planning? How many people today know whether a room temperature of 30 degrees centigrade is hot or cold? The lesson: planning for a marketing database will not do anything for the bottom line. Only an actual functioning database will get you the benefits you seek.

Some Cautions

- A marketing database will cost money. It requires a budget and top-level support to overcome the many obstacles in its formative years.

- Marketing databases are new, charting unexplored territory. They raise issues, such as personal privacy, which, if not handled properly, could bring down the wrath of consumer groups and the dead hand of federal regulation on what promises to be an innovative and useful marketing strategy.

- A marketing database requires very imaginative and creative leadership within the company if it is to succeed. Such leadership is hard to find. Unless that kind of talent can be found, all the committees and planning will come to nothing.

WHERE WE ARE GOING

Those who have caught the database marketing bug (including the author) are very excited about it and its possibilities for making America a better place to live. It is not just a better way to sell products and services; it is a way of bringing back something that we have lost during the mass-marketing fervor since the 1960s. It is a way of restoring the personal contact with customers that we all enjoyed in earlier years, when you knew your merchants and they knew you, recognized you, appreciated you, and did personal favors and services for you on a regular basis.

Database marketing, when done properly, will restore loyalty and personal recognition as important aspects of the business relationships which all will come to experience and enjoy. It will be more individual, more personal, more satisfying. It should help us get the products and services we want, and should help to reduce the costs of those products and services.

Across America, the message has spread. Hundreds of marketing databases are being built. Probably your principal competitors have already started. Once their databases are up and running, they will be learning how to reduce attrition and how to win over your customers. Don't give them too much of a head start!

Part I:

What Is a Marketing Database?

Chapter 1

What Marketing Databases Do

In my youth I had an Irish governess named Annie Kearney who came over from the "old country" about 1880. Whenever she encountered a silver coin—a dime, a quarter, or a half-dollar—she would bite it to see if it was genuine. She taught me to do this, and to this day I can tell silver from other metals by biting. It was a skill apparently needed in the Ireland of her day, and perhaps also in early 20th century America. Counterfeiters were active.

The average person has little use for this skill today. Counterfeiters seem to have gone into retirement and the government isn't making coins out of silver anymore. It is one more thing that we don't have to worry about.

In fact, there are hundreds of things that we don't have to worry about anymore:

- The products we buy in a supermarket are pure, fresh, and safe (albeit laced with government-approved food additives and preservatives). This was not always so.

- If you put your money in a checking account or a savings bank, the money is safe—it won't disappear even when the bank goes belly-up due to mismanagement (although the taxpayer eventually ends up paying the bill). From 1930-1933 there were 7,763 banks that went bankrupt, and most of their depositors lost everything.

- Insurance companies, in general, can be relied upon to pay you what your policy says they will pay.

- Cars do not disintegrate as soon as you buy them (as many did in the 1950s).

- Radial tires, in general, last for 50,000 miles without ever going flat or losing air. (I spent much time in my teens and twenties changing flats and having relatively new tires recapped because they were worn smooth.)

- When you buy a dishwasher or a computer, it works. And if it doesn't, the manufacturer and the dealer will stand behind it.

- Money for many people is no longer a problem. Most households today own at least one credit card with a substantial credit limit. Almost every household has a checking account, most with overdraft protection.

What has brought about this happy state of affairs where the consumer has so few worries? Many things:

Mass advertising and mass marketing. A major company simply cannot afford to risk many millions of dollars and its market share advertising something that has basic flaws, so they are more careful than they used to be about what they offer for sale.

Intense competition. There are three or four major producers of almost everything that a consumer or a business could possibly buy. Competition improves quality and lowers prices.

Widespread information. Through TV, newspapers, magazines, radio, yellow pages, and a walk through any large supermarket or department store, the average person is exposed to much more reliable information about availability and prices than can possibly be absorbed.

Constantly advancing technology. Technology is racing ahead. Every week new products come out with surprising new features. The public has come to accept and expect this. There is little resistance to trying something new. Competitors hasten to match each innovation.

Easy credit. Almost anyone can buy almost anything on credit. This has made it immensely easier to sell and to buy.

America today is a much better place for the consumer and the business customer than it once was. Products are better, and the level of trust is higher. We now worry about much higher-level issues: stress, keeping our families together, finding time to fit in all our desired activities. We have moved several notches higher on the Maslow scale of values.

MASLOW SCALE OF VALUES

In 1950, Abraham Maslow wrote a paper which changed thinking about human values. He described a hierarchy of values for all people. At their most basic, people need air and food. They will sacrifice everything else if they cannot breathe or they are starving. When these needs are satisfied they look for shelter from the elements.

Above security needs comes love: to love and to be loved. And above love is the desire to belong: to a family, to a group, to a company.

Above love and belonging is self esteem: pride in yourself and what you do, and a confidence that you can do your work well, that you are an effective person—living your life as it should be lived. This is the level that most people are striving for, and that we hope to facilitate with our products and services. Cars are sold on the basis of pride and self esteem. The American Express Gold Card or the President's Club of a hotel chain cater to this need.

The highest level is self fulfillment, or what Maslow called "Self Actualization." In this state people feel that they are truly living a life that brings out their most creative possibilities: a musician who writes what he considers a great symphony; an author who writes what he believes is a wonderful book; a marketing professional who successfully creates a functioning and profitable marketing database. Selling Cadillacs or Mercedes to people at this level will not be enough. They already have self esteem, pride, and confidence; you have to find a way to help them to achieve self actualization.

The interesting thing about the values that Maslow noted is that once you have attained a level, you worry about the next higher level.

Figure 1-1 Mankind Tries to Satisfy Higher Needs.

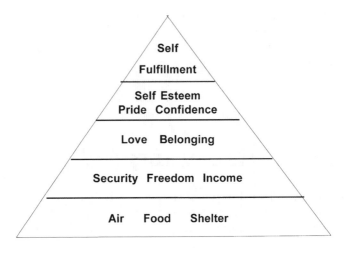

Adapted from Abraham Maslow 1908-1970

People rarely look down to see how far they have come. They look up to see how far they have to go. People seldom say "Well, at least I have enough air to breathe."

If we are going to reach customers, Maslow would argue, we must appeal to their current value needs. There is no point in offering love or belonging to a starving group. Nor does it help to offer basic food or shelter to someone who already has a job and a family.

WHAT CUSTOMERS WANT TODAY

What do customers want today? What are those higher levels that we have moved to?

Unique Products

Our basic needs for products are satisfied; now we want something a little different. We have caught up with the Joneses, now we want to catch up with our own personal, special needs. We don't want a standard dining room table, we want a 5 foot oval glass table with brass legs that exactly fits in an area on our glass-covered patio. We don't want regular dog food, we want dog food especially made for our very old dog who is getting fat and has halitosis. We can't find these things in a department store or supermarket, and it is a waste of time asking for them there.

Special Services

In the last few years, my wife and I have been working at our offices until almost eight o'clock every night. We have become like most two-income families: not enough time to shop. We are looking for plumbers and air conditioning men who will come in and fix things without our having to stay home to let them in; someone who will take care of our trees and fertilize our lawn while we are away; a delivery service that will leave things at the door. We shop by catalog and telephone.

My wife and I rent about two movies every week. I waste at least an hour and a half every week choosing them. I really want a video store that knows me and what I like, and would get a movie ready for me two times a week so I could just swing by and grab it. I haven't been able to find such a store.

Information

Despite the barrage of information coming at us from scores of sources every day, we find it difficult to acquire the information that we need in our relatively complicated lives. We have bought a slick software package for our computer, but we really can't figure out how to make it work properly. We need some expert to show us. Where can we find such an expert? The salesmen in the stores either don't know or are too busy to show us. There is probably an article in some magazine that would be very helpful, but how do we find the right article in the right magazine?

Attention

Everyone seems too busy to talk to you. Many employees in large stores either don't have the information that we need or are too busy and distracted to be of any help.

I have at last reached the point in my life where I am able to save some money every month. For several years I searched for someone who could give me some practical and helpful advice on what to put my money into: CDs? Bonds? Stocks? IRAs? Real estate? Annuities? I tried them all and, in the process, lost a lot of money in the stock market. I was looking for someone that I could talk to who would take some interest in me and my financial situation, not just in selling what he was selling. I finally found such a person. I talk to him on the phone. He knows and understands our financial goals. He has our complete financial history on a marketing database, and he discusses our financial situation with me whenever I call him. He has never steered me wrong. I am saving more, paying (somewhat) lower taxes and I do not worry about losing my nest egg.

Recognition

Several years ago I joined the American Airlines Admiral's Club. It provides me with access to a private lounge in many major airports complete with a bar, conference rooms, telephones, clean rest rooms, free crackers and cheese, magazines and newspapers, television, Xerox and fax machines, personal computers, and airline reservation service. There is an annual fee, and everyone who has the money can join it. But belonging to it, and being greeted with special service with my reservations, is really worth the money. For that annual fee, I have bought some recognition that makes me feel a little better when I am in a strange place thousands of miles from home. Membership has its privileges, and one of them is recognition.

DATABASE MARKETING MEETS THESE NEEDS

We can summarize the higher level needs today as:

- Unique Products

- Information

- Service

- Personal Attention

- Recognition

How does database marketing help to meet these higher level needs?

A marketing database consists of a large collection of information about each customer and prospect. Most of the information is provided by the customer in orders, telephone calls, and surveys. The information is arranged on a database that can be called up instantly whenever the customer is on the telephone, or has written a letter.

The telephone system can be tied to the computer in such a way that the computer learns the telephone number from which each incoming call is placed and automatically looks up that number in its database, bringing the complete customer record effortlessly to the screen as the operator is receiving the call. The system enables Customer Service or Sales to recognize customers by name and remind them that their previous sales and interests are considered and used as guidelines in meeting their needs.

Behind the database is a huge warehouse of products, more diverse than could be stocked in any single store or in all the stores in a single city. The sales staff has a product database at their fingertips which lists everything the company makes, not just the most popular items. They can get customers exactly what they want.

Figure 1-2   How a Marketing Database Works

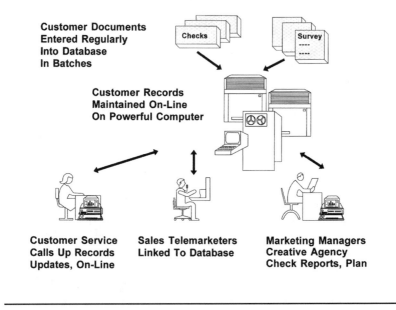

**Customer Documents
Entered Regularly
Into Database
In Batches**

Checks

Survey

**Customer Records
Maintained On-Line
On Powerful Computer**

**Customer Service
Calls Up Records
Updates, On-Line**

**Sales Telemarketers
Linked To Database**

**Marketing Managers
Creative Agency
Check Reports, Plan**

Also behind the database is a network that provides more information about this line of products than could be provided in any store. Does the customer want to get a replacement for the glass screen on the front? Know how to change the filter? Know what attachments come with it and what they cost? For technical questions, the customer can be routed to an expert—perhaps even the individual who designed it. He or she can find out when it was shipped, by what carrier, and when it is likely to arrive.

The database permits personal services. We all have become accustomed to the super service provided today by travel agencies. They can book us on complicated tours across the country, have hotel rooms and rental cars waiting for us at each stop, and deliver tickets and boarding passes to us, with a printed itinerary, the next day. All it takes is a short telephone call. It works because at the travel agent's fingertips is an airline computer database network which is linked to most airlines, hotels, and car rental services.

A marketing database takes that concept one step further. A marketing database tells the travel agent that you prefer window seats, you always use a VISA® card of a certain number, you prefer American Airlines® and are an Advantage® member, you always fly economy class, you prefer The Hertz Number One Club Gold cars, the St. Francis in San Francisco and the Plaza in New York. The agent knows where to deliver your tickets without asking, knows your spouse's name, and your office phone number. You needn't repeat all these facts every time. They are on your database record.

DIVERSIFYING YOUR PRODUCT MIX

Database marketing will have a profound effect on the product and service mix of the companies that take it seriously. The general effect will be to widen the line, to diversify and add new flavors, features, and sizes.

When Coca-Cola® decided in their executive wisdom to change the formula of their product, the public revolted. People were outraged. Coca-Cola had to bring back the old formula as "Classic Coke®" and, at the same time, decided to introduce Cherry Coke®, Caffeine Free Coke®, and other innovations, so that Coca-Cola ended up with more products and shelf space in the average store than they had before. The consumers spoke, and Coca-Cola listened. The result was a remarkable resurgence for a company that had been perceived as being in decline.

But Coca-Cola was more than a household word. It was an American institution, which a mere board of directors was not meant to tamper with. When you decide to change your product, you may not be so lucky. There won't be any protest meetings. Your unhappy customers may just decide to shift to buying your competitor's product, and you won't have a clue as to why. Your first reaction may be to fire your advertising agency, on the grounds that the right words can sell anything. If you do get a new advertising agency, let us hope that the replacement suggests a marketing database, because it is one of the surest ways of really listening to the "Heartbeat of America."

All of us have said, many times, "why don't they just . . . ," completing the phrase with, "make a product that would . . . ," or "make their product easier to . . . ." How do you get through to the executives who make these decisions and tell them what you think? It is almost impossible.

I had an experience which really bothered me. Several years ago, I became addicted to Shape®, a dry powder food sold in supermarkets. Shape powder mixed with milk made a great breakfast drink (similar to Carnation Instant Breakfast). It was filling; it helped me to lose weight. One day, the product just disappeared from the stores. I was frantic. I went from store to store—no one had it. I called Giant Food, and was told that the manufacturer had stopped producing it. "Could I buy up some of his residual stock?" I asked. Yes, it was possible. A couple of weeks later, Giant Food delivered a special order of twelve cases to me. I was able to enjoy it for about six months until I ran out forever.

Today, of course, similar products are everywhere, but it took more than ten years—I have gone on to other things for breakfast. How many other people like me were upset at this product's disappearance? Who knows. Certainly the manufacturer didn't know, and made no attempt to find out. Why didn't he continue to make it, since there was obviously a market for this type of product? It is everywhere today. The main reason was that in those days we were in the midst of mass marketing. Manufacturers were fighting for shelf space in supermarkets. If your sales did not warrant a decent display, you pulled out altogether. There were no alternate channels of distribution. Sell big or die. The same thing was happening to television shows, where Nielsen ratings doomed excellent show after excellent show because they did not have ratings as good as other shows.

Database marketing promises to change this picture. By setting up a dialog with your customers you should be able to anticipate what they want: not just what they think about what you are producing now, but what they would like to see you produce in the way of changed products and services in the future. With the knowledge that you accumulate, you will be able to make wise decisions about changing your products and services, broadening your market, and finding alternate means of delivering products which may have a multi-million dollar sales potential, but are too small for supermarket shelf space.

WHAT DO COMPANIES WANT?

It would be an oversimplification to concentrate too much on the personal services side of database marketing. It is true that the main advantages *for the customer* are the recognition, personal attention, information, and diversity of products which a marketing database provides. Marketing databases also provide very practical benefits for the company which maintains them. What are they?

Repeat Business

Your best prospects are your own satisfied customers. Most companies don't realize this even today. They use coupons, rebates, cash back, and discounts to win over customers that they already have. A marketing database builds customer loyalty and builds repeat business. Marketing database theory studies the *lifetime value of a customer:* from this, any company can learn how much they can afford to spend on acquiring a customer because they know how much that customer will be worth to them in repeat business.

Reduced Costs

A repeat sale costs, at most, half of what the first sale cost (and possibly much less than half). Overall, a lot of repeat business can bring total costs down and profits up.

Increased Loyalty

Loyalty means more than simply repeat sales. It means that customers spread the word for you. It means that they will support you if you fail (occasionally). It means that they will buy new products that you are launching just because they are loyal to your present products.

Market Segmentation

Some companies feel that the chief advantage of a marketing database is its ability to separate out categories of users: loyalists, occasional users, switchers, competitive brand loyalists. Once you have identified these types you can design marketing strategies to win over the competitive brand loyalists while keeping your own customers satisfied.

Prospect Identification

Many companies have no clear idea of who is buying their products. They hire agencies to make up colorful ads, which seem to do the trick because their market share does not decline. But they don't really know who these customers are. Marketing databases identify them. Once you have profiled your customers, you can use lists and media surveys to locate new prospects who match that profile.

Product and Service Feedback

The world changes rapidly, particularly in a competitive, capitalistic democracy like ours. What was a perfectly good product two years ago may be outdated today. All companies must be alert to market trends: to what their customers are telling them about what they want. There is no better way to stay on top of the market than an actively functioning marketing database that maintains a two-way dialog with consumers and provides weekly reports on what they are asking for and thinking. If you don't listen to your customers every day, rest assured that your competitors will.

Other Company Benefits

Marketing databases do other things for a company:

Internal Restructuring. They can bring Marketing, Sales, and Customer Service together into a single system which will reduce costs, improve sales, and reduce harmful infighting.

Lead Qualification and Tracking. They can be used to set up a system to profile leads before salesmen get them, and to track action on them from inquiry to contract, thereby increasing sales and reducing the cost of sales.

Improved Internal Information. They can be used to set up a reporting system within the company which will bring everyone from top management through sales, marketing, product development, inventory management, advertising, and accounts receivable into the information loop.

Better Dealer Relations. They can be used to improve relations with your dealers by giving them instant notice of leads and data on the prospects.

CONCEPTS FOR MARKETING DATABASES

Following are some examples of the ways that companies can use the marketing database concept to provide a profitable dialog with their customers.

- An electronics company packs a warranty card inside every electronic clock shipped out. The card asks the name, address, and other information about the customer which will be useful later: Does he have a VCR? Does he have a CD player? Does he have a Walkman? What is his education level? What is the household income? What is his age? His occupation? Are there young children in the house? Where did he learn about the clock? Magazine, Newspaper, TV, Radio, Direct Mail, saw it in the store?

When these cards come in, they are keypunched and used to form a database which is used to market other products made by the manufacturer.

- An agricultural chemicals manufacturer who has built a database of every farmer in America. He knows what they produce, how much, what chemicals they need — and when. He has their addresses, phone numbers, fax numbers (yes, most farmers have fax machines today), and in some cases their e-mail addresses (yes, they all have computers!). Using this information, the manufacturer can send timely and helpful information on weather, crops, diseases, insects, seasonal problems, governmental regulations, and credit availability. They aim to be the farmer's advisor and friend; in the process of which, they become his chemical supplier.

- A baby food company sends out coupons to every mother of newborns in America. The coupon is coded so that, when redeemed, the company knows exactly who redeemed it. The coupon also asks additional questions and promises a second, even more valuable coupon by return mail if the mother fills out the questions and checks a box on the coupon. The coupons form the beginning of a database which can follow the child through infancy to preschool, school, and college, thus winning brand loyalty for the company's food and related products.

- A quick-lube company has all customers fill out a work order form. This form triggers a follow-up mailing three months later inquiring about the service and asking many other questions that will be useful later, and also enclosing a new lube coupon. The work order forms become the foundation of a database that will track these customers from car to car.

- A car sales promoter obtains a tape of all the automobile registrations in his state (about half the states in America rent these lists). Then he goes to automobile dealer showrooms throughout the state, promising to fill their showrooms on a specific Saturday morning with people wanting to test drive the latest models. He mails coupons to car owners within driving distance of the showroom, promising a free gift and a chance in a drawing for a car if they will test drive on Saturday. The owners have been selected by demographics and make, model, and year of their present car. When they respond, they go into a respondent database. They will receive other mailings.

- A bank compiles a list of all its customers—which is often not as easy as it sounds. Normally in banks, each account is a separate listing with a separate name and address. Loan accounts are often on different computer files and in a different format from deposit accounts. Putting the entire Customer Information File (CIF) together by household is a major undertaking which most MIS departments find overwhelming. Once the database is compiled, the file is enhanced with geodemographics and lifestyle codes, and the bank begins a series of personalized mailings encouraging cross-selling of other bank products. When the customer does buy another product, his record is flagged as someone responsive to direct marketing. He will be approached again.

- American Express® is probably the most effective credit card company in the world in terms of database creation. They pioneered the concept of *membership* in which each card holder is a member of American Express and has certain privileges which are associated with the membership. They take pains to learn what kind of customer you are and use this knowledge in their marketing activities.

- A pet food manufacturer introduces a new high-end product not sold in stores. The announcement is made on TV, in print, and by direct mail. Customers call an 800 number to order food shipped once a month automatically, with pre-paid home delivery (you needn't be there). As each call is received by the operators, the information goes directly into an on-line database where a record of all the customer's prior purchases are stored. The operators thus are knowledgeable about the customers, and can ask them for feedback on the product.

- A cosmetic manufacturer requires each customer to have a facial exam by a trained specialist before buying its products. Customers are then admitted as lifetime members with all of the pertinent data recorded in a database. All subsequent purchases are tracked by point-of-sale units triggered when the customers pass their membership cards to salesclerks in one of 400 department store outlets. In this way, very personalized customer service and follow-up can be maintained— "For as long as you own your face"—with resulting brand loyalty and increased sales.

- A cruise line has passengers fill out a comprehensive questionnaire during the cruise (there is plenty of free time). The data is used to trigger personalized follow-up mailings announcing new ships, new cruise locations, and new features, and suggesting that you name some friends who might like to share your joy. These prospects are immediately sent to the travel agent who originally booked the passenger. This travel agent is a key part of the database and is a *specific target* in subsequent follow-up mailings. The travel agent has life and death power over cruise bookings: no one knows as much about the differences between various lines; the travel agent can steer customers in any direction. The database is thus a means of cultivating the travel agent as much as (or more than) the passenger.

- A drug company maintains a database of doctors who specialize in the ailments which their drugs alleviate. Salespeople visit these doctors, leaving samples and discussing the products. The salespeople have laptop computers which are used to plan their weekly activities and to record the results of each call. On a regular basis, they transmit the results of their activities to a central database, which thus contains details on what is happening in the field, what the doctors are thinking about the product, how the samples are moving, and how well salespeople are doing their jobs. If a doctor visits one of their booths at a convention or answers a coupon in a medical publication, the information is logged in the doctor's record in the database. Direct mailings to the doctors announce new products and send monographs on existing products as they come off the press. Gifts and other emoluments go to the participating doctors. Patients are guided to the doctors by coupons reimbursed by the drug manufacturer.

- Another drug manufacturer maintains a database of 7 million households in which reside persons who suffer from specific ailments remedied by their drugs. These people were discovered by household questionnaires which included a valuable premium for response. A series of newsletters about health which focus on the ailments in question go directly to the households which have responded to coupons. The sufferers may be prompted to visit specific doctors, with coupons. They may receive monographs on the products.

- A video store keeps track by category of what movies its clients rent. As new releases of interest to the clients appear (comedy, children's, sports, musicals), clients receive personalized announcements. They are invited to become members of the "sneak preview" club in which they receive notice of new movies which are not among the latest bestsellers. As club members, they learn first of these movies and they fill out an extensive evaluation of the movie, which is then averaged in with other responses to develop a "viewer's guide" available to all members. The "sneak preview" works in several ways: it helps promote the rental of older movies; it builds brand loyalty for the store; it helps the store know what movies to buy. The store also gives credit towards valuable prizes for each movie rented. Monthly mailings notify the members of the points they have accumulated, and encourage them to rent a few more in order to qualify for a valuable gift.

- A major telephone company keeps track of all of its yellow page listings in a database. The database has the type of ad, size of ad, history of advertising, the heading, and other information. Each year there is an annual season for each book in which subscribers can sign up for a new ad. The database is used to *compare and contrast* the ads taken out by (unnamed) competitors of each subscriber in the same and other books published throughout the system. In this way, an auto rental company can learn something about its competitors which would otherwise take considerable research to find out: how many other auto rental companies take out ads, and the size of those ads compared to its ads not only in the local book, *but in all other books in the system.*

- A supermarket establishes a frequent buyers club for house-holders who live near the store. To join, members fill out a family history questionnaire, and are given a special card to use when shopping at the store. Before going through the checkout line, they hand in their card. As each item is run through the scanner, their purchase is recorded in their own database record. In this way, the supermarket knows exactly what everyone bought and when. But more importantly, the store learns a great deal about its patrons which it can use in planning promotions, stocking new items, and giving better service. When a family starts buying diapers and baby food, a set of special marketing programs is triggered; if they start buying pet food, a different program ensues. The database earns revenue for the store through renting the names to manufacturers of baby food, pet food, or other products to use in *their* databases.

REQUIREMENTS FOR MARKETING DATABASES

Any good marketing database must meet certain requirements:

Custom Design. There is no such thing as a good generic marketing database—it must be custom designed for the company that is using it.

Dynamic. Constant change in the data, the software, and the applications are the rule in a good marketing database. Just as you cannot maintain market share by selling a single product without change in the same way year after year, you cannot market to your customers in the same way. They will tell you things you will have to listen to. Their ideas will force you to modify your marketing plan. A revised plan means a revised database.

Huge. Any marketing database must maintain a tremendous amount of information about every customer. It will require extensive memory and a very powerful computer.

Universally available. Many parts of the company must be able to access the database at the same time. If it is available only to customer service or marketing it is not yet doing its job.

Equipped for ad-hoc queries. All good marketing databases provide a means for users to get less than 60-second answers to any query ("How many women in California have bought products A, B, and D in the first six months of this year, who have not bought anything since? Show that by age range and income level."), no matter how large the file and how complex the query.

Profitable. Built into any marketing database must be an accounting system which shows clearly what the database is costing and what benefits it is providing. All good marketing databases, in addition to improving company profits, also can demonstrate how they are doing so by means of very precise systems of measurement.

Separate from the billing file. A properly functioning marketing database is not on the same system with other company MIS functions such as general ledger, payroll, inventory, production control, or customer accounts. There must be a data link between them so that the database can keep up to date on sales and shipments. But marketing requires that the records be organized by customer or household, not by product. The database must contain several features not present in normal MIS functions, among them on-line access, seven-day-a-week activity, constant software changes, addition of prospects and leads, as well as customers, merge/purge, profiling involving multiple regressions and other statistical functions, and matching of the file with outside data sources.

Controlled by a DBA. All functioning marketing databases are under the control of a Database Administrator (DBA). This is someone in Marketing who has the final word on all software and data changes in the database. The DBA does not have to go through MIS or other layers to issue orders to the service bureau or others who manage the software. The DBA determines the priority of users on the system, and assures that the database improves the company bottom line through dynamic marketing and customer services.

Fully accountable. All successful databases pay their way in the company's marketing program, and can prove it by lifetime value analysis. Unlike advertising, which has to use surveys and anecdotes to justify its budget, marketing databases can show in very precise terms just what are the benefits and costs of each marketing strategy. Some things work, and some things don't. Database marketers can prove which is which.

SUMMARY

Consumers today have more confidence in the products and services they buy than consumers thirty years ago. They have fewer money worries. They have easy credit.

Customers today are seeking higher levels of satisfaction than can be met by mass marketing. They are looking for:

- Unique products and services.

- Special services.

- Information.

- Personal Attention.

- Recognition.

Marketing databases meet these needs in a way that cannot be matched by mass marketing methods. The first reason for having a marketing database, therefore, is that it is the only way to meet today's customer's needs.

Companies install marketing databases because they provide several important benefits to the company:

- More repeat business.

- Reduced costs of sales.

- Increased customer loyalty.

- Ability to segment the market and treat each customer differently.

- Ability to profile customers and identify prospects.

- Ability to learn from customers how the product is being received, so that products and services can be improved.

- Marketing databases tend to bring Sales, Marketing, and Customer Service into a single system which reduces costs and company infighting.

- Marketing databases disseminate information and reports throughout the company.

- Lead tracking and dealer relations can be improved.

A marketing database must meet certain requirements:

- Custom design—each company's database is different.

- Dynamic—software must be constantly changed.

- Huge—a good database requires a huge mainframe and company-wide access.

- Separate from the billing file—and from other MIS computer functions.

- Directed by marketing—under the control of a Database Administrator.

- Profitable—it must improve the bottom line, and prove it.

Chapter 2

The History of Database Marketing

Almost all of the techniques discussed in this book exist today. Somewhere in America, they are being tested and in many cases are working successfully. But not more than 10 percent of the companies in America are actively using the full potential of database marketing. Why is this so?

There are a number of reasons:

- There are some products for which database marketing does not work, and will never work. It is not profitable for the manufacturers of most of the products sold in the typical supermarket to maintain a database of the ultimate consumers of these products, although the retailer can keep these same people profitably on his database.

- In many companies, the compensation system is still based on selling products not on satisfying customers. Database marketing cannot take root unless marketers are rewarded for building loyalty, referrals, and increased total customer sales.

- In other companies, the central information systems staff has successfully resisted marketing's attempt to outsource their customer databases. Few satisfactory database marketing programs can be carried out on systems built or maintained by central MIS operations.

- The most important reason, however, is that it is difficult to design creative database marketing strategies and sell them to top management. The programs described in this book are—in many cases—fascinating. They are exciting. They are, however, complex. They require marketing skills of a high order. There are not yet enough really creative people who understand how to build customer loyalty.

HOW IT ALL BEGAN

Database marketing is the culmination of a long chain of successful developments in marketing and selling products and services in America, beginning with the earliest advertising, through mass marketing, direct marketing, coupons, catalogs, and frequent-flyer clubs, to the beginning of real database marketing today.

The position of database marketing in American business today is similar to the position of the automobile in American society in 1900. The automobile is essential to our present lifestyle, but the automobile requires a very elaborate infrastructure to make it work. In 1900, all this was in the future. A few rich people had cars. There were almost no paved roads, bridges, parking places, service stations, mechanics, laws, signals, insurance, or financing. We built all this step by step as the need arose, without a real plan; without really knowing where we were going or what it was doing to our lifestyle.

The same is true of database marketing. It too will have a revolutionary impact on our lives—perhaps not as revolutionary as the automobile, but fully as widespread and pervasive. Well into the next century, database marketing will be so built into our business system and culture that it will be impossible to conceive of life without it. Every successful business will use it. It will be difficult to sustain a successful sales program for goods or services without it. Competition will insure that this is so.

Let us explore how we got to where we are today, and what is likely to happen in the future.

MEDIA DICTATES THE MARKETING METHOD

Every system for advertising, marketing, selling, and delivering goods has been influenced, if not built around, the media which existed at the time. From the earliest years, print advertising existed. The newspapers which carried ads were local, with most of the advertising limited to businesses within the delivery area of the paper. There were few national brands. The birth of direct marketing came about with the expansion of the railroad system after the Civil War. The first national direct mail effort was the Montgomery Ward catalog in 1884, followed by the Sears Roebuck catalog in 1897, and the Spiegel catalog in 1905. Sears' success was only possible because the mail system, by that time, was beginning to reach most of the cities and rural communities, and the railway express was beginning to develop the capability of delivering goods to catalog recipients. By 1902, Sears had an annual business of more than $50 million from their catalog.

One of the next milestones in direct marketing was the founding of the Book-of-the-Month Club in 1926 by Harry Sherman and Maxwell Sackheim, based on their experience in direct marketing. This pioneering effort really set the pace. By the mid-1900s, more than half of all hardcover books were sold by direct mail.

But for most of the twentieth century, catalog marketing was always considered a backwater, an aberration, an obscure method for unloading second-class goods on rural people. The real money was thought to be only in national advertising.

National brands became possible through national media: big city newspapers linked to national advertising agencies, magazines with national circulation, the radio and, later, television. When national advertising was born, a whole new world opened up for merchandising. The public and the business community were mesmerized by the riches, the fantastic profits that resulted from delivering the right message about soap or cigarettes through these new national media. The nation became fascinated by Madison Avenue, symbolized by the "Hucksters" and "The Man in the Gray Flannel Suit." Advertising developed its own rules, culture, systems, agencies, and profits.

Successful advertising aims at creating a powerful image of a national brand in the minds of consumers. Manufacturers wanting this service were trained not to expect immediate results. The introduction of a new product required tens or hundreds of millions of dollars of advertising designed to stimulate a sequence of related events:

- Awareness of the existence of the product and its name (Camay, the soap of beautiful women);

- Knowledge of the product and what it could do for the consumer (softer, lovelier complexion);
- Image—what life would be like if only one used the product (admiration, adoring glances, the skin you love to touch);
- Preference for this product over other products (unlike cheap imitations, Camay . . .); and
- Purchase—the actual sale of the product (available at fine stores everywhere).

Building this sequence of events took years. No one expected a new product to break even in less than a year; rather, it could take two years or more. But the rich benefits of creating a brand name image paid off in huge sustained sales to loyal customers for years to come. Soap and cigarette manufacturers (to mention only two) became rich. Advertising agencies became rich. Magazines and television became rich.

Figure 2-1 Advertising Spending 1920-2000

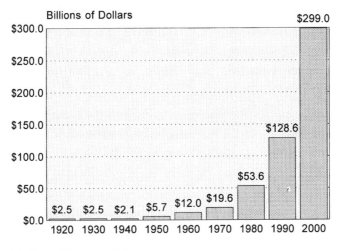

Robert J. Coen, McCann-Erickson

Figure 2-2   Advertising Spending Ratios in the 1990s

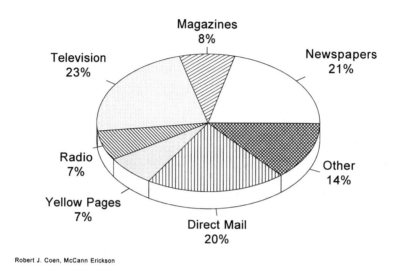

Robert J. Coen, McCann Erickson

SUPERMARKETS

After World War II, this whole process was changed by the introduction of a new media: the supermarket. I classify a supermarket as a media because, like an advertisement, it offers the manufacturer a chance to display his product, together with a message on the package, to millions of potential buyers.

I remember when the first supermarket came to my community. I grew up in New Canaan, Connecticut during the Thirties and Forties. We always shopped for groceries at Gristedes or the First National store. These were modern shops with large overhead fans instead of air conditioning, and products stacked from the floor to the ten-foot high ceiling. To shop, you got the attention of a clerk at the main counter and asked him to get items for you. He would scurry about the store to find them, piling them up on the counter. For items stacked high, he had a long stick with a grabber on one end and a hand-operated squeezer on the other. Customers didn't wander about the store; they were waited on.

I remember the curiosity with which we drove to Stamford to investigate the first supermarket in our area. How strange it was to push a shopping cart down the many aisles, grabbing packages out of sight of the employees. "This will never work," we said, "if you let people handle the products before they have bought them, they will steal you blind."

But, of course, it *did* work. Supermarkets sprang up everywhere, squeezing the "regular" grocery stores out of business. Perhaps the ultimate triumph of this worldwide movement appeared in 1987 in Lago Ranco, an impoverished backwater community in the south of Chile: dirt roads, ruined buildings, and about ten pathetic tiny shops displayed rusting cans and distressed vegetables. But over the door of each shop was a hand-lettered sign proclaiming the establishment to be a "Super-mercado."

With the growth of supermarkets, the customer played a much bigger role in the product selection process. The appearance of the package and the shelf space devoted to it in the store became more important, almost, than what was actually in the box. An interesting case study several years ago detailed the effort that went into designing and testing consumer response to the box of a new breakfast cereal for a national manufacturer. After they created a box that consumers really responded to, they spent a couple of months at the end of the process figuring out what to put into it.

While advertising was directed at the consumer, a good part of it was also aimed at the owners of the supermarkets. If they were going to accord shelf space to a new product, they wanted to see evidence of a huge national advertising campaign to support it. The campaign would bring customers into the supermarket looking for the product or give them awareness and knowledge of it. This awareness would tempt a purchase when they encountered it while they walked down the aisles looking for something else.

During the 1950s and 1960s, we entered the era of mass marketing through the fast-growing new supermarkets. The vast spaces in these stores permitted the stocking of three or four brands and two or more sizes of each product, and a much wider variety of new products. Advertising designed to get this lucrative shelf space really took off. Everyone was looking for an edge, a gimmick to beat the competition. For a while, people went crazy with "green stamps," which were handed out in every store with purchases—after you filled up several books with them, you could exchange them for suitcases or a set of china. They were the rage for several years, but have now died out almost completely. They were designed to stimulate loyalty to a particular supermarket chain, since each one offered different, non-exchangeable stamps.

Then came the next media: the coupon. "Twenty-five cents off" proved to be a powerful draw. Millions of people began clipping their daily papers and opening their mail to save up stacks of coupons for their weekly shopping expedition. The beauty of coupons, as compared to general advertising or stamps, was that you put something into people's hands to remind them of what they wanted when they went to the store. *And* that same coupon was left with the store manager to remind him of why you came into his store.

THE ROLE OF DIRECT MARKETING

Direct marketing is any technique designed to provoke a direct response to the advertising stimulus. Catalogs, 800 numbers, and coupons are all a part of it. Direct marketing differs from general advertising in that the response is direct, immediate, and measurable: you send out 100,000 letters and measure the response exactly. Usually the response can be predicted in advance. Good direct marketers are often correct to a fraction of a percent.

But direct marketing has never had the glamour of general advertising. Direct marketing operates out of the national limelight. It is involved with catalogs, with direct mail, and with free-standing coupons inserted in magazines. There is some direct response TV (DRTV), of course, and its use is growing, but it is still small compared to general advertising on TV.

One of the most important boons to direct marketing came about in the 1950s with the introduction of plastic credit cards. Diner's Club and American Express came first, followed by the "bank cards," Visa and MasterCard. These cards really permitted mail-order transactions to take off as never before.

DIRECT MAIL HAS BECOME PROFESSIONAL

The low-profile direct mail industry has attracted some big bucks. The industry continues to grow at about two to three times the rate of growth of the U.S. economy. The telemarketing industry, both inbound at 800 and 900 numbers and outbound, is growing even faster. Mail order is growing faster than retail sales. One major retail chain with 400 department stores added direct mail to its proprietary card customers as a sideline. After five years they were making more profit each year from the direct mail sales than from the 400 stores put together.

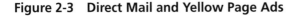

Figure 2-3   Direct Mail and Yellow Page Ads

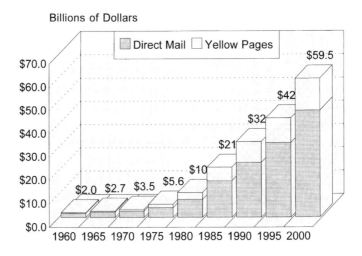

Extrapolated from Robert Coen, McCann-Erickson

Direct mail is really the foundation of database marketing. One of the best books on direct mail is *The Complete Direct Mail List Handbook,* by Ed Burnett. Burnett, one of the most respected men in the business, has been at it for a long time.

Direct mail professionals pioneered working with lists of customers and prospects and matching them against census data. They built up national lists of households which contain amazing amounts of information about what goes on and what is spent in each one. They pioneered the Recency Frequency Monetary (RFM) analytical techniques described in this book, and the concepts of demographic overlays, clustering, and modeling. Above all, they created a very accountable profession where results can be measured and predicted precisely; there is a maximum of bottom-line and a minimum of mumbo-jumbo or advertising hype.

Computer Technology Leads Direct Mail to Database Marketing

In the early years, almost all direct mail lists were kept on magnetic tape. Direct mail and telemarketed response was "keypunched" and compared with output to determine the percentage return down to minute fractions. The "two percent" rule became known and accepted: in any successful direct mail campaign, you will achieve a two percent response or better. The corollary—that 98 percent of your letters will result in no response—was also accepted as a part of the cost of doing business.

When direct mail people began working with computers, they noticed some things that were going on around them:

- The price of mainframe and micro-computers was actually going down every year, while the machines themselves were growing more and more sophisticated and powerful.
- The sophistication and usefulness of computer software was growing: merge/purge, statistical modeling, geocoding, and clustering was becoming easier and cheaper.
- Relational database technology combined with full-screen access techniques made it possible to locate a wealth of information on a single household out of 95 million households

and display it on the screen within seconds of access time. The data could be updated with new information, and returned to its database location at the touch of a button. All of this could be done by fifty or more operators working with the same database of 95 million households simultaneously.

EARLY BEGINNINGS OF DATABASE MARKETING

No one knows just who was the first person to use the term "Database Marketing" to describe their work. A lot of people in the direct marketing business were experimenting with the concepts during the 1970s and early 1980s. One of the first who was successful at it was Tom Lund.

In 1969 Tom founded the Customer Development Corporation in Peoria, Illinois, initially as an ad agency serving State Farm Insurance and a major consumer finance company. Both companies had the same objective: they had large customer lists, and wanted to sell more to those customers. Both had national field organizations that were at the heart of their delivery system, and both wanted to set up a system that would drive a constant flow of business into the field organization.

Tom hit on the idea of building a computer system that would mechanize the sales and service techniques employed by the best agents and managers. But he soon found out it was difficult to do—in 1969. The technology did not exist. One of the objectives was cross-selling, but the data centers couldn't even determine who had purchased more than one product. He was told that what he wanted would require ten year's work and $40 million in programming.

So Tom became a pioneer. His agency bought their own computer— a very expensive proposition in 1969. The clients wanted more research. They also wanted a direct mail program, because the field managers wanted traffic. Combined with branch variables, that meant hundreds of different lettershop lots every month. He couldn't find a lettershop willing to handle such a project. So he set up his own.

They started producing personalized computer letters. These personal letters had to be signed. In those days there was no such thing as laser imaging and digitizing so they had to go into the hand-signing business. "We ultimately were signing more than a million letters each month, making Peoria, Illinois the world capital for writer's cramp," Tom Lund explained.

"The most difficult problem to solve was inventing a way to make the system interactive. The best agents and managers told us that if you asked a customer to buy something, and he did, you should recognize that fact and talk to him differently next time. Plus, the computer had to remember everything it had said to an individual customer to keep from repeating itself. There was no software available anywhere that would handle that kind of history. We had to hire programmers so that we could write our own."

To mimic the way good agents selected the best customers, Lund used RFM analysis from the mail order industry. Within a year he was generating continuous traffic for the branches, altering the product mix as the client required.

The result of this work was the creation of a new type of company with a combination of services never before put together under one roof. "In a management presentation for one of our clients, I described us as a database marketing agency, and the name stuck."

Tom Lund took these early successes and went on to make CDC what he describes as "the largest financial services database marketing firm in America." CDC converts customer, prospect, and membership information into marketing databases. These databases are then used for behavioral research, predictive modeling, and strategic planning to create and initiate a selling system that includes personalized communications and other cross-selling programs to support a client's sales network.

Direct marketers aim at making a sale. The entire industry prides itself on the accountability of each individual mailing or campaign as a distinct entity. You invest so much money and you get so much return—period. Each campaign is self-contained.

Of course, the campaigns are related. Direct mailers, figuring out how soon after the first mailing the next mailing should be sent out, discovered the recency principle, which almost flies in the face of common sense: the customer most likely to buy from you today is the customer who bought from you last week, rather than the one who bought from you three months ago.

American Express Scores a Breakthrough

At the same time that Tom Lund was building CDC, the folks at American Express (and elsewhere) were looking at the customer in a different way. They didn't look at each sale, but at the lifetime value of a customer. They were able to take this longer view for several reasons:

- At the time, in 1978, they had one of the largest active lists of consumers in America.

- They also had at their disposal one of the best computer systems available to direct marketers.

- Most of the activity at American Express was financed by American Express customers and clients (the merchants who honored the cards), rather than by direct sales from American Express itself. This fact meant that American Express was able to observe and measure responses to thousands of different product offers by hundreds of clients, something that few other companies in the country had the luxury of doing.

- Finally, American Express had enlightened management which employed some very sharp people and gave them the freedom and resources to experiment and learn.

The results, as they say, are history. Database marketing has now multiplied and prospered throughout this country. The database marketing concept is based on the *lifetime value* of customers. It aims not at the first sale, although that is essential, but at all the sales that come after that. Direct marketing or mass marketing still has the honor of the first sale. After that, you add the customers to a marketing database. You begin a dialog with them. You provide them with products and information. They provide you with sales, loyalty, and more information. You listen to them and respond to their ideas and wishes. They appreciate the recognition you accord them and respond with more sales, more loyalty, and more information. This goes on for a lifetime. It can make them resist the coupons, cashback, limited-time offers, and discounts offered by the competition. They are your customers for life.

SUCCESSFUL DATABASE MARKETING IS DIFFICULT TO ORGANIZE

Database marketing is very difficult to organize in any company. It is complicated. It involves not just the list of customers (which is usually fairly easy to come by, although not always), but the entire company in an effort to make good on the promise of recognition, response, and results which constant contact with customers requires.

A marketing database connects you to your customers every day. They are writing to you, or more likely, telephoning your sales or customer service staff with inquiries, orders, or requests for detailed information. "What is the status of my order?" "How do I assemble this thing that I just received?" "Don't you make one of these for left-handed people?" You get all the questions that have accumulated for thirty years while people sat out the mass marketing and catalog revolutions.

There are more than 500 ad agencies and almost as many consultants who specialize in direct response advertising. Most of them want to get involved in database marketing, although few of them really know much about it. Very few of them have yet developed the kind of creative leader who can put a database project together.

If direct marketing is complicated, and it is, database marketing is many times more complicated. There are now national organizations which recognize this profession. The first was the National Center for Database Marketing established by Skip Andrew in 1987 and now run by Cowles Business Media and the Direct Marketing Association. They host two annual conferences in Orlando and Chicago with over 100 speakers and 1000 or more attendees each time. The enthusiasm is contagious. You can feel the excitement. It has become almost a religion to its devotees. Why?

Because you can offer something to customers that they really want—an audience, recognition, and information—and get from them something that you really want—loyalty and sales. You both feel that the relationship is mutually satisfying and profitable.

This message is so exciting for its proponents that they run around inside their companies buttonholing everyone trying to get *them* enthusiastic about the idea. What they find is what all other religious fanatics before them have discovered: it is easier to get excited about a concept than it is to make it a part of the society and social environment you are living in. To get a real marketing database going takes a creative genius and a substantial corporate commitment of money and resources. This commitment must be wrung from higher management who may not yet have embraced the religion, and from lower level parts of the company who, in some cases, may actually be opposed to the changes which database marketing will bring. Sales may be opposed to surrendering the names of their contacts, or to using your leads. MIS may be opposed to allowing you to set up a marketing database outside of the central computer, while also protesting that the database takes up too much space or too many in-house resources. Dealers may fight the idea of the company having direct contact with their customers.

Database marketing really began to take off in the mid-1990s. Graduate schools began to offer courses and even degrees in the subject. By this time, almost every major corporation in America had appointed someone with the designation of Director of Database Marketing. There had been major national successes and major national failures.

The successes?

- MCI Friends and Family—one of the most powerful applications of database marketing that has been so successful in generating new business through referrals, that AT&T and Sprint had to spend several years devoting most of their ad budgets to fighting it.

- Hertz Number One Club Gold—an innovative system for pampering their best customers with super service, and capturing all of their business with no discounts.

- American Airlines Advantage—a powerful method for maintaining customer loyalty year after year after year.

Some of the failures included:

- Quaker Direct—a $20 million dollar failed effort to build relationships with Quaker Oats customers by mailing them coupons. (Hint: coupons do not build loyalty!)

- Reward America—a $200 million dollar failed effort by Citicorp to capture the names and purchases of supermarket customers and sell the resulting data to national manufacturers. (Hint: the manufacturers didn't know what to do with the names they already had. They weren't in the market for more.)

- Air Miles—a huge loyalty program with 40 corporate sponsors and 2.2 million members which died after only a year. (Hint: it required members to clip out and mail in proofs of purchase. People couldn't be bothered.)

The methods are chronicled in the pages of this book, and in marketing magazines, each of which today accords sections, and often whole editions, to database marketing.

The National Center for Database Marketing is mobbed at every one of their twice a year conferences. The Database Marketing Institute in Arlington, Virginia is sold out in their four times a year seminars for industry leaders. There have been a dozen books published in the U.S. on the subject, and more are coming out each year.

Database marketing has arrived. But it is still difficult to do. The objectives are clear. The methods are known. To design and carry out the strategies that will win customer loyalty, boost sales, win referrals, and boost lifetime value, however, is not easy. The future of database marketing will be created by some very resourceful, imaginative, and dedicated marketers.

SUMMARY

Database marketing is the culmination of a long chain of developments in marketing, including:

- National advertising and brand consciousness;
- The growth of supermarkets and the mass marketing of the 1970s and 1980s;
- The success and professionalism of direct mail;
- The sophistication and reduction in cost of computers; and

- The relative affluence and sophistication of modern consumers, who want more personal attention and diversity of products.

Throughout this book I have provided hundreds of examples of database marketing. Some of them are case studies; many of them are proposals which are under active consideration by major corporations. Some are only dreams which may never achieve reality. All are intended to spark your imagination, to give *you* the religion.

Database marketing is so hard to organize and carry out, and requires such a high level of creative talent, that in many industries it may never get off the ground. But from all indications, the idea has taken root across a wide spectrum of American and European business today. It is not just a passing fad. What we make of it in our businesses is up to us—the future is in our hands.

Part II:

The Technical Side of Database Marketing

Chapter 3

What the Database Marketer Needs to Know About Computer Hardware

This chapter will tell you what you, as a database marketing planner, will have to know about computer hardware. To make it easy for later reference, the terms defined here are also listed in the glossary at the back of the book.

Hardware refers to computers and the peripherals plugged into them. Software refers to the programs that make computers work. We will cover software in the next chapter.

THE IMPORTANCE OF HARDWARE

The kind of hardware you select to store your database can determine the kind of work you can do efficiently. If you select the wrong machine, it is possible that your database will never get off the ground, and will never be able to realize the benefits for your company that you are seeking. You should not choose a computer that is too small to hold all of your customer records and to permit you to find them instantly and update them. Marketing databases require huge processing power; probably a bigger machine than your company uses for other applications. The computers that already exist in your company for other functions are probably not suited to a database marketing application even though they may be ideal for doing payroll, general ledger, processing customer orders, or maintaining inventory. Don't make the mistake of thinking that a computer is a computer is a computer. There are big differences, and you must know the differences before you start or you will fail to reach your objective.

Another "don't": don't assume that the computer professionals in your company know anything about database marketing and are capable of advising you on what type of hardware you need. Some of them may be, but most are probably not knowledgeable in this field because it is so new and so different from other computer applications.

Your company's computer professionals in most cases have a vested interest in seeing that your marketing database is installed on the hardware already present in your company. After all, it is their hardware. Their power and influence in the company are built on their ownership of this hardware. If applications like yours are farmed out to other equipment, what will happen to their position in the hierarchy?

For this reason, these very professionals may be your biggest obstacle in your quest to establish a marketing database. They will insist that your database be installed on their hardware (whether or not the hardware is suitable) and that they control the programming of the database (since they program all applications on the computer). At first this may seem like an ideal solution, since you certainly don't want to have to hire your own programmers or to become proficient at this skill yourself.

However, putting your database on the existing hardware is probably a trap because it will undoubtedly be accorded a lower priority than the computer's other applications. You will be unable to get the programming time, the hardware attention, or the clout you need to get your database going. It will take you months (or even years) longer to get your database up and running than it would if you put your database on another, better suited computer. Finally, it will probably cost your company more to install it than it would to set the database up on an outside service bureau computer.

Types of Computers

There are basically three types of computers: Mainframes, minicomputers, and microcomputers (commonly called PCs).

Minicomputers. Minicomputers are midrange between a PC and a mainframe. For applications where you maintain a medium-sized database (200,000 or less) they may be very good. For a large marketing database, they are really not powerful enough.

An IBM AS/400, for example, does not have the combination of processing power, input-output capability, multi-user ability, software availability, and multi-tasking flexibility that are available on mainframes. Mainframes have some telling advantages in database marketing: control, recovery, integration, high volume data access, and large-scale database and network management. The factors behind all of these advantages are software availability and concentrated processing power, which most minis lack.

A large television station used an IBM AS/400 mini for their financial operations, their broadcasting operations, and their membership program. About 300 staff members throughout the station were connected with the mini by terminals on their desks. This particular type of mini is very good at managing on-line operations. ("On-line" means the ability to serve many different users simultaneously.) But it was poor at batch operations; the ability to process marketing functions, like updating membership files, from external data such as mail responses or telemarketers' tapes.

Finance and broadcasting were very happy using this system. Their software had been written several years before and ran with minor modifications day in and day out. Marketing, however, was in very deep trouble. To increase membership, the marketing staff constantly came up with new initiatives, revisions of forms, special appeals, special reports, and selects for direct marketing and telemarketing. All of these initiatives required extensive programmer time.

These initiatives swamped the programming staff. The other computer applications (finance and broadcasting) used only one programmer each, whereas membership consumed three. The software for the mini was difficult to write, and there was not enough off-the-shelf software designed for marketing applications available for minis. The result was that membership could not get the support that it felt it needed.

Mainframe Computers. These are the big ones, most of them made by IBM. These monsters used to require special air conditioning and raised floors. The newest ones do not. Attached to them are five types of devices:

Figure 3-1 Types of Database Hardware

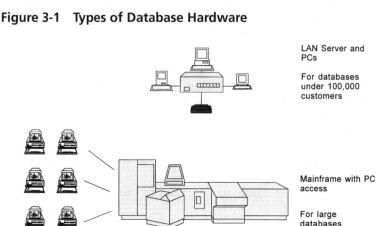

LAN Server and PCs

For databases under 100,000 customers

Mainframe with PC access

For large databases

- Disks (sometimes called DASD) on which your database resides,
- Cartridge or tape drives (used to get data into and out of your computer),
- Printers,
- Communications gear (used to connect the computer with the outside world by telephone lines), and
- PCs or Terminals used for entering commands and viewing data.

Personal Computers. PCs (or microcomputers) are just like mainframes, except they sit on a desk, don't need air-conditioning or raised floors, and are less powerful. They are very sophisticated and are being improved and radically upgraded every year.

PCs also have internal disks and communications gear. PC Servers are large PCs that serve several PC users who share the disk and software located on the server.

For database marketing, as we know it today, you must have a mainframe computer for a large database (anything over 200,000 customers), or a powerful PC server (for smaller databases). You will want to access your database through a PC on your desk which is connected to your server or your mainframe, either directly or through a telephone line.

MIPS, Chips, Bits, and Bytes

A five MIPS (Millions of Instructions Per Second) mainframe computer used to be considered fast. Many mainframes today will do 100 or more MIPS. Of course, speed alone is not a worthwhile measurement. You need to know what other work is going on at the same time on your computer. Mainframes work simultaneously for scores or hundreds of users at the same time. Each user is doing a different job. Even the fastest mainframe can perform slowly if it is bogged down with heavy number-crunching activities while you are trying to access your customer database.

For PCs the measurement is the *chip and the speed in megahertz*. A computer chip is about the size and weight of your fingernail. It has thousands of printed circuits and electronics which have been shrunk by photographic wizardry to infinitesimal size. It costs tens of millions of dollars to develop one chip. To make the second copy costs only a few cents. Inside every PC there is a chip. The original IBM PC and all competing brands used an 8088 or 8086 chip, which was considered very good until the 80286 chip appeared. The '286 was about ten times as fast and powerful as the '86. It was the hottest thing for about a year until the '386 arrived. Following this were the '486 and the Pentium which were faster still. This improvement will continue until the outer limits of chip creativity are reached; and no one knows when that will happen. Chips are also rated in speed—megahertz. For database marketing today you will need a minimum of 90 megahertz for most applications.

Another measurement of mainframes and PCs is *memory*. Memory is a measure of how much information a computer can hold while it is working on a problem (or program). The more memory, the faster it works, and the more complex things it does. Most mainframes today have many million bytes of memory. Memory for them is not a limiting factor. Today, PC memory is so cheap that almost any that you buy will have 4,000,000 or more bytes, although 8,000,000 is probably required for any normal database marketing activity.

A *byte* is a unit of memory. It is a character or a number. The letter A is one byte. So is the number "6", or an *. Computers store information in their memory or on disks or tape reels as bytes. Normally, a byte is composed of eight *bits* or a group of 1s and 0s. The character A when written in bits is:

1100 0001

B is:

1100 0010

What is on a disk, a magnetic tape, or a cartridge, then, are groups of bits (1s and 0s), which, grouped together, form bytes, which represent letters, numbers, and other characters.

Figure 3-2   Hardware Components of Database Computers

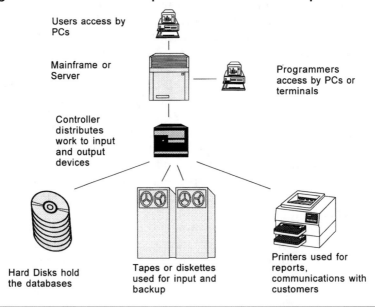

Users access by PCs

Mainframe or Server

Programmers access by PCs or terminals

Controller distributes work to input and output devices

Hard Disks hold the databases

Tapes or diskettes used for input and backup

Printers used for reports, communications with customers

Disk Memory

Disk memory is very important to database marketing because your database is stored on a disk. Disk memory is measured in *megabytes* (or millions of bytes). Disks are *direct access devices.* That means that every byte on a disk has a special disk *address.* The computer can find that byte and go directly to it if it knows the address.

Marketing databases require a lot of space on disks because they hold a great deal of information about customers and prospects. For example, in addition to names and addresses, you will want to keep records of all purchases, products bought, amounts paid, and the dates and source code of the marketing activity or media that produced each sale. You may also want to record every telephone call made to you. You will also keep the results of survey questions with such information as family income, number of children, type of automobile, or hundreds of other things.

On one of the databases which we are maintaining in our company we have household records on 330,000 customers. But when you total the records we are keeping on all of their purchases, we have 28 million records on these 330,000 customers. The average number of bytes in these records is about 100, so we need 6300 megabytes (6.3 *gigabytes*) to hold this marketing database. But that is not all. Databases require a lot of extra space to insert *new records* which are created every day in the course of sales activity. Plan for this extra storage room. For our 330,000 customer file we actually have set aside 8 gigabytes (8000 megabytes) for the entire file. While 8 gigabytes in the early 1990s used to take up a lot of floor space, modern smaller disks have brought the space required down to briefcase size. Computer technology is still on a roll.

On-Line versus Off-Line

Catalog marketers have been keeping records on customers for more than twenty years. Most of these records have been kept on computer tape. A computer tape reel is 1/2 inch wide and holds 2,400 feet of magnetic tape. At a rated density of 6,250 bytes per inch, this tape could hold the records of about 300,000 customers. The big difference between tape and disk is that to find the record of any one customer on a tape, you must read through all 300,000 customers; on disk, you can go right to the customer if you know the address on the disk.

Because of the difficulty of working with tapes or cartridges (a cartridge holds the equivalent of three tapes), catalog marketing was often done in *batch mode*, meaning that many transactions from many customers were gathered (once a week or month, for example) and then run simultaneously, making a new updated tape in the process. This was very efficient, but it doesn't work well for database marketing. Off-line batch records typically impose limits on the amount of data that you can keep on a customer; and, using tape, you can't call a customer's record to the screen when he or she calls you on the telephone.

There is no substitute for having customer records on-line on disk when doing customer service in support of database marketing. Every time you get a piece of information from a customer—an order, a return, a coupon, a survey response, a telephone call, a change of address—you will want to update or enter the information into the customer's record immediately, not a month later. The Customer Service function of database marketing typically requires many different people working with customer records at the same time, and they need to be confident that they have the *latest information* about customers when they are talking to them, writing to them, or servicing their orders.

Access Time

Having a lot of MIPS in the mainframe is not the whole story. If your mainframe is busy much of the day with other company work not related to marketing (and this is usually the case), this other work will have a tendency to dominate the computer. You may find that your marketing operation is pushed onto the back burner while the computer gets out the payroll, sends out the bills, maintains the inventory, or runs the factory. You will notice this most in delays in *access time*.

Consider the following scenario. Mrs. Clara Fowler calls customer service because her order did not arrive. She is irate. You are sitting at a computer terminal connected to your database. You enter Mrs. Fowler's name and wait for her records to appear. You wait 10, 20, 30 seconds—still no record. Meanwhile, Mrs. Fowler is steaming. You try to keep up a pleasant conversation. It may begin to occur to Mrs. Fowler that maybe the delay with her order and the fact that you can't retrieve her records are *related facts.* She may suspect not that the customer database has a low priority, but that the *Fowler household* has a low priority.

When designing your marketing database and dealing directly with the computer systems people who will make it happen, you must set standards for access time to records. Typically, any record should come up on the screen within one second after you request it, no matter whether your computer holds 100,000 customers or 10 million. In busy times, access time could slip to three seconds, but you must get an ironclad guarantee that it will *never* be more than five seconds; if you can't, you should seek some other location for your database. You simply cannot run a satisfactory customer service operation with access times in excess of five seconds. Your customers will not like it, and your staff will revolt.

Communications

If you are located in the same building as your PC server or your mainframe computer, communications will not be a problem for you. Your PC will be wired directly into the server or mainframe. But in most database marketing applications, the mainframe or server is in one place and your customer service or marketing staff is somewhere else. You must set up a communications system.

Remote communication with a database is usually achieved by telephone lines. Where many people are using the database (such as on customer service), you will want a *dedicated line.* This is a private line rented from the telephone company which connects point A with point B. Using such a system, fifty or more operators can use the database at the same time over the same line. This is accomplished by an electronic marvel called a controller. All users' terminals are wired into the controller, the controller is wired into a *modem* and the modem is plugged into the dedicated telephone line. When this line gets to the mainframe, it goes through another modem and a communications unit which separates each of the many different conversations going on over the line so that the computer recognizes and deals separately with each of your service people.

You must also take line speed into consideration. Slow line speed means slow access time. Communications line speed is measured in *baud rate*. (Never mind what a baud is!) The minimum speed suggested is 14,400 baud; a good customer service operation, with lots of operators, really requires a 56,000-baud *digital* line. Digital lines have much cleaner data, less dropping of the line, and better communications. What you need will vary in each case.

Three Views of Customer Data

There are really three ways to store and access customer data: for operational, customer service, or marketing functions. Each method needs different data, and different access methods.

- *Operational Files* are maintained in situations in which the customer is sent a periodic bill. In such cases you keep track of purchases by account number. In a company, MIS normally maintains such files. They seldom have historical or other non-accounting data. They are used by accountants to keep track of the money. They are not very useful for marketing.

- *Customer Service Files* are organized on a household or company basis, rather than by account number. Such files exist so that you can talk to customers on the telephone. Such databases usually have past years' purchase history, plus a record of past customer service calls. Good customer service is essential to good database marketing, but customer service files are not very useful for marketing purposes. Customer service files are usually organized by customer, rather than by account.

- *Marketing Files* contain all the data in customer service files, plus other data: demographics, survey responses, and promotion history. Marketers don't need to look up individual customer records. Instead, marketers need to do very rapid ad-hoc counts and selects as a basis for the design and analysis of marketing programs. Marketing files are usually organized by household or company, rather than by account or customer.

Three File Types

Type	Data Organization	Data Maintained	On-Line View	Ad-Hoc Counts & Selects
Operative	Account Number	Current Year	None or Account Status	None
Customer Service	Household or Company	Current Year and Past Years	All Customer Data Service History	None
Marketing	Household or Company	All of the above plus promotion and response history, surveys, demographics	Data indexes (no individual customer data)	Very Rapid Ad-hoc Counts & Selects

In many cases, these three files may be most economically stored on three separate computers: one for MIS, one for customer service, and a third for marketing. This may be much easier than trying to make the MIS file work for all three. We will be discussing this subject further in the next chapter on software.

Figure 3-3   Three Related Databases

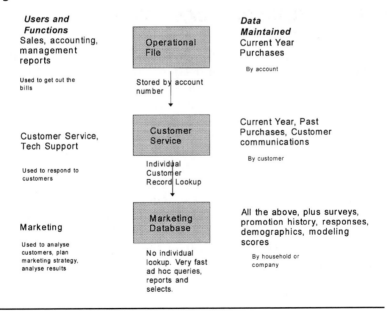

Users and Functions
Sales, accounting, management reports

Used to get out the bills

Operational File

Stored by account number

Data Maintained
Current Year Purchases

By account

Customer Service, Tech Support

Used to respond to customers

Customer Service

Individual Customer Record Lookup

Current Year, Past Purchases, Customer communications

By customer

Marketing

Used to analyse customers, plan marketing strategy, analyse results

Marketing Database

No individual lookup. Very fast ad hoc queries, reports and selects.

All the above, plus surveys, promotion history, responses, demographics, modeling scores

By household or company

Nightly Backup and Down Time

One other point that should not be overlooked is the problem of down time and disaster. Computers are always going down for one reason or another: hardware problems, software problems, power problems. It is going to happen, so plan for it. Once you get deeply into database marketing, the database will dominate your business, and the computer, which is the heart of your database, can make or break you.

Insist on nightly backup on tape of all the information on all of your customers. Insist that the computer staff has written procedures on how to restore your database after a breakdown and that their staff is trained in these procedures. Your computer will need an Uninterruptable Power Supply (UPS) system with a diesel generator.

Finally, be sure that your telemarketing operators have pre-printed forms and instructions so they can keep working when the computer goes down. Train your staff to handle a one-hour downtime, a one-day downtime, a three-day downtime. Don't just assume that it won't happen.

PUTTING YOUR DATABASE ON A PC

Given the growing power of PCs and the increased size and speed of their disks, why not use a PC instead of bothering with a mainframe with all the attendant problems of an unresponsive MIS staff and slow programmers? This question has occurred to hundreds of would-be marketing database planners.

If your customer database is small—as are most business-to-business databases—you can hold and access all of the information on a PC. This may seem like the ideal solution, until you consider what really needs to be done with a customer database.

You must run merge/purge to eliminate duplicates and update your customer records with new additions, deletes, changes of address, responses, purchases, and customer service inquiries. You should back up your database every night, maintaining a copy onsite and offsite. When you do selects for a mailing, you will have to run postal presort software to get proper discounts. You will have to format your output for labels or laser letters.

Can you do all of these things on a PC? Of course. Software is available. In the process, however, while doing them you will stop being a marketer, and become a slave to your PC database.

These are programmer or operator functions. The most difficult function to perform in database marketing is dreaming up and implementing marketing strategies that build customer loyalty and repeat sales. Time spent doing PC housekeeping takes marketers away from their main goal: building customer lifetime value.

You are far better off having your marketing database maintained by computer professionals—on your staff, in MIS, or at an external service bureau—than asking marketing professionals to become part time programmers. The PC stand-alone solution may sound simple and seductive. It is a trap.

PC TO MAINFRAME CONNECTION

Mainframes have the processing power needed for a marketing database, but they do not have, and probably will never have, the sophistication of a personal computer. This is because there are a few hundred thousand mainframes in the world, and millions upon millions of personal computers. All the great software of the future is going to be written for the personal computer, not for the mainframe. Think of the mainframe as the offensive line of a major football team. The PC represents the backfield: running, passing, and coming up with new plays all the time. PCs have color, graphics, statistics, versatility, and software. Because they are so impressive, some people make the mistake of thinking that they are suitable for database marketing themselves. Try putting the backfield of any major football team up on the line and see how long they last.

What you need for successful database marketing is a system which combines the power of the mainframe with the sophistication and software of the PC. Fortunately, it is not difficult to arrange this combination. Nowadays, PCs and PC Servers are easily linked to a mainframe. The central processor can do all of the heavy lifting, while the PC provides the access, graphics, spreadsheets, reports, and user friendly features.

One of the most difficult problems for mainframe programmer staff is the preparation of user reports. As a marketer, you will want a large number of very specialized reports that tell you what is going on in your customers' minds. Report preparation takes hundreds of hours of mainframe programmer's time, and eats up your marketing budget.

The beauty of a PC is that you have Lotus, Excel, Harvard Graphics, SAS, SPSS, and scores of other software packages that can make more beautiful reports and graphs than could ever be constructed on a mainframe. You can grab data from the mainframe database using ad-hoc queries (see next chapter) and convert that data into dozens of different reports using your PC.

The ideal solution, therefore, is to have your database maintained on a mainframe where professional programmers and operators run all the updates, merge/purge, and backup functions, while your marketers use PCs linked to the mainframe to do ad-hoc queries and produce printed reports. You can also do this if the PC is linked to a server— but be sure that you have a full-time server programmer somewhere whose job it is to run all the database software functions, so that your marketers do not get bogged down in infrastructure functions.

Mainframes, regarded by some as pitiful, helpless giants, become the offensive line of a winning database marketing team that includes the most advanced PCs, with their inexpensive but sophisticated software, directing operations from the backfield.

The real key to the hardware problem is personnel. Database marketing requires skilled and involved professional programmers who will manipulate your database to do the updates, cleaning, merge/purge, and produce your output. If your database is on a stand alone PC, there is no room for these professionals. You are on your own. You will have to forget about marketing and become a programmer. Your marketing program will suffer.

The Small Database Problem

Much of what is written here deals with the handling of large customer files—from 50,000 to 50 million customers or more. Some marketers, however, particularly those with business-to-business applications may have extremely small customer and prospect files—often less than 5,000 records in all. With such small files, it is normally not cost efficient to outsource your database. You will have to maintain the data in-house on a PC server. Just because the numbers are small, though, the complexities still exist. You should consider outsourcing.

In the next chapter we will offer some guidance on software for small systems.

DIFFERING HARDWARE ROLES

Different people in your organization will have different applications for the marketing database. Your customer service people will be answering telephone calls, calling up customer records, and entering data. They will need high-speed terminals to view the records, linked by high-speed telephone lines.

Your marketing research staff will be using the database to do modeling using neural network software. They will want to have their PCs linked to the database so that they can download customer data, and upload the algorithms developed by their models.

Your database marketing staff will want to be linked to the database with PCs that permit them to do instant ad-hoc counts, reports, and selects. They will want to try out hundreds of what-if scenarios to understand the motivation of their customers.

Your mainframe or PC server programmers will be accessing the database to do regular updates, address cleaning, identification of duplicates, nightly backup, and other housekeeping functions.

At the same time, your mainframe or PC server programmers will be running event-driven software (which you have designed) that writes letters to customers on their birthdays, or when their cars are three months or three years old, or thanks them automatically for a purchase, or notifies them that they now qualify for "Gold" status. This kind of software is best done by professional programmers, rather than having to have marketers remember (or forget) to call it up every day.

You may want to give your direct marketing agency access to the database so that they can help you to design marketing programs directly from their offices. You may want to link an external telemarketing bureau to your database if they are helping with customer service or sales. In most cases, though, these telemarketers will simply upload to you daily data which results from their activities.

If you have regional sales or marketing offices, you may want to give them access to your database by long distance telephone dial-up or leased lines.

Finally, you yourself, the database marketer, will want direct access to the database so that you can monitor what is going on, and design your marketing program.

In planning your marketing database hardware, therefore, consider the needs of each unit that is likely to use the data base, and plan their hardware needs. They will not all be the same.

Keep It Small

A fundamental mistake that most beginning database marketers make is thinking too big at first. If your database is going to be successful, there are steps you must go through. The first step is building a small test database. This database, while a pilot, must still be a real database with real customers with whom you have a dialogue. Try it first with your top 10 or 20 percent of customers. You will learn a lot—about what data to keep, what to discard, and what type of hardware and software works best. After you know that, then go on to make your bigger database.

If you start from the beginning to make the ultimate database with millions of records and all the bells and whistles, you may never actually build a database at all. Why? Because the costs and complications will bog you down. It will take you a long time, and you won't learn anything during the planning process.

SUMMARY

- Your database should be stored on a mainframe or a PC server which has a full time programming staff available to do the database housekeeping functions.

- In considering choice of hardware, bear in mind what other work will be running on the machine. If the machine is often busy, your database response may be too slow.

- Your users should access the database by means of PCs linked to the mainframe or server.

- Disk space requirements will be very extensive.

- Customer Service needs to look up individual records. Access time for an individual record lookup should be a few seconds.

- Marketers do not need to look up individual records. Instead, they need to do ad-hoc queries. Users should be able to do ad-hoc queries that run in less than a minute, no matter how large your file.

- You may be better off outsourcing your database to a professional service bureau than relying on your MIS staff or part-time marketers.

Chapter 4

Software for Database Marketing

When cars first appeared, people had the idea that anyone who wanted to drive one ought to learn how its motor worked, what a carburetor did, what pistons were, what a timing gear did. Nowadays we leave all that to the mechanics. The average driver never looks under the hood. If he can drive the car, and keep gas and oil in it, that is all he needs to do to be a fully functioning automobile driver and owner.

Some people today feel the same way about computer programs. They know what they want the computer to do for them. All they need to do is to tell the programmer their desires and let the programmers do the rest.

The analogy is not a good one. Automobiles have matured over the last 100 years. Computer programs have not had time to do that. Even though cars are now manufactured all over the globe by hundreds of different companies, they are all basically the same. They all have the same components. If something is wrong with the car, you don't have to explain anything to the mechanic; you just say that the brakes need adjusting.

But there is no such universal understanding about computer programs. There is no agreement on what a customer record should look like, how to store it, how to update it, or how to report on it. If you travel around America looking into computer programs that deal with customer records, you will find hundreds of different ways of dealing with the same fundamental situation. Some of them are brilliant. Some are terrible. Most are just variations of a barely adequate system.

To be successful at database marketing, you have to come up with great creative ideas which involve manipulating your customers' records to support and expand a mutually profitable long-term relationship. The things you will ask the programmers to do will not be simple. Many of them will require the programmers to do complex things that they have never heard of before. You will be pushing the outer edges of software capability. To get the programmers to understand and create what you want, you are going to have to understand them and the media they are using: software.

A better analogy than the automobile driver and the mechanic is the analogy of the first designers of jet airplanes and the engineers who created the early models. The designers knew what they wanted aerodynamically, but they had to understand the materials and problems of the engineers if their designs were ever to result in a satisfactory jet. For these reasons, therefore, we will cover a bit of history and database theory to explain the software that underlies successful database marketing.

MAILING LIST CONSTRUCTION

Databases began as *mailing lists.* These were, and are, flat sequential files of names and addresses and other data kept on a magnetic tape. A typical mailing list record for a household looks something like this:

Field	Size
NAME	30
ADDRESS	30
CITY	20
STATE	2
ZIP CODE	5
ID NUMBER	6
DATE	6
Total	99

Size refers to the number of bytes (characters) allowed for the information in the field. The total size of the record (in this illustration) is 99 bytes. I should emphasize that there are absolutely no standards for what the record fields and the record size should look like. Every computer center in the United States has a different format for customer records. There are no government industry standards. It is total anarchy—or free enterprise (depending on how you look at it). Typically, in a sequential file, each record is strung out on a magnetic tape immediately following the previous record:

```
   BACH         BARNES        BORK        BUSH
|_____|_____|_____|_____|
```

In this example, each record is 99 bytes long. The bytes consist of magnetic bits on the tape. Each bit is either magnetized (on) or not magnetized (off). Eight bits make up a byte. Different combinations of on and off bits determine whether the byte is an A or a B or a C . . . or a 1, 2, 3, etc.

If you have 200,000 names recorded on your tape in alphabetical order, you will have to go through almost all of the tape to reach someone named Williams. If you want to reshuffle the names and sort them in zip code order, you must put these names on a disk where a sorting program will do the job in a few minutes (or an hour, depending on the speed of your computer and how busy it is), and put them back on tape in the new order.

Many catalog lists were kept on a magnetic tape just like this. Nine-track 6250 bytes per inch magnetic tape is standard in the industry. If you rent a list of names from anyone, the list will come to you on a nine-track tape. The data is written on the tape either in EBCDIC (an IBM protocol) or ASCII (everything else). Any large computer service bureau can read any EBCDIC or ASCII tape.

There are many different functions that must be performed on such a tape: sorting, selecting, and updating.

Updating consists of adding new names, deleting old names, and modifying (changing) existing names. Typically, as a result of an ad campaign, you may receive several thousand responses on order forms or coupons. When these are received, you send them for keypunching. In keypunching, someone sits at a typewriter-type keyboard of a small computer and enters each name and address. A program has already been written to assure that the names and addresses will end up in the correct *format*. In our case, it will be our 99 byte format. The output of our keypunching will be a magnetic tape of the new names. We will probably use this tape in a program to prepare labels so that we can mail to the respondents whatever they ordered with the coupon. After the respondents' requests have been fulfilled, we are then ready to add the names on the respondent tape to our master tape so that we can update the master. To update our master tape from this transaction tape, we will run both tapes through an update program.

The first step in the update is to sort our transaction tape in the same order as the master tape (in our illustration it is in alphabetic order). A computer program puts our transactions on a disk attached to the computer, and reshuffles the records into alphabetic order. Then the names are put back onto tape. Now both tapes are run simultaneously.

Figure 4-1   Tape Updating

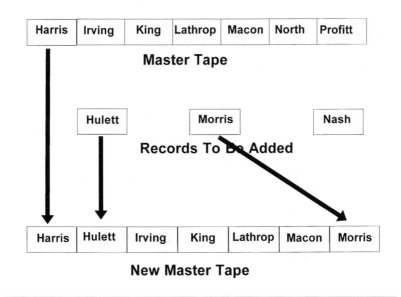

In the update program, a new master tape is created with the combined names. Arnold goes before Bach, Benson before Bork. Suppose we add "Bush" to a file that already has that name. We have a problem: if one is George Bush and the other David Bush, we put David first and we are done, but if both Bushes are George Bush at the same address, we have a duplicate. The update program has to contain instructions for what to do in this case (delete one and mark the master to show that there was a duplicate, for instance).

This rather elemental discussion of sequential file processing illustrates a point: flat sequential files have both good and bad qualities. It is easy to run batch updates on them and to sort them. You can run simple counts on them. But if you are going to use them for complex reporting or to update one record at a time, they just are not satisfactory.

Adding Order Records

Sequential files become complicated when you want to add customer orders to them. You can increase the record size and add the orders to the format:

EXISTING 99 BYTES PLUS . . .

ORDER DATE	6
SKU ORDERED	8
QUANTITY	6
AMOUNT OF ORDER	8
CELL CODE	6

"CELL CODE" refers to the outgoing promotion which brought the order in. "SKU" refers to the number of the item purchased.

Of course, this format is useless if a customer has ordered two items and you want to record the purchase of both. One solution to this problem is to make space for ten or twelve different orders after the name and address. If the customer ordered more than the maximum, you would delete the oldest order, adding a counter in the record for total number of orders. Another method is to create variable length records with the length of the record being determined by the number of orders. The programs for sorting and updating variable length records can become complicated and costly.

A third widely used solution is to have a separate order file not connected to the customer file at all. It would look something like this:

ID NUMBER	6
ORDER NUMBER	8
ORDER DATE	6
CELL CODE	6
SKU ORDERED	8
QUANTITY	6
ORDER AMOUNT	8

Figure 4-2   Customer and Order in Separate Files

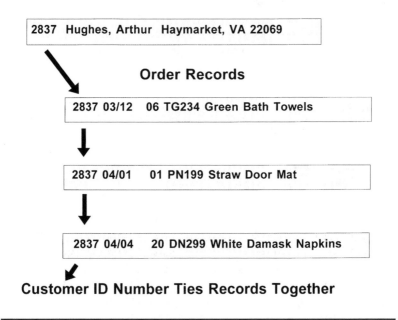

In this arrangement, "ID NUMBER" is the ID of the customer. "ORDER NUMBER" is a chronological number stamped on each outgoing order. With this system, each customer can have as many orders posted to the system as needed: some customers can have thousands of orders; most customers have only one or two. If you want to know how many orders a given customer has placed, you would have to run both the customer file and the order file in a program that matches the ID Number.

ADVANTAGES AND DISADVANTAGES OF SEQUENTIAL FILES

Sequential files have the advantage of being the cheapest way to store data.

The disadvantages are:

- Producing marketing reports is a nightmare. For large files of millions of records, it may take two weeks or more for a data processing shop to produce the reports you need.

- Updating can only be done in batches. For this reason, it is done infrequently—probably once a month. Your files are never current.

- You cannot find any record instantly. If your customers call you on the phone, your best research tool is a thick printed book of all the customers.

- Duplicates build up and are hard to find and consolidate.

Clearly sequential files offer many disadvantages. Yet many customer files are still maintained in this way. For a marketing database, however, we need something else—a relational database.

RELATIONAL DATABASE

Marketing databases are maintained as relational databases on disk. There are other methods, of course, but there is really no other way to have instant access to all parts of your customer file, and still do reports, counts, and selects.

Instead of putting your records on a tape, a relational database stores them on a disk where they are instantly retrievable by their location. You can pull up Mr. Williams' record just as fast as Mrs. Bach's. The program tells the disk seek arm where to look. It goes there and reads the record. The program finds Mr. Williams by means of an *index*. An index is a disk file consisting of a name and a location:

Name	Location
WILLIAMS, ARTHUR	23145
WILLIAMS, CAROL	83290
WILLIAMS, DAVID	11092
WILLIAMS, EDWARD	33325

The index is created when the record is stored. If you add a new record for Betty Williams it will be placed in any free space on the disk; you can update the index so you can find her:

Name	Location
WILLIAMS, ARTHUR	23145
WILLIAMS, BETTY	999120
WILLIAMS, CAROL	83290
WILLIAMS, DAVID	11092
WILLIAMS, EDWARD	33325

Order records are stored in the same way. Every order record contains the ID number of the customer. You can have an order index that looks like this:

Order Index

Customer ID	Order Record Locations
11092	223876 774334, 887653, 223014, 888375, 764111
	223877 223145, 443526
	223878 110299, 993267, 337265

Records can be indexed by more than one field. For example, you might want to find customers by their zip code or telephone number. You would have an index for each one:

Telephone Number Index to the Customer File

Telephone Number	Customer Record Location
703 742-4470	293847
703 754-3477	983726
703 784-1234	112938
703 784-9487	887362

Figure 4-3   Disk Files Are Random Access

Tape Files Are Sequential

ler	Smith, Alfred	Smith, Andrew	Smit

Disk Files Are Random Access

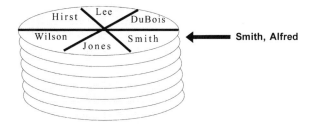

With a disk database, if you know the address on the disk, you can access any record instantly.

With a relational database, then, you build a large number of indexes. Each index permits you to access parts of your data instantly by telling your program where it is. What does this mean for your marketing database?

- Your telemarketers can instantly call up any customer record and get all the information they need on orders, telephone calls, complaints, shipments, billing problems, and family relationships. They have a way of immediately knowing everything they need to know about customers.

- Your telemarketers can quickly update any record (add a new order, change a credit card number or an address, add or delete a record).

- You can create reports very rapidly on the status of your marketing program, reports that would take weeks using many other systems. (More on reports later.)

- You can do sophisticated statistical analysis or modeling with the data. You can do complex segmentation. You can quickly add data to your records (enhancement), and match your customer file to other outside data files. The sky is the limit.

However, there is a downside. There is no such thing as a free lunch:

- Your relational database will take up a lot of space on disk. Besides providing space for your existing customer records, you must provide space for new customer records and future orders. And you need lots of space for your extensive indexes. Disk space today is dirt cheap, but many information management staffs do not yet accept that.

- The software for your relational database is very complex and expensive. Depending on the size of your system, you may be spending a lot of money on database software.

- Complex software *always* has built-in errors or bugs. Something is always going wrong for unknown reasons. You must have a very alert system staff which is constantly watching the database and patching or restoring it when it "goes down." It may go down several times a month.

- The more indexes you add, the slower the response. If you have thirty indexes on your customer record, every time you try to change any data in the file, the program will have to update (rewrite) thirty indexes. That takes time, and you will feel it in slower response. A batch update (where you are updating several thousand records from an outside tape in a single session) can take many hours to complete.

- Because you have this wonderful relational database, you will think up scores of new functions and improvements that you will want to add to it. You will want to add the names of the children in the household and their ages. When you write to a customer, you may want to suggest that you have new school outfits which would be "just perfect for Sarah and Jonathan." Writing letters like this can really make a marketing database profitable, but this functionality comes at a cost of many hours of programmer time to write the code to make it all happen. Do you have the ability to convince the programmers to devote the time required?

- Finally, a relational database is often very difficult to update in batch mode. Assume you have a large file (say 10 million) and you have a lot of transactions from a mass mailing that you want to use to update your large file (say a million transactions). Some relational databases can take 24 hours or more to do the updating even on a very large and fast mainframe. Why? Because of all the indexes that have to be updated at the same time.

REPORTS YOU WILL NEED

There are two types of reports that you will absolutely need to have to make a marketing database work: *ad-hoc reports* and *custom reports.*

Ad-hoc reports are created by sitting at your PC and entering queries. For example, suppose you are working with a cellular phone database. You want to know more about the usage patterns of heavy use consumer customers in Ohio and Pennsylvania during peak daytime hours broken down by price plan. An ad-hoc query using MarketVision or similar software might go like this:

IF (STATE IS OH, PA) AND (MONTH IS JULY) AND (CUSTOMER IS CONSUMER) AND (USELEVEL IS HIGH) AND (MINUSED WITHIN 0900, 1700) COUNT PRICEPLAN BY TIMEUSED

This will result in a cross tab showing customers organized by various price plans across the top and minutes used down the side.

The answer to this query should show up on your screen in less than a minute. If the answer is not what you are looking for, you alter the query and wait another minute for the answer. The resulting cross tab can be printed on your PC printer, or graphed using a PC graphics package. If you want to develop a marketing package to a group of these consumers, you say:

SAVE SELECT AS OHPAHIGH

The software will save the records of these customers on disk with the unique name you have created. You can then convert these records into labels or letters.

Ad-hoc queries are the heart of successful database marketing. You learn a great deal about your customers by this kind of analytical work. In many ways it is better than modeling, since models usually take a long time to run, and require the services of statisticians. With ad-hoc queries, any marketer can ask the questions and get instant answers all day long.

Custom Reports

The other reports you need are custom reports that you design, the programming staff sets up, and that run automatically every night, every week, or every month, depending on your program and your needs. These reports will show such data as:

- Results of leads received by salesman, dealer, district; number of contacts, refusals, sales.

- Responses to most recent mailing by cell code, household income, customer recency, frequency, monetary level. Return on investment from the mailing.

- Coupon redemptions by cell, sales territory, coupon type, product type, etc.

- Calls received by Customer Service, broken down by type of call, product, hour of the day, length of call.

Every day when you come to work, these custom reports have been run the night before and are sitting on your desk, in neat laser printed forms, and three-hole punched for insertion in ring binders, ready for your review and notification of top management.

If you have a good relational database and a good programming staff, these ad-hoc and custom reports will be easy to do. They are vital to your marketing operation: if for some reason you cannot get these reports, do not take no for an answer. You cannot expect to run a marketing database without them.

CHANGES IN YOUR DATABASE

Database marketing is dynamic. You are trying to reach your customers and prospects in new, exciting ways. Once you set up your database, you will discover many new uses for the data, some of which will be very successful, and some of which will not work out well at all. You can only find this out by experimenting constantly, testing, and trying new things. There is no such thing as the perfect marketing database.

The beauty of relational databases is that new fields can be added with little difficulty. Let us say that when you first set up the database, there was no thought of having data in the customer record like household income, educational level, or number of children. You now have such data available and want to add it to the database so that you can use it in modeling. It should be possible to add this data from an outside tape in a matter of a day or two.

When you set up the database, be sure that everyone involved understands that you will be making many changes in the future. You need these changes to maintain your customer base and market share. If you cannot make changes, be assured that your competitors will.

Relational database software is available for mainframes and PC servers. What is harder to find is ad-hoc query software which works well with a relational database. Before you select any system, test out the ad-hoc query language with a test database of the size you are considering for your customers. Be sure that the language is easy to learn and use, and that it works rapidly. There is really no point in setting up a wonderful relational database if you cannot get at the data yourself.

You should not need programmers to enable you to produce almost any kind of ad-hoc report from your customer database.

SQL, for example, is the standard IBM mainframe database query language. Don't even consider it. Marketers cannot learn it easily, and some SQL queries take hours to run. One mainframe system that handles queries rapidly is MarketVision by ACS, in Reston, Virginia. There are others.

Other Required Software

Relational database software is only the beginning. To support a marketing database, you will also need the following:

- *Merge/Purge software*, to detect duplicates.
- *Zip code, address, and name correction software*, to clean up your records, to make them personal and acceptable to your customers.
- *Geocoding software*, which permits you to determine the census block group of each customer and append demographic and lifestyle information to your customer records.

(All of the above software is available from Group 1 Software, whose mainframe products are probably the IBM of the direct marketing business.)

- *On-Line access software*. There are really two ways of working with a customer marketing database. The first way is to look up an individual customer record. Customer Service, typically, needs this access. Ideally, the database should be linked to the telephone system using ANI (Automatic Number Identification — see Chapter 17) so that when a customer calls you on the telephone, but before you answer the telephone, your computer already knows who it is who is calling (because of the telephone number) and has gotten the customer record up on the operator's screen. This is the type of software that hotels use to know the name of the guest who has pushed the "room service" button.

Marketers and market research people, however, don't need that type of record access. A marketer doesn't need to look up one customer record. Marketers need to do segmentation, ad-hoc queries, and profiling. They need to do counts, reports, and selects.

Since there are two ways of looking at customer database records, you may well want to have two different types of software, or two separate databases. One database would be used for customer service, and the other for marketing. The customer service software would give instant access to any one record, but would be useless for ad-hoc counts. The marketing software would do instant counts, but not provide individual record lookup at all. This is by far the most common and useful way to maintain databases. Those who try to combine both functions in a single system are bound to be disappointed: both record access and ad-hoc counting will be too slow.

- *Statistical modeling software* which permits you to do multiple regressions, neural networks, mapping, and graphics. Question: should you use mainframe statistics software or PC statistics software? Answer: get used to using PC modeling software. It is much less expensive, faster, and easier to use. All the new software is being written for the PC, so you can get the latest thing.

- *Custom software prepared for your particular application.* For example, as each customer is added to the database, you may want to assign a dealer code, sales district code, UPS district code, salesman code, or other special identifier. You may want to add RFM codes or other special data of use to your company. Software to add all of this information must be written by the programmers assigned to your database.

The functions of most of this software are covered elsewhere in this book. I have listed them here merely to remind you that wherever your marketing database is housed, the computer requires a lot of expensive software and the skilled resources of a trained staff to make it work.

BATCH UPDATING

Most marketing databases are updated periodically in batch. Batch updating means saving up all your changes and making them all at once in a big batch. The opposite is on-line updating, in which you make the changes in your database every time you receive new data, such as a telephone call or an order. Operational files (billing files) are usually updated on a daily basis. Customer service files are often updated on-line, while the customer is on the phone.

Marketing databases normally do not need to be updated more often than monthly. The reason is that marketing usually consists of a group of specific campaigns or initiatives that are conducted on a periodic basis. You need an updated file before every outgoing communication. If you have a preferred customer club, and want to send monthly statements showing the points earned, you need to update your database a couple of days before the mailing.

Why not update your marketing database every day? Because it costs more to do this than it is worth.

A complex marketing database may contain millions of pieces of data. The update process may take many hours. The reason for updating is to have all data fully correct before you select records for mailing. There is no need to do it more frequently.

Updating usually involves gathering data from many different sources. Here is a diagram of the updating process for a cellular telephone company marketing database:

Figure 4-4   Cellular Telephone Company Update

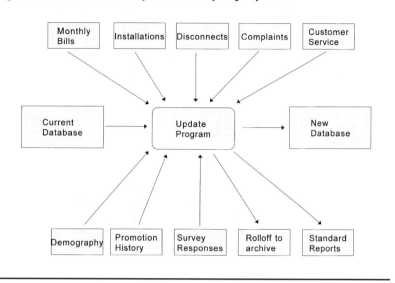

In this process, five different tapes are assembled from five different units of the company. In addition, tapes or disk files of outgoing promotions, responses and survey responses, are put into the process. Special software has to be written to merge all of this data together in the update process.

Not shown in this diagram is the householding process. Some companies or individuals may have more than one telephone. On the billing file, these telephones may show up as separate accounts with separate bills. For the marketing database they must be consolidated.

The update software is obviously custom made for this particular database. In many cases, the update software will have to be rewritten every month. Why? Because the format of some of those input tapes will probably change — for reasons unrelated to the marketing database. If a new survey has been completed, the software to insert it into the customer records has to be written. Most service bureaus have one or two programmers working almost full time just preparing for and carrying out the monthly update of one of their client's databases. It is a complex job.

Event Driven Communications

Also not shown in this diagram is the software for event driven communications, which is present in all good database marketing programs. You may be sending letters to people on their birthday (or before their child's birthday). You may be writing them a letter when they have owned their car for three years, inviting them to come in for a test drive of the new models. You may be keeping track of the supplies they have been ordering and want to send a reminder when your records show that they need to order more. There are all sorts of event driven communications which are helpful for the customer and profitable for the supplier.

Devising and maintaining such software is a very big job. It is, furthermore, a job for a professional programmer, not for a marketer who is doing it part time. It is unlikely that your MIS department will be able to write or maintain such software. It is best outsourced to a firm that specializes in database marketing.

Setting Up Control Groups Using an Nth

Your job, as a marketer, is thinking up the events, and devising the communications. As a part of the process, you will want to see that control groups are set up in your database. A control group is a group of customers who do not receive the communications that are sent to other customers.

Why not? The reason is so that you can measure the performance of those that get your newsletters, promotional letters, and event driven communications, versus the customers that do not receive them.

It could be that your newsletter is not doing you any good at all. You can test that by seeing if people who receive the newsletter buy more, or have higher retention rates than people who do not receive it. To set up a control group, or any test group, you must use a procedure called an Nth. To pick a control group of 10,000 customers out of 200,000, you select every 20th record and mark it with a "C" or some other mark. When you select people for the newsletter, omit everyone with the "C".

Later, create an ad-hoc report that compares the sales to people with a "C" with everyone else.

Inserting RFM and Lifetime Value Codes

In the update process, you will want to create special pieces of information. For example, every record should have a space for the "most recent date" in which the customer made a purchase or a change in his service. This date is used for creating recency codes (see Chapter 7). You will want to keep a running total of the frequency of purchase and the total dollars spent. You will want to insert RFM codes (Chapter 7), and Lifetime Value Codes (Chapter 10). There is no off-the-shelf software that will do these things.

THE ISSUE OF PRIORITY

One thing that you may not know is that it is possible to set priorities for each user of a computer. Most mainframes have scores or even hundreds of jobs running at the same time. Many users are hooked up to the computer simultaneously. The mainframe works by doing a little piece of a job—for example, it asks a disk controller to go and find a customer's record on the disk—which takes several milliseconds; while it is waiting for the record to come back, the mainframe will look for something else to do. It has a long list of jobs in process, called a queue.

The mainframe will run down this list and pick another job to work on. It will make this decision based on the priority assigned to each job on the queue. Once it has selected a job, it will work on that job until it gets to an interruption, such as the need to send information to a printer or tape drive. The mainframe is then ready to pick another job off the queue. Eventually it will get back to the original job because the disk controller has reported back with the customer's name.

The priority assigned to each user or each job determines how likely it is that the mainframe will pick that job off the queue. When I worked at the Department of the Treasury in Washington many years ago, we used the Federal Reserve Bank of New York mainframe to do much of our processing. For some reason, the NY Fed assigned our operation a very low priority. As a result, simple jobs that I wanted to run would often take four or six hours to finish—jobs that on another machine could be completed in less than a minute. Your marketing database could be caught in the same trap unless you assure yourself of a high priority for database marketing on the machine you are using.

INSIST ON EXCELLENCE

Once you start serious database marketing you will discover that your marketing database *becomes your company*—at least it does to your customers.

We have all visited stores which appear dirty; trash litters the entrance and the aisles. What we are looking for is often out of stock, and no one seems to care. In fact, it is hard to find anyone who seems to take any responsibility for the store at all; they are all just employees, putting in their hours to get paid. They can't or won't answer questions or be helpful. Unless there is nowhere else to shop, we try to avoid these stores if we possibly can. Why don't the owners of these stores see them from the customer's point of view and clean up their act? Who knows?

With database marketing, you can easily fall into the same trap. Imagine a customer service operation with a telephone line that is always busy; when you do get through, the operator has never heard of you, can't find your name on the database, can't make changes in your order because it is "out of my hands." The supervisor's approval is needed for that, but the supervisor is "unavailable."

You present an image of your company every day. If you write letters to your customers, and they receive duplicate letters addressed to A Hughes and Arthur Hughes, this is your image. If your customer billing or order records are several weeks behind, and the invoices incorrect, this is your image.

All these things *can* be fixed. You can present a first-class impression to your customers all the time, in all parts of your operation, but it will not be easy. You will need first-class software and a first-class programming staff. You will need to train all your personnel in the use of the system. You will have to monitor what is happening from the customer end, and constantly *insist on excellence*.

The essential software problem is this: because modern database marketing software is very complicated and very expensive, it is easy to get snowed by the experts. They will tell you that what you want to do cannot be done or will take a very long time or will be prohibitively expensive. In most cases, these experts are dead wrong. Today, database marketing software and hardware is so versatile that you can do virtually anything that you can imagine or visualize. Furthermore, if you let yourself get rolled by your experts, rest assured that your competition will not let that happen. *Insist on excellence.*

PROGRAMMING STAFF

A marketing database will not run itself. It will absolutely require one or more full-time programmers who know the database intimately. You will need a formal change order system for modifications of the database. Someone must become the Database Administrator (DBA). The DBA should be able to issue written orders to the programmer to make changes and improvements in the software for the database. The DBA must meet with the programmer or the programmer's boss on an almost daily basis to find out how things are going and to make sure that your requests are logical and reasonable.

Bear in mind that it is possible to make grave errors in writing database software which will seriously affect your customers. One line of code designed to correct one problem can cause unforeseen problems in thousands or hundreds of thousands of other customer records. The error may not show up for several days. Then your telemarketers will report strange happenings: people getting birthday cards when it isn't their birthday, or frequent shopper points when they haven't shopped.

You will soon find that you need a system for testing all changes in the software before they become operational. You will probably need a *test database* in addition to your *production database.* All of your software will run on both databases. New software must be written and tested extensively on the test database before it is shifted over to the production database.

You will get to know your programmers quite well. You will need to have a good relationship with their supervisor, and you will need the capability to call on extra programming resources in a crisis.

Software for the Small Database

If you have a small database (under 10,000 customers) you will probably not be able to outsource it, because the cost per record would be too high. You will have to maintain the database on a PC server. I have been asked many times for recommendations on the best software. I am sorry to say that I can make no specific recommendation. I have tried several: ACT!, PC File, Q&A. Each of these has some merit. None of them are really as satisfactory as custom-designed software on a mainframe. New and improved PC software comes out almost every month. My advice: look around and experiment. Talk to people with similar problems. I have found a person that provides advice in this field: Rich Bohn, President of The Denali Group in Issaquah, Washington (206 392-8943). He reviews all the PC database software, and publishes a newsletter about it.

SUMMARY

- Marketing databases must be stored on disk using relational database software. This software is expensive and will require programmer attention to keep it working properly. It will require a very large amount of disk space.

- You will want to store a vast amount of data in your database. Each new piece of data will require the addition of one or more indexes so that it is instantly retrievable and can be integrated into your reports. When the database is set up, it must be understood that you will be adding new types of data on a regular basis.

- You must be able to run ad-hoc reports from your desk in the marketing department, accessing any indexed field, and getting the output in a few minutes without any assistance from a programmer.

- You will need one or more programmers constantly available to make the changes, program the reports, and keep your database working properly at all times. There must be a Database Administrator (DBA) who will keep tight control of what happens to the database.

- You will need a test database and a production database. All changes must first be tested thoroughly on the test database.

- You will need software for merge/purge, zip code and address correction, name correction, statistical analysis, geocoding, updating, RFM scoring, Lifetime Value analysis, and event driven communications.

- The DBA must know and understand your software and programming staff. You must know enough about software so that you do not get snowed by the experts. You must insist on excellence.

Chapter 5

How to Build Your Marketing Database

At some point your company has to start building the database. In this chapter we take you step by step through the process.

HOW LONG SHOULD IT TAKE?

Very important first question. I have a definite answer: while the particular database depends on the type of situation and use in your company, in general, your initial database should be up and running within *one year or less.*

How can I be so dogmatic? Won't many databases take years to design and build? Of course, but those databases may in fact never be built. They will be in the planning stage for several years, and never reach the operational phase. Why do you need to move so fast?

- Computer hardware is evolving very, very rapidly today. What is state-of-the-art today will be obsolete in three years, and not even still maintained in five. If you take too long to plan and build your database, when it emerges it will be designed around obsolete equipment. It will not be state-of-the-art and everyone will know it.

- Computer software is changing almost as rapidly as hardware. The same comments apply.

- There are powerful forces in every company which resist change, particularly the fundamental changes brought about by a marketing database. The longer the planning stage, the more opportunities the opponents have to kill your project in its cradle. You must get it up and running before this happens.

- No marketing database can be built without support at the top of the company. Someone at the top must believe in it and have acquired the money to make it happen. In any dynamic company, things change quickly. It is hard to retain your senior interest and funding over a several year planning phase. When you are ready to implement, either your backer will have been transferred or promoted or the funds will have been diverted to something else. You have to produce something and *show that it works* in a short time, or your project will wither and die.

- By waiting, you are losing money. An effective marketing database more than pays its way in increased sales and increased customer retention. The longer you wait to start, the more sales and customers you will lose. Get out a calculator and figure out how much it will cost the company for each month delay in becoming operational. These opportunity costs are *real*, not hypothetical.

- By waiting, you permit your competition to surpass you. Don't assume that they are waiting for you to make the first move. If you have a leisurely three-year development plan, you may find that when your database is ready, your competition has a two-year head start and is much more proficient at it than you are. Database development plans are seldom trumpeted in headlines. They are developed quietly and tested one-on-one with customers. You may have no idea how far along your competition is until it is too late.

- Developing and making your database operational is only the start of a long learning curve that will transform the way you handle customers. The database by itself is nothing. It is the way you use it that will make the difference. Once you have it, you must train staff throughout the company: customer service, sales, billing, delivery, acquisition, telemarketers, and direct-mail production. You will have to change your forms and procedures to take advantage of the increased knowledge and contact with customers. None of this can begin until you have a database. And the staff training and learning curve may take more than a year itself.

- What if your company is too big for a one-year process? Impossible. What you must do is begin small—start with the top 5, 10, or 20 percent of your customers. Make them an elite group or club. Develop your marketing database just for them. Extend it to others only when you have a sound concept that is working well—*but you must get started.*

Recently I sat for several hours with the planning committee of a major bank which was developing a long-range marketing database plan. The committee had already decided to build the project in-house, and was heavily staffed with MIS people. They planned to use the existing terminals throughout the bank as their mechanism, so that more than a thousand different people could tap into the database at the same time once it was up and running. But when would that day come? Their subcommittees reported one by one, adding additional requirements. At first, they had planned to get up and running in three years. That was a year ago. Now they were working on a five-year program which would meet the needs of all sections of the bank. What would they do in the way of direct marketing in the meantime, we asked?

"Oh, we have a program that we developed several years ago which we will keep pursuing until our database is ready."

We nodded, saying nothing. But, as we compared notes after the meeting, we recalled that the marketing staff's perception of the failure of the current direct marketing program was the reason that we had been asked to come to the meeting in the first place. That failure was now forgotten as the group concentrated on their five-year objective. One of the first steps the group had decided upon was to "lock in" the hardware design of their terminals so that their MIS staff could know what equipment to purchase during the next five years. We left the meeting shaking our heads.

SHOULD THE DATABASE BE BUILT IN-HOUSE?

There are some examples of good marketing databases built on in-house computer systems, but from my observation these are the exception. There are important and telling reasons why most companies look to an outside service bureau to build their marketing databases:

- Unless your company is very unusual, your MIS staff does not have the software and experience to mount a marketing database. As you recall from the chapter on software, you will need a very large relational database with about a dozen other major types of software including merge/purge, geocoding, statistical modeling, on-line direct access, ad-hoc reporting, custom reporting, on-line telemarketing, and so on. This software is very expensive, and takes several months to learn. The MIS staff must dedicate at least two programmers to install it and learn to operate it. This may be a difficult commitment.

- For this reason, setting up a database in-house is almost always much more expensive than an outside contract. Outside service bureaus experienced in marketing databases already have all of the necessary software and have trained their staffs to use it. Their costs are spread over several clients' accounts, so they don't have to charge you a lot of initial costs when you become a client.

- The hardware requirements are significant, and usually much more than your MIS staff and budget will normally support. From the beginning they will be telling you that your disk requirements are excessive. They will try to talk you into down-scaling your project so that it will fit on their equipment.

- The in-house priorities will usually work against you. After all, the MIS in your company exists for some very definite reasons, none of which involves marketing. They are grinding out the payroll, sending out the bills, maintaining the inventory, and controlling the manufacturing process. All these projects take priority over marketing, and most of them have a long backlog of program revisions and improvements scheduled and promised. It will be six months or more before they can fit your application into their schedule. Their slow-moving schedule will wear you down.

- Even worse, the MIS culture is at variance with your marketing dynamism. Most marketing databases require almost constant testing, modification, retesting, and shifts in approach. A programming staff of two or three is kept constantly busy on a full-time basis making changes in your database to support your learning curve and the dynamics of marketing. There is no such thing as a marketing database that runs itself. But your MIS staff will have difficulty reconciling that kind of resource allocation with their other applications. When they write a payroll, billing, or inventory program, it is expected to run flawlessly for the next several years. MIS will expect you to draw up a firm list of software requirements in detail so that they can budget the application. The idea of changing it every week as experience dictates will be a difficult sell.

- Yours may be the first on-line operation in your company. If it is, it will be a shock to MIS. They are used to bringing the computer down any time they need to fix something. If your database has now got fifty customer service and acquisition telemarketers on-line all day and half the night including Saturday and Sunday, MIS will find that they have to make their fixes between 2:00 A.M. and 5:00 A.M. It will make them very grumpy.

- There is a more subtle reason for going outside. MIS is not your contractor. They are a sister function to marketing, with responsibilities to the entire organization. Once your database is firmly committed to inside, and funds have been expended to get it started, you are just another user. When you announce that you need some rapid changes, you may find that your changes have been shunted to a six-month queue, like everyone else's. There will be nothing you can do about it—kiss your dynamic database plans goodbye.

On the other hand, you should be able to control an outside company. Put them on a short leash. Be sure that your contract specifies that you get rapid action on your requests with rewards and penalties built in. Be sure that you are the Database Administrator, and that you call the shots on what is done, when it is done, and how it is done. *You,* not your contractor, will run the database. This is the tremendous advantage you will have in building your database at an outside service bureau.

What About a Data Warehouse?

Many MIS departments have been busily constructing data warehouses for their companies. A data warehouse is a large storehouse of data from all parts of the company combined together for management analysis. Such projects are expensive and time consuming. Their proponents insist that such warehouses should also be the basis for customer marketing databases. Many marketers have been fooled by these proponents into thinking that a warehouse could serve their needs. Think again.

If you tie your marketing fortune to such a project you may not only be disappointed, you may end up out of a job.

One of the experts on database marketing, David Raab, a consultant specializing in database systems, points out that the two concepts, which look similar from the outside, are really very different in their content and usefulness.

Scope of data: A warehouse contains full company data including sales, employees, vendors, inventory, etc. A marketing database has sales and customer data only. Years may be consumed in building the warehouse, while a marketing database may usually be constructed in four or five months at the outside.

Customer level data: Warehouses have complex software that cleans data and makes it consistent. A marketing database must do the same, but then must put all data about a customer together, using specialized merge/purge software rarely found in a data warehouse.

Drilling Down: Most warehouses aim at consolidating data for management reporting purposes. Users often work with the data by downloading relatively small summary tables to PC servers. Marketing databases are the opposite: the goal is to find out as much information about a single customer as possible. The marketers want to build one-on-one relationships with customers. Data warehousers want to summarize what is going on. The two approaches are inconsistent. In the struggle, marketing needs seldom win.

Customer contact: Marketing databases must maintain mailable addresses and correct phone numbers for all customers. Obtaining, updating, and cleaning this customer data is seldom done in a data warehouse.

Sheer size: Customer marketing databases and data warehouses are both huge. But marketing systems must continually read all of the millions of bytes of information about each customer's purchases, promotions, demographics, and survey responses to facilitate personal correspondence. Warehouses may store as much information, but usually read only small portions or summaries at any one time. Networks and PC systems designed for warehouses often cannot handle the massive flow of customer data needed for marketing.

Reading and writing to files: Users of data warehouses normally do not write data to the warehouse. They query the warehouse and prepare summary reports. Marketers, on the other hand, are always writing data to their databases: recording customer calls, orders, complaints, promotions, responses, and surveys. Question: can the marketers get the warehouse controllers to change their entire scheme so that customer data can be updated with regularity? Not likely.

Marketing databases have operational functions: Marketers insert RFM codes, lifetime value estimates, model scores, key codes, no-mail codes, and frequent buyer points. They set aside test and control groups and gold card groups. All these functions must be automated and built into the marketing database software. Adding these functions to data warehouse software ranges from difficult to impossible.

Conclusion: Don't get trapped in a warehouse.

A data warehouse and a customer marketing database are two different animals. They should not be combined. If marketers agree to the combination, several things will result:

- Costly delays: The combined project will take months or years longer than would the building of a customer marketing database. The project will be much more expensive.

- Frustration of goals: Forget about your dynamic customer relationship building ideas. There is no way that a data warehouse can give marketers the kind of close relationship with their customers that is the goal of database marketing.

- The end of database marketing in your company.

SETTING UP A DATABASE PLANNING TEAM

You will need a database planning team with someone from marketing as its clearly defined director. On the team you will need people from marketing, market research, sales, customer service, billing, dealer support, MIS, and someone from your creative direct agency. As soon as you have selected your outside service bureau, add it to the team. You may also want an outside database marketing consultant and an outside telemarketer.

As you assemble the team, you will soon realize that there are two basic types of people involved with a marketing database. I call them *constructors* and *creators.* A constructor is a person who is interested in putting the pieces together to make a database work. He or she may be interested in the hardware, the software, in accumulating the names, converting them to the correct format, arranging the telemarketing system and such. Creators are people who come up with the creative ideas for using the database to provide more service to customers, to increase sales, to build loyalty, to reduce attrition, and to generate repeat business.

Creators are seldom very interested in the nuts and bolts of a database which so intrigue the constructors. They are often bored by these details. But don't be misled by that boredom into thinking that you can build a working database without the creators. *Building a marketing database without creative ideas and leadership is a waste of company money.* Databases don't run themselves. They won't earn you a nickel without some very creative ideas which will serve to offset the costs and go on to generate real profits. Make sure your team includes both kinds of people.

Don't make your initial objectives too grandiose. Keep them within bounds so that you can get up and running fast. You can make long-range goals, but don't let them dominate. Remember, *the best is always the enemy of the good.* Shoot for the good now, with the best to come later. The principal initial objective will be to compile the information for your marketing database and to make it available for several purposes:

- Determining who your best and worst customers are, and initially, developing programs to retain and support your best customers.

- Segmentation and direct mailing or telemarketing to your customers for upselling, cross-selling, and retention.

- Supporting a vigorous customer service operation which has access to the database and can add information to customer records based on their contacts.

- Enhancement and augmentation of the customer information base with surveys, demographics, and lifestyle.

- Analysis and profiling of your customer base.

- Using your profiles to develop useful lists of prospects and generate leads.

DEVELOPING A STANDARD FORMAT

The first step in creating the database is to identify the information you will retain on each customer. Do not be overly influenced by what you already have on your customer lists. Quite often, the initial data is just barely adequate. For example, you may find that your customer list looks like this:

First Name	10
Initial	1
Last Name	12
Address	25
City	15
State	2
Zip	5

Fine. But what is missing here?

Title (Mr., Mrs., Rev., Rabbi, Captain)

Suffix (Jr., Sr., M.D.)

Fuller middle name (J. Richard Stokes becomes J. R. Stokes when all his friends call him "Dick")

Address and city may be truncated on the database and may look funny when used on letters—"20900 MacNaughten Pkwy. N" fills up 25 characters, with no space to put the apartment number.

You will want to create a new format that allows enough space for all the fields and adds many more: telephone, second address line, sex, spouse name, work phone and so on. Think ahead of everything that will be useful for future personalized correspondence and customer service and put those fields in.

Of course, you will want to add fields for household income, family size, educational level, home value and type, and complete purchasing history with your company. You may want makes and models of automobiles, age, children's names, sex, and ages. You also will want fields for response to direct marketing efforts (dates, source codes, amounts) and results of correspondence and telephone calls.

Can you afford all these fields? Can you afford not to have them if your competition moves heavily into database marketing? Remember, bytes are cheap, and they are getting cheaper every year. One hundred twenty-five bytes of information is enough to hold the typical customer file of name, address, phone, and other data.

Database Costs for Storing 125 Bytes of Information

Year	$/125 bytes
1973	$7.13
1987	$0.05
1991	$0.005
1995	$0.002

The end result of your efforts should be a comprehensive format for your customer records which will serve for the initial conversion of your present lists to your new database. This initial format will last for only a few months after your database is created. You will discover many gaps which you must fill in the early months. Prepare for dynamic changes in your format. With a relational database and competent programmers, this should be no problem at all.

Figure 5-1 Computer Costs Are Falling

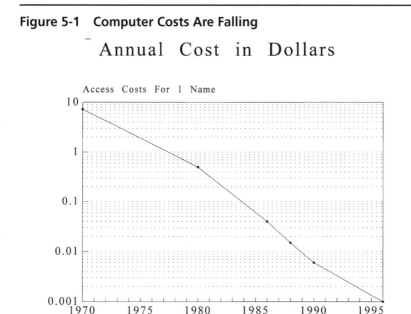

Annual Cost in Dollars

DETERMINE YOUR INDEXES

You have determined the format of your database records, and at the same time, you have to determine your indexes. An index (as already explained) is an external disk file which tells you where data in your database is located, and how many of each piece of data exist. Fields that are indexed can be retrieved much faster than other fields. Indexed fields can also be used for ad-hoc and custom reports without the need for ever calling up the customer records. What types of fields need to be indexed? Some examples:

- Geocode
- Age
- Sex
- Zip code
- Telephone Number
- Telephone Area Code
- Last Name
- City
- State
- Total Purchases Since Inception
- Most Recent Purchase Date
- Earliest Purchase Date
- Most Recent Purchase Amount
- Cell Code
- Highest Single Purchase Amount
- Credit Limit

DESIGNING CUSTOM REPORTS

As a part of the planning process, you will have to determine what reports you expect to get from the database on a regular or periodic basis. Everyone can play a role in report design. Here, interests will diverge: market research will have one set of interests, sales another, advertising a third, and marketing still another. You want special reports on customer service activity, on response by cell code, on sales by SKU, on sales by store, or by salesman. You will want to know how many people have bought from you often, or recently, or in large amounts.

In a marketing database, your programmers will have to write software code for each of these custom reports. Each report should be given a name or a number, and made available to everyone on a menu screen. Then, when the database is set up, individual users can access this menu screen and call for the reports to be printed for them on printers in their offices or nearby.

Go Slow on Customization

Before you spend a lot of money on custom reports, consider what you can do with a PC. If your database is located on a PC server or a mainframe, you can always use Windows to download the data into a spreadsheet like LOTUS, Excel, or a graphics package like Harvard Graphics. Once the data is in one of these programs, you can easily convert it to produce any type of report that anyone wants—at virtually no out of pocket cost. My recommendation is that you plan on using spreadsheet reports at first until you discover some reports that simply cannot easily be produced in that way, and are essential to your operations. Then call in the programmers.

Custom Report Menu Screen

R01   Sales by Zip code
R02   Sales by Month
R03   Sales by Cell Code
R04   Sales by SKU
R05   Sales by Customer Frequency Level
R06   Sales by Customer Recency Level
R07   Customers by Income level
R08   Customers Total Purchases by Occupation

Enter Rept No. ____   Begin Date __/__/__   End Date __/__/__

What Data Should You Keep?

Every year new devices are created that provide us with more and more customer data. Supermarkets, for instance, now provide their customers with plastic membership cards which are scanned at purchase time so that all the items purchased can be stored in the database record of the card holder. It is a wonderful idea, but, if all the data captured is stored in the database, it will prove to be unworkable.

Keeping track of every tube of toothpaste, bar of soap, and everything else that a household has bought in the last two years will consume a fantastic amount of disk space. It will be very expensive, and will make counting and reporting ponderous and slow. What's more, it may be a waste of money.

Here's how to decide what data to keep: figure out your marketing program for the next year or two. Then decide what information you will need to carry out that program. The chances are almost nil that the date and time of day of the purchase of a tube of toothpaste will have any significance at all for your marketing program. Better to keep track of total purchases by the household per month—if you want more detail, you could get it by department. You could also keep track of each visit, and the day of the week.

Database marketing provides incremental sales, incremental profits. You have to build a lifetime value table to determine whether the incremental profits from your marketing efforts will be more than the incremental costs of the database. Build a lifetime value table (see Chapter 10) before you decide how much data to store in your database.

DESIGNING USER ACCESS

When your users want to see names on the marketing database, what will they see? Can they call up individual customer records? If so, what will they use to call them up? Names, zip codes, customer number, telephone number, company name, SIC code, contact name? These questions have to be decided.

Next you have to decide what the screen will look like. A customer service representative should have a screen that is considerably different from that needed by a researcher or someone in marketing. Screens can, of course, show anything that is stored in the database. Besides the screens that show individual records, you will want screens that permit you to count, select, and download information and records. You may want to select out a list of all customers who have purchased more than $10,000 in the past sixty days for a special mailing. When they are selected, you may want to mark their records as having been selected for mailing number SPL002 on March 24. Then when the responses come in, you can compare them with the outgoing numbers. All of this may be possible from your menu screens if you set them up that way. When these names are selected, you could arrange for a service bureau to send each selected customer a laser letter.

This is the type of advance planning you can do at this point. As a result of such planning, you may go back and revise your record format because the old format lacked some of the data needed to support your ongoing activities.

Now comes the hard part: who will have access to all of this data? Modern database software permits you to assign passwords and access codes to all users. You can have 200 or more people in your company working with your database at once or you can restrict access to only a handful of people. As Database Administrator, you are in a position to make that judgment, supported by your planning team.

You have to decide how those who will have access will gain it. If you are all in one building, the service bureau can arrange a single direct line over which as many different people can access the database at once as the line will allow. For a 14,400 baud line, that would be about forty-eight different people. For a 56,000-baud line, you can have more than a hundred.

Do you want them to view the database with a PC or with a terminal? PCs are getting so inexpensive that they have become the choice means to access marketing databases since they have many advantages over terminals. With their hard disks, they can receive data from the database and load local programs such as spread sheets and graphics to display the data; with their PC printers, they can print any mainframe reports or listings or labels directly from the database.

HOW DOES A MARKETING DATABASE RELATE TO EXISTING FILES?

This question comes up constantly, and has to be faced head-on. We can restate it this way: should the marketing database be a separate database, stored in a different place from the other company computer records, or should you try to modify your existing files to give them the characteristics of a marketing database?

Figure 5-2   Three Related Databases

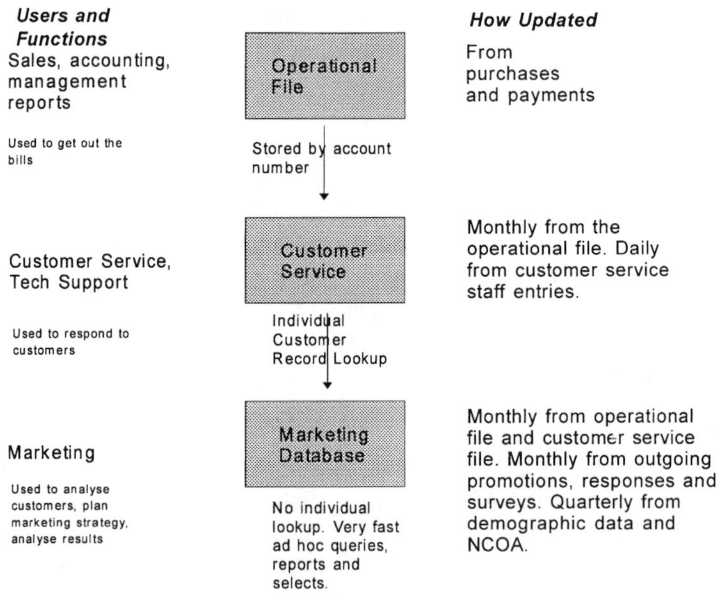

Users and Functions		How Updated
Sales, accounting, management reports	**Operational File**	From purchases and payments
Used to get out the bills	Stored by account number	
Customer Service, Tech Support	**Customer Service**	Monthly from the operational file. Daily from customer service staff entries.
Used to respond to customers	Individual Customer Record Lookup	
Marketing	**Marketing Database**	Monthly from operational file and customer service file. Monthly from outgoing promotions, responses and surveys. Quarterly from demographic data and NCOA.
Used to analyse customers, plan marketing strategy, analyse results	No individual lookup. Very fast ad hoc queries, reports and selects.	

To do marketing, you will want to manipulate a customer file in unpredictable ways. You will want to add many enhancements (demographics, lifestyle, survey data). You will want to segment the file and do mailings, posting the responses by cell code. You will want to run multiple regressions, profile the data, and add prospects and leads to your list. If at the same time with the same database you have to mail out monthly bills, post payments and partial payments to bills, collect utility taxes, and cut off service for non-payment, your marketing activities are bound to get in the way, and, in many cases, to be shunted aside in favor of more pressing requirements.

How, then, can such companies build a marketing database? They simply spin off a copy of the customer base every month, every week, or every night, for that matter, and use that copy to update and refresh the marketing database. The two functions must be kept separate. Marketing is a very important function: it should stand on its own and not be secondary to operational activities.

Isn't keeping two copies of a customer file more expensive than keeping just one? In most cases, the answer is no. Computer disk space is very, very cheap, and getting cheaper every year. Computer programmer's time is becoming more and more expensive. A good marketing database requires constant program changes as a result of testing, experience, retesting, and dynamic new ideas. If you are working with a *live* database used for billing and accounting, your programmers will have to work twice as hard when making changes in your marketing programs because of the constant worry that some of their marketing changes would impact the billing and accounting system. In most cases keeping two separate databases is actually cheaper than combining them.

You should not try to convert a customer file used for accounting and billing into a marketing database. Make a weekly or nightly copy, and use the copy to refresh the marketing database. It will be cheaper to do it this way, and more satisfactory for marketing purposes.

WHERE DO YOU GET CUSTOMER NAMES?

For the bank or the insurance company, the answer is easy. But what about the furniture manufacturer? Who is buying your beds and dining room tables? If they bought dining room furniture, what about showing them what you have for living rooms? Furniture is always sold by dealers, almost never direct. Why should you get the names of the ultimate consumers, and what can you do with them?

Of course, by now, we know the answer to these questions. Dealers are often too small to set up a database. You can help them by building a database of ultimate customers to establish brand loyalty. You work with the dealers to furnish them leads for more sales. You have to get those names, and start to cultivate them yourself. How do you do it?

Obviously, you have to pack a registration card in with each item you sell. You have to make it very worthwhile for the consumer to fill in that card. What can you offer? Cash back, low-cost accessories, a catalog, a sweepstakes? You experiment and test. Make the registration card a survey form: find out the household income, education level, house value and style, furniture style, presence of children and so on.

How do you get names if you are a retailer? It should not be difficult. Many retailers have their own credit cards. Others write down the names and addresses for deliveries. You may be able to purchase names of people who have charged their purchases of your products on their credit cards. Supermarkets have established frequent-buyer clubs. Video stores have it easy. Movie theaters have set up sweepstakes and "Sneak Preview Club" enrollments. Once you determine that you are going to have a database, you and your employees can come up with hundreds of creative ways to learn who your customers are. Reward your employees for getting the names, and reward your dealers.

One major electronic retailer, Radio Shack, has never failed to amaze me. I have shopped there for thirty years. They have scores of stores in cities across the country. Every time I buy anything from them, even a fifty-cent battery, I have to write down my name and address. Yet I have never received a single piece of mail from them. What do they do with all these names? Who knows? They certainly don't have a marketing database with me on it.

HOW TO CONVERT NAMES

The names and addresses of customers you obtain to use for your marketing database will never be in the correct format which you have established for your marketing database. That is a given. But it is not really a problem. Most service bureaus have software that will convert anything from one format to another at very low cost and in a matter of minutes. I mention this simply to alert you to a step that must be taken before the database can be loaded. If you are trying to maintain your database in-house, your programmers may see this file conversion as a major exercise. If they do, try to get it done by a service bureau.

Before the names can be loaded, you must do a merge/purge to consolidate duplicates. You will also want to do an *edit check* on the data to go into your database. Check the SKU numbers for validity, the dates, cell codes, and dollar amounts. Every field should be checked by an edit program which knows what is within the correct range and what is nonsense. Records which fail the edit check will have to be corrected or, at least, the bad data should not be entered. The same edit checks should be built into the database if it is to be updated "live" by your telemarketers. The edit checks won't let them enter "Ten" in a numeric field, or AL in the state field, if the zip code shows that the customer is in Alaska.

Figure 5-3   Steps in Database Construction

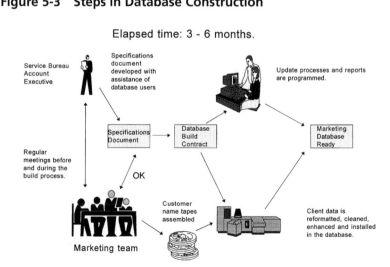

Elapsed time: 3 - 6 months.

Service Bureau Account Executive

Specifications document developed with assistance of database users

Update processes and reports are programmed.

Regular meetings before and during the build process.

Specifications Document → Database Build Contract → Marketing Database Ready

OK

Marketing team

Customer name tapes assembled

Client data is reformatted, cleaned, enhanced and installed in the database.

You may also want to enhance your data at this point. This means finding out the geocode (including zip code, carrier route number, census tract, and block) using special software, and appending demographic information (assumed income, house value). You may also want to append lifestyle information which you have available, plus age, sex, motor vehicles owned and such.

LOADING THE DATABASE

Now we are ready to load the database. This is a big step. All the previous steps, the conversion, the duplicate elimination, the editing, the enhancing, have been working with a *flat, sequential file*. Programs that accomplish this work very rapidly. Depending on your mainframe and how busy it is, you can usually run an edit check, for example, of a million names in a half hour or less. But when we come to load the database, the time involved increases considerably.

As we were planning our database format, we determined the indexes. Loading the database now brings these indexes into play. As each new name is added to the database, all the indexes have to be updated. This will take a long time, even on a fast computer. To add a million names to a database with thirty indexes may take all night or even longer. Fortunately, modern computers can do many things at once. Normal operations don't stop just because you are loading the database. But batch operations to load or update records in a marketing database will always be very slow.

This is not necessarily true of getting data out of a marketing database. Simple counts and reports should come back in a matter of minutes, even from a database of several million names. If you want to select a half a million names from your database, based on criteria that you have developed during previous counts and reports, the process is as follows.

Figure 5-4   Loading a Database Takes Time

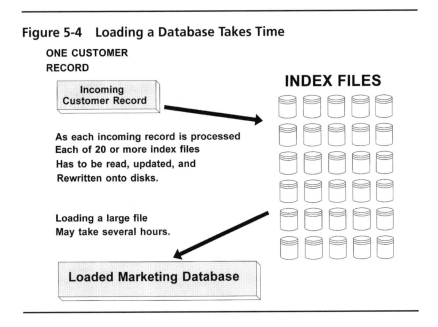

Enter the select criteria from your terminal or PC, and ask the database, using a menu screen, to store the resulting names on a disk file named XXXXXX. The computer will then tackle this task, finishing up, notifying you when it has been done. At that point, you should fax to the service bureau detailed instructions on what to do with the selected names ("Make a tape and send it to XXXXX; give me a set of cheshire labels and send them to XXXXX.") Some of the software systems make heavy weather of this selection process, taking several hours or longer. There is good marketing database software that will accomplish most selects in less than a minute even from files of millions of names. Shop around and be sure you have the best.

DETERMINING PRIORITIES

As planning for the new database begins, you will have to consider the question of priorities for your database functions. Your DBA will play a central role in determining what the priority of each function should be.

Figure 5-5   User Priorities Should Differ

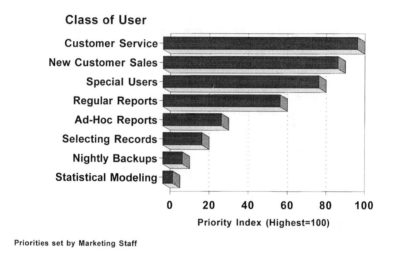

Priorities set by Marketing Staff

Generally speaking, your computer will tackle the command with the highest priority (lowest priority number) before it tackles anything else. Of course, if you assign everything priority 1, then nothing has priority and everything is equally slow. You have to decide what should take precedence for "priority" to have any meaning or impact.

For database marketing, here is a rough idea of the priority you should assign, from highest priority to lowest priority:

1.   Customer service screens.

2.   New customer acquisition telemarketers.

3.   Screens of individuals who are entering data or communicating with the database on an individual basis.

4.   Regular and custom reports.

5.   Ad-hoc reports.

6. Selecting records from the database.
7. Nightly batch updates and backups.
8. Market research multiple regressions and other modeling statistical functions.

DEVELOPING A MARKETING PROGRAM

This is the most important part of the database building process: it is the reason that you build the database in the first place. You would think that it would be the first thing that you do, but in fact it is usually the last, and is often short-changed.

It is amazing how many companies fail to put together a functioning database marketing program in the first year. They spend all the money on putting this product together, and then when it becomes operational, they don't use it. It just sits there. One bank we knew had great plans for their database. By the time they had it set up, the person in charge had left. Those who remained had no real concept of how to use the database, so it languished. The bank got little real use out of it.

Another company built a database of two and a half million customers who had bought their product. When the database was set up, no one had any real idea of what to do with the names. Almost a year was occupied in developing concepts for test mailings. Meanwhile, the names grew stale.

Why is it that marketing databases get built and then not used? I have a theory:

There are two personality types involved in this business. The type of practical hard-headed personality who can put a database together is quite different from the creative person who can visualize how to use it. The *constructors* worry about hardware, software, list acquisition, merge/purge, edit checks, user access, screens, reports, and quality control. The *creators* say "OK. Great. We can deal directly with Sally Warren one-on-one and offer her super service, recognition, diversity, and information. From her we can get loyalty and repeat sales. But what do we have to *do* to get this process started?"

That is the hard part—that is the reason this book exists. It is pretty easy to find constructors. They are located in any good service bureau, and in some cases, in marketing or customer service. But finding a creative person who can dream up practical applications and sell them to management is much harder.

Of course, a database is totally worthless unless it is used. A part of your planning has to go into thinking through those first twelve months:

- When will we select our best customers and categorize them all? How will we reward loyal customers?

- What direct-mail steps have we planned? When will they go out?

- How will Customer Service be set up? How will we publicize it? How will we train employees in use of the database?

- How can we use the database to cross-sell and up-sell our customers? What practical steps will we take, and when?

- How do the salesforces and dealers fit in to the database? What will we be doing for and with them in the first twelve months?

Figure 5-6 Database Infrastructure Functions

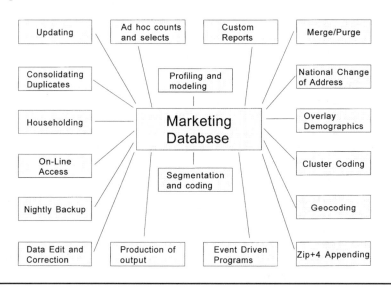

When you put it all together, as we have in Figure 6, you can see what has to be done to maintain a marketing database. Not all databases will be this complex, but most of the good ones will. In developing your plans, go around the circle of this chart, and ask yourself how you will handle each of these functions—whether you will need it, how your software will handle it, where you will get the data, etc.

SUMMARY

Marketing databases must be dynamic instruments of change within the company. They must be used to build customer loyalty, to increase sales, to support dealers, and to beat the competition. In almost every chapter of this book are hints about what you must do. Some will work in your company; many will not. Study these hints, find the right ones, add your own ideas, and put them together in a plan that will work in your company.

- A marketing database should be up and running within one year from the time it is first approved.

- Waiting too long can be costly to the company and to the success of the database.

- If your company is planning on such a huge database that more than a year is required to create it, scale back your plans and build a smaller database which can get up and running fast. You learn more from your database after it is set up than you do in its construction. It is relatively easy to make changes to an established database.

- Almost all marketing databases are more efficient and cost-effective if built on a service bureau mainframe rather than on inside equipment, because few MIS staffs have the software or experience and MIS may not have the programmers needed.

- The MIS culture may find it difficult to accept a software system that requires the constant changes needed for a dynamic marketing database.

- MIS will probably assign a lower priority to the marketing database than it does its operating functions such as payroll, inventory, billing, and manufacturing. The marketing database could be strangled in red tape.

- In dealing with an outside contractor, you must have an in-house DBA who maintains tight controls.

- To plan the database you need a team consisting of marketing, market research, sales, advertising, customer service, MIS, your creative direct agency, your service bureau, and an outside telemarketer.

- You must develop a format for the data you will keep on each customer. Be creative here; do not be constrained by your current format.

- Bytes are cheap. Collect as much information as you need to build a very imaginative customer database.

- Decide what fields should be indexed. Indexes make reporting and access very fast, but each additional index slows down the update and loading process.

- Designing reports will help you in the planning process. Every member of the team should design reports that are needed by his or her function in the company.

- The DBA can determine who in the company will have access to the data, and can assign access codes and passwords.

- Access can be by a PC or a terminal. If everyone in your company already has terminals, there are ways to route the marketing database to them.

- A marketing database should stand on its own and not be considered a modification or addition to existing company databases. In particular, the marketing database should not be kept as a part of customer accounting records, unless these records are created by use of the database for direct marketing.

- Keeping the marketing database separate from other company customer records may seem to be more costly, but will save money in programmer time, which is the most expensive part of any database.

- To keep the marketing database current with other customer files, a copy of the customer files should be spun off on tape periodically and used to update and refresh the marketing database.

- Getting customer names for the database is often a creative process in which everyone must come up with good ideas.

- Converting names from one format to another is very easy for any service bureau—don't make it into a major project.

- Loading a marketing database is usually a very slow process, because of the updating of the indexes. Be prepared for a full day or more.

- Your DBA will have to determine the priority of every user of the database. Customer Service screens should have the highest priority.

- As a part of the planning process, you should develop a marketing program for the first year of the database. The program will help you to be sure that the database is designed properly. It is very important that you make use of the database right away so that you can learn about your customers and how to make the database improve your bottom line.

- You will need to assemble a first-class team to run your database. It must contain both *creators* and *constructors*. Without both types, it will fail.

Chapter 6

The Personal Computer and the Mainframe

Most of us who are active in database marketing came to this profession from somewhere else. We each bring to our jobs different backgrounds which influence the way we do our work, or approach the problems. My personal experience, therefore, may explain my point of view, and may serve to illustrate some principles about our subject.

I first got into the data processing field in 1958. I was working for the US foreign aid program (what is now called the Agency for International Development, or AID) as Director of the Program Methods Division. Through a bureaucratic maneuver, I managed to acquire the Agency's Electric Accounting Machine Branch—a group of about 20 people who ran the IBM punched card accounting operation—there being no other method of computing in those days.

AID at that time was close to a two billion dollar operation. Most of the accounting was done on IBM punch cards. Data entry clerks punched the data (made rectangular holes) in the stiff IBM cards—about the size of bank checks. These cards were then run through a series of machines—sorters, calculating punches, and printers—which did the card reading, the mathematics, and the reports necessary for accounting.

WIRING BOARDS

Each machine was "wired" for each individual job. Colored insulated wires were plugged into removable plug boards—large heavy square blocks of Bakelite with hundreds of individual holes, each of which controlled some machine function. To do a simple job like multiplying hours worked by rate of pay, it was necessary to plug wires into the holes representing the columns in the cards that contained the hours worked, to plug the other end of the wires into holes connected to one of several calculating registers in the machines. Other wires would be plugged in to move the card columns which held the rate of pay to another part of the register. Finally, wires from the output of the register would be plugged into to a punch control area where the pay amount would be punched into other columns of the same or another card.

Wiring the boards was wonderful fun. When completed, a board for a complicated job would have hundreds of individual wires and weigh twenty or thirty pounds. I went to IBM classes part time for more than a year to learn how to do this. My goal was not just to be a good supervisor for the unit, but to get essential knowledge so that AID could acquire its first business computer.

To get a computer in those days—1960—a Federal agency had to get permission from the Bureau of the Budget, a part of the Executive Office of the President. The thirty-page justification that I wrote, when finally presented, was rejected on the grounds that our agency, with a mere $2 billion budget, could not afford a computer.

THE PEACE CORPS

Shortly thereafter, John Kennedy was elected President. He appointed his brother-in-law, Sargent Shriver, to head a new agency, The Peace Corps. I, among others, was given responsibility for providing services for this new Corps.

After I had gained Sargent Shriver's confidence by doing various administrative jobs, I asked him how he was planning to process the hundreds of thousands of expected applications for the Peace Corps. Seeing that he had not thought about this question in any great detail, I suggested, "Why don't you use the foreign aid agency computer?"

He grabbed at the idea at once. I neglected to mention to him that we didn't have a computer, and had been turned down when we tried to get one.

Armed with this requirement for an agency close to the President's heart, I had no trouble getting the Bureau of the Budget to change their decision, and give us permission to acquire an IBM 1401 computer. There was only one obstacle. IBM was backlogged in delivery of these machines, and required a 9-12 month wait. Fortunately, I discovered that Ted Watson, Chairman of IBM, was also Chairman of the Peace Corps Advisory Council. By getting an audience with Watson, I was able to get delivery of the computer within 90 days, complete with two full-time IBM engineers who would stay for six months to program it, and teach me and my staff how to do the same.

That is how I got into data processing, learning to program the 1401, which had many similarities to today's mainframes: raised floors, special air conditioning, tape drives, high security, etc.

FROM DATA PROCESSING TO DIRECT MAIL

Shortly thereafter, I was promoted to higher level management and economist positions (I am basically an economist), and left data processing behind. I found myself in 1977 in the Carter White House, representing the Treasury Department on a reorganization task force. The previous year, I had married Helena, a Spanish instructor at the American University. Shortly after we married, she received a pink slip from American. She spent most of the Carter years trying to find another professional job. For these years, despite her graduate training, she took secretarial typing jobs. Seeking something more professional, she hit on the idea of becoming a computer programmer.

So that Helena could learn programming and we could spend our evenings together, we both went to a community college at night studying COBOL, operating systems, and all that a modern programmer should know. After two years, when she went for interviews as a programmer, she was told that she lacked experience. Undaunted, we set about to create a data processing company to give her the necessary experience. The company we created, Automated Systems Associates (ASA), provided software services. We printed up a nice brochure, rented a list of 2,000 names of data processing companies in the Washington area, and spent our weekends sticking labels and stamps on envelopes, stuffing them with brochures.

The very first significant job we got was from ACS, Inc., a direct mail company in downtown Washington. They wanted us to install their first computer—an IBM Series/1. Just at this moment, however, Helena got a job teaching Spanish, and could not fulfill the ACS contract, so I was stuck with it.

To do this, I acquired a helmet and a bicycle. ACS was several blocks from the White House through heavy traffic. I parked at ACS each morning about 6:30 AM to work on the ACS computer. By 8:45 AM I was at work at the White House. By 5:45 PM I was back at ACS until about 8:00 PM when I went home.

My employers at ACS (who later became my partners), Manny Kandel and Ben Spaisman, had a very successful direct mail business personalizing first and third class letters on IBM System 6 machines. Their clients were political and non-profit groups. I knew next to nothing about direct mail at the time that they employed me for this job. They and I had the idea that once you programmed a computer to do direct mail, it would run itself, like a washing machine. You just put dirty clothes and soap in, and clean clothes came out a half hour later. Their contract with me was to get the computer running, and to write ten standard programs that would do all the work required by their clients.

FROM DIRECT MAIL TO DATABASE MARKETING

Of course, we soon discovered that computers do not run themselves. Every new job we got required some revision of one of our existing programs—or an entirely new program. Besides that, when the ACS clients found out that we had a computer, they began to send us bigger and bigger jobs, with more and more personalization. ACS extended the ASA contract, and gave us more and more work. Because of the computer, ACS grew in size from 12 employees when I first began work for them to more than 70 employees fifteen years later. The majority of the new employees were programmers. When ACS got big enough, I retired from the government and became an ACS partner.

I spent my first six years with ACS writing a large body of what is now standard database marketing software. I wrote merge/purge to find and consolidate duplicates, address and zip code correction to standardize addresses, and editing and error correction routines to keep garbage from getting into the databases. I also had to write postal presort software to get postal discounts, and gender finding software so you could say Dear Ms. (or Mr.) Hughes. I wrote name correction software so that IBM would not come out as "Ibm" when it was upper/lower cased. Most important, I had to write update software so that each database could be modified each month by the many different inputs necessary to keep it current: changes of address, additions, deletions, new purchases, responses, promotion history, and demographic overlays.

When we upgraded from the Series/1 to large IBM mainframes, we found that much of this standard software could be purchased from Group 1. The database updating software, however, had to always be written by hand, because every modern marketing database is completely different from every other database. In addition, the formats, inputs, and output requirements were always changing. Marketing just does not stand still. Marketers keep coming up with new surveys or offers which require modification to their databases.

Our growing staff of programmers and operators were kept busy doing merge/purge, designing new reports, modifying databases and update programs, backing up customer data every night, and hunting for duplicates and errors in the data or the programs which could spoil the relationship with the customers.

We acquired a number of non-profit databases early in the game. Our first significant commercial database was with Compaq Computer Company. For eight years we built and maintained their database which was based on owner registration cards. As the work increased with Compaq, we jointly came up with the idea of owner registration diskettes—an interactive diskette that was packed into every new Compaq. It asked the new owner hundreds of questions, the answers to which were stored in the diskette. A self-mailer brought more than 1,000 disks a day to our new facilities in Reston, Virginia where we uploaded the information into our mainframe computer.

Soon after we began work for Compaq we went on to add dozens of other marketing databases for pharmaceuticals, telephones, banking, insurance, baby food, pet food, diet products, automobiles, cruise lines, ski resorts, and financial services. The world was waking up to database marketing, and we grew with it.

As our business grew, I got further away from programming and more into marketing. I discovered what most marketers know today, that once you have good software and a trained staff, building and maintaining a database is comparatively easy. The hard part is thinking up profitable ways of using a database in marketing. These methods must build lasting relationships with customers to keep them loyal and increase their spending rates. If a database cannot be used to accomplish these functions, it makes no economic sense to build it. To keep our database business, therefore, we had to help our clients with strategy. For that reason, I became a marketer: working with our clients to figure out ways to create two-way dialogues which provide services and information to the customer, and repeat sales to the client.

THE ADVENT OF THE PC

As personal computers advanced in sophistication and processing power, we discovered how versatile and useful they could be in the database marketing world. Mainframes can hold millions of records, run massive updates, and support a hundred simultaneous databases, programmers, and users. But they can't create great graphics. They lack the spreadsheets, word processing, and statistical software available on PCs. They lack the user-friendly graphical user interfaces that permit a marketer to manipulate his or her database with a mouse!

Figure 6-1   What Happens in a Typical Database Update

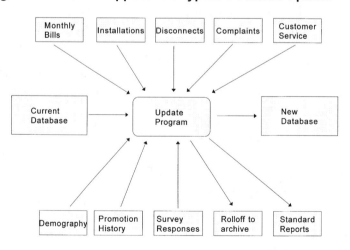

For this reason, we had to build PCs into our database picture, installing them as the front end so that the user was able to have her entire customer database at her fingertips, available to do reports, ad-hoc counts, selects, graphics, modeling, and "what if" scenarios. All of this hands-on contact with the customer data had to be so user-friendly that the user never was aware of what went on behind the scenes.

As our clients became more and more versatile in their marketing programs, their databases became the heart of their marketing efforts. Any loss of data, or error, could damage customer relationships. Every night, customer data had to be backed up on-site and off-site. Database update programs involving a dozen different data sources had to be run off-line, behind the scenes, so that the new databases were cleaned, deduped, and ready for use when the marketers needed them to maintain their customer relationships.

DRAWING MAPS OF SERVICE AREAS

Some companies have used their PCs to draw maps of their service areas, plotting the locations of their customers, their competitors, etc. Such maps today can include streets with street names, census block numbers, and other data in any area, size, or shape. Data on incomes, home values, spending habits, or savings propensities can be shown on maps in color plus tables including percentages, averages, medians and so on. An example of such a map is the Market Potential Index Map shown in Figure 6-2.

Figure 6-2   Market Potential Index Map

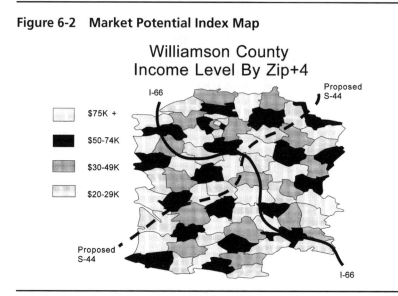

Williamson County
Income Level By Zip+4

Used by such companies as JC Penney, Aetna, McDonald's, Amoco, Southland, Pizza Hut, Sears, Mobil Oil, and Citicorp, this PC software can be used for presenting, mapping, and analyzing customer and prospect data. With software prices starting at about $25,000, plus a fast PC and color plotter, you can turn your marketing office into a data powerhouse with maps and reports on consumers and businesses anywhere in America or Canada. The software can be programmed to accept and display on maps data from such sources as Dun and Bradstreet, Equifax, Arbitron, Neilson, or your own customer data.

Banks use such maps to show where many bank products (checking accounts, savings accounts, consumer loans) are being used, and where the competition is strong.

On the downside, such maps take a long time to draw. Even with a fast PC and color printer, you must allocate between fifteen minutes and an hour for production of each map with any degree of detail. Even when you have finished the map, management will want to see a list of the customers or competitors, and it is from such lists that the real decisions will be made. You might even skip the map.

The other problem is that such maps are really part of market research, not database marketing. Such maps will not help you to set up a two-way dialogue with your customers or to correspond with them.

THE SCREEN IMAGE IS NOT THE DATABASE

Some marketers, unaware of the complex activity in database updating that must go on behind the scenes, begin to think that what they see on their PC screens is the database; that all they need for database marketing is a very large and powerful PC. They make the same mistake that my partners Manny and Ben made so many years before—thinking that a computer by itself could do the work, once proper programs had been written and installed.

Of course, that is not true. Any active database requires full time programmers who are constantly modifying the database format, redoing the update programs as new data and new requirements are developed. Each of our active databases requires one or more application programmers, plus operators who do the backups and the extracts. These people are supported by systems programmers who must constantly install new releases of the many software programs used in database marketing. Finally, almost all inputs to the databases must be first processed by production programmers to clean the addresses, correct the zip codes, perform merge/purge, overlay external demographic data, latitude/longitude coordinates, geocodes, etc.

Figure 6-3   Database Infrastructure Functions

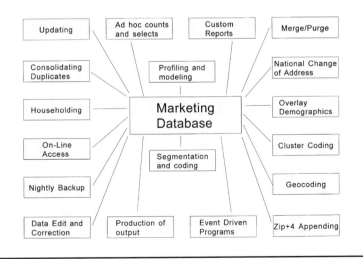

Marketers don't know how to do any of these things, and they shouldn't have to. Once a marketer decides to put his customer marketing database on a PC which he handles himself, if he is to do the job right, he must become a programmer. He will find that in learning to do, and carrying out all of the functions shown above, he ceases to be a marketer at all. He will become a slave to his PC. In the trade-off, his company will have lost its attempt to build relationships with its customers, and gained a group of marketers who waste their company's money "reinventing the wheel" as amateur programmers.

PCs Updated from Diskettes

Some providers have a practical solution to this problem. They have a mainframe that creates and updates a client's marketing database. When the database is ready, the client receives a bunch of diskettes or CD ROM disks which he uses to transfer the database to his PC or PC Server. He can then work with this data, counting, reporting, graphing, and selecting. When he wants output, he calls the mainframe provider and asks them to make the same selection that he made, producing labels or letters to customers. In some cases, instead of a telephone call, he can send the request electronically over a phone line, or send the provider a diskette. For small jobs, he can select customer names and addresses on his PC, producing letters with word processing software. Okra Marketing in Tampa, Florida, provides this service to more than 330 clients. Banc One uses this method.

BANC ONE DIRECT MARKETING

Banc One Corporation, headquartered in Columbus, Ohio, is a holding company with fifty-two banks. A few years ago the corporation created a central unit for Direct Marketing Services, headed by Bobbie Hagen. Every quarter, each bank submitted a tape of their customers. The seven million name customer tapes were processed by an outside service bureau. The relational database was housed on a PC in the bank's central office. Using this PC, Bobbie Hagen could perform sophisticated analysis leading to about sixty different promotions every year involving mailings of about 3,500,000 plus outbound telemarketing.

Ms. Hagen was able to learn a lot about the bank's customers from this database. She tried appending demographic information from an outside supplier. The appended data did not improve response significantly. She found that the best predictor of customer response is RFM analysis (see Chapter 7). Using RFM she could do predictive modeling, which helped the bank to improve profitable response.

Not all of Banc One's banks participated in all of the central programs. A typical promotion involved five to thirty banks. The bank affiliate paid for the mailing, but the Direct Marketing department handled all tracking and analysis. The bank affiliates picked the promotion that featured the product they required for their bottom line.

Almost every campaign was a combination of direct mail and telemarketing, with the in-house telemarketing staff working the telephones. A customer was targeted by modeling for a particular product. If the customer did not respond as expected, he or she would get a telephone call, which helped to close the sale. In this way, Bobbie Hagen got responses as high as 45 percent on a credit card mailing, and lesser but very profitable responses on scores of other promotions.

Is this Database Marketing?

This type of predictive modeling using RFM is really direct marketing, rather than database marketing. Bobbie Hagen gets the responses entered into her database only once a quarter. The system, however, put her bank way ahead of most of the competition in terms of learning the best segment of the customer base to target. The only way to learn direct marketing is to try it, and for Banc One it was a great success.

For direct marketing programs, therefore, a stand-alone PC fed by a service bureau on a periodic basis may be the ideal solution. Many banks and business-to-business marketers use this solution. It is not database marketing, however. It is difficult or impossible to maintain a two-way dialogue with customers using this method. If a customer calls you with a question or a complaint, the relevant facts should be inserted in the customer record so that future correspondence can use this information to provide helpful and relevant communications. To say, "I am glad that you pointed out the problems with the payment envelopes. As you can see, the envelopes we are now using are a size larger—thanks to you, Mrs. Sawyer" will keep Mrs. Sawyer a customer for life.

This is difficult to do with a PC database fed by monthly diskettes. Any data you create during the month will be wiped out by the next monthly batch of diskettes. I know of no easy way around this problem. If, however, all you want is better targeting of your marketing dollar, and don't care about dialogue, the PC-mainframe-disk transfer system is a workable and cost effective solution.

FROM PCs TO SERVERS

Another solution is to eliminate the mainframe altogether and put your entire customer marketing databases on a PC server. PC servers are really very large PCs which are accessed simultaneously by many different PC users—exactly like a mainframe. Every year, servers grow in power as better disks, faster chips, and newer software are added.

Advantages. The advantages for complete database maintenance on a PC server over a mainframe appear to be several:

- The hardware seems to be less expensive. Server disk is inexpensive and can be increased almost without limit. Mainframe processors and disks tend to be expensive, requiring MIS departments to impose arbitrary restrictions on the data that the marketing staff wants to acquire and access.

- The server can be under the control of the marketing staff, not the central MIS department. MIS departments are notoriously unresponsive to marketing needs, due to marketing's labor intensive demands for database modifications, updates, etc. MIS often relegates marketing to the end of months-long queues of units in the corporation waiting for service. By freeing themselves from the "dead hand" of MIS control, marketers can begin to do real database marketing.

- Servers are PCs, and therefore can hold the modeling, graphics, spreadsheet, and word processing software not available on a mainframe.

Disadvantages. The disadvantages of using PC servers as the basis for a marketing database are also significant. They are these:

- There is some marketing software written for a PC server. Mailer's Software of San Clemente, California, Mirus of Plano, Texas, and Dydacomp of Montville, New Jersey, to mention only three, sell PC software for list conversion, address standardization, duplicate elimination, zip correction, geocoding, latitude-longitude determination, postal presort, gender resolution, etc. The PC software covers the same ground that mainframe direct marketing software does. The problem is that the mainframe software does not run by itself. It requires skilled programmers to modify it so as to get satisfactory results. The same is true of PC software, except that the makers do not provide their customers with source code, so, in fact, it cannot be easily modified. If you can't modify the software, however, you will be unable to do adequate database marketing.

- Most of the behind-the-scenes work on a mainframe marketing database is done by application and production programmers. Any active database will need such people plus an operator doing backups and extracts. Someone has to train these people and supervise them on a day-to-day basis. On a mainframe, these technicians are part of a larger programming staff which works on many different jobs. With your server, the staff is normally devoted only to one application. For proper database maintenance, therefore, your server will require a very high labor budget for programming staff costs. Very few marketers, seeking funding for a database project, have the foresight or budget clout to build in the staff increase needed along with the comparatively modest cost of their initial server hardware and software.

- PC server databases almost always cost more than their mainframe cousins. The costs of labor in a client/server environment are steeper than most industry participants originally thought. Research by the Gartner Group in Stamford, Connecticut indicates that more than 70 percent of the costs of computing in a client/server environment are labor costs, not technology costs. The costs of training, program development and modification, system maintenance, and system planning are routinely ignored in figuring the cost of a client server. Without sufficient funds in these areas, projects may fail.

Managers should expect a much more labor-intensive endeavor than they experienced in a traditional mainframe environment. The costs of labor in a client/server environment can be as much as four or five times more than the costs on other computing platforms, according to Peter Burris, of the International Data Corp. Jeffrey Jordan of Price Waterhouse puts it this way: "Many of our clients are under the misconception that deploying a client/server application is a one shot deal. They fail to understand that computing needs, like business needs, change and grow constantly, so applications must change and grow as well."

Alan Young-Pugh of Deloitte & Touche points out that "The cost of keeping the technology updated and understanding how new software versions will affect what already exists and what changes must be made to accommodate the updates is an issue many managers have not anticipated."

SOLUTION: OUTSOURCE

If server stand-alones or PCs updated by diskettes have drawbacks, what is the solution to database marketing? On the one hand, keeping the marketing database on the MIS mainframe will probably put your marketing plans in a MIS straitjacket which will prevent dynamic marketing. A PC server, which seems like an escape, will probably cost much more, and will not have the software to do an adequate job. My solution is to outsource: find a service bureau—there are a large number of them by now—which has the experience, software, and trained staff to build and maintain your database, and which can provide access to all of your users by linking the service bureau's mainframe to your server or to PCs on your user's desks.

You will then have the versatility of the PC—windows, graphics, statistics, reports, modeling, plus the ability to keep all sorts of customer data and use it in your marketing. At the same time, your housekeeping functions will go on efficiently off-site where trained systems and application programmers are using the experience gained from maintaining many similar databases to provide efficient service for yours. Labor costs will be lower. Why? Because the programmers working on your application will also be working on other databases. Your users will not have to become part time programmers and your marketing database will be state of the art.

Some advice on outsourcing: Database marketing should be dynamic and constantly changing. Don't expect your database management firm to be a vendor, providing specified services for a specified price. Look on your service provider as a marketing partner. Let them understand from the outset that their job is not to maintain your database, but to help you with your marketing needs. Ask them to suggest better ways to develop customer dialogue, to create meaningful communications and surveys. Have them help you by computing customer lifetime value, by computing recency, frequency, monetary cells, and reporting on your success in increasing the lifetime value of each cell. Have them help you in the design of your forms and communications so that the data can be rapidly stored in the database, and used in future communications and strategy development.

SUMMARY

- Database marketing is more labor intensive than most data processing functions. It requires special software and constant program modifications not required in most other applications.

- Mainframe software has been developed over the last twenty years which provides effective support for database marketing functions. Service bureaus exist which can build and maintain databases.

- PCs can do graphics, mapping, spreadsheets, word processing, and modeling better than mainframes. PC software is evolving rapidly. PC hardware gets better and cheaper every year. PCs should be used as the front end for any database marketing application.

- A stand-alone PC cannot be used effectively to do database marketing because it will require the marketing user to perform the scores of tasks done by mainframe programmers, including program modification and updates.

- Providing PCs or PC servers with periodic data from a mainframe database is a partial solution to this problem, but falls short of real database marketing because it is difficult or impossible to retain customer data generated between periodic mainframe updates.

- Keeping a marketing database on the MIS mainframe usually proves unsatisfactory for marketing because MIS will resent the labor-intensive dynamic changes in software and structure demanded by a modern database marketing program.

- The solution is outsourcing the database to a service bureau which builds and maintains the database, providing daily access for marketers by a direct link between their PC server (or individual PCs) and the service bureau mainframe. Users get behind-the-scenes maintenance combined with the versatility and power of the PC.

- Such outsourced service bureaus should be considered partners in the marketing program rather than vendors of services. In this way, the marketer can get professional help with the real challenges faced in database marketing.

Part III:

Building Relationships with Your Customers

Chapter 7

How to Select Your Best Customers

WHY DISCRIMINATE?

This is a chapter on how to select your best and your worst customers, and how to rank them so that you can give your best service to your best customers. The obvious question is, why? Why not give super service to all your customers?

The answer is that it is much more profitable to discriminate. The old 80/20 rule is true of almost every business: 80 percent (or some other high percentage) of your business dollars comes from the top 20 percent of your customers. If you want your business to grow and become more profitable, you should lavish your attention on this top 20 percent. In addition, you should develop programs to influence the *next* 20 percent to emulate the buying habits of the top 20 percent. But if you make a major effort to serve and influence this top 40 percent group, you will not have the resources left to make a similar effort on the bottom 60 percent. Investigation may show that the absolute bottom 20 percent may be costing you more than they bring in: you may be losing money on them. So you should develop ways to spend less money on these losers.

But there are other, even more powerful reasons for discriminating:

1. It is much more costly to acquire a new customer than to retain the customers you already have.

2. Therefore, it is a mistake to concentrate on acquiring new customers without first doing everything in your power to keep your existing ones.

3. The more you know about what keeps your customers happy, and keeps them your customers, the better you will be at acquiring new ones. Studying customers and ranking them is part of the process of getting to know them.

WHO ARE YOUR BEST CUSTOMERS?

The concept is very simple: your best customers are those who:

- have bought from you most recently;

- buy from you frequently; and

- spend a lot of money on your products and services.

On these three principles rest all the laws and the profits.

Let's discuss each of these factors in turn. In this chapter, for illustration, we are going to assume that you are using your customer database as a mailing file. In this way, we can measure the results of each mailing to validate the principles of Recency, Frequency, Monetary (RFM) analysis which we will explain. But don't be misled into thinking that the principles apply only to direct mail: customer segmentation is central to database marketing as well. Many people who have arrived at database marketing from some background other than direct mail (from general advertising, retailing, or sales, for example) make the mistake of assuming that this RFM analysis technique is only of use in direct mail. This is not so. The examples we use for testing the RFM principles in this chapter are taken from direct mail, but the results—customer discrimination—are crucial to successful database marketing.

Recency

Recency is a very powerful factor. Obviously someone who bought from you last month is a better bet than someone whose last purchase was three years ago. But does this apply to all gradations of recency? Analysis will show that it does. Here is how you can prove it to yourself.

From your most recent offer to your *existing customers,* sort them by the most recent data that they made a purchase from you. Divide the entire sorted file into five equal groups. If you create a chart to show the performance of each of the five groups (quintiles) it will look something like this:

Response Rate by Recency of Purchase

Recency Quintile	Months Ago*	Number Mailed	Number Responded	Response Rate	Index of Response
5	0 - 3 Months	24,000	1464	6.10%	197
4	4 - 6 Months	24,000	1032	4.30%	139
3	7 - 9 Months	24,000	600	2.50%	81
2	10 - 15 Months	24,000	432	1.80%	58
1	16+ Months	24,000	194	0.81%	26
Total		120,000	3722	3.10%	100

* Quintiles are exactly equal, so the months ago column is only an approximation. In real life, the "Months Ago" numbers will be odd days, not even months.

The Index of Response is computed by dividing the average response rate (3.10) into the actual response rate (6.10, 4.30, etc.) for each group and multiplying by 100. It shows that your most recent purchasers are almost twice as likely (197) as the average (100) to buy again. If you were to calculate the cost of the offer, assuming you mailed the same piece to everyone, it could be that you actually lost money on the lowest quintile, while your profits from the top quintile customers were probably excellent.

Figure 7-1   Response by Recency

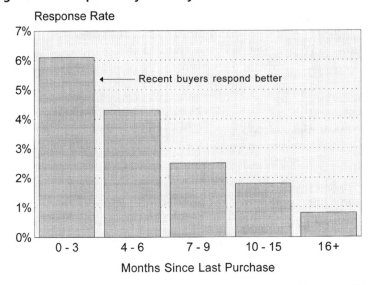

Response Rate

Recent buyers respond better

Months Since Last Purchase

The lesson here is obvious: lavish your attention on your most recent customers. Provide them super service. Contact them frequently. Let them know you are thinking about them. It will earn you profits, and will help you retain the most valuable group of customers that you have.

Frequency

Recency is only one part of your analysis. From the same offer you can break your customers down an entirely different way: by *frequency*; by how many times they have bought from you since they first became your customers. Look at these numbers:

Response Rate by Frequency of Purchase

Frequency Quintile	Number of Purchases*	Number Mailed	Number Responded	Response Rate	Index of Response
5	1000 - 100	24,000	1204	5.02%	162
4	99 - 60	24,000	1102	4.59%	148
3	59 - 11	24,000	606	2.53%	82
2	10 - 2	24,000	444	1.85%	60
1	1	24,000	366	1.53%	49
Total		120,000	3722	3.10%	100

* Quintiles are exactly equal, so numbers are only an approximation. In real life, the numbers will be odd amounts, not even ones as shown.

Figure 7-2   Response by Frequency

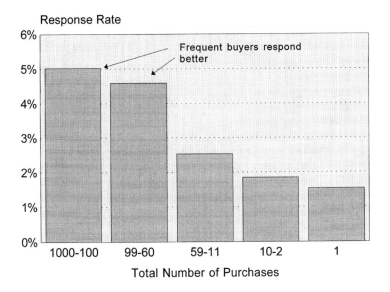

Customers who buy from you many times are much more likely to buy again than those who buy seldom. Of course, some one-time buyers are folks who will be ten or more time buyers eventually; they haven't had a chance to make all those purchases because they just came on board. That is why your lowest quintile on a frequency rating normally does better than your lowest quintile on a recency rating. Again, remember, these frequent buyers are your best customers. You need to structure your services and benefits with this in mind.

Monetary

Finally, let's rank response from customers by *monetary sales,* by the total dollar value of their purchases since they first started buying from your company.

Response Rate by Total Monetary Amount

Monetary Quintile	Total Dollar Purchases*	Number Mailed	Number Responded	Response Rate	Index of Response
5	$80,000 - $2,400	24,000	1119	4.66%	150
4	$2,399 - $1,000	24,000	1056	4.40%	142
3	$999 - $100	24,000	709	2.95%	95
2	$99 - $30	24,000	456	1.90%	61
1	$29 - $1	24,000	382	1.59%	51
Total		120,000	3722	3.10%	100

* Quintiles are exactly equal, so dollar amounts are only an approximation. In real life, the dollars will be odd amounts, not even ones as shown.

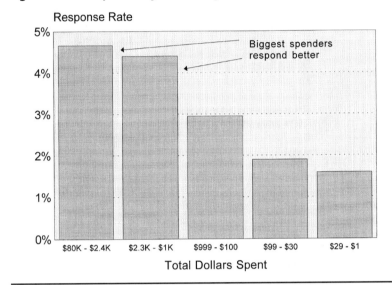

Figure 7-3   Response by Monetary Amount

Monetary amount can be calculated in several ways, each of which has benefits. You can measure:

- amount of total purchases
- amount of purchases in last twelve months
- amount of average purchase

BUILDING RFM CODES INTO YOUR DATABASE

Now that you understand the principles, you can combine these three vital customer behavioral measurements into a comprehensive coding scheme that will give you an excellent segmenting system for your customer database. Using RFM codes, for example, you will be able to predict the response to future mailings with some degree of precision. You will learn who your best customers are so that you can accord them different treatment. You can decide who to spend promotion dollars on, and who to drop from your active customer list.

The first step is to put RFM codes into each customer record. Here's how to begin.

Creating a Recency Code

To put a code for recency into each customer record, your database records have to have one key date: the most recent purchase date. For a utility where the customer gets monthly bills, the date would be the last time the customers changed their service. For a department store, it would be the last time they charged something.

Figure 7-4   Creating Recency Codes

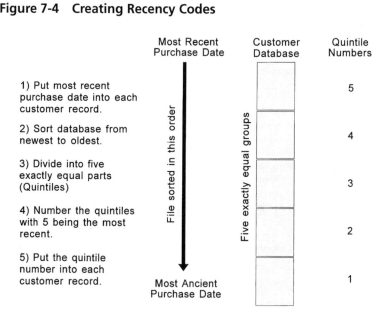

Using your PC or mainframe, sort all the customer records by this most recent date, putting the most recent at the top and the most ancient at the bottom. Divide the database into five equal parts (quintiles) and code the top 20 percent with a "5", the next with a "4", etc. Every record in the database now has a new piece of data stored in it: a single digit, a recency code, which is either 5, 4, 3, 2, or 1—5 being the most recent and best.

These recency codes will change from month to month as existing customers fail to purchase again, and old or new customers buy your products. You must update these codes on a regular basis. Once you have written a program to insert these codes, it will take but a very short time to do this on even the largest customer files.

Creating Frequency Codes

Frequency codes are created exactly like recency codes. You put into each customer record a number representing the number of times that the customer has bought from you. For a utility like a telephone company, this number would be the number of months that the service has been connected. A bank would have the number of transactions (deposits, checks) since the account was opened. A supermarket or department store would record the number of visits to the store as shown by use of the store's credit or check cashing card. An oil company would have number of trips to the gas pump, etc.

Sort the database by this number, from the highest frequency to the lowest frequency. Divide into five equal parts (quintiles), and number each quintile from 5 (the highest) to 1 (the lowest). Put the quintile number into each customer record.

Customer records will now have two new numbers side by side: Recency and Frequency. The numbers will range from 55 to 11, with 55 being the most recent and most frequent.

Creating Monetary Codes

The last step is to repeat the exercise by adding a monetary code to each record. Again, each record should have a number representing the total dollars of purchases since the customer first came on board with you (or since the database was created). Sort the file from most dollars to least dollars. Divide into five equal parts (quintiles) and number from 5 (greatest dollars) to 1 (least dollars). Put the quintile number into each database record.

Your RFM numbering scheme is now complete. Each customer will have three numbers (side by side) in their record, ranging from 555 (most recent, most frequent, highest dollar amount) to 111 (oldest, least frequent, lowest spender). There will now be 125 RFM "Cells" in your database. Every time you update your database, you should recalculate the RFM cell of the customer—and store the old cell number in the database record. Why keep two RFM cell numbers? Because you want to measure which people moved up and which people moved down as a result of your marketing activity.

USING RFM CELLS TO PREDICT RESPONSE

Now that you have your customers coded by RFM cell, we can use these numbers in a very powerful way. Let us suppose that you have a customer database of 1 million customers (or any number). You want to do a test mailing to a small number so as to be able to predict the response of the full customer file in advance. That way, if the test is a failure, you need not waste money on promoting the whole file.

The first step is to select a test group from your database. Your test group, for example, could be 40,000 customers. How do you select 40,000 to be sure that they are exactly representative of the 1 million in your customer base? You use a procedure known as an "Nth". Forty thousand divided into 1 million is 25. To create an exact Nth, you take every 25th record from the master file to create your test file.

Figure 7-5   Creating a Test File

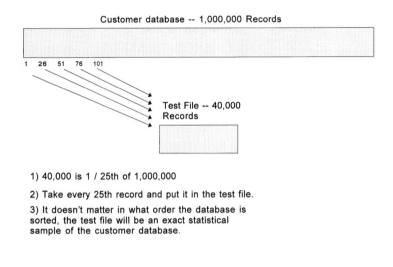

Customer database -- 1,000,000 Records

1   26   51   76   101

Test File -- 40,000 Records

1) 40,000 is 1 / 25th of 1,000,000

2) Take every 25th record and put it in the test file.

3) It doesn't matter in what order the database is sorted, the test file will be an exact statistical sample of the customer database.

Now that you have your test file, you can do a test mailing. The test file will also be coded by RFM cell, since those RFM numbers were in the selected records. Let us suppose that you make an offer of some product or service to these 40,000 test customers. Let us suppose that 711 respond and purchase the product. The response rate is 1.78%. (711/40,000). This may not be a very gratifying response, but since your file is coded by RFM, you can learn a great deal from the results of the promotion.

Table 7-1 on the next page shows the results of your test promotion. There are 125 RFM cells in all. There were 320 customers in each of the 125 RFM cells. The response rate for each RFM cell is calculated individually.

This analysis should be done on a spreadsheet like Lotus or EXCEL. To get the data, you put the customer ID number (or the RFM cell) on each outgoing communication. Ideally it should be on the label and on the response device (post card or personalized order form). When your responses come in, you have to train your mail openers, or your telemarketers, to look for or ask for this number so that you can compile the following chart. This is very important. Without this vital data, your test is not worthwhile.

Table 7-1   Result of Test Mailing to 40,000

Cell Position	RFM Cell	Number Mailed	Number Responses	Resp. Rate
A	B	C	D	E
1	555	320	31	9.69%
2	554	320	30	9.38%
3	553	320	28	8.75%
4	552	320	20	6.25%
5	551	320	19	5.94%
6	545	320	26	8.13%
7	544	320	20	6.25%
8	543	320	18	5.63%
9	542	320	16	5.00%
10	541	320	12	3.75%
11	535	320	14	4.38%
12	534	320	10	3.13%
13	533	320	10	3.13%
14	532	320	9	2.81%
15	531	320	7	2.19%
16	525	320	13	4.06%
17	524	320	10	3.13%
18	523	320	8	2.50%
19	522	320	8	2.50%
20	521	320	7	2.19%
21	515	320	12	3.75%
22	514	320	7	2.19%
23	513	320	8	2.50%
24	512	320	8	2.50%
25	511	320	16	5.00%
26	455	320	8	2.50%
27	454	320	6	1.88%
28	453	320	4	1.25%
29	452	320	4	1.25%
30	451	320	5	1.56%
31	445	320	9	2.81%

(continued)

Cell Position	RFM Cell	Number Mailed	Number Responses	Resp. Rate
A	B	C	D	E
32	444	320	8	2.50%
33	443	320	5	1.56%
34	442	320	3	0.94%
35	441	320	4	1.25%
36	435	320	8	2.50%
37	434	320	7	2.19%
38	433	320	4	1.25%
39	432	320	2	0.63%
40	431	320	3	0.94%
41	425	320	8	2.50%
42	424	320	6	1.88%
43	423	320	4	1.25%
44	422	320	3	0.94%
45	421	320	3	0.94%
46	415	320	7	2.19%
47	414	320	5	1.56%
48	413	320	3	0.94%
49	412	320	4	1.25%
50	411	320	3	0.94%
51	355	320	6	1.88%
52	354	320	5	1.56%
53	353	320	4	1.25%
. . . .
125	111	320	0	0.00%
Total		40,000	711	1.78%

HOW TO PREDICT THE ROLLOUT RESPONSE

Since all of your customers are coded by RFM cell, and we have learned the response of each RFM cell to a test promotion, we are now in a position to predict what the response would be to a rollout mailing to the entire file of 1 million. Before we do this, however, we should establish certain principles which apply to RFM analysis.

In the first place, rollout promotions never have a response rate that is as good as the test. Why is this so? Because marketers can never conduct a fair test. They always tend to bias their test in some way that cannot be repeated in the rollout. The reason, I think, is that no one wants to have an unsuccessful test. You tend to mail first class, instead of third class. You pick the best month for the test—which cannot be repeated in the rollout, etc.

Because rollouts never do as well as the tests, you must discount your test results when using them to predict the rollout response.

You can use any discount percentage that seems appropriate to your situation. I use a standard discount of 15 percent, meaning that the rollout response rate from any RFM cell will be only 85 percent of what the test response rate was.

Now that you can predict the response to a rollout mailing, you should only mail to RFM cells for which you can safely predict a profit. Which are the profitable cells? Ones that are predicted to have a response rate greater than break even. The formula for the break even rate for any mailing is this:

Break Even = Cost per mailing piece / Net Profit from each sale

For the promotion that we are using as an example, let us suppose that your in-the-mail cost per piece is $0.74, which covers the creative, printing, personalization, mailshop and postage. Let us suppose that the net profit from each successful sale is $45.00. The break even response rate, therefore is:

Break Even = $0.74 / $45.00 = 1.64%

This means that any RFM cell whose rollout predicted response rate is exactly 1.64 percent will break even. Above that it will be profitable, below that it will lose money. The profit potential of each cell can be computed on a spreadsheet using this method:

RFM Cell Profit Potential Calculation

RFM Cell	Test Response Rate	Discounted Rollout Prediction*	Index of Profit Potential**
A	B	C	D
455	2.50%	2.13%	29.6
454	1.88%	1.60%	-2.6
453	1.25%	1.06%	-35.2
452	1.25%	1.06%	-35.2
451	1.56%	1.33%	-19.1
445	2.81%	2.39%	45.6

 * 85% of Test Rate
** ((C / 1.64%) * 100) - 100

Once this spreadsheet calculation is done, you can create a graph of each cell that will show clearly which to mail and which to avoid:

Figure 7-6   Response by RFM Cell

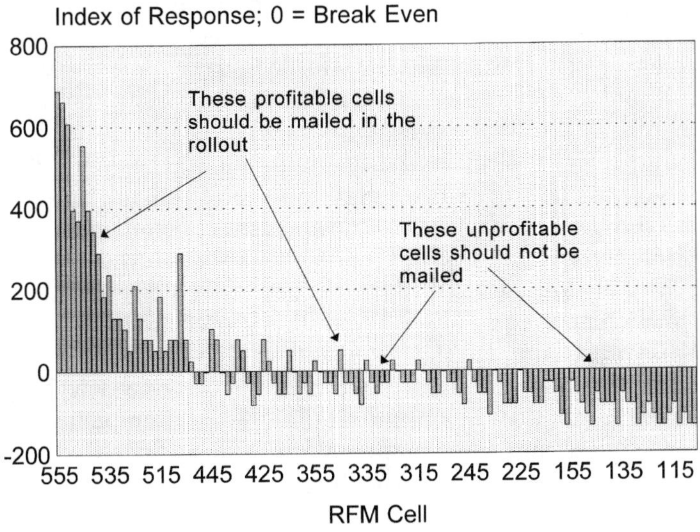

Index of Response; 0 = Break Even

These profitable cells should be mailed in the rollout

These unprofitable cells should not be mailed

RFM Cell

(chart x-axis: 555 535 515 445 425 355 335 315 245 225 155 135 115; y-axis: -200 to 800)

When we graph the response of each rollout RFM cell, the picture looks like Figure 7-6. As you can see, some RFM cells did very well. Some broke even. Many lost money. What do you do with this information? You mail only to the RFM cells with a predicted response rate of break even or greater. Here are the results of using the test results to mail all of the customer file, and only the profitable cells:

	Test	Full Rollout	Selected Rollout
Number Mailed	40,000	1,000,000	264,000
Cost Per Piece	$0.74	$0.74	$0.74
Mailing Cost	$29,600	$740,000	$195,360
Response Rate	1.78%	1.51%	3.45%
Number Responses	711	15,126	9,121
Net Revenue Per Sale	$45.00	$45.00	$45.00
Total Revenue	$31,995	$680,670	$410,445
Net Profit	$2,395	($59,330)	$215,085

If you mail to all 1 million customers, it will cost you $740,000, and you will gain 15,126 sales netting $45 each or $680,670. Many of the RFM cells you mailed to were losers. The result of mailing all 1 million would have been a loss of $59,330. This loss was completely unnecessary, since you had already done a test mailing using the RFM cell information. You can predict these losers in advance by using your test results for each RFM cell, and discounting them. The only RFM cells which you can be fairly sure of getting a profit from are those with a predicted rollout response rate of 1.64 percent or better. In the last column, only those RFM cells were mailed. There were 264,000 of them in all. It cost only $195,360 to mail them. They brought in only 9,121 sales for a total revenue of $410,445. The resulting profit was $215,085.

Can you be sure that the test results will be valid for the rollout? Of course not. There are all sorts of things that can go wrong. The time of year of the rollout cannot be the same as the test. Competitor's products or services may have made an appearance since the test. The economy could have taken a downturn. All true.

But, this type of prediction using RFM is extremely powerful. It is better than any model based on demographics. We are trying to predict the behavior of customer groups based on their past behavior and the behavior of other customers who resemble them in their purchasing behavior. It is as close to certainty as you are ever likely to get in database marketing.

LOOKING AT CUSTOMERS BY RFM CELL

Once you have coded your file by RFM, you have an entirely different way of looking at your customers. You can pick certain cells and give them special treatment. You can design promotions to get certain RFM cells to move up. By keeping track of the previous RFM cell of each customer after an update, you can determine which way they moved.

Figure 7-7   Lifetime Value by RFM Cell

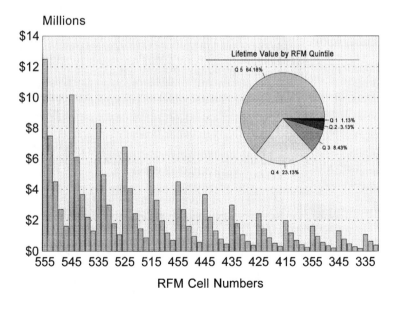

The previous graph shows the results of looking at customers by lifetime value (see Chapter 10). Using the methods that we will be developing in Chapter 10, we have computed the lifetime value of the customers in each RFM cell. In these charts, a company that has 780,625 customers has computed the lifetime value of each RFM cell. You will note the interesting shape of the bar graph. Every five RFM cells, the lifetime value is greater than the previous cell. The reason is clear: the last digit of the RFM cell is the monetary digit. Lifetime value (which is a forward looking concept, but computed based on past performance) is a combination of the customer's propensity to respond and remain as a customer (retention) and the customer's spending rate (for which we use monetary amount (M) as a basis for computation).

SUMMARY

- All customers are not alike. The top 20 percent probably give you between 60 percent and 80 percent of your business. The bottom 20 percent may cost you more than they are worth. Many businesses are aware of this, but have no easy way to distinguish one customer from another, or to treat them differently once the distinction has been made.

- Recency, Frequency, Monetary Analysis (RFM) is a time honored method of easily finding the best customers so that they can be treated differently. Generally, it is much more profitable to spend your energies and resources trying to hang on to your best customers, than to waste your time dealing with your worst customers.

- To use RFM you must have a customer database which retains purchase history. Once you do, it is a simple matter to write software that will put three quintile codes into each customer record (one each for recency, frequency, and monetary amount). These codes should be recalculated with each update of the database, after storing the old codes in the customer file. Using the old and new RFM cell codes, it will be possible to tell if a customer is becoming more profitable or less profitable. Special status benefits can be given to customers who are moving in the right direction.

- It is also possible to use RFM coding in a test mailing to determine the response of each RFM cell to the offer. The results of such a test can then be used to predict the response to a rollout mailing. By avoiding mailing to RFM cells whose response is below break even, virtually any test mailing—no matter how poor—can lead to a profitable rollout mailing.

- RFM coding gives you a very powerful marketing tool which is, in fact, much more useful than any computer model based solely on demographics. RFM analysis can be done using a spread sheet like Lotus or Excel. One does not need to understand statistics to make profitable use of RFM.

- RFM can also be used in connection with lifetime value analysis. As such it will help you to decide how to make the most effective use of your marketing dollars.

- RFM will help you build better relationships with your customers. You can't afford to talk to everyone. Use RFM to find out who your most important customers are, and talk to them.

Chapter 8

Building Customer Loyalty

We have already determined who our best customers are through RFM analysis. How do we "lavish attention" on them?

To approach this question, let's go back to the old corner grocer. When we last saw him, he was standing in the front of his store meeting his customers as they came in to shop. He calls them by name, and asks about their families, vacations, houses, jobs. He doesn't say, "What are you going to buy from me today?"

Perhaps the customer has a request or a complaint. He listens; he agrees with her. It *is* too bad that they were out of rosemary last week, and that she had to go over to that horrible supermarket to buy it. "We have your rosemary today, a little late, of course. We won't run out of that again soon, I can tell you that. We also have some fresh salmon, and I know that Dan loves our salmon."

"Can we get some coconut extract? I'll have it for you Tuesday morning. When do you need it? . . .Oh, oh. I'll run over to the warehouse myself after lunch, and have some for you this afternoon."

What is he doing? He's wrapping that customer in a cocoon of loyal services, kindnesses, and understanding that will keep her buying at his store forever. How can he make any money driving to a warehouse for an 85-cent bottle of coconut extract? He can't. What he is doing is maintaining the loyalty of a customer whose lifetime value to him is several thousand dollars. He thinks long-term. He isn't thinking about the sale. He is thinking about the loyalty of Sally Warren and her family, and what that means to his business.

Can we hope to duplicate the activities of this caring man with our marketing database? Never. But we can try to come close, and that is the focus of this chapter.

If you look at what the grocer is doing, you can break it down into specific actions and reactions by the customer. When you walk into his store:

- You are recognized and greeted by name.
- Your family and prior history are remembered.
- Your prior transactions are remembered.
- Your special preferences are remembered.
- Your special requests and complaints are listened to, and *something is done about them.*

We can do many of these things on our marketing database. Let's first visualize the telemarketing situation. We have a telemarketer who is responding to calls on an 800 number. As soon as the call comes in, we have to decide whether this is an old customer or a new one. How do we do that?

One possibility is to equip our telemarketing terminals with ANI, the equipment that tells us instantly the telephone number of the calling party. ANI gives us the area code and number. As soon as we enter that into our system, our computer can do an automatic search of a telephone number index and determine that the person calling is customer number 1234567. Her record comes up on the screen. We have her name, address, credit card number, prior history and so on—everything needed to make the call. Instead of "Hello," we could say, "Mrs. Warren! Good to hear from you again." Knowing the number of the calling party as you receive the call provides the following advantages:

- Allows you to treat incoming calls from non-customers differently depending on where the call comes from. Even though they are all calling the same 800 number, the call can be taken by different sales personnel based on territory.
- Lets you tell the caller who the nearest dealer is, since you know the geographic area.
- Flags your loyal customers so you can greet them personally by name and give them expedited service.
- Enables your computer to call up the customer's entire record on the screen so that the operator can speak knowledgeably at the very outset of the call.

WHAT TELEMARKETERS DO

Imagine Mrs. Warren's reaction. Instant recognition. She is pleased, flattered, surprised. She feels at home with your telemarketer *even though this particular operator has never spoken to her before.*

If you recall the old-fashioned telemarketer, you can hear the traditional exchange: "May I have the catalog number of the first item, please." But that is not what our marketing database operator is going to say at all. "How was your trip to Spain? Did you stay at one of the Paradores?" (What does this have to do with selling luggage? Nothing. It has to do with the lifetime value of Sally Warren.) "How did your overnight suitcases work out on the Spanish Railway system?"

Our operator is compensated on two things: sales (as at present) and *recorded information.* As Sally Warren and the operator chat about life, the operator is entering important information into the database. The information: "Lock forced on suitcase on Spanish railroad. Camera stolen. Dan promoted to head of engineering department. She is buying leather briefcase for him." This information is converted by the operator and the software into some simple codes that can be used later to provide better service to the customer.

"You have a lifetime guarantee on that suitcase. If anything happens to it, we replace it at 50 percent of its original cost. Shall I send out a replacement for the one that had the lock smashed? . . . Oh, sure, I know the number. It is the green carry-on bag with the red satin interior. We will send one out next week. Now here is what we have in briefcases . . . ."

But Sally doesn't want to buy this briefcase over the telephone. This is too important. It is for a party to celebrate Dan's promotion. She wants to learn what is available and then go and see the ones she is interested in at a local store. A briefcase with a built-in calculator, a holder for business cards and such, in maroon leather strikes her fancy. We give her the telephone number of the luggage departments of several local stores that stock this briefcase. And we give her a code number over the telephone. If she buys at any of these stores, she gives the clerk the code number and receives a $5 credit on her MasterCard account.

Why the $5 credit? She is in the market for the briefcase. Isn't this just a waste of money? Perhaps. There are two good reasons for this credit. The first is that, when she gets to the store, she may see a competing brand that looks better. But she won't have a $5 credit on that brand. The real reason for the $5 is to get her to *use the code number*. This code number will assure that her purchase of this briefcase will get into the database. We now have tied two things together: Sally Warren's desire for a briefcase for Dan's promotion, and the fact that she bought one of our briefcases. We have the model, color, style, and date recorded. One more strand in the cocoon of knowledge and relationships which will bind the Warren family to our company.

Another feature of the code number is that we will know which dealer sold her the briefcase. As far as we are concerned, dealers are customers too: very important customers. We are keeping track of the fact that we steered Sally Warren to Fisher's. And a whole new story opens up from that.

ENTER THE DEALER

Just as we want to keep the Warren family loyal and buying, we want to keep Fisher's and the other dealers loyal, stocking our merchandise, and cooperating with our programs. We will never make a direct sale without also suggesting that customers call a local dealer, giving the names and telephone numbers of these local dealers. We sell at list price. The dealers discount. We tell everyone that. We deliver by UPS. The dealers also deliver.

The dealers have come to understand the value of our database. Every month we give them a printed record of the business we have supplied to them through the database. And what's more, we give each dealer a direct access to our database through a terminal at their store!

This is modern database marketing. Many dealers will be equipped with a small PC or terminal (which costs only a few hundred dollars) and an automatic dialer which puts them in direct contact with the marketing database. When a customer walks in to buy a name-brand product made by a firm with a marketing database, it will be automatic to dial up that database during the sale process. Not only can the sale be entered, and the customer given a rebate (if any), but the dealer can also have access to valuable information about customers which permits the dealer to understand them, talk with them knowledgeably about their former purchases and lifestyles, and, in the process, offer them better service: possibly cross-selling or up-selling based on prior history.

The dangers of untrained personnel in the dealer's store messing up the database with their entries is significant enough that safeguards must be built in. The dealer's access must be essentially "read only" meaning that his staff can access and read data from the database, but not update or change it. This protects the database from being accidentally destroyed. The software *does* permit the dealer to enter some new data: the current purchase, the code number and so on. As this data goes in, it is checked by an edit program to insure accuracy. If the dealer tries to enter an SKU which does not exist, he will get an error message. The same thing happens with the code or other data. The date and time of purchase and the dealer ID is entered automatically by the system.

The customer may be a member of a special "gold card," preferred customer class based on prior sales history with a particular manufacturer, or with the dealer. If so, this fact can automatically be triggered by the sale—even if the customer did not present a "gold" card at the point of purchase. The Visa, MasterCard, or American Express card number will be automatically registered by the dealer at the time the card is presented. If the customer is on the "gold" list, the store record or manufacturer's database record will be called up and displayed. At the same time, of course, if he or she is a customer with a bad credit history, presentation of the card will also trigger appropriate action at the point of sale. No more looking up information in a thick pamphlet. The credit card verification process will turn up the good and bad information, and bring up the appropriate database.

But we are getting ahead of the story. Let us return to the corner grocer for a moment, and explain this "gold card" concept.

Preferred Customers

Not all customers are equal, as we have already seen. Some must be courted. Some are not worth bothering with. Some are new, and we must be very nice to them until we can learn more about them.

The corner grocer knows this. He knows that if he is too chatty with his preferred customers, he may "turn off" new people who have just come in and who are beginning to feel that one must have a long prior history to buy anything in this store. The preferred customers are aware of this, too. They realize that he cannot spend all day with them. He gives them a knowing wink as he leaves them to turn to the newcomers to say in a loud voice, "Well, what can I do for you folks?" Such gestures convey to preferred customers that they are "in" and that these newcomers are not; to the newcomers, he is warm and welcoming.

How do you let database customers know that they are "in?" There are many ways, and still more will be developed as time goes on. This process lies at the heart of the loyalty program. What is loyalty?

Essentially, it is a two-way relationship. The seller makes you feel that you are known, appreciated, welcome, and *better than most*. You are conscious that he does things and will continue to do things for you that he probably wouldn't do for everybody. You trust him to look out for your welfare, and you impart to him information about yourself which you would tell only to a friend.

How can you show a customer that he or she is special? The answer depends on your business and your creative ideas. Here are some ideas:

Offer a Special Card. Gold, platinum, silver. Be sure it reads "Loyal member since XXXX." The software to put this on the card takes four lines of code. The benefits to you can be worth millions of dollars. I have had many such cards for years. I feel that somehow the company is going to give me better service because I have been with them for twenty years. Of course, that isn't true of many stores or companies today, but it will be increasingly true in the future.

The card may have a special 800 number on it different from your regular 800 number that puts the customer directly through to a special operator for loyal customers. American Airlines has such special service for their gold card members.

The special card represents a special status. The experts at this are companies in the travel business. Some hotels have different classes of business customers. Special cardholders who are frequent guests get extra-special service. The hotels train their employees to recognize these guests and to treat them in a special way to emphasize the hotel's responsibility to maintain the loyalty bond. This is also true of many airlines and car rental agencies. These institutions are pioneers in the marketing database industry, and have much to teach everyone else.

Create a Club. The Bank of Boston did an analysis of their depositors to isolate the high-income segment. They inducted these depositors into a luxury service club. Elaborate and elegant direct mail was sent to the club members, encouraging them to mix their investing with living with the arts, music, and social events. The direct mail contained invitations to prestigious events such as polo matches, exclusive art auctions, and concerts. This successful club produced valuable leads which resulted in millions in additional deposits and investments.

Give "Points" to Frequent Flyers. This is a controversial issue. Do frequent flyer credits really build loyalty? Many experts say no. They say that programs that award points or miles don't really build loyalty at all. What they do is provide incentives for doing business with one company over another. They help maintain market share in a hotly competitive environment—especially where the competing products are seen as being similar.

Have these incentives really created loyalty? The acid test is whether market share changes if the program is canceled. Just how long would that loyalty last if all your competitors in your category were to continue their programs after you stopped yours?

In a true "loyalty" program, there has to be something more; something that appeals to another personal need in the consumer. Some component of your program has to make your customer feel special and appreciated: that you recognize his or her importance to you. For true success, there must be *recognition*.

You must be able to tie some tangible level of special service to the amount of business you get from a customer. Many airlines have figured out a way to pick their most frequent travelers out of a coach seat and plunk them into an empty first class seat, thereby developing an emotional sense of loyalty. The future will see loyalty marketing mature beyond its status as a direct marketing tool. The databases we create and the technological tools we've developed, perfected, and continue to enhance will completely reshape the way business is transacted.

I recently acquired Gold status with American Airlines. It wasn't easy. You have to fly 25,000 miles with American Airlines in one calendar year. If you have less than 25,000 miles at the end of a year, you have to start all over again from zero the next year.

Last year I called AA about Christmas time to learn my balance. They told me that I had 24,600 miles.

"You're going to give me the Gold, aren't you?", I asked.

"No, you have to have 25, 000 miles."

"Can't I pay you something for the missing 400 miles?"

"No, I'm sorry Mr. Hughes, you have to fly it."

So, the next day I bought a ticket (for $44) to Raleigh Durham (about 200 miles away). I flew down there at 7:00 AM, got an immediate return flight, and was in my office by 11:00 AM. I got my Gold.

Was it worth it? You bet. I get on flights earlier than everyone else (along with the women with children and the handicapped). I now fly first class everywhere I go on American without having to pay for it. I can call 24 hours in advance to reserve first class space, which is usually available. They not only give me free "stickers" for first class upgrades, they also give me 25% bonus miles every time I fly.

What is the benefit to American Airlines? I choose that airline over any other one. I often fly circuitous routes to be sure that I fly American. No one else gives me first class for the price of coach. They have me hooked — and I do an awful lot of traveling. By making the hurdle sufficiently high — 25,000 miles in a calendar year — they make me feel that I have earned my gold status (and I have!), and then they give me very valuable and appreciated rewards. What are the costs to American Airlines? Significant, but much less than the extra patronage that they get out of Arthur Hughes.

By using today's technology—and tomorrow's—we can place in the hands of the customer interface personnel valuable personalized information that helps them treat customers in a prescribed manner based upon their value to the marketer.

The more we can link marketing databases to operational systems, the better we can serve the customer. And it will be this higher degree of personalized service, combined with effective incentives, that will develop true, long-term loyalty.

Communicate Often. Not to sell, but to ask opinions. "Is the new service/product well-received? Do you have suggestions?" And, if they do, take some action and *let them know* what you have done. Encourage their calls. Listen to them; make them feel appreciated.

Several years ago I spent $100 and became a member of a think-tank institute in Washington. It was everything I wanted: they showered me with newsletters and policy papers on important public is-sues and invited me to seminars. I went to one seminar, a week long live-in sojourn at Dartmouth University, with outstanding speakers from all over the country. On the strength of that seminar, at which I got to meet all the members of the staff, I increased my voluntary an-nual payment to $250. Here was the kind of institution that was inter-esting, and, I thought, was interested in me.

That was my big mistake. After a long overseas trip to a politically hot country, I sent the president of the institute a twelve-page analysis of the political and economic situation in the country, asking for his views. He never answered. I sent a follow-up letter a month later. Still no answer. Two months later I sent another follow-up letter. I finally received a letter after three months from a low-level staffer who said that he disagreed with my analysis. He didn't thank me for preparing it. I got the impression that he thought that my letter was a nuisance and a waste of his time.

My mistake was thinking that they had me on a marketing data-base. Actually, they had me on a mailing list. It was intended to be a one-way communication. They sent out the policy papers, I sent in the money. My attempt to write a policy analysis paper just did not fit into the mailing list system that they had going. I cut my annual contribu-tion back to $100.

My lifetime value to this institute went from about $2,500 to about $1,000 due to one unanswered letter. I would have been happy with a one paragraph letter from the president (drafted by his secretary or someone else) saying, "Thank you for your very interesting letter on xxxxxx. I am passing it on to our foreign policy group as input to their thinking on this very important country. I appreciate your taking your time to write to me."

There is a point here: marketing databases permit any organiza-tion to maintain one-on-one communications with their customers or members in a *mutually profitable* relationship. They create the *illusion* of a close relationship. It lies in your hands to determine whether this illusion is to be maintained and supported, or shattered by your re-sponses to customer input.

Once you have set up a database, many of your customers would like to feel that the flow of information and products from you to them and the orders and payments from them to you has created a friendly, close, mutual relationship between them and your company. But if in setting up your database you do not provide for two-way communication, customers will eventually realize that they are corresponding with a computer, not a person. The illusion of mutual interest will be shattered, and you will lose loyalty and sales or contributions as a result.

Total Organizational Commitment. Customers see your company as an organic whole. What you do as a marketer can be completely destroyed by what happens in customer service, sales, billing, delivery, or technical support. You may be building loyalty like mad, while your billing department is treating these same people as deadbeats and your delivery department is dropping off damaged packages two days late. For loyalty programs to work, you need:

- strong support at the top of the organization;
- the ability to communicate to everyone in the company who the preferred customers are;
- an agreed upon method of treating these customers by all departments who have any direct contact with customers;
- promulgation of your loyalty goals throughout the organization, and an employee training program to support them;
- active support by your retailing arms, whether they be stores, hotels, agencies, or dealers; and
- a marketing database accessible throughout your organization, which is constantly updated with accurate information about the activities of your preferred customers.

LOYALTY MAINTENANCE CASE STUDY— A HOTEL PROGRAM

An interesting case study of loyalty maintenance is this story of a frequent guest program in a major hotel chain.

A direct response agency was recruited to develop a program to help the guests of the hotel chain identify themselves with the chain, instead of just with the particular hotel they were staying in at the time. The chain was anxious to build a system-wide loyalty in their guests so they would seek out the chain's hotels in every city.

To make the program work, the agency realized, they had to assure that guests received the same high quality of personal recognition at any of the chain's hotels, whether in New York or in Hawaii.

The objectives of the program were:

- To identify the chain's most frequent guests;

- To figure out a way to facilitate consistent, superlative service worldwide;

- To provide special recognition to the best customers;

- To generate incremental revenue, because the program had to pay its own freight and deliver substantial return on the investment; and

- To provide a strategic marketing tool for the chain.

They started with an existing customer base, but the records available were skimpy. The chain had been a participating member in United Airlines' Mileage Plus Program, which provided the names and addresses of the hotel guests who received Mileage Plus credit. United Airlines let them append additional travel history regarding origin and destination cities, frequency, and class of travel and average nights away from home.

Some of the hotels did maintain guest data. All the data available was merged into the rapidly building database. Some of the gaps were plugged by information from a major credit card company. The chain was able to find otherwise unidentified frequent customers by their credit card history. Most credit card companies keep a very detailed file.

To segment the database, the direct agency developed a Preference Profile, which requested information from each hotel guest. They combined the information they wanted to know from both operational as well as marketing perspectives, which the information research had shown that customers were willing to provide. They were surprised at the willingness of customers to supply information useful for the database.

Once the information was stored in the central database, they set up a system that made it available throughout the hotel chain, everywhere the customer was likely to interact with the company. By electronically linking it with the reservation system, they were able to send preference data along with reservation data down the line to each hotel. The information included special instructions for each individual. The information was put on-line for both the reservations center and the customer service center.

To be sure that all customers were properly recognized, each active member of the chain's frequent guest club received a personalized plastic card, color-keyed to the amount of business they had given the chain. Royal blue indicated a moderate level of activity; gold signified the very highest.

To know whether they were generating more revenue through the system, they had to know what revenue was coming in. So the database was updated constantly. Letters of appreciation went out automatically, including gold cards when that level of activity was reached.

The database also measured the results from special offers extended to individual members. The hotel could monitor the effectiveness of offers and efficiency of packages on a one-to-one basis. The database was also used to help individual hotels in the chain test and validate their own individual promotion programs.

Some of the information for the database was provided by a sweepstakes. People were asked to select their desired resort vacation. The sweepstakes generated interest and activity on its own, but also enabled the chain to construct specifically targeted offers to members based upon their stated interests in specific types of vacations.

The loyalty program was a great success. The hotel was able to prove that the incremental revenue produced far exceeded the projections for the program. And the increased utility of the database exceeded nearly everybody's expectations.

The key to the success of this loyalty program was linking the marketing database information to operational systems throughout the hotel chain, so that everyone knew who the preferred customers were and could give them super service. This helped to build a profitable long-term relationship with the best customers.

Figure 8-1 Building Customer Loyalty through Dialogue

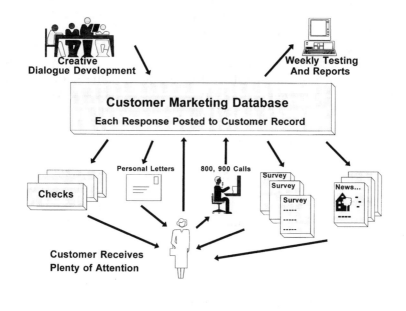

MISSED OPPORTUNITY: THE AUTOMOBILE INDUSTRY

Many industries have yet to explore the tremendous possibilities which exist in database marketing.

Several years ago, my wife and I both purchased identical Dodge Colt Vistas with four-wheel drive. These were really wonderful cars: very roomy, plenty of power, and with the traction needed to get up to our house on top of a mountain in Virginia. We bought the cars brand new from a Virginia dealer. But in the four years we owned them, we never received a single letter from the salesman, from the dealer, or from the Chrysler Corporation, thanking us for the purchase or making any suggestions for the future.

When the cars were three years old, we began to think about trading them in. Do they still make Colt Vistas, we wondered? Have they added any new features? Or should we go back to Subarus? It was obvious that all the automobile companies were spending a fortune on general advertising, but we saw no ads relating to the type of car we were interested in. General Motors, to mention one, spent more than a billion dollars that year on general advertising, but practically nothing to reach out and communicate with its current customers. It is obvious that some of the automobile companies, at least, had forgotten one of the oldest rules in marketing:

Your own customers are your best prospects for future sales!

Everyone accepts this in principle, but very few companies act on it.

How difficult would it be for the automobile companies to divert a small percentage of their general advertising budgets to establishing a loyalty link with their existing customers, and what would be the results? Consider the facts:

- Automobile ownership, second only to home and telephone ownership, is one of the best-documented and publicly available sources of information available today. In more than half the states, motor vehicle registration information is provided for a nominal cost by public agencies. Everyone with a new car has to go to the dealer periodically for scheduled maintenance. It would be a simple matter for dealers to forward to a central source the fact that vehicle #1234567890H678 was still being driven by Arthur Hughes of Haymarket, Virginia.

- Automobiles are probably more expressive of the lifestyle and personality of their owners than anything else purchased today. Many people are in love with their cars: the car says who they are and what they like. Most people are far more loyal to their cars than they are to their brand of soap, shoes, or shirts. The loyalty on the consumer side is there, but it is not being reciprocated by actions on the part of the manufacturers.

- The time when the average person is ready for a new car can be pretty well determined from reliable statistical sources. There is very little guesswork involved. No one knows when the average person is going to fly on American Airlines again, but AA maintains a very accurate marketing database trying to insure that when we do go it will be with them. Yet all automobile companies know almost exactly when their customers are going to need a new car, *and they are doing almost nothing about it.*

• There are frequent stories appearing about particular car salesmen and car dealerships that have had phenomenal success with direct marketing to their current customers. Some salesmen send hand-written notes to their customers on their birthdays and anniversaries. They have proved that it works, and works very well. Buick, Ford, and Volvo have launched very promising loyalty building programs. They have built marketing databases which are used to send letters periodically offering discounts on accessories and tips on maintenance. But most of the major manufacturers have done little or nothing to pick up and build on this experience.

My Chrysler Story

Annoyed by Chrysler's lack of database marketing awareness, I sat down and wrote a letter to Lee Iacocca, Chairman of Chrysler at the time, and told him that I owned two brand new Chrysler products, but had never heard a word from the company. I told him that he should have a database. He should be building a relationship with people like me who own their products, keeping track of me, leading to suggesting that I take a test drive of a new Chrysler product after my cars are three years old. I poured out my heart to this man, giving him a lot of the philosophy that you can find in this book.

Well, of course, I never got an answer from Lee Iacocca. But, I did get a telephone call from the Manager of Sales for the Eastern Region of Chrysler in Baltimore. He called me at my office in Reston, Virginia. He said:

"Mr. Hughes, I have your letter here to Mr. Iacocca. Now Mr. Hughes, I want to assure you that we do have a database. I've looked you up, and you're on it!"

Fine, but what were they doing with their database? Since that time, I have never received a single letter, fax, or phone call from

Chrysler. What is the good of my being on some computer database spinning around in Detroit somewhere? It is a total waste of money.

Three years later, I attended a Database Marketing Conference in Chicago. At one of the sessions, the lecturer asked everyone in the audience to identify themselves and their company. One man said he was with the Chrysler Corporation, in charge of their 25 million name customer database.

Twenty-five million names! The lecturer was very impressed. He kept genuflecting towards the Chrysler man during the remainder of his talk. When it was over, I went up to the Chrysler man out in the hall. I said:

"So you are in charge of the Chrysler database?"

"Yes, I am."

"Well, tell me. What are you doing with your database?"

"Oh," he said, "we have it on a UNIX platform."

For those that don't know, UNIX is a type of software. The man was a constructor. He saw his job as being that of keeping the names clean, up to date, and accessible, in case anyone in the corporation could come up with an idea for using the names some day for marketing.

Chrysler was pouring millions of dollars down a database rathole. You can't make money with a database on a computer. You can only make money if you use the database to build customer loyalty. Why did Chrysler fail? I have an idea.

Twenty five million names is a huge file. It probably includes owners of cars and trucks going back several years. Any time anyone comes up with an idea for using the database to write to the customers, they multiply the idea by 25 million, and the cost is astronomical. So they give it up.

What should they do? Pick the top 200,000 names as a test, and pick out an identical 200,000 as a control group that they set aside. Forget the remaining 24,600,000 names—for now. Experiment with this 200,000 test group. Develop relationship building programs for them. Chrysler can certainly afford to mail a few times to these 200,000 new car owners. Track them to see if the programs do any good. If the programs work, more of the test group will buy Chrysler products than the control group to whom nothing is sent (the current situation for all Chrysler owners). The database can be used to prove that what they are doing has validity—or doesn't.

When they develop something that works, then expand the program to the top 1 million—keeping 1 million as a control group. Go step by step, experimenting, learning, becoming successful in building profitable relationships with their customers.

Getting 'Em Back

Cellular phone providers have a terrible problem: their customer base is in a perpetual state of churn. Customers are constantly bombarded with competitive offers which are hard to refuse. To attract a customer today, you almost have to make an expensive offer: a free phone or free air time. You try to tie customers up in a long term contract that will repay your investment. This works, but they bolt as soon as the contract period ends.

BellSouth Mobility has all of these problems. With over 1 million subscribers in their 28 cellular systems, they are growing at a rate of 45 percent per year. They are adding over 2,500 customers a day—but they are losing over 500 customers per day as well. While business, on the whole, is very good, it is depressing to have to support this high level of churn.

BellSouth Mobility is not unique. On average, the cellular industry churn is about 18 percent of the customer base per year. It costs an average of $350 to add a customer. Active customers average only $60 per month in revenue. Customers who leave early may cost more than they are worth. Because of this problem, Ed Evans, director of field operations for BellSouth Mobility, decided to investigate the reasons why customers were leaving so as to develop a program for getting them back.

Ed used one of BellSouth's markets with a population of 1 million, and 65,000 subscribers. In this market, BellSouth had a 65 percent market share. Their goal was to win back 10 percent of their lost subscribers. To begin with, they wanted to know why they left, whether they would come back, and what it would take to get them to do so.

They called a large sample of the lapsed subscribers. Here is what the customers said about their reasons for dropping the service:

- 12% No longer needed the service.

- 18% Company no longer pays the bill.

- 24% Moved out of the coverage area.

- 34%   Switched to the competition.

- 12%   Other reasons.

Ed decided to concentrate his attention on the 34 percent who switched to the competition. He set up four focus groups of former customers who were currently active on the competitor's system. They asked each focus group member to compare the two systems, identifying advantages and disadvantages of each system. They asked them to explain why they switched, and whether they would be willing to switch back.

What they found out was quite interesting. Most of those leaving BellSouth felt that the BellSouth system coverage was better, customer service was better, and the billing system was better. So why did they leave? Here is what they said:

- BellSouth did something that upset me.
- BellSouth wouldn't issue a credit ($0.50) for a dropped call.
- BellSouth gave free phones to new subscribers, but not to me.
- BellSouth wouldn't give me the current (free air) promotion.

Many indicated that they might switch back, but that they were currently under contract.

They would want a free phone or free airtime to return.

Reactivation Strategy.   Armed with this knowledge, BellSouth made two decisions: they decided to give the fifty cent credit for all dropped calls. Next, they tried a free phone or free airtime direct mail offer to 3,500 customers who switched to get them to switch back. The mail piece reaffirmed the advantages cited by the focus groups, and included a coverage map.

The results were disappointing, to say the least. After thirty days they had only a 3 percent response rate, resulting in only 1 percent reconnection. The effort cost them $800 per reconnected customer. It was definitely not a profitable test. To find out why it failed, they held focus groups of people in the promoted test group.

Everyone interviewed thought that the offer was a strong one, but they explained:

- I'm under contract with the other guys.
- I moved and didn't see the offer.
- I lost the card they sent me.

Back to the drawing board for BellSouth.   To counter these objections, the company next tried a repeat of the same direct mail offer to 1,000 former customers. But, this time, they sent it only to customers who left eleven months before—i.e., those with contracts with competitors which were about to run out. They followed up each letter with a telephone call.

The letter produced an 8 percent response rate and a 3 percent connect rate. The telephone call increased this to a 10 percent connect rate. The cost per customer dropped to $325 each. This, at last, was profitable. Since that time, BellSouth mails to about 1,000 people every month, using the same selection criteria. The reconnect rates have stayed good. They are expanding the system to their other 27 markets.

Conclusion.   Getting customers to come back begins with understanding their thinking. BellSouth skillfully used a number of tools that enabled them to come up with a winning strategy rapidly and at a reasonably low cost. Their methods included:

- *An active marketing database.* The entire BellSouth effort was possible only because they maintained a database of current and former subscribers. They were able to do ad-hoc queries which enabled them to understand what their customers were doing and thinking, and to use this knowledge in planning their marketing strategy.

- *Surveys and focus groups.* Calling former customers and setting up the focus groups was an excellent idea, which paid off in increased knowledge.

- *Timing of the offer.* Once BellSouth learned the secret of making the offer in the eleventh month, the answer seemed obvious. But it wasn't obvious at all when they started.

- *Testing on a small scale.* How many companies with a million customers begin with a test mailing to 3,500? Not many. The bigger you are, the more likely you are to waste money on large-scale tests which often fail.

- *Putting themselves in the customer's shoes.* The result of the testing was a genuine understanding of the customer's thinking. Figuring out that the eleventh month was the right month, knowing what offer to make, learning that dropped calls were important—all contributed to the success of the effort.

- *Drawing intelligent conclusions based on financial analysis.* Too many marketers would approach the reactivation problem with a single mass mailing. BellSouth didn't do that at all. Each effort was carefully studied and measured. From what they learned, they tried to get inside the heads of the lapsed subscribers so as to figure out what they were thinking. The combination of the right offer, at the right time, based on careful testing, is certainly the hallmark of database marketing at its best.

The Catalyst Project

Austin Rover, the biggest British-owned car manufacturer, has a marketing database program in operation, as reported by Chris Richards in *Direct Marketing* magazine. The strategy is a series of time-related communications throughout the life of a car. Once the customer is in the database, he or she receives a welcome letter, warranty and service reminders, special offers, and a sequence of sales propositions once the car has reached a certain age.

The system works well, but it rests on two shaky assumptions: that the customer's replacement timing coincides with the computer program and that the customer wants to buy the model chosen by the database. Systems Market Link (SML), a London direct agency that set up the Austin Rover program, decided that they needed more information and that the information could come directly from the car owner.

They developed a glossy, high-caliber magazine called *Catalyst* designed to maintain a dialog with existing customers and to warm potential customers to Austin Rover. To obtain a subscription to the magazine, a car owner fills out a questionnaire about the customer's current car, replacement plans, and the type of car he or she wants next. In addition, the customer indicates his special interests from six choices: sports, dining, home and garden, entertainment, female interests, and travel. As an added inducement to complete the questionnaire, they offered a sweepstakes.

The magazine is produced by split runs so that every reader gets a personalized magazine, with the features he or she has requested. The response rate to the first issue was close to 40 percent. Questionnaire data is entered into the database and kicks off a multimedia campaign including direct mail and telemarketing. Each dealership is connected with the database so that they know what the consumer wants to buy and when.

Once the day for car replacement comes near, the prospect is qualified by the dealership through a telemarketing program, and sent a VIP pack (Vehicle Information Portfolio) specific to the model range interest indicated on the database. Personalized and designed to be retained for reference, the VIP is accompanied by an invitation for a test drive and purchase incentives targeted for the lifestyle of the recipient.

Once the buyer has made a purchase, a customer retention program takes over. It uses the database to issue a sequence of essential letters that maintain a caring dialog between customer and dealer about the manufacturer's warranty, servicing, and government safety checks, as well as strategically timed dealer phone calls until six months before the next purchase is due.

Central to the program is the Catalyst Collection, a selection of high-quality products and services offered exclusively to purchasers of new cars. The catalog offers armchair shopping at its best, with a choice of activities which can range from wine-tasting weekends to a session on a DC-10 flight simulator.

Participating dealers must have their staff trained by SML in telemarketing technique, or contract the telemarketing work out to a SML marketing agency. The Catalyst program has created a stir in marketing circles in Britain, with the potential for being modified to serve other industries.

Figure 8-2 Everyone Helps to Build Loyalty

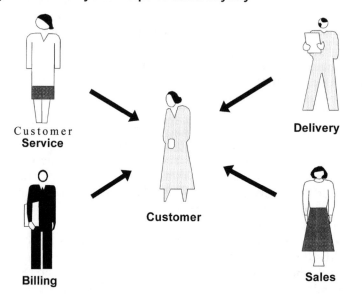

Customer
Service

Delivery

Customer

Billing

Sales

Prediction

I will make a prediction. Database marketing in the American automobile industry will be one of the major success stories in the future. They have tried everything else: cash back, TV specials, four-page spreads in major magazines, quotas on imported cars. Now they are going to try to market cars to their own loyal customers through marketing databases. They are going to experiment with loyalty marketing. Once one does it, they will all do it; this has been the history of the auto industry.

SUMMARY

Once you have identified your best customers, you must work very hard to maintain their loyalty.

- Loyalty is not maintained by money or points or anything that you can count. It is maintained by *recognition*. You must find a way to use the database to recognize your best customers and to *let them know* that you recognize them.

- You must provide them special services. You must listen to them when they say something, remember it, and *act on it*. Then you must tell them what you have done.

- You must work very hard to get everyone in your organization—sales, customer service, billing, delivery—to participate in your loyalty-building program.

- You must have an accurate and constantly updated marketing database which is accessible to everyone who deals with customers, so they will recognize them and know their preferences, and respond appropriately. There must be a way that these individuals can *input data* into the database as they learn of customer needs and requests.

- Some of the things that you can do to maintain the loyalty of your best customers include:

  — Equip your telemarketers with ANI, which can provide the name and customer record of each caller while he or she is calling you on the telephone.

  — Encourage telemarketers to take down customer information which can be used to build a bond between your company and the customer.

  — Include the dealer in the loyalty loop: encourage customers to visit the dealers with inducements, telephone numbers, etc. Let the dealer know that you are doing this.

  — Give customers special cards which identify their customer buying status.

  — Create your own buyer's clubs.

  — Communicate with your loyal customers often. Be sure that your communication is two-way: that you listen as well as speak.

- Hotels, airlines, and car rental companies are masters at loyalty building today. We can learn much from them.

- Most American automobile manufacturers are far behind everyone in loyalty building. They sell a big ticket item which is easy to follow, yet they manage to lose track of their customers and ignore them as soon as the sale is over.

- A successful loyalty program requires total organizational commitment by your company. It can pay rich dividends

Chapter 9

How to Maintain a Dialog with Your Customers

Pop quiz: What is the difference between a mailing list and a marketing database?

Answer: There are many differences, but the principal difference is that a mailing list is designed for one-way communications: products and literature out, orders and money in. A marketing database is designed for two-way communications: either party can initiate communications. Each party thinks about what the other has said, remembers it, and modifies his or her behavior based on the knowledge and understanding of what the other party wants.

This tells us that a vital part of the design and functioning of any marketing database is the development and use of creative response mechanisms, whereby you can get feedback from your customers on what they are thinking and *what they want.* A marketing database is not just a list of customers which you use for segmentation and mailings. The database should be designed as a computer simulation of the mind of the old corner grocer: a thinking machine that stores up information received from the customer, retains it, and *modifies its behavior* based on that information.

Whenever you design a marketing database, then, you have to think: How are we going to get customer feedback? What are the methods whereby we can get data about how our programs are being received? How can we store this data? How can we modify our future communications to show that we have remembered what we learned, and are acting differently because of it? In short, we have to plan for customer response.

There is one fundamental rule: make every contact with your customers a learning experience for you. Find out more information from your customers about them and their lives, their desires, their opinions, so that you can be more helpful, more understanding, and a better friend in the future.

COUPONS

In some ways, direct marketers seem like a herd of sheep. Somewhere they got the idea that coupons help to increase sales (as they clearly do), so they are investing billions of dollars in them. More than 4,000 manufacturers send out more than 300 billion of them every year. Many customers look for them in their newspapers, magazines, and mailboxes. They save them and use them in their shopping. Although there is some cheating, most people actually buy the products listed on the coupon, and, in some cases, buy some product that *they might not otherwise have bought* because of the coupon. What could possibly be wrong with that?

Figure 9-1   Coupon Distribution by Media

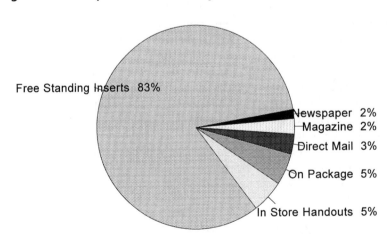

Free Standing Inserts 83%

Newspaper 2%
Magazine 2%
Direct Mail 3%
On Package 5%
In Store Handouts 5%

Nothing. Except that the same money might have been spent in other ways which would have produced more sales and more profits. Direct marketers have learned the coupon lesson so well, and they see their competitors using coupons so consistently, that it has become a vast and expensive game which no one can afford not to play: if you don't send out coupons, your competitors will grab your market share. If you experiment with some other technique, and it does not work, you will lose market share. Most direct marketers thus are set on coupons: they won't listen to any other possibility, even though they know all of the faults of the coupon system.

What are these faults?

- Ninety-eight percent are thrown away unused (no real loss). Redemption rates began to fall in 1993 for the first time since 1970. Coupon servicing costs about $3 billion per year. Manufacturers spend an average of $0.95 for every coupon redeemed.

- There is a non-negligible percentage of cheating: people who take your sixty cents but buy some other product.

- A high percentage are used by your own customers, who would have bought your product anyway. Shoppers who use the coupons save about $4 billion per year.

- Coupons encourage the public to concentrate on price and rebate as the only reason for choosing one brand over another.

- Coupons do not build brand loyalty, they tend to destroy it.

- The coupon redemption system is so cumbersome and slow that it takes many months from the time they are sent out until you receive reports on how many were redeemed, and to which offer the public responded best.

- As a result, you seldom learn anything about your customers from these coupons. You can hold in your hand coupons which your customers held in their hands several months ago. But from that piece of paper you can tell nothing about who they are, why they bought your product (if they did), what their purchasing habits are, or what they were thinking about. You have missed a golden opportunity for getting responses and building a database.

Figure 9-2 What Happens to Coupons

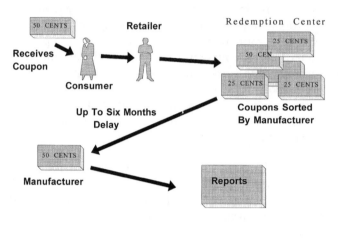

Redemption Process Can Take A Full Year

What are the alternatives to the coupon treadmill?

INSTANTLY REDEEMABLE CHECKS

Several companies have developed a substitute for coupons in the form of a check (which we will call the INSTA-CHECK) that offers you an opportunity to find out exactly who is redeeming your coupons within days after your promotion is started. The INSTA-CHECK is an actual check, processed through the normal U.S. banking system back to your bank within the federally prescribed one-week clearing process. But the INSTA-CHECK is also a survey form which can be used to capture information.

The INSTA-CHECK looks like a coupon. On the back, however, it has space for the endorser's name, address, city, state, zip code, phone number, and signature (required by the bank). The remaining space can also be used for a few survey questions.

The INSTA-CHECK has the bank's code number printed in magnetic ink characters which are read by the bank clearing system's machinery. Because this magnetic ink has metal particles in it, you cannot produce a valid Xerox copy of the check. Without the metal particles, the bank's system will reject it.

The clearing process is entirely different from the coupon redemption route. When coupons are redeemed they are bundled and given to the store manager. Eventually, the coupons are sent to a regional redemption center where they are painstakingly sorted by hand, by product and company, and counted so that the stores can get paid and the companies can be billed. As a by-product of the payment process, reports are generated which will tell the manufacturer (months later) how many coupons were redeemed, and for what.

INSTA-CHECKs are handled entirely differently. The customer must endorse the check and hand it to the checkout clerk. The clerk then puts the INSTA-CHECK in *with the other checks*, not with the coupons.

When the store presents the INSTA-CHECKs with their regular checks at the bank every day, they receive immediate reimbursement (weeks ahead of the coupon reimbursement). Within a short period (an average of three days) the check is processed through the Federal Reserve clearing system, and arrives back at the manufacturer's bank. The bank charges about eight cents for processing. As soon as the checks arrive at the bank, the manufacturer can have them keypunched. Voila: here are the names and addresses of customers, two to four weeks after they bought the product (depending on keypunching time), together with whatever survey data was included on the check. These names can be used to build and to update the marketing database.

General Mills used the checks in Honey Nut Cheerios. Their offer resulted in a 30 percent response. This was extremely high in comparison with coupon redemption rates. Direct mail coupon redemptions vary from 5 to 14 percent. Freestanding inserts are redeemed at a rate of less than 4 percent. Newspaper redemption is about 2 percent. Yoplait Yogurt did a promotion with INSTA-CHECKs in a freestanding insert. The INSTA-CHECKs included a survey of the customer's most frequently purchased brand. In this case, some customers redeemed so many that Yoplait suspected fraud. Their follow-up mailing to these customers included a survey of customer satisfaction with an additional check, which proved that the survey results were valid.

Pillsbury used INSTA-CHECKs to introduce a new brand of pizza. They were very pleased with the results. Eighty percent of those cashing the INSTA-CHECKs filled out all of the survey questions on the reverse side. Pillsbury built a marketing database with the survey results which told them what competitive brands were used in the household, which family members liked the pizza and so on.

Figure 9-3   Insta-Checks Come Back Fast

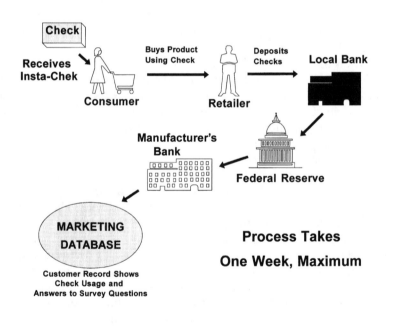

REBATES

"$1 rebate coupon enclosed!" You buy the product, and inside is a coupon you send in to get $1, or $2, or $5, or more. You have to use the coupon, and you usually have to include an IPC seal, or proof of purchase, or something else. By the time you have met all the requirements, found an envelope and affixed a postage stamp, you may have used up the rebate in energy and frustration. But millions do send these rebate coupons in. They can be a wonderful way to start a database.

Unfortunately, very few manufacturers who offer these rebates are using them to construct a marketing database. I find it hard to understand why they offered the rebate in the first place, unless it was just another sales gimmick. Here they have the name and address of a purchaser. A golden opportunity. Yet if you go from company to company, you will find that somewhere in a back room they have a tape of 50,000 customers who have received a rebate or responded to an offer of a premium. No one has any idea what to do with these names; so they just sit there and get out-of-date. Twenty percent of Americans move every year. After two years, 40 percent of your file has moved somewhere else. As for the rest, after two years, they have forgotten that they ever sent in the rebate coupon, and probably have forgotten about you and your product. There seems to be a great deal of push in creative departments thinking up these sales ideas, and practically no long-range planning involving the question of what do to with the results.

I think the reasoning goes this way: "The customer sees $1 off on the package. He likes what he sees and buys it. When he gets home and realizes what a nuisance it is to get the $1, he gives up. Fine. No need to give him a rebate, and *he has bought the product!* So what if some clowns send in for the $1? Punch their names, send them a buck and forget it."

With this kind of reasoning in your company or your advertising agency, you will have an uphill battle trying to get a marketing database started. If you can turn it around, however, you may find that the rebate respondents represent a place to start building your database.

ORDERS WITH SURVEYS

The easiest way to begin a two-way dialog is often overlooked. It is the order form. Here is a piece of paper which comes from your customer to you. She is writing down her name and address and the products she wants. Why not also get some other information that you need and can use later?

How many children under the age of 10 in the home?
What magazines do you read?
Do you have a compact disc player?
Do you live in a house or an apartment?
Do you have a child in college?
Are you planning an addition to your home?
Does anyone in your family suffer from diabetes?
Are you planning a trip overseas?
How did you find our catalog?   [ ] clear and informative
                                    [ ] hard to read
                                    [ ] thin on descriptions

You create questions that will have some relevance to your business. They should be asked in a non-threatening, voluntary way, which makes it clear that you can buy the product without answering the questions. You will be amazed at the response. In a well-crafted database environment, the answers to these questions can be the start of a real dialog with customers.

Of course, the process of creating a dialog is a new one for most companies. Design of the order form is usually left to the creative agency. Processing of the orders is handled by a different department. No one will know just what to do with the responses. As the marketing database planner, you will have to get everyone together to plan your strategy. Once the responses are safely in the database, you will have to plan how to use them as a part of an intelligent dialog. This calls for creative marketing strategy of a high order. You will have to be not only an imaginative marketer, but also an effective coordinator of several parts of your organization for these survey questions to do you any good. Customer service personnel will have to be trained to work the questions into their talks with customers. Outgoing letters will have to have paragraphs derived from the survey responses. Your company may not be ready for intelligent use of survey data, but you will have to start sometime, because your competitors are thinking about it right now.

POINT OF SALE RESPONSE

A cosmetic and skin-care company which we shall call Eugenia had a different problem. Women came to them for total facial care. They had skin-care specialists trained to study a customer's face and to make recommendations on a series of creams and treatments which would bring out the best. Customers were typically given a lifetime membership, and expected to buy about $700 worth of products every year, following the recommendations of the specialists.

Eugenia has more than 400 outlets across the country, most of them located inside large department stores. When the specialist is not on duty, a regular sales clerk from the store makes the sales. Sales are good. They have a database of members. Members had plastic membership cards with a membership number and the number of the program that was appropriate for their face. The problem was, Eugenia didn't have any response data. They didn't know what their customers were buying. Store clerks were supposed to send in one copy of the sales slip with the member number written on it, to be keypunched centrally, but the system was spotty and had fallen into disuse.

The system they finally decided to adopt was suggested to them by a database consultant. It was based on the little credit card verification (Datacomm) units found all over America. Eugenia plans to buy these units, and put one in each outlet. They will add a magnetic stripe to the back of the member's cards. The stripe will hold the member's name and number. The Datacomm units contain an automatic dialing device, a modem, and a small computer. When a member's card is passed through the slot, the Datacomm unit automatically dials up the Eugenia database, going though an 800 number. The Datacomm sends across the telephone line the customer number, the date and time, and the store number. In response to prompts on the screen of the Datacomm, the clerk enters her number, the SKU numbers of the products purchased and a code for any special promotion that the customer may have mentioned which prompted her to visit the booth. That is all. The process takes less than a minute, and the database now knows who is shopping where, at what time of day, what they bought and, in many cases, why.

Figure 9-4   Sales Tracked Automatically

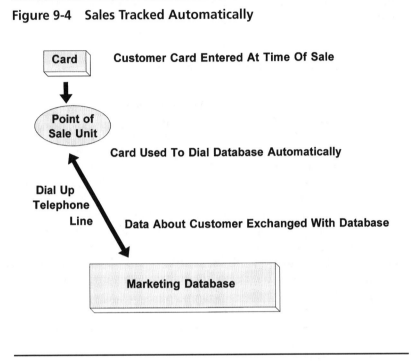

Card — Customer Card Entered At Time Of Sale

Point of Sale Unit

Card Used To Dial Database Automatically

Dial Up Telephone Line

Data About Customer Exchanged With Database

Marketing Database

The beauty of this system can be demonstrated when they begin test promotions in various cities. By studying the responses, they can tell store-by-store and hour-by-hour how many respond to a particular promotion, versus those who just wandered by the outlet.

It will be easy to identify customers who fail to buy products when they should, which was impossible previously. When the database detects someone who has clearly run out of product, the software can initiate a friendly reminder letter. If this does not do the trick, telemarketing follow-up is appropriate. For this system to work, it has to be of benefit to the customer. The reason why database marketing works is that both parties gain from it. If you are thinking of database marketing as a targeting device, forget it. Think of it as helpful service, and you will succeed.

DATA FROM DISKETTES

A major manufacturer of microcomputers has been one of the leaders in database building. From the moment of their inception, they packed with every computer they sold a comprehensive registration card with more than twenty different questions in addition to the name and address. They inquired about the type of computer purchased, from whom, whether it was bought by an individual or a company, the occupation, income, and age of the user, the principal application, whether it replaced a current computer, and if so what make and model, whether the purchaser had considered other brands and what they were, and many questions about the configuration of the computer, the peripheral equipment and software purchased, the type of company the user worked at, the size of the company, and much more.

All of this data was keypunched into the company's owner registration database. The company developed a unique series of cross-tab reports displaying all of the above data. The information was used by product planning, by advertising, by market research, by direct marketing, by dealer relations. But they wanted more.

They had two problems: they felt they weren't getting a high enough percentage of completed cards, and they weren't getting the answers to as many questions as they wanted. At the suggestion of a database marketing service bureau, they switched to using a registration diskette. They created a colorful interactive diskette which they packed with every new computer. The program welcomed the customer, then put them through a query session which enabled purchasers quickly to provide the company the numerous data elements needed for its database. Most of the data was furnished to the owner on pop-up menus; he or she had only to choose from several choices offered. The choices were hierarchical:

"Did you purchase a printer?" [If no, it would automatically skip the next series of questions.]

"Was it thermal, daisy wheel, laser, dot matrix, ink jet?" [Laser]

"Which brand of laser printer (choices shown)?" [Hewlett Packard]

"Which model Hewlett Packard Laser Printer (choices shown)?"

At first, of course, the diskette was tested on a single product. They were ready to can it if the response was poor. What happened? They doubled their response rate. They were getting double the number of customers. They introduced one innovation which tipped the odds in their favor: they automatically entered everyone who sent in a diskette in a quarterly sweepstakes to win a computer. Now, as new computers are added to the line, a diskette is packed inside rather than a card.

One feature of the diskette response that is interesting is the open-ended, free-response question. There are eight questions which ask such things as "Why did you choose our computer?" "Did you get good service from your dealer?" "How do you like your new computer?" They did several things with such free-form data. First, they coded the responses into the database, so they could count them on their reports: X percent did not like the new diskette unit; Y percent felt that the dealer should have had more training; and so on. But they went beyond this. The free-form responses were printed out separately and sent to the appropriate department: Customer Service, Dealer Relations, Product Design. These departments studied the responses. That is using your response—that is database marketing!

The company sells its computers heavily in Europe and elsewhere in the world. They are packing their diskettes into computers going to Europe, with responses coming back in French, German, and other languages. They have trained the organization to read and code these responses, and to provide the proper response to the purchasers.

SUPERMARKET CUSTOMER BUYING CARDS

One of the best ways of knowing what your retail customers are doing is the Ukrop's Valued Customer card. Ukrop's, a twenty-one store supermarket chain in Virginia, provides its customers with cards with a unique bar code in a system which is used by many chains throughout the country. Each customer's card is read at the checkout scanner. Everything the customer buys is then scanned, as usual, but the results go into a special database in the store that keeps track of everything that the Hughes family bought.

Figure 9-5 Supermarket Customer Cards

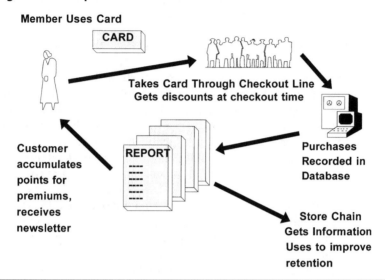

Why do the customers participate? They get automatic discounts. What does Ukrop's get out of it? A way of building a relationship with their customers. They can communicate with them and build customer loyalty. Ukrops used their regular scanners which created the invoices and posted their inventory system. With the Valued Customer Cards, they gained sales data pertaining to households. They can also track purchases by zip code areas or areas around a new store—information that they didn't have before they introduced the cards. If a customer stops buying, Ukrop's can, and does, write and call. If they have done something wrong, they can attempt to rectify it.

Ukrop's uses their marketing database to mail out over 200,000 newsletters every month: *Ukrop's Valued Customer News*. The newsletter reports on new food products coming out, new store openings, news about pesticides or prices. "Before we had the valued-customer program, we didn't really know who our customers were. Today we do," said Carol Beth Spivey, Ukrop's manager of advertising and marketing. "If a competitor opens a store in the area, we can see which customers are dropping us. Then we can write to them and invite them back."

Returns suggest that the card program increased sales for Ukrop's by 10 percent. But what about the big picture? What happens when every store chain has a similar card program? Won't that wipe out the advantages? As Gary Arlen, publisher of *Electronic Shopping News* said, "Retailing is a me-too focus. When someone finds the formula, they'll all do it."

Of course, he is correct. But looking at such card programs strictly as a means of increasing sales misses the point entirely. To make adequate use of such a card, a retailer has to establish a marketing database. "It is not easy or cheap to set up a program like this," according to Carol Beth Spivey. The very act of establishing this database forces the company to begin to know their customers, to understand their purchasing behavior, to build better loyalty programs, to improve service, and to change the behavior and policies of the store. The response derived from such a system provides information of tremendous value to retailers, if only they can organize properly to take advantage of it. Clearly, stores like Ukrop's which do pioneer with this system will have the jump on all the others who do so later.

To argue that such cards will be of no value when all stores have them is like arguing that automobile service garages should not install engine diagnostic machines because all other garages have them. The fact is that a diagnostic machine permits the garage to do a much better job of servicing a customer's engine rapidly and correctly. They are essential to providing good service. That is why the retail customer card system, or something like it, will be adopted by most large chains, I predict, in the years ahead. The supermarket card system is explored at length in Chapter 24 of this book.

DIRECT RETAIL CONNECTION

Advanced Promotion Technologies of Pompano Beach, Florida provides a different system from that of Ukrop's. APT has a unique customer card system called the Vision Value Network. More than 1,000 terminals are installed in the checkout lanes of supermarkets. These terminals are connected by satellite hookup from each store to a customer marketing database maintained on APT's mainframe computer. Each unit delivers to each customer in the checkout line:

- Targeted promotions and advertising
- A frequent shopper program
- Financial services

To use the system, the shopper inserts her frequent shopper membership card into the terminal at checkout time. As it reads her card, the network accesses her household database record, complete with purchase history and demographics. While waiting in the line during scanning of her purchases, the terminal can show her a live action video, provides her with printed coupons, recipes, frequent shopper point totals, and financial services receipts. The interactive terminal can ask her questions enabling the retailer and the manufacturers to interact with her, storing her responses in her database record. The cost of using the terminal is about 6 cents per transaction.

To join the system, a shopper fills out an application form that requests information on the size of the household, the children's ages, pet ownership, major appliances, and household income.

Manufacturers use the APT data to identify heavy category users who do not use their brand, thus permitting them to offer a trial-inducing high value coupon. They can identify key audiences, eliminate mis-redemption, and decrease their marketing costs. Retailers can use the system to increase customer loyalty, convert secondary shoppers, and get manufacturer support of their card programs.

The system will only work if the customer benefits from it. These benefits must be substantial, including:

- Valuable, meaningful offers
- Rewards for store and brand loyalty
- Free gifts
- Easy to read price and product descriptions

RESULTS OF THE APT SYSTEM

In one test of the Vision Value Network system in action, sales of tested brands increased by 7.7 percent, and market share of the product in the test areas grew by 9.2 percent. The number of trips per month by card holders increased by 15 percent after the system was installed.

The household spending increased by 18 percent. VVC members tend to be heavy spenders to begin with as compared to non-VVC store shoppers. Despite this, after a year, the average VVC household increased their average order size by about $1. The system enabled participating stores to take households away from other chains. Secondary spending per household increased by 25 percent while primary spending grew by 18 percent.

A WEIGHT-LOSS PROGRAM

The manufacturer of a weight-loss powder to be mixed with milk was quite successful in his primary sales. People were responding to the advertising and making a first purchase, a two-week supply for fifty dollars. But repeat purchases were running about 5 percent. Clearly, a marketing database was needed. After several false starts, the company finally hit on a solution which promised to turn things around.

Figure 9-6   Report on Weight Loss

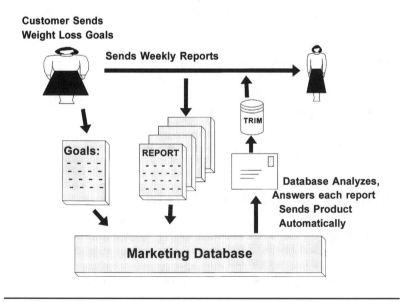

They developed a concept whereby they stopped describing their product as a product, and started describing it as a program. Purchasers were called members, and each was expected to sign on to reach a specified goal: a loss of so many pounds, a reduction of cholesterol of so many points, a reduction of blood pressure, or a slimmer waist. With the first purchase, each member fills out a fitness statement with personal goals. The statement is forwarded to the company, where it is entered into the database. In addition, members are given weekly report cards which they return, listing the amount of exercise, their eating habits, and their progress towards the goals.

Meanwhile, back at the database, there was much activity. After the first fitness statement is received, the database generates a personalized letter from the fitness director congratulating the member on his or her selection of a goal; in some cases, warning the member against such a drastic change in eating habits or too rapid a shift to strenuous exercise. The personalized comments are built up from an analysis of many data elements in the fitness statement: age, weight, height, previous exercise level, blood pressure, cholesterol level and so on.

As each weekly report is received, the database generates a personalized analysis, again in the form of a laser letter, congratulating members on their progress, sympathizing with them on problems reported, making helpful suggestions on exercise, eating, relaxing.

Telemarketers are trained as "Fitness Specialists." Customer service will have the entire database available to them on their terminals so they can see the customers' records as they consult with them. The most important single element in the package, however, would be the weekly report returned by members to the database. This initiates the two-way communication which is essential to successful database marketing.

THE 800 NUMBER

Of course, the best response device ever invented is the 800 number. Invented by AT&T in 1961, it really took off in popularity in the 1980s and 1990s. The service is continuing to expand. Originally, many companies saw the 800 number as an order-taking opportunity and a method for customers to let off steam. Today, it is viewed as an essential customer response device: a marketing tool that feeds information into a marketing database.

Many companies which have invested heavily in their 800 number operation have found that it pays off. Answering the telephone is much more user friendly than forcing customers to write letters. The telephone improves the ability to service customers and thereby build loyalty.

The GE information service center receives more than 3 million calls a year. Some calls prevent the needless return of an appliance by allowing a representative the opportunity to explain to customers how to operate appliances that they don't understand. The system also supports dealers who are featuring GE products by providing those dealers' names first to callers who want to know where to buy it.

When people call an 800 number, they are usually trying to tell you something or to ask questions. Fine. Answer the questions. Then listen to what they are saying and make a note of it. Tell them what you are going to do with their ideas. Be sure that something *does* happen: put customers' ideas into the database, code them, and make sure they get follow-up letters or phone calls afterwards. Then, ask them some questions. Get information which you can use. All customer service reps should have a list of questions that the company is interested in asking, in general and about this particular customer.

Kraft General Foods is using their hot line to get consumer opinions on packaging colors, product tastes, annoying advertisements, and hot microwave containers. Kraft acted: they redesigned Kool-Aid boxes due to consumer complaints and rearranged the vents on packaged microwave meals to avoid burning customer fingers. Con-Agra, Inc., rewrote instructions for its Healthy Choice frozen dinners to clarify how to cover them before microwaving. Customers calling Warner-Lambert told them that Efferdent, which is designed to clean dentures, works wonders on toilet bowl stains. The calls gave them an idea for a new product. One company modified their advertisement of a child unrolling toilet paper after parents called to say that the ad set a horrible example for children.

CODING RESPONSES

Your database design must include a plan for coding responses. That means developing a series of alphabetic or numeric codes that summarize what the customer is trying to say to you. For example:

BE   Billing error

PD   Product damage

DP   Delivery problem

DE   Product design problem

AD   Problem with the advertisement

HP   Happy with the product or service

SV   Problems with service or response

Operators can be trained to enter these codes. Pop-up windows on their screens can be used to jog their memories. Your system must be flexible, so that you can add codes.

Some codes do not require any action; some codes do. Your software should be designed to distinguish these, and to call up screens for action by the proper people. Your codes should also be used for reports, so you can monitor on a regular basis how many people are calling with delivery problems or what have you.

E-MAIL COMMUNICATIONS

More and more marketers are experimenting with e-mail as a method of customer feedback and communication. Some are building e-mail databases:

- NBC created an affinity club, called NBC-TV Viewers Club. Membership was free, if members agreed to accept e-mail from the network's advertisers. Developed by CKS Partners in Cupertino, California, the club provides members with a newsletter, and incentives to watch shows. Members can choose the kind of show that they like to watch. Planned are games where members earn points towards merchandise and prizes. NBC's Home Page on America Online generates from 7,000 to 10,000 e-mail inquiries per week.

- Preview Vacations Online solicits members for their Vacation E-Mail List. Members supply information about their preferred destinations, travel habits, and the best time to call. When the service develops vacation offers that match members needs, the members are contacted about special bargains. Members can book their trips before the vacations are offered to the general public. Using their entry in America Online, the service attracted 500,000 members during the first few months.

- Club Med through World Wide Web is offering a brochure and $50 gift certificate and e-mail messages to members who sign up for information about the vacation resort.

- DealerNet provides a chance to win a new Nissan Sentra for those who provide their e-mail address when accessing the company through World Wide Web.

- Saturn offers prospective car owners, who supply information and their e-mail address through Prodigy, a free brochure and a chance to make suggestions on the kinds of car that they want Saturn to build.

- Chrysler-Plymouth through Prodigy is collecting e-mail addresses from people considering the purchase of a new car.

- Tribe Z is the name of a membership club launched by Coors Brewing Company's Zima brand. Members can specify how much e-mail they want to receive from the Zima Tribemaster. Accessible on the World Wide Web, the club promises members special online club areas and digital gifts, managed by Modem Media of Westport, CT. Members have been offered Zima Logo Patches, Zima coupons, entrance to a special area of the Web, and a directory of other tribe members.

How to Get On the Internet

If you are going to reach the new generation, you might try getting your company on the Internet. What that means is setting up a "Web Site." By the mid-nineties, very few marketers had any success in selling products through the Internet—but thousands were trying. Ultimately, many will succeed. Your initial success is not as important as what you will learn by making the attempt.

The cost of setting up a site is remarkably low. You can set up a "Home Page" for $5,000, or a sophisticated multimedia web for $25,000. Quality is important, however. Thousands of marketers are doing the same thing. If what you put out there is boring, the blasé browsers will ignore it completely.

One group that has been on the Net for some time is the Electronic Newsstand (http://www.enews.com). By the mid-nineties, they had 220 magazines each of which offered one free article to browsers, plus the opportunity to take out a subscription. They were getting about 85,000 "hits" per day, but only a very few subscription sales—between two and ten a day per magazine.

The Internet is a confederation of close to 40,000 separate but linked computer networks. There are no fees for users or marketers. There is no central registry of users. Marketers are required to register with InterNIC.

How does a user get into the Internet? You can go through one of the on-line services such as America Online, Prodigy, or CompuServe. Microsoft Windows 95 makes access to the World Wide Web very easy and inexpensive.

For a marketer, here are the steps you need to go through to get on the Net.

- *Get a Service Bureau.* Find an experienced service bureau which will do the work for you. It's too technical for a company to do on their own. Besides, having an outsider maintain your site will keep hackers from intruding into your private company files.

- *Create a winning home page.* The Home Page is everything. If it is interesting and inviting, you will get lots of hits. If not, you are wasting your money and time. There are a great number of competitors. The home page alone, however, is not enough. Browsers who like it will quickly click to your inside pages. If they are dull and texty, you will lose them. Designers cost $100 an hour, and may spend days creating your pages. Be sure they do a good job. Sony spent almost $500,000 launching the Sony On-Line home page.

- *Register your name with the InterNIC (nethappenings @is.internic.net).* You will have to pay a fee.

- *Look for partners.* If you are a ski resort, partner with makers of sportswear, ski equipment, or skiing magazines so that anyone browsing their site will click a button for you, and vice versa. Partnering is vital for success.

- *Develop a strategy for what to do with the browsers.* This is the hardest part. Are you going to sell them something direct? Or send them to a chain of stores? Or send them a fax or newsletter? Or get them to answer some survey questions? Or enter them into a sweepstakes? Or give them a coupon?

Modem Media in Westport, Connecticut is an example of a modern interactive agency. They harness television, computer, fax, and telephone media to design, create, produce, and manage interactive relationships with their client's customers. They set up interactive telephone programs for Coors and AT&T. They set up an interactive fax system for Thompson Linearfax which not only gets product information into callers' hands within seconds, it does so for 30 percent less than conventional mail costs. They set up the JCPenney Electronic Shopping system on the Internet. Their telephone-based promotion for Keystone Beer provided a Fishing Hotline Guide which managed over 2,000 weekly fishing condition reports covering 500 locations and 200 species of fish.

The point? Relationships. If you're a fisherman and beer drinker, you'll thank Keystone at the grocery store when you toast your catch at the end of the day. Here is the home page that Modem Media set up for CBS television:

Figure 9-7 CBS Television Home Page

I can tell you right now that what you will be doing after one year on the Net won't look anything like what you do the first day. But that is all right. This is a new medium. You will have to learn by trial and error what works and what doesn't.

Fax Communications

Every business today has a fax machine. Business-to-business communications now rely on fax more than on letters—a dramatic shift in only a decade. What most marketers have not realized yet is that fax is making major gains in the consumer market as well. I predict that well before the year 2000, faxes will be as common as VCRs in middle class households. How can marketers take advantage of this situation?

- *Product data on demand.* Computers can generate and send faxes on demand, as a result of customers calling up voice response units and pushing buttons. All software manufacturers now supply information by voice response and fax. It is quite inexpensive for the manufacturer because very little labor is involved. Once you have written and stored the coded information in your PC, linked it to your automated voice response unit, each PC can handle hundreds or thousands of customers per day, finding out what they want, and sending it to them.

- *News on demand.* The Los Angeles Times offers *Financial Fax.* For a monthly fee, customers can follow fifteen stocks with data sent to them by fax on a daily basis. Several other newspaper examples are reported in Chapter 19.

- *Fax bulletin boards.* Don Peppers and Martha Rogers, in their innovative book *The One to One Future*, suggest that businesses can provide bulletin boards. Each subscriber has his unique PIN number. Fax messages are left in the bulletin board. The messages are actually stored on a computer. When you dial up the correct number and enter your PIN, you receive what is on the bulletin board on your fax machine. They report on the Government Access and Information Network (GAIN) which allows fax customers to tap into government databases stored on their equipment. The Art Co-op lets you dial a code number for the artist you are looking for, whereupon your fax will spit out a complete list of prices for the artist's work.

  Using fax bulletin boards, companies can communicate directly with hundreds of thousands of different customers, sending each a different and personalized message, for a fraction of the cost and inconvenience of direct mail or telephone calls.

- *Fax response ads.* Shearson Lehman, the brokerage house, runs ads periodically in *The Wall Street Journal* offering printed copies of industry reports as a means of acquiring customers. The reports arrive within a couple of weeks. Peppers and Rogers suggest that Shearson should send their reports instantly by fax, thus improving the currency of the information, speeding up the customer acquisition process, and reducing the cost of the entire operation. Even better, they suggest that Shearson charge a fee for the reports, while allowing their current clients, using an PIN number, to get the reports free. Non-customers giving their credit card number would be charged $10, which would be rebated if they subsequently become Shearson customers.

- *Customer portfolios.* Peppers and Rogers suggest another use for the fax machine. Brokerage customers, bank customers, and others receive a monthly tabulation of their portfolio holdings. There is nothing in between. Why not have customer's portfolios updated on a daily basis on computer, and have the customer able to dial up at any time to receive a faxed copy of his present portfolio. Cost? Very little to the bank or brokerage house, providing that they maintain their customer data on a real-time basis. Advantage? A closer relationship with the customer who thinks of the brokerage house or bank as a daily correspondent, not a once-a-month reporter.

- *Product information.* Doctors, realtors, and law firms need the latest information on medicine, houses for sale, and legal decisions. Publishing this information in a journal or book is a stone age way of getting it to your customers. Peppers and Rogers suggest regular fax transmissions on subjects of interest and concern to the recipient. What if some doctors do not have a fax machine in their office to receive the pharmaceutical house's research reports? Give them a fax machine, they suggest. It would beat the cost of a salesman's visit, and promote a close relationship between the doctor and the supplier.

Interactive TV

That black box on top of millions of TV sets may be the next communications medium between you and your customers. Cable TV companies are now offering access to the Internet, and a chance for viewers to respond directly to ads or surveys that they see on their screens.

The explosion of methods for contacting customers is so great that anything that I write in this book on this subject will quite likely be obsolete in a couple of years.

What I suggest is that you explore all of these options: e-mail, fax, interactive TV, the Internet, in addition to mail, phone, and personal visits. Some of these techniques will survive. You should get on top of them to find out what you can use, and what you must cast aside.

Two publications that should help you to do this are: *Interactive Age* (708) 647-6834 and *Inter@ctive Week* (609) 829-9313.

KEEPING TRACK OF AND FIELDING RESPONSES

Responding to your customers will keep your database planners and programmers busy all the time. If you have an active program, the diagram of the response activities can get very complicated. In brief, here is what has to happen:

- Every outgoing message from you has to have a source code assigned to it. The table of source codes is stored in a promotion history file. Also in the file is the cost of the outgoing message, the date, the number sent out, and a trigger to a series of program steps telling the computer what to do when someone responds or doesn't respond.

- When a response comes in, it could be in the form of a letter or card, e-mail, fax, a telephone call, an order, a visit by the customer to one of your showrooms, or a non-response—no customer activity after a certain number of days.

- The response itself can have many gradations:
  - Send literature
  - Call me
  - Answers to survey questions
  - Here is a check or credit card, send product
  - Send product and bill me
  - Send a salesperson to visit me
  - Get lost—not interested
  - I don't live here any more, wrong address
  - Nothing . . .
  - And many more

Each of these responses should call forth a specific action from you which has to be planned out in advance. First you diagram the activities, and then you have your programmer write into your database software the steps to be taken in response. Figure 9-8 is a sample diagram of just a few of the steps you will need to take in response to one simple mailing.

"Why," you may ask, "do you go to the bother of diagramming these activities? The diagram makes the activities seem more complicated than they really are. Don't you just put the 'Yes's' into one pile, and the 'No's' into another, and get to work?"

Figure 9-8   Planning Customer Response

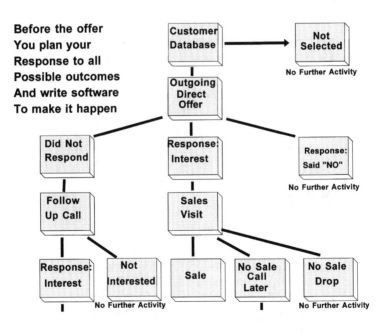

Good old-fashioned thinking. It works fine with a simple direct-mail campaign, but not with database marketing. You have to draw diagrams and write programs because any active database will be developing scores of different initiatives in a single year. You need to be sure that each one is a *test*. You need to produce reports that show you, for each initiative:

- How many went out, how many were responded to, week by week until the responses die out. What was your percentage response?

- How much each one cost to send out, and how much revenue was generated. What was your return on investment?

- How many people responded in each of the possible ways.

- How many answered the survey questions, versus those who ordered product or took some other action. There should *always* be some survey questions.

- How many bad addresses were there?

- How many people didn't respond at all, and why?

- What type of person responded, versus the type that did not respond. What type made a purchase, versus those that just asked for literature?

- Which of the packages (envelopes, texts, offers) got the best response, and which got the worst?

- How many people responded in unexpected ways: by writing an unexpected question or comment on the card, or asking an unforeseen question in the telephone call. You must tabulate these unexpected responses, and react to them. They can be very important.

How do you get all of this information into your reports? In the first place, your telemarketers need special screens which permit them to call up the customer's record (or create a new record in the case of a response from a prospect), and enter these responses into fields already pre-programmed into your database. If the responses are in writing, you will have them keypunched, off-line, by outside keypunchers. The tape they generate will be run against the master database to insert the responses into the customer records, just as if you were getting the responses by telephone.

Don't count on the programmers to design your reports. You will have to do that. It takes time and is very demanding work. It is easier to create a report than it is to think it up. Be sure the report provides *relevant information* which you can use to take other steps to improve your program.

ACTING ON THE RESPONSES

Reporting on the responses is just the beginning. How often have we heard the phrase "Allow six to eight weeks for delivery." That is fine for direct marketing, but it isn't database marketing. You can't maintain much of a two-way dialog if you take six to eight weeks to respond. "Next-Day Service" should be your goal, even if you cannot move quite that fast.

The way you fulfill the response is usually by means of some sort of computer generated-action:

- The computer will generate labels to be affixed to the literature or the product ordered, and it can be shipped out the next day.

  ACS in Reston, Virginia has a unique system called High Priority Messaging (HPM). Using distributed printing sites throughout the country, ACS has clients with active telemarketing centers that receive orders for products or customer service calls seven days a week. These clients are linked electronically with the ACS data center. There the names and addresses are merged with codes inserted by the telemarketers indicating the products ordered, or the text of the outgoing response message. The ACS mainframe creates the message to the customer and has it printed the same day at a printing plant closest to the recipient. The letters, printed by color laser, go out to the customers, timed to arrive within 48 hours of the telephone call or order receipt. That is the kind of speed that is required by modern database marketing.

- The computer will produce a thank-you letter with personal references throughout the body of the letter, based on data in the customer's database record. "Thank you for calling us on October 12. We sent out the replacement motor housing by UPS the next day. Please call us again if you have future needs."

"The XR50 has been one of our most successful products. Many customers like you, Mr. Soule, have been using them for years. Others have traded up to our new XR100, released last year, which does the job in half the time. For your information, I am enclosing a brochure on the XR100 which is available at hardware stores everywhere. If you decide to step up to the XR100, you should use the rebate coupon which I have included with the brochure. This coupon gives you a special discount *because you are a loyal customer who is trading up from an earlier model*. And, if you have a moment, you might fill in the enclosed service questionnaire. We would like to hear from you what you thought about our customer service operation. It takes just a couple of minutes to fill out the questionnaire. It will help us to give you better service in the future."

- The computer will generate lead cards which will be assigned to a salesperson or dealer automatically, printed on a printer in the dealer's office, and will trigger an automatic lead tracking sequence.

- The survey response will be planned in advance to put the customers into a special category:

  — if they make more than ten business trips a year, you will code them for a different sequence of follow-up letters than those who make less;

  — if they are over 60 years old, it puts them in a special class;

  — if she has children under 12 in the house, you need to react properly;

  — if they took a trip abroad in the past twelve months, they are going to be invited to take another.

- *Bounce back* is a concept invented by catalog mailers. It works this way: when someone buys an item from one of the small catalogs sent by direct mail, they "bounce back" with another copy of the *same catalog*. Why? Because these small catalogs are usually tossed out once used. If your customers found one thing they liked in your catalog, there is probably something else in the same catalog which would appeal to them. With each sale, there is usually a "rush" of brand loyalty for that particular catalog, which is soon dissipated because the catalog is no longer around. You have a tiny window of time to build brand loyalty. Bounce back helps to widen that window.

Some catalogers have refined bounce back to a fine degree. When you buy children's clothing from their general catalog, they bounce back with a specialized child's clothing catalog. It requires computer programming to be sure that that happens automatically.

All of this requires advance planning, diagramming, and elaborate computer programming. Remember what you are doing: you are trying to recreate the thinking that goes on in the brain of the old corner grocer. What would he do with each of these pieces of information? He would turn each one to his advantage, making appropriate suggestions on purchases, advising his customers on particular specials *of presumed interest to them.*

That is what you will have to do. But you will be handling several hundred thousand customers, not just a few hundred. There is no time to make little stacks of responses.

Your systems planner makes up a diagram of the sequence of events. You check it. Then the programmer translates the diagram into a series of computer program instructions. Then these instructions are tested with dummy data, in every possible combination of response, to be sure that you are not skipping something.

For example, you may be sending out the literature promptly but not also acting on the information that the customer is a senior citizen, and receives a special offer *in the same envelope.* You may be wasting postage on a second senior-citizen mailing.

Testing is one of the most difficult parts of response tracking, and one of the most neglected. Quality control: without it, database marketing falls apart.

HOW MUCH DIALOG DO YOU NEED?

Dialog is expensive. Letters, telephone calls, e-mail, faxes cost money. How can you justify dialog programs to senior management, and to yourself?

There is a simple way to answer this question. Any form of dialog should be continued if it improves customer lifetime value. Build a customer lifetime value table based on your existing customer database. Then design a new one that has built into it the benefits and the costs of the type of dialog you are proposing to install. See if the dialog improves lifetime value. How can it do that? There are really only five possible ways. You should institute and continue a system of dialog if it results in:

- *Improved Retention.* Customers keep buying from you longer with the dialog than without.

- *Improved Spending Rate.* Customers purchase more after the system is installed than before.

- *Improved Referral Rate.* Customers recommend you to their friends and relatives, and these referred people become customers.

- *Reduced Marketing Costs.* It costs less to market to customers than to prospects. You can show that your marketing costs are less with the dialog.

- *Reduced Direct Costs.* It may be that customers with whom you are having a dialog will cut your actual costs by buying directly from you products that you previously had to sell through a middle man. Example: software upgrades, supplies.

If you have no purchase history from the past to compare current spending levels to, (but you have now built a database so you can track spending), you might consider setting up a control group. This would be a group of customers, similar to the rest of your database, to whom you send no mail, and make no phone calls. You have no dialog with these people. Compare their spending habits with those with whom you maintain a close daily association. By comparing the retention rate, referral rate, and spending rate of these two groups you can prove to your CFO that your expenditures for maintaining a dialog are worth it (or not worth it!). Don't maintain a dialog because it is "a nice idea". Do it because it is profitable. Be sure you can prove it.

SUMMARY

In the design of any marketing database, you must plan on effective ways for the consumer to contact you, to respond to you, to tell you things: unexpected things, important things, trivial things. A marketing database is a mechanism for two-way communication.

- You provide a way for consumers to contact you with their ideas, thoughts, complaints, compliments, suggestions.

- How do you do this? By mail, phone, fax, e-mail, the Internet, interactive TV. There is an explosion in communications. Be sure you are with it.

- You store what you learn from your customer in the database so that you can remember them, quantify them, act on them.

- You design your database software so you can poll the database constantly for unresolved issues, new ideas, gripes, types of questions being raised.

- You act on what you learn from your customers.

- You reach out and tell your customers that you have listened, remembered, and acted. Give them credit for their ideas or for pointing out flaws in your product, delivery, advertising.

- You remind them of how much you appreciate their business.

- While you are telling them what you have accomplished with their ideas, you ask for more.

Result: true two-way communication.

Chapter 10

The Lifetime Value of a Customer

Many marketers use the term, "The lifetime value of a customer." Few of them, however, know how to compute it. Even fewer know how to use the concept in their business planning. By the end of this chapter, you will know all of these things.

The lifetime value of a customer is the net profit that you will receive from transactions with a given customer during the time that this customer continues to buy from you. Some customers buy once and disappear forever. Their lifetime value is the profit on that one transaction. Others keep coming back. The old corner grocer was intuitively aware of the lifetime value of all of his customers, even though he probably never sat down and figured it out as we are going to do. He worked very hard to recognize his customers and do services for them so that they would keep coming back. He worked every day to increase the lifetime value of his customers. You can do the same thing with database marketing.

Once you know the lifetime value of a customer, you can use it in planning your marketing strategy. Every marketing initiative you undertake (such as setting up a customer service operation with a toll free 800 telephone line) has certain costs. It also may have certain benefits in improved customer relationships, increased sales, and increased retention. How can you be sure that your new customer service is the right move for you? If it has the effect of increasing your customer lifetime value. For your particular business, a toll free customer hot line may actually cost more than it is worth, and you should not invest in it. On the other hand, it may be quite profitable. Lifetime value computations can help you determine that before you invest the money. That is why lifetime value is such a useful concept.

To understand lifetime value, we are going to do some computations. First we will determine the lifetime value of the average customer as your business exists right now. Next, we will determine what the revised lifetime value is likely to be after you undertake some new marketing strategy. We will see if your average customer lifetime value has gone up or down as a result of your efforts.

MARY ANNE'S CLOSET

Let us take as an example Mary Anne's Closet, a small chain of stores offering children's clothing. Let us assume that Mary Anne has successfully set up a number of retail stores, but has never done any database marketing. At this point, they have about 100,000 customers per year, with annual sales of about $12 million. Their annual profits are about $3.6 million.

Learning about the concept of database marketing, their marketing director, Kelly Baumgartner, decided to set one up. Starting from scratch two years ago, she began with a list of the names of customers to which something had been delivered. She sent them all an inexpensive plastic card with their name and a number on it. She told them that they would receive a 5 percent discount on certain items if they showed the card when they shopped. She also encouraged people visiting the store to sign up for a card. After two years working at this, she had collected names, addresses, purchase history, and some other data on 10,000 of her customers, which she punched into her PC.

By tracking customers over the two years, she discovered an amazing fact: only 30 percent of the customers who shop at Mary Anne's Closet ever come back. Even the store managers couldn't believe it. They told anecdotes of customers that they recognized who were "regulars" and shopped there all the time. But, alas, their anecdotes were not statistically useful.

From the store's sales records, she was able to estimate the amount that the average customer bought in a year—$120. She also knew that Mary Anne usually marked up wholesale clothing by 100 percent. Adding 20 percent for shipping and other variable costs, she figured that the store's costs were about 70 percent of sales revenue. She arranged all of this information on a spread sheet in her PC using Lotus. Here is what she found:

Table 10-1   Mary Anne's Closet

Revenue	Year1	Year2	Year3
R1 Customers	10,000	3,000	900 (3)
R2 Retention Rate	30.00%	30.00%	30.00%
R3 Spending Rate	$120	$120	$120
R4 Total Revenue	$1,200,000	$360,000	$108,000 (4)
Variable Costs			
C1 Percent	70.00%	70.00%	70.00%
C2 Total Variable Costs	$840,000	$252,000	$75,600 (5)
Profits			
P1 Gross Profit	$360,000	$108,000	$32,400 (6)
P2 Discount Rate	1.00	1.16	1.35
P3 NPV Profit	$360,000	$93,103	$24,000 (7)
P4 Cumulative NPV Profit	$360,000	$453,103 (1)	$477,103 (8)
L1 **Customer Lifetime Value**	$36.00	$45.31 (2)	$47.71 (9)

How she did the calculations for the figures listed in parentheses:

(1) $360,000 + $93,103
(2)   (1) / 10,000
(3)   3,000 * .3
(4) $120 * (3)
(5)   0.6 * (4)
(6)   (4) - (5)
(7)   (6) / 1.35
(8)   (1) + (7)
(9)   (8) / 10,000

Let's explain what she did.

In the first place, she tracked 10,000 specific people during their first two years at the store. There were, of course, about 90,000 other customers that she could not keep track of, because they did not have a card. She ignored them for the purpose of this table.

Of those 10,000 customers, only 3,000 made any purchases in the second year. This is shown in line R1 under Year2. These were the only 3,000 of the original 10,000 left. From that fact, she was able to determine the store's retention rate at 30 percent, which she showed on line R2. The retention rate is:

R = (Customers in Year2) / (Customers in Year1)

From overall sales figures, she knew that the average customer spent $120 in a year, so her total revenue from these 10,000 customers in Year1 was $1,200,000 (line R4). She figured that 70 percent of that revenue was cost—50 percent merchandise, and 20 percent other variable costs—so her total costs were $840,000 (line C2).

Her profits, therefore, from these 10,000 customers were $360,000 (line P1).

Fixed and Variable Costs

Every business has both fixed and variable costs. Fixed costs include the buildings, overhead, debt service, etc. Variable costs are those that vary with the level of production or sales. Database marketing lifetime value calculations normally use variable costs exclusively, rather than including fixed costs. The reason is this: most database marketing is incremental. There is already an ongoing business for which the fixed costs were incurred. Added to this ongoing business, a company decides to increase its sales, increase the retention level, increase referrals, etc. by means of database marketing. There is normally no need to increase fixed costs to permit database marketing. For this reason, including fixed costs in the calculations will distort and undervalue the benefits to be derived from database marketing by making the erroneous assumption that fixed costs must increase with increased sales.

The Discount Rate

Because Kelly majored in Business Administration at college, she knew how to use a discount rate. The reason for using a discount rate is that future profits are not worth as much as present profits. The profits that she will realize from customers in Year2 and Year3 are not worth as much in today's money as profits she is realizing today in Year1. To add apples and apples (instead of apples and oranges) she has to convert future profits into today's money. She does this by discounting future profits so they can be added to present profits to find out the value, in today's money, of the future profits she will get in the future from today's customers.

The discount rate she uses is based on the market rate of interest, plus risk. For Mary Anne, at this point in time, the market rate of interest is 8 percent. Mary Anne can borrow money at that rate. But to compute the discount rate, Kelly is doubling that 8 percent to get 16 percent. Why? Because there is always risk in a business like Mary Anne's Closet. There is intense competition in this field from other similar stores, and from department stores, Wal-Mart, and catalogs. It is a rough world, and Mary Anne may not be around in three years to profit from it. So she wisely doubles the rate of interest to allow for risk.

The formula for the discount rate in any given year, then, is:

$$D = (1 + i)^n$$

In this formula, "i" is the interest rate (including risk) and "n" is the number of years that you have to wait. Figuring the discount rate for Year3 (two years from now), the formula becomes:

$$D = (1 + .16)^2$$
$$D = 1.35$$

To figure out the present value of any profit that you plan to receive in the future, you simply divide that profit by the appropriate discount rate. In the case of this year's profits, the discount rate is 1—there is no discount.

There is an exception to this rule, however. Suppose in your business your typical customer pays you in 180 days, instead of immediately. You might want to discount even this year's profits by a certain amount to allow for the six month's wait. In that case, your discount rate in Year1 would be:

$$D = (1 + .16)^{0.5}$$
$$D = 1.08$$

In this book, we will not be spending much time on such technical details. You may want to, particularly in a business-to-business database where the amounts of money and the waiting times are significant. Our main concern in this chapter is to understand and work with the principles of lifetime value, not these very fine points.

Net Present Value Profits

To get the net present value profits in any given year, (Line P3) Kelly divides the profits in that year by the discount rate. In Year1, she divides $360,000 by 1 and gets $360,000. In Year2 she divides $108,000 by 1.16 and gets $93,103.

The cumulative net present value profits (Line P4) she gets by adding the NPV profits in any year to the cumulative NPV profits from previous years. In Year2, therefore, she adds the discounted profits in that year ($93,103) to the discounted cumulative profits in the previous years ($360,000) to get $453,103 which are the total cumulative discounted profits from the original 10,000 customers at the end of two years.

Customer Lifetime Value

To get her final figure, customer lifetime value (Line L1), Kelly simply divides all her cumulative net present value profits by the original 10,000 customers. She learns that the lifetime value of any new customer after one year is $36.00. After the second year, the value is $45.31. After three years, it is $47.71.

Why divide all of these numbers by the original 10,000? Why not divide Year3 cumulative profits by the 900 customers that are still left? Because that would be a useless number. What Kelly is determining is the lifetime value of every new customer that walks into the store and signs up for a card. That number has built into it a lot of facts and assumptions. It assumes that 70 percent of these customers will disappear and never come back after the first year. It assumes the average spending rate is $120. It assumes costs are 70 percent, etc. It is really a terribly useful and important number to Kelly, because she can use that number to test her future marketing strategy, and predict her success, before she spends a lot of marketing dollars.

Projecting into the Future

Year3, for Kelly, hasn't happened yet. She is using the information that she collected for Year1 and Year2 to project what Year3 will be like for the loyal 900 customers who still remain out of the original 10,000. Lifetime value tables, therefore, are a combination of facts from the past, and projections into the future. The past really is unimportant for any business. The future is vital. The use you can make of the past is to understand the trends of your business so you can better predict the future. Customer behavior, after all, tends to be somewhat predictable. What you cannot predict is the market: your competition, prices, changing tastes in products and services. So you hang on to what you can count on—the demonstrated behavior of your customers—and try to make something useful out of it.

Kelly's Birthday Club

Now that she knows the lifetime value of Mary Anne's customers, Kelly has decided to do something to change things in a positive way. She is going to do a little database marketing.

Fortunately, when she captured the names and addresses of her card members, she was thoughtful enough to also capture the name of the child for which the clothes were bought, and the child's date of birth. That information is stored in the database in her PC. It is vital information.

Each month, she plans to run a PC program that pulls out the children who have birthdays in the next month. She has bought some birthday cards and a laser printer that will print on the cards and on the envelopes. She has gotten the store management to agree to provide a special 20 percent discount coupon for any card-carrying-customer who is buying a present for a child that has a birthday that month. In addition, she has bought a supply of huge "Happy Birthday" balloons and helium gas containers for each store that will be given as a gift to each birthday child who comes to the store—whether they use the 20 percent discount coupon or not.

What Kelly wants to figure out is what this program will do to her customer lifetime value. She makes some assumptions:

- *Retention Rate.* The program will certainly bring some of the 70 percent dropouts back to the store. After all, they know where the store is. They have shopped there once. They filled out a form to get the card. The balloons and the 20 percent discount offer may well bring some of these folks back for a second visit. She estimates that she can raise her retention rate from 30 percent to 50 percent with this program.

- *Referrals.* Word of mouth is a great advertising technique if you can get it to work for you. Kelly plans to ask card holders to recommend others who might also be interested in being included in her "Birthday Club". Some parents, grandparents, uncles or aunts may well be interested. To motivate them to suggest others, Kelly plans to reward them with a little gift. How many new customers can be referred in this way? Kelly guesses that she might get 8 percent of her existing customers to recommend others.

- *Spending Rate.* Of course, there is also the likelihood that this birthday program will increase the customer spending rate. Why? Because most people have more than one child's birthday to worry about—whether it is their children, their grandchildren, their nephews, nieces, etc. If they make a purchase for one child's birthday, and like the idea, some of them will probably use the discount for another birthday. Kelly projects the average spending rate will go up from $120 per year to $150 per year.

Lets see what Kelly's Birthday Club might do for Mary Anne's Closet:

Table 10-2   Mary Anne's Closet with the Birthday Club

Revenue	Year1	Year2	Year3
R1 Referral Rate	8%	8%	8%
R2 Referred Customers	0 (1)	800 (5)	464
R3 Retained Customers	10,000	5,000	2,900
R4 Total Customers	10,000	5,800 (6)	3,364
R5 Retention Rate	50%	50%	50%
R6 Spending Rate	$150	$150	$150
R7 Total Revenue	$1,500,000	$870,000	$504,600
Variable Costs			
C1 Direct Percent	70%	70%	70%
C2 Direct Costs	$1,050,000	$609,000	$353,220
C3 Birthday Club Mailing & Gift	$50,000 (2)	$29,000	$16,820
C4 Birthday Discounts @ $4	$40,000 (3)	$23,200	$13,456
C5 Referral Gifts @$5	$0 (4)	$4,000	$2,320
C6 Total Costs	$1,140,000	$665,200	$385,816
Profits			
P1 Gross Profit	$360,000	$204,800	$118,784
P2 Discount Rate	1.00	1.16	1.35
P3 NPV Profit	$360,000	$176,552	$87,988
P4 Cumulative NPV Profit	$360,000	$536,552	$624,540
L1 **Customer Lifetime Value**	$36.00	$53.66	$62.45

Table 10-2   *continued*

Assumptions on which the numbers are based:

  (1)   Assume referrals buy in Year2
  (2) $5 per customer: mailing & balloons.
  (3)   20 percent will use discount, spending average of $50 times
          20 percent
        discount divided by total customers on database
  (4)   No referrals in Year1
  (5)   Referral rate of 8 percent times Year1 total customers.
  (6)   Retained customers plus referred customers.

If Kelly is correct, she will have 3,364 active customers in Year3 (out of the original 10,000) instead of only 900. The club could push the customer lifetime value in Year3 up from $47.71 to over $62.

Note that all of her expenses are figured in: the cost of creating and mailing the birthday gifts and giving away the balloons, the cost of the discounts given to those who request them, and the cost of referral gifts given to those who refer others to the store.

THE MEANING OF KELLY'S CLUB

What does it really mean that lifetime value has been increased from $47 to $62—an increase of about $14.74 per customer. What does that really mean for the bottom line?

To understand the significance of Kelly's idea, we have to make some assumptions. Let's assume that, based on Kelly's computations, the store decides to make a major effort to get as many as possible of the 100,000 customers who shop there every year to join the club—instead of the modest effort that Kelly has made up to now. How many of the 100,000 can they get to join? Perhaps half of them? After all—this is a store for children's clothes. Clothes are a very common birthday gift. They are using the club to remind people who are already in the store to buy something for a child that they have a club which will benefit both the child and the gift givers. This club gives the purchasers a much more powerful reason for taking out a card than the occasional 5 percent discount that Kelly used in the first place.

All right, suppose that the store does go all out on this idea, and they sign up 50,000 people for Kelly's club. What will that mean for the bottom line? An increased lifetime value of $14.74 per card member times 50,000 members represents an increase of $737,000 in Mary Anne's total profit, or a net gain of about 20 percent. It is the kind of thing that can really give a boost to a marketer's career.

Let's look more closely at what Kelly has accomplished so that we can understand the meaning of lifetime value.

Net Change in Customer Lifetime Value

	Year1	Year2	Year3
Before the Club	$36.00	$45.31	$47.71
After the Club	$36.00	$53.66	$62.45
Change	$0.00	$8.35	$14.74
Times 50,000 Customers	$0	$417,500	$737,000

You will note that in Year1, Kelly's program produced no profit gains at all. This is normal for database marketing. Using database marketing, you can often produce impressive gains in customer acquisition by better targeting of your efforts. But you can rarely change the short range profits resulting from increased customer retention, which is the long range objective of Kelly's club. I can hear the Chief Financial Officer telling her at the end of Year1:

"Well, Kelly, what have we gained from all of your balloons and birthday cards? Exactly nothing! We have spent a fortune, and we are right back where we started. Lets go back to the old ways. We were doing just fine."

But Mary Anne's management is more enlightened than the CFO. They understand Kelly's computations, and they can see the pot of gold at the end of the rainbow. They have accepted the idea that you have to think long term. They see the power of the increased retention and increased spending rate. They also appreciate the very real gains through the referral program. Kelly has educated them, and it is working.

Suppose That Lifetime Value Does Not Increase

We have been painting a rosy picture here. Kelly has tried something new, and it seems to work. Not all database marketing ideas do pay off. Probably half of them don't. That is one of the most important reasons for drawing up a lifetime value table in the first place. By costing out her programs carefully and estimating her potential benefits conservatively, Kelly can learn in advance whether each new marketing initiative has the potential for success. Of course, even if Kelly's birthday club seems to be a success on paper, it could still be defeated by poor execution or some other miscalculation. But Kelly has a solid and financially possible plan. She has a better than average chance of success.

What should you do if you draw up such a lifetime value table for a new marketing program for your business, and it shows that lifetime value will not increase—or may even decrease? That's an easy one. Don't do it! Keep it to yourself. Think up something else, tinker with it to cut your costs, or find a way to boost your benefits.

WHAT CAN DATABASE MARKETING ACCOMPLISH?

From Kelly's experience, we can see that database marketing can affect lifetime value in three ways:

- *Increased Retention.* Retention is the real meaning of customer loyalty. Successful database marketing always boosts retention rates. Retention is powerful. Take a look at what Bain and Company estimate to be the effect on profits of a 5 percent increase in the retention rate in various industries:

Figure 10-1   Increased Profits from Retention Increase

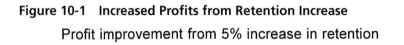

Profit improvement from 5% increase in retention

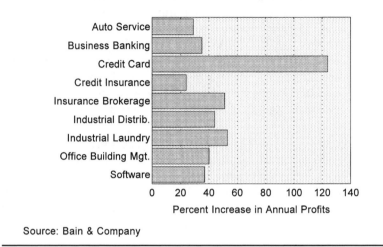

Source: Bain & Company

- *Increased Spending Rate.* Not only do customers keep buying longer, they spend more per year, if your program is providing benefits for your customers.

- *Increased Referrals.* Happy customers love to tell their friends about your business. You can capitalize on that by making it easier for them to recommend you and your services.

You should consciously aim any database marketing program at these three objectives, and measure its success against these basic yardsticks.

OTHER ACCOMPLISHMENTS

There are two other things that you can often achieve by successful database marketing that are not readily apparent in Kelly's club. They are these:

- *Decreased Marketing Costs.* Before Kelly's club, Mary Anne's Closet used print ads, yellow pages, and occasional radio spots at Christmas time. They were really scattering their shot, since their audience is parents or grandparents of children under 8 years. Once Kelly builds up her database of 50,000 customers, she can try direct mail to these customers. It is highly likely that the money spent in this way might be more powerful than the same money spent in general advertising. Of course, it would not replace general advertising. Direct mail to customers does not help acquisition, but it can boost the spending rate of existing customers in a very economical way.

- *Decreased Direct Costs.* Once Kelly has a functioning database of 50,000 loyal customers, she can try something else. Why not send out a catalog with the option of buying by phone, mail, or store visit? She will discover what many large retailers have learned, that direct sales can be more profitable than retail sales.

A large department store chain with 400 stores nationally began a syndicator's promotion program. Under this program, promoters with a product to sell (fleece lined jackets, encyclopedias, dresses) approach the store with deals: let us use your customer list and your name. We will put up all the money for the mailing, and send it out. You collect the money from the sales. We will fulfill. You make 20 percent of the profits. The store has a large database of customers who have the store's proprietary card. Each customer's record holds the annual sales by department. The store knows, for example, if the customer bought children's, or women's, or men's clothing. They know the total level of sales for each household. They can furnish the syndicator with a list of names that is targeted to the right audience. The results? The store now makes more profits annually from their syndicator program than they make from all of their 400 stores combined!

Why Three Years?

If you look at Kelly's lifetime value chart, you will see that she has projected the value over only three years. Why not five years or more? Good question.

Some companies should build lifetime value tables that are much longer than three years. For example, telephone companies, life insurance, banks all should build long term lifetime value tables. The nature of their business is long term. Automobile companies should build five or six year tables. Why? Because most new car buyers buy again in Year4, not Year3. Some wait for Year5 or later. You need to understand your customer's motivation and thought processes. You need to understand what he uses his car for, what it means to him, how many miles he drives in a year, whether it is for pleasure or business or both. You need to look long term, and collect a lot of data about your customers which is built into your table.

For Kelly, three years is probably the right size table. Remember the audience: relatives of kids under 8. The retention rate is low—for fundamental reasons.

Where Did She Get Her Numbers?

Where did she get this number for the referral rate of 8 percent? Where did she get the idea that she could boost her retention rate from 30 percent to 50 percent, and her spending rate from $120 to $150? This is, of course, where marketing savvy comes in. She doesn't know these things, of course. She makes an estimate based on what she has learned about the customers and the business, and what she thinks is possible. They are really objectives, which she can test.

In Year2, she will be able to learn whether these projections were correct or not. Each number she used can be verified with scientific accuracy. If the referral program is producing referrals of 10 percent instead of 8 percent, she will know that, and she can revise her tables. If the spending rate is only $145, she will learn that and redo her projections. Everything in these tables is measurable and revisable.

Think of how different what Kelly is doing from what marketers usually do. They think up an idea like the Birthday Club, and promote it as a "good idea". They sell it. No one knows what it will accomplish. Once it is in place, there are seldom any ways of measuring its success. If the store management does not think long term, the idea will be dropped at the end of the first year, on the grounds that it costs too much, and is going nowhere. Without a lifetime value table, this idea would probably die.

WHAT YOU CAN DO

If you have built a customer database which tracks customer purchases, you now have in your hands all the information necessary to build a lifetime value table for your customers. Track your customers from year to year to determine your retention rate.

"What about people who take out a card in Year2 or Year3? How do I show them on the table?", I can hear you asking. Simple. For those people this is their Year1. You add them in to the Year1 group and track them. In other words, Year1, Year2, Year3 are not calendar years, like 1997, 1998, they are customer years which are peculiar to each customer.

Build your table on a PC spreadsheet like Excel or Lotus. Determine your retention rate and your spending rate. Determine an appropriate discount rate. If you have actual spending rates in your database, use these. Otherwise, you can construct the spending rate from overall sales figures, and your estimates of the total number of customers.

Most marketers don't know how to compute the store's variable costs—which in Mary Anne's case we determined to be 70 percent. What are they in your case? You will have to figure that out. It helps to know that you can estimate the number without weakening the validity of the table. If you use the same number in your base lifetime value table as you do in your revised table (with your new marketing program initiatives), it won't matter much whether you use 70 percent or 80 percent or some other number. You can still use the table to predict whether lifetime value is going up or down as a result of what you plan to do, and that is the basic purpose of the exercise.

EVALUATING STRATEGY

Once you have built your base lifetime value table, as Kelly did, you then must build a revised table for every new marketing initiative that you dream up. Make up your new retention rate, your new spending rate, your referral rate. Plug in the costs of all the activities that you are planning. Then see if lifetime value goes up or goes down. If it goes down (as it may in many cases), modify your idea or drop it. Try something else. If your idea doesn't work on paper, it sure as heck won't work in practice.

In Kelly's table, she put all of Mary Anne's customers into a single table, and you can do the same thing with your customers. Once you have done this, however, you can get much more sophisticated. You may want to create a lifetime value table for senior citizens which is different from your table for young families with children. If it is a business-to-business database, you may want to create lifetime value tables by SIC code groups, or by size of company. You may want to estimate the lifetime value of each RFM cell (as explained in Chapter 7). There is really no limit to what you can do with this useful tool.

There is one caution, however: Don't get carried away. The purpose of lifetime value calculation is to evaluate strategy. You make up a new set of tables every time you come up with a new strategy to see if it makes economic sense. Don't make up scores of lifetime value tables if they have no relation to possible strategies. If other words, don't waste time playing with your computer, when you should be dreaming up great database marketing ideas.

SUMMARY

The lifetime value of a customer is the net profit that you will receive from transactions with a given customer during the time that this customer continues to buy from you. Its purpose is to evaluate strategy. Since it includes both the costs of a database strategy and the possible benefits, a lifetime value table can be used to show if a proposed strategy is likely to be successful.

To build a lifetime value table, you need to have a customer database that tracks consumer behavior from one year to the next. In constructing the table you will learn that you need to know:

- *The Retention Rate.* What percentage of customers keep buying from you in the second and third years after they first come to you.

- *The Spending Rate.* How much money the average customer spends with you in a year.

- *The Variable Cost Percentage.* Usually calculated as a percentage of revenue.

- *The Discount Rate.* Which is based on the market rate of interest (usually doubled to include risk).

Once you have built a base lifetime value table on a spreadsheet like Excel or Lotus, you then dream up some new marketing strategy. You test that strategy by building a new lifetime value table. This new table includes the costs of implementing your new strategy, and the benefits which it will probably bring. A new feature of this table will also be a referral rate: results of a strategy to get one customer to recommend your product or service to another customer. There are five (and only five) possible benefits to lifetime value from a database marketing strategy. They are:

- Increased retention rate—making customers more loyal through recognition, services, information, helpfulness.

- Increased spending rate—more sales from existing customers due to your new strategy.

- Increased referral rate—getting one customer to recommend another.

- Decreased marketing costs from better targeting.

- Decreased direct costs from changing your channel of distribution using your database.

Lifetime value tables sometimes show that a proposed strategy will not increase lifetime value, it will reduce it. This is wonderful. Don't implement the new strategy. The table has saved you from spending thousands of dollars on something that won't work. This is one of the chief benefits of a lifetime value table.

Chapter 11

Providing Services to Your Customers

If Nancy sells a book to Dan for $10, what is the book worth? If you said $10 you would be wrong. If it were worth exactly $10 there would have been no trade, no transaction. Would you go to town with a $10 bill, take it to the bank, exchange it for an identical $10 bill, and drive home satisfied? Of course not.

To Nancy, the book is clearly worth much less than $10. After all, she had to bring the book to their place of exchange, wait while Dan examined it, run the risk that he would decide against buying it and waste her time. Nancy wants the $10 much more than the book. The book is probably worth $9 or perhaps even $5 to her.

To Dan, the book is clearly worth much more than $10. After all, he is exchanging a $10 bill which can be used to buy a meal, a haircut, or transportation, for a book which probably has very little liquid exchange value. He had to believe that the book would provide him with information or entertainment worth far in excess of $10—perhaps $11 or even $15—to be willing to give up his $10. Just try going to a restaurant and offering the book in exchange for a meal, or giving the book to a cab driver in exchange for a ride to the airport!

This example shows that in a free exchange, there is profit, sometimes a lot of profit, to both parties. If the book was worth only $5 to Nancy, she has walked away with $5 profit. If it was worth $15 to Dan, he too has a $5 profit.

This is the core reasoning behind customer service. Companies trade something that does not cost them much, information and helpfulness, for something that is worth a lot to them—customer loyalty and continued sales. Customers trade something that does not cost them much, loyalty, for something they really value a great deal: information about the product, and helpful service in using it, understanding it, or getting it repaired.

If the database is the trunk of the tree, customer service is the fruit. In the past, companies thought of customer service as a losing proposition. They spent a lot of money on an 800 number and operators to staff it—but where are the sales that would justify this expense? Better to print up clear instructions, paste them to the outside of the box and forget it!

But, of course, all that is now in the past. Most companies have gotten the message that contact with customers can and should be a mutually profitable experience. They have learned that one of the most important commodities that they have to sell is information. Prospects and customers want information:

- about what is available, and how much it costs;

- about where to get it, and how to get it;

- about how it works, how you put it together;

- about what to do if you can't get it to work;

- about upgrades: things that go with it, plug into it, make it more useful and attractive; and

- about spare parts.

MAINTAINING CUSTOMER CONTACT

With this as a background, it is easy to see how a marketing database can be used to maintain a one-on-one relationship with each customer. Every time a customer writes a letter or makes a telephone call, one of your customer service reps can get your customer's record instantly up on the screen. Visible will be all the contacts, all the purchases, all the data about this customer. "Yes, Mrs. Warren, did the baby car seat arrive in time? Was your daughter happy with it?"

This time Mrs. Warren may be calling to order something else, or she may be calling with an inquiry or a complaint. No matter what it is, the substance of the call should be recorded in her file for later reference. (This is what the corner grocer did. He remembered that you asked when peaches would be in stock. When the peaches came in, he reminded you of it, and you thanked him for remembering.)

How do you keep track of such telephone calls in a marketing database? In two ways: coded records and free-form records. The free-form records are made while Mrs. Warren is on the phone. They might read like this: "UPS man left car seat at wrong house. OK now. Invited to wedding on May 14. Can suggest luggage gift at $100? Can bride exchange for credit if wants other?" The free-form record will have the date, the customer ID, and the free-form ID.

When the call has ended, the customer rep will review the free-form record, and enter suitable codes into a coded record. There will be a code to send a gift catalog and gift coupon to Mrs. Warren, an exchange certificate letter, a wedding gift reminder code for three weeks before May 14, and a UPS delivery error code. These codes will trigger mailings and reminders for outbound telemarketing. For example, there could be a telephone call late in May. How was the wedding, and what did she end up buying as a gift? (If it was not luggage, maybe it was something that we should have in our catalog.)

The coded record will be used to prepare reports: problems with UPS, coupons sent, catalogs sent, customer events and such. Every time Mrs. Warren calls, her free-form records will show on the screen. After a year, they will be automatically purged, to be replaced by the coded records only.

Disk Space

"Keeping all this information is going to require a tremendous amount of disk space," I can imagine you thinking. "Hughes has really gone overboard if he thinks that we can keep all that information in our file of 6 million customers. We will go broke."

Old-fashioned thinking. As detailed earlier, new advances in computer technology has caused the cost of maintaining data on disk to drop every year. It will continue to drop.

Your competitors have already realized this and are developing marketing databases which will hold this data. And what's more, *you won't be able to find out about it* because marketing databases are private, one-on-one affairs. Mrs. Warren will think that it is because their customer rep remembers their many phone calls (even though the rep is not always the same person). As time goes on computer disk space will be dirt cheap, and no longer a worry.

Total Company Involvement

When you get your database set up, your company's entire operations will change in ways that will be dictated by your database. Customers will ask for service, and expect it the next day (not in "six to eight weeks"). If you offer the old service, they will go elsewhere. You will be able to do a much better job of predicting sales and consequently predicting needs for inventory replenishment.

Product design will rely more and more on the intelligence provided by the database. As we move from the mass marketing of the past, it has become obvious that customers want more products and services in ever-increasing varieties. What these varieties are can be learned from the database.

CUSTOMER SERVICE FUNCTIONS AND ATTRIBUTES

What do you expect of customer service? Let's make a list:

Cheerful, helpful, interested. A fun person to talk to. A sense of humor. Someone who is really interested in people.

Intelligent and knowledgeable. Customer service reps must know not only your products but your *business*. It is not enough to know that you have fourteen different computer models available; they have to know what each one does, and why someone would buy one over another. They have to have at their fingertips (not necessarily in their heads) the answer to any question that could be asked. They have to know how to use their fingertips to get that information. They have to be smart enough to figure out what customers are trying to find out so that they can supply it.

Linked to technical resources. No one customer service representative can know everything. But somewhere in your company there is someone who knows what the customer is asking about. Your telephone system has to be such that reps can quickly send callers to the right place for an answer. Ideally, however, they should be able to talk to the resource on the intercom first:

"Roger Harris is on the line. He has a scanner which produces a bitmap. He wants to know if our product can read the bit map. He has version 2.0. I think that he may need an upgrade to 2.2, but I am not sure. Can you talk to him and be sure that that is what he needs. If so, give him back to me, and I will place an order for him."

The technical link requires something more than a good customer service rep and an excellent telephone system. It requires that almost *everyone* in the company understand and be prepared to play a role in customer service. The whole company has to become *dedicated* to thinking that providing information to customers is an *important part of their jobs*.

When someone asked the old corner grocer how big a turkey was needed to feed fourteen people, he didn't say, "Don't bother me. I have a delivery truck broken down and ten orders to get out." Somehow he found a moment to tell you, "A pound and a half per person, and sometimes a little extra. We will have some fresh ones coming in on Wednesday morning. Can I save one for you?"

In the same fashion, when customer calls come in, your technical personnel, billing clerks, and shipping staff have to realize that responding to this call right now is as important as whatever they were doing when the call came in. The message of customer service has to permeate the whole company, or your reps will have a hard time projecting a helpful image.

Delegated real authority. There comes a time when someone has to say to a customer: "That is too bad, Mrs. Michaelson. You know that we stand behind our products 100 percent. No one should have to put up with what you have gone through. I am going to send you a replacement today, right this minute. It should get there in two days, three at the outside. There is no charge. Please call me and tell me when it arrives, and if it is working OK. I want to be sure that you are happy with us and our products."

Figure out what decisions you can delegate to your experienced customer service reps, and *delegate them.* This delegation will have important benefits for you. Customers will get better, more responsive, speedier service, and your reps will begin to feel that they are important in the company. They will take a greater interest in their work, do a better job, represent you better. They will become "old corner grocers."

Of course, when they do give away replacement products, or refunds, they have to record this information in the database—that is how the replacements and refunds get to the customer. The database triggers an order or a refund check.

The fact that the decision is in the database means something else: there will be reports generated. You can see how much each rep has given away each month. The authority you have delegated carries responsibility with it, and accountability. You know, and the reps know, that there will be a printed report every month on refunds and exchanges. If there is a question, they have a complete database record on every transaction. They can document what they did, and why they did it.

Thus, your database makes it easier for you to delegate responsibility. And this delegation enables you to provide quicker and more responsive services to your customers.

Motivated to sell. People used to think that customer service was an information function, and not in the business of selling. That was old-fashioned thinking. Today we know that customers are busy people. Both the customer and his or her spouse are working. They don't have time to fool around. If a product or service that they need, want, or would be beneficial to them is available, they want to know about it and be able to place an order for it right then and there.

That is the whole point of this chapter: a successful sale means that both parties walk away with a profit. Your customer service reps have to understand this, and use this understanding in selling upgrades and new products.

Willing to fish for and record information. In the modern supermarket, when you ask a clerk where you can find canned Polish ham, the clerk says "Against the wall, near Aisle 8." That is all—there is no more to the exchange. But when your caller says, "Do you have cruise ships that go to Jamaica?," this should open up a whole line of information-gathering. Not only do you tell the caller that, in fact, you do not go to Jamaica, but you do go to Aruba, the Virgin Islands, and a dozen other nearby places. And you also try to get other facts:

Who is the customer?

How many people might be going?

Has the caller been on a cruise ship before?

What was good or bad about the previous cruise?

Where else have they been on vacation?

What travel agent do they usually use?

What occasion prompted the call—a birthday, an anniversary, a retirement party?

What does the caller's spouse do for a living?

Do they know someone else who has cruised?

Would they like to receive literature, video?

When was the caller thinking of going?

Is this information relevant? You bet it is.

Can your customer service rep record it? It depends on how good your database system is.

Can you put the information to profitable use? Again, that depends on you and the resourcefulness of your company and your marketing database system. The result of this call should be a phone call or a letter to the customer's travel agent or one of your preferred agents, with some very hot information.

TRAINING CUSTOMER SERVICE REPRESENTATIVES

Equipped with screens that show a customer's entire history and potential, the customer service representative becomes one of the most important sales forces that your company has. You will have to completely revamp their training, not just to know how to work the database, but in the techniques of selling, cross selling, and upgrading. They will have to know everything about the products that you sell, but also about the competitor's products and "competitive advantage." They must be trained to lead the conversation in certain directions. The menu screens available will help to profile the customer against available products and services. The rep can suggest the correct additional product or service through using the right questions at the right time.

Customer service reps must be trained in responsiveness. If your company culture says they should not sell, you will have to change your culture. Professionals in this field often need training in sales techniques: initiating the right questions, asking for the sale, following up. You will need a high-powered planning staff to design the training and support the effort.

At first, you may want to use an external telemarketing company to provide your customer service staff. A good service bureau can get you started immediately with experienced telemarketing staff. The costs of outside start-up are usually much lower. And the outside staff can handle the staffing problems of evenings and weekends which are typical of 800 number respondents.

Customer service reps receive their compensation not only in the number of customers that they handle, but also in the number of sales that they can make. They have the entire product line with quantities and prices available on pull-down screens. If the product is insurance, they will be prompted for about twenty questions that they should ask to qualify the customer for the product, as well as information they should provide to whet the customer's appetite for the upcoming appointment with the salesperson. The selling script is contained on each screen, so the rep does not need to look elsewhere to figure out the right question to ask or answer to provide.

Besides training your customer service reps, you will want to train a hundred or more other people in the company on their roles in customer service. You want them to know how they should react when they get a call: what they can say, how important the function is and *what to do with the caller when they have finished providing the information.* They must learn not to drop the ball. Keep it in play, and pass the ball back to customer service for the score. Customer service is everybody's job. You may also want to be sure that whatever your technical people discuss with the customer is entered into the customer record. Either they can do it themselves, through their direct access to the database, or they may call the customer service rep to do it. Either way, the database should have that information.

COSTING OUT CUSTOMER SERVICE

How can you decide whether you should expand your customer service? By determining if it will increase lifetime value. In some cases, the expansion cannot be justified because it will cost more than the increased revenue that it will bring in. In the following example, a business-to-business one, the Harris Equipment Company is providing high-tech equipment sales to industrial customers. They have about 5,000 customers at present. They do not have an 800 number. Customers who have problems call the company's catalog number or—for the largest customers—call their salesman. The marketing department proposed that they add an 800 number staffed with personnel trained in Harris's products.

Marketing estimates that an external telemarketing staff of five persons will be required.

Their annual expenses are estimated at:

Salaries	$250,000
Telephone Costs	$ 80,000
Training	$ 20,000
Database Costs	$ 50,000
Total	$400,000

The long term benefits of having such a staff are estimated as follows:

- Increasing the retention rate from 60 percent to 70 percent and higher.
- Generating 6 percent referred customers per year.
- Increasing the spending rate from $4,000 to $4,200 and higher.

Putting these numbers together, marketing came up with the following charts. They show that in the initial year, the benefits are less than the costs. By Year3, however, the expanded customer service should be resulting in more than $2 million in increased incremental profits.

Harris Equipment Company before Customer Service Expansion

Revenue	Year1	Year2	Year3
R1 Customers	5,000	3,000	1,800
R2 Retention Rate	60.00%	60.00%	60.00%
R3 Spending Rate	$4,000	$4,000	$4,000
R4 Total Revenue	$20,000,000	$12,000,000	$7,200,000
Variable Costs			
C1 Percent	70.00%	70.00%	70.00%
C2 Total Variable Costs	$14,000,000	$8,400,000	$5,040,000
Incremental Profits			
P1 Gross Profit	$6,000,000	$3,600,000	$2,160,000
P2 Discount Rate	1.00	1.16	1.35
P3 NPV Profit	$6,000,000	$3,103,448	$1,600,000
P4 Cumulative NPV Profit	$6,000,000	$9,103,448	$10,703,448
L1 **Customer Lifetime Value**	$1,200.00	$1,820.69	$2,140.69

This was the base lifetime value. Here is the result of expanded customer service:

Harris Equipment Company with Expanded Customer Service

Revenue	Year1	Year2	Year3
R1 Referral Rate	6.00%	6.00%	6.00%
R2 Referred Customers	0	300	228
R3 Customers	5,000	3,800	3,078
R4 Retention Rate	70.00%	75.00%	80.00%
R5 Spending Rate	$4,200	$4,400	$4,600
R6 Total Revenue	$21,000,000	$16,720,000	$14,158,800

Variable Costs			
C1 Percent	70.00%	70.00%	70.00%
C2 Direct Costs	$14,700,000	$11,704,000	$9,911,160
C3 Customer Service @ $80	$400,000	$304,000	$246,240
C4 Total Variable Costs	$15,100,000	$12,008,000	$10,157,400

Incremental Profits			
P1 Gross Profit	$5,900,000	$4,712,000	$4,001,400
P2 Discount Rate	1.00	1.16	1.35
P3 NPV Profit	$5,900,000	$4,062,069	$2,964,000
P4 Cumulative NPV Profit	$5,900,000	$9,962,069	$12,926,069
L1 **Customer Lifetime Value**	$1,180.00	$1,992.41	$2,585.21

If Harris has 5,000 customers, here are the gains from the customer service expansion:

Gains Through Expanded Customer Service

Lifetime Value	Year1	Year2	Year3
Before Expansion	$1,200.00	$1,820.69	$2,140.69
After Expansion	$1,180.00	$1,992.41	$2,585.21
Difference	($20.00)	$171.72	$444.52
Times 5,000 Customers	($100,000)	$858,600	$2,222,600

As you can see, in the first year, the lifetime value went down. The costs of the customer service outweigh the short term benefits. Looking at the picture over three years, however, there are substantial rewards. The benefits of a long term program like customer service can seldom show short term gains.

Will the improved customer service produce these projected gains? Only experience will tell. The important thing is that the company is quite clear at the outset what gains are expected. The gains are specified and measurable. That being the case, both marketing and customer service will be developing programs designed to make these things happen. It will be possible to see as early as Year2 whether they are going to be achieved or exceeded (are programs generating referrals at the 6 percent rate? Is the spending rate going up? etc.)

SUMMARY

All calls and contacts with a customer should be logged into a marketing database. These calls and contacts should be instantly recoverable when the customer calls again so that your rep can knowledgeably discuss the customer's purchasing history and life. The database should permit your rep to continue an uninterrupted dialog with your customers whenever they call and talk with a complete knowledge of the past, *even though the last company rep who spoke with this customer was someone else.*

- There is plenty of inexpensive disk space available on which to store all this customer information. The disk space is much cheaper than the value of the information to you.

- The way to determine whether information should be retained is to ask, "How can we use this information to increase lifetime value? Will lifetime value go up?"

- Everyone in the company will have to play a role in customer service, once the database is set up.

- Customer service reps have to be:

  — cheerful, helpful, interested

  — intelligent and knowledgeable

  — linked to technical resources

  — delegated real authority

  — motivated to sell

  — willing to fish for and record information

- Training of customer service reps is important to successful database marketing.

- Plans for expansion of customer service should be tested in advance by building a set of lifetime value tables. Expand the service only if the tables show that it will be profitable. Don't do it because it is a "nice idea."

Part IV:

Reaching Out to Prospects

Chapter 12

Profiling and Modeling

Our database contains purchase information and survey data from our current customers. Their responses and purchase histories will help us to select our best and our worst, and to develop programs to keep the best happy and buying.

But companies do not live and grow by current customers alone. New customers are needed to grow, and to balance the inevitable attrition. What kind of new customers do we want? The answer must be: ones similar to our most profitable customers. That is the challenge discussed in the next chapters: how to find people who resemble in their purchasing habits the best customers that already exist on the file.

At this point, all we really know about these best customers is their purchasing history. They buy often and in large amounts, and they have purchased from us recently. But if we go to any external source of possible customers, whether it be a rented list, convention attendees, responders to an advertisement, or people who walk into our store and apply for a credit card, we may not be able to get information about them which would classify them for us in this useful way. Are there ways, in advance, in which we can select people who will have purchasing behaviors which meet our expectations?

Perhaps. There are now a score of well-explored methods for finding new customers, none of which is foolproof, but some of which offer an improved chance of finding the type of people that we want. All of them are expensive. Some will cost more than they are worth. But in some cases they will be exactly what we need, and will pay us rich dividends.

Profiling, which we are going to explore now, works under a single premise: the desirable behavior of our best customers can be traced back to some combination of measurable qualities in their lives or lifestyles. Other people who share these lifestyles will exhibit similar behavior.

On the surface, this seems a weak premise. You and your next door neighbor may have identical homes, identical jobs, incomes, and families, but you are as different as night and day. He likes sports, drinks heavily, and dresses badly. His children are a wild bunch. You read books (thank goodness for that), have well behaved children, like classical music and dinner theater. You buy excellent clothes and keep them neat and clean. Your purchasing habits are probably very different from those of your neighbor. Yet, compared to people in other subdivisions in other parts of town, the two of you look very much alike. Neither of you resemble the family on welfare only three blocks away, nor the owner of the water works who owns half the town. You are different from the farmers who bring produce to the market every morning, and the science teacher in the high school who is saving up to buy a cross-country skiing outfit.

Here are some similarities: you and your neighbor have identical mortgages. You have to buy outfits for two school children. You have the same doctor and dentist bills. You get three weeks vacation a year which you spend somewhere else. You have lawns to mow, cars and heat pumps that break down, and two college educations to save up for.

So for some vendors selling certain products, you and your neighbor may exhibit similar behavior. Our job, with our database, is to find those qualities which work *for our situation* and use them to select future customers.

The method we will use is to add to (or append to) our customer file as many known qualities about these customers as we can discover. We will use computers to help us know whether these qualities serve to separate our good customers from our poor customers. When we find some group of qualities that seem to work for us, we apply them to some group of unknown new prospects to see if these prospects are worth pursuing. The qualities we are seeking are those which:

1. Can be found out and recorded about our customers.
2. Serve as a significant discriminating factor between good customers and poor customers.
3. Can be found out and recorded about prospects who are otherwise unknown to us.
4. Help us to pick the good prospects from the poor ones.

Figure 12-1 Preparing a Customer Database

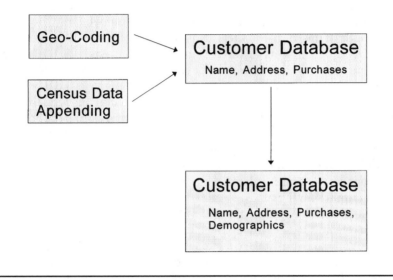

There are many sources of such new information. In this chapter we are going to explore only one of them—demographics. Subsequent chapters will cover other enhancements, such as clustering, and lifestyle information.

DEMOGRAPHICS

The technique of using demographics is built and based on the U.S. Census. In the latest version of this massive exercise undertaken every ten years, the government has broken the country into 7.5 million or more blocks for which it obtains and supplies data. A block has a small number of families, such as twelve or fourteen. In most cases all of the dwellings in a block contain households which are similar in terms of income, home value, age of head of household, presence of children, educational level, ethnic background, occupation of head of household and so on. This is not, of course, universally true. Of necessity some blocks are very heterogeneous in makeup. But, across the country, the vast percentage of blocks are made up of similar households.

A certain percentage of the households in each block are asked to fill out the "long form" in the census. This long form asks more than a hundred questions about the background and lifestyle of the household members. When the forms are tabulated, the census staff determines the set of lifestyle factors which are dominant in the block. So, for each block, the census assigns to all fourteen families the same average income, home value and such. This is mere chance, of course. By chance, the census may select the richest family on the block or the poorest to represent the entire block. As a result, some block data may be quite unrepresentative. But overall, with 7.5 million blocks surveyed, the chances are that the data on most blocks is fairly representative of most families on the block.

As part of the census, the computer has been supplied with all of the streets and house numbers included in each block. These are preserved on magnetic tape. So a mailer with a tape of customers or prospects can match their addresses with the census files to determine the "geocode" of each household, the geocode being nothing other than the census number of the relevant block.

To assign demographics to a household, therefore, a mailer runs a tape of prospects against a census tape and geocodes it. Then he or she transfers (appends) to each household from census data the income, home value, and other attributes of the block to which that household belongs.

Qualifications

This method is fraught with error. In the first place, the dominant household income in the block—even if it is representative—may not be the household income of the particular household we are studying at all. But, statistically speaking, it is as close to the real truth as we are likely to get.

The second qualification is that census figures will become more and more out of date as the years go by. How do we adjust for the changes that will take place each year?

There are several commercial firms that do projections. They use national, state, and county aggregate data on income changes to adjust block income levels by appropriate percentages. They use information on housing starts at the county level to apply back to home construction in particular blocks. They use information which may have come to them about ethnic shifts in neighborhoods to adjust the ethnic percentages in blocks. They apply home value increases in particular areas to recompute home values in each block. This attempt by individual companies to do this job accurately in a nation of 250 million people broken down into 7.5 million blocks will obviously yield only approximately correct results. In some blocks, the resulting numbers will be just plain wrong. No private company has the resources to research every intersection in America every year to see what has been happening so that they can update their statistics. Take all this information with a grain of salt.

DEMOGRAPHIC INFORMATION AVAILABLE

The type of information we can determine from demographic overlays is staggering:

Household and family income

Source of income

Per capita income

Poverty level percentage

Percent households with children

Marital status of heads of households

Median age

White-black percentages

Home value

Percent professional, technical, managerial, clerical

Percent sales, craftsmen, operatives, blue collar, service

Percent farmers, laborers

Schooling of adults

Persons per household

Type of housing unit; number of rooms

Length of residence

Age of construction of units

Energy source for heating, cooking

Number of bedrooms, bathrooms, telephones, air conditioning

Public water supply, sewer

Rental versus home ownership

Date moved in to residence

Rental value

Percent married, widowed, divorced

Motor vehicle ownership

Ethnic makeup

Principal type of employment

Male and female employment

Mortgage information

College and school attendance

Social Security and welfare recipients

Ancestry

Travel time to work

Military service

Language spoken

Urbanization

The headings presented here represent only an introduction to the information available. Under ancestry, for example, there are twenty-one different pieces of data, from Dutch to Ukrainian.

How do you get this information applied to your database? The simplest method is to make a tape of your names and addresses and send it to one of the hundreds of firms which will add updated demographic information to clients' tapes. For a fee, which is probably about $30 per thousand names, or three cents per name, they will add (append) as much (or all) of the above information to every name in your file for which you have a correct street address. We must make space in our database for this additional information, and it will become a part of our marketing program for the foreseeable future. We have vastly expanded our data base and its possible uses.

A few cautions are in order. New streets are being created every day. Many of your customers may live on new streets which have not yet found their way into the commercial compiler's list of geocodable streets. In other cases, the address may be useless for geocoding. Route 1, Box 378, will deliver a letter fine, but may not be sufficient for determining the block. In some cases, the geocoder cannot match more than 60 percent of the households on your list with a valid geocode.

What do you do when you cannot geocode a particular address? The answer is that you use the zip code to assign to the household the demographic information at the zip code level. There are 7.5 million blocks, but only 36,000 zip codes. Clearly information at the block level is much more pinpointed and accurate than zip code level data. Paradoxically for this valid reasoning, some studies show that demographic analysis performed at the zip code level works just about as well in predicting behavior as block group level data. Zip code analysis is much cheaper since it is quicker and easier to do. In some cases you can save money and not sacrifice accuracy by doing your demographic appending at the zip code level. Experiment and see what works best for your company.

The other caution has been already mentioned: what is true of the block may or may not be true of your customer's household. Don't get into the habit of thinking that appended demographic information is true data. It is *approximate* data.

Is Appended Data Correct?

Before you invest a lot of money with a vendor doing enhancement, do a small test to convince yourself that the vendor's methods and his data are correct. Take a file of a few thousand names where you already know the actual age and income. Mix this file with other names, and ask the vendor to enhance the file with age and income. Check the results. You will probably find a soberingly high percentage of error. Glenn Hausfater of Precision Marketing Corp., Northbrook, Illinois, did just that with two vendors. He found that each of them appended totally incorrect information to his test names about half the time.

True Age Versus Appended Age

	Names Classified as "Under 25"		Names Classified as "Over 25"	
True Age	*Vendor 1*	*Vendor 2*	*Vendor 1*	*Vendor 2*
Under 25	12.5%	6.4%	3.6%	3.9%
25-34	6.3	26.9	13.4	14.2
35-44	18.8	20.5	12.9	11.9
45-54	12.5	10.3	11.1	10.6
55-64	6.3	10.9	13.4	14.3
65+	43.8	25.0	45.7	45.0
Total	100.0	100.0	100.0	100.0

In this test, more than 40 percent of the names overlayed as being "under 25" by Vendor 1 properly belong in the "over 65" category. For both vendors, more than half of all names tagged as "over 65" actually belong to a younger category.

Figure 12-2 Errors in Appended Data

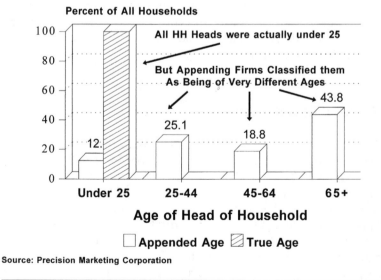

Source: Precision Marketing Corporation

In short, beware: you may be paying good money for erroneous information—and what's worse, you may be basing a multi-million dollar marketing campaign on these errors. It is easy to assume that because a vendor is a large corporation with a good reputation and a massive mainframe, you will be furnished with reliable and correct information. That is not necessarily so. You must check everything.

Tiger System

An interesting feature of the census data is the TIGER mapping system upon which the 1990 census was based. TIGER (Topographically Integrated Geographic Encoding and Referencing) is a computerized map of the entire United States that can be directly related to census data. TIGER mapping displays every street, road, railroad, and river in the country. This mapping system permits marketers to create accurate maps of their market areas. These maps can show clearly the location of all their customers. From surveys they can also learn the spending, wealth, and income of their non-customers, which can also be accurately mapped.

Determining Which Factors Relate to Behavior

The next step is a difficult one: difficult to accomplish and difficult to justify by the laws of common sense. Out of the hundreds of facts that we have appended to our customer file, we must find those few which best "explain" the differences in behavior between our customers. We have already coded our customer file using RFM analysis so we know our good customers and our poor customers. Can we use a simple factor, such as income or home value, to pick the good ones from the poor ones? Let's use a simple example as a model.

Analysis of 2000 Customers by Value of Home

Type of Customer		Value of Home			
	Total	*$200K+*	*$100-199K*	*$50-99K*	*Below $50K*
Good Customers	1000	200	600	150	50
Poor Customers	1000	50	400	300	250

This chart is typical of the disappointing results you get from demography. It is clear that people in $200K-plus houses make better customers, but common sense might have told you that. If the world were made up only of people with homes of this value, our marketing job would be a lot easier than it is. Unfortunately, we must make our sales in the world as it is, not as we would like it to be. As for the rest of the chart, home value is only a weak discriminating feature.

Figure 12-3   Customers by Home Value

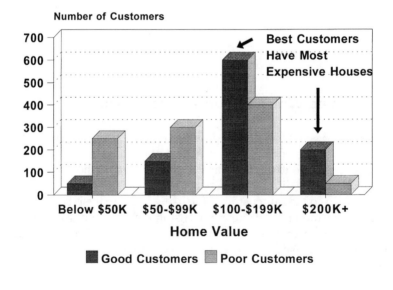

Let's try another feature: own versus rent.

Analysis of 2000 Customers by Own versus Rent

Type of Customer		Home Ownership	
	Total	*Own Home*	*Rent Home*
Good Customers	1000	700	300
Poor Customers	1000	300	700

Figure 12-4   Customers by Own vs. Rent

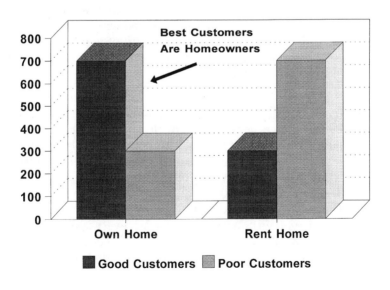

Here is what appears to be a much more powerful discriminating factor. You can run counts by each of 100 different demographic factors to try to pick the ones that work best for your product or service. To really dig down into your data, you should explore modeling.

MODELING

Many newcomers to database marketing assume that they should be doing modeling with their customer database. They are not sure what it is. They have heard that it is expensive, and that all the big boys do it. If you go to any database marketing convention, a goodly portion of the speeches are made by vendors of modeling. Yet when you ask a meeting of database marketers for a show of hands of the people who have used modeling in their work, you seldom see more than 15 percent of the hands go up. Is it the wave of the future, or what? Let's try a few definitions.

In the first place, there are two uses for modeling in a customer or prospect database. The first is predictive: to predict what a group of customers or prospects will do when presented with an offer. The second is descriptive: to understand the makeup of your customers so that you can market better to them. Lets discuss predictive modeling. There are several universal steps:

The test group. In predictive modeling, you typically begin with a small test group of customers or prospects which is representative of a much larger group. To be sure that the test group is statistically representative, you use a selection procedure called an Nth. An Nth is very easy to do on a computer. If you want a test group of 30,000, for example, out of a large group of 600,000, you begin by dividing 30,000 into 600,000. The result is 20. There are twenty 30,000s in 600,000. To create your test group, you write a program to select every 20th record from the 600,000. The resulting file of 30,000 people will be an exact statistical replica of the 600,000. It will have the same proportion of income, age, zip codes, etc.

In addition to creating the test group, you should also create a control group. This is a similar group of people (again selected by using an Nth) which is used to test the validity of any model you may develop. We will discuss the use of the control group below. The control group could also be 30,000 or some smaller size, such as 10,000.

The offer. The second step is to make an offer to the test group of 30,000 and the same offer to the control group. Some of them will accept the offer, and most will not. Let us say that 2 percent respond and purchase, and 98 percent do not.

The analysis. The purpose of the analysis is to determine what measurable qualities in the test group separate the responders (the purchasers) from the non-responders. If we were to find, for example, that most responders have moved into their residence within the past three months, and most non-responders have moved earlier than that, we would really be on to something. We could use that information to make an offer only to those people in the 600,000 who have recently moved, and ignore the rest. We could improve our response rate from 2 percent to some very much larger number. The profits could be tremendous.

Figure 12-5   Creating Test and Control Groups

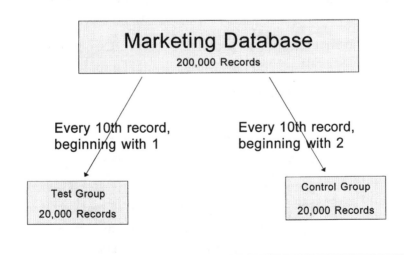

Unfortunately, it is very, very rare that you can find some simple explanation for response like that. In many cases, you can examine everything that you can learn about a group of prospects (age, income, home value, etc.) and not find a single factor that really separates the responders from the non-responders. In such a case, modeling won't do you any good. You cannot get blood out of a turnip.

How can you know whether there are measurable differences between the responders and the non-responders? One method is to use an overlay.

The overlay. Most customer and prospect files lack demographic data such as age, income, value of home, etc. As already pointed out, you can get this kind of information appended to your records by paying a small fee to an outside service bureau. You should do this with your test and control files. The cost of appending data to a file of 30,000 is quite small—less than $1,000. Be sure to get as much data appended as possible (for the test and control files) so you can be sure you haven't overlooked anything.

We should note here that you will never get data appended to every one of your records.

There are always new addresses or box numbers for which no appending is possible. We will ignore this problem for the moment. Once the data is appended, you can use your ad-hoc query facility in your marketing database software to pose a whole series of queries, for instance:

COUNT PERCENT RESPONDERS, NON-RESPONDERS
BY INCOME RANGE

This might produce a table like this:

	Percent *Responders*	*Percent* *Non-Responders*
< $20K	10.00%	10.00%
$20-$29K	15.00%	15.00%
$30 -$39K	20.00%	30.00%
$40-59K	30.00%	20.00%
$60-99K	15.00%	15.00%
$100k +	10.00%	10.00%
	100.00%	100.00%

Figure 12-6   Responders and Non-Responders by Income

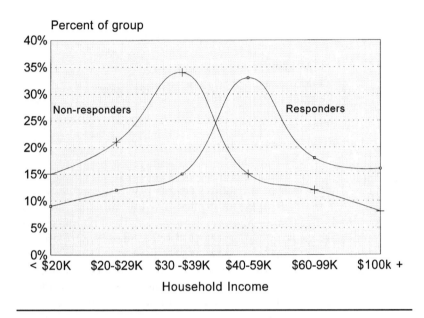

Percent of group

What this shows is that while both responders and non-respond-ers have a similar bell-curve shape when displayed by income range, the non-responders tend to be lower income people, and the respond-ers tend to be upper income people. You have a little piece of informa-tion that may be useful in distinguishing one from another based on income. You can go on to do lots of other ad-hoc queries like this one. Some may show no differences at all. Others, like this one, may show some differences. If there are enough differences, you may be justified in calling in a modeling expert.

What the modeler can show you is something that is very difficult or impossible to demonstrate with an ad-hoc query: how much each one of a number of factors can be combined to separate responders from non-responders. Her model will develop a series of weights which can be used to score your database. A weight is a number which can be multiplied by a value in your customer's record. For example, let's suppose that the modeler discovers five factors that seem to be useful in separating responders from non-responders. The output of the model will be a series of weights like this:

Factor	Weight
Presence of children	.130
Household income	.050
Value of home	.042
Age of head of household	.022
Length of residence	.012

The real weights that the model produces will not actually look like this, since they are to be multiplied by quite different numbers (incomes are in thousands, ages are in years, length of residence may be in months, etc.). For purpose of our discussion, let's suppose that these are the real weights so that we can compare them.

In this example, for your offer, presence of children in the home is a very weighty factor in separating respondents from non-respondents, whereas length of residence is much less important. What the model will permit you to do is to run a program which takes each of the relevant factors in your customer (or prospect) record, and multiply it by the appropriate weight. These weights are then added together to get an overall score. The score can be converted into percentages, so that every customer in your database can have the model score placed into his record. The score represents the likelihood of purchasing a given product (the one tested). Scores range from 99 percent (almost certain to buy) down to some low number that is well below 1 percent (almost certain not to buy).

To prove that the scores the modeler has created are accurate at predicting customer behavior, you can apply these scores to your control group, which got the same offer. If the model is accurate, the scores will accurately predict which of the people in the control group bought the product and which did not. Since you have already made the offer to the control group, and you know whether they bought, you can instantly see how correct the model is. If the model does correctly predict who bought and did not buy in the control group, you have really got a powerful tool.

Scoring the rollout universe. On the assumption that you now have scores which accurately predict behavior, you can take the following steps.

- Overlay: Pay the money to have your entire prospect universe (the 600,000 in our example) overlayed with the required demographic data. You don't need a lot of data at this point—just the data required by the model.

- Scoring: Compute the scores for all records in the prospect universe. You can then rank everyone by their score. You may divide them into ten equal parts (deciles), with the most likely to purchase being in Decile 1, and least likely to purchase in Decile 10.

- Promote the best deciles: Now that you have an accurate way of predicting response rates, you should not make the offer to your entire prospect universe. Make the offer only to those deciles that you think will be profitable. Skip the unprofitable ones.

In the following example, we have done a test mailing, used the results in a model, appended data to the full file of 600,000, scored the file, and mailed those deciles that the model predicted would be the most responsive. Two thousand prospects in each of the remaining deciles are also mailed as a test of the model to be sure that we didn't miss anything.

Model Decile	Average Model Score	Number Prospects	Number Mailed	Number Sales	Response Rate
1	85.00%	60,000	60,000	2,880	4.80%
2	72.00%	60,000	60,000	2,352	3.92%
3	54.00%	60,000	60,000	1,680	2.80%
4	44.00%	60,000	10,000	162	1.62%
5	31.00%	60,000	5,000	55	1.10%
6	27.00%	60,000	2,000	19	0.94%
7	22.00%	60,000	2,000	18	0.88%
8	16.00%	60,000	2,000	16	0.80%
9	11.00%	60,000	2,000	15	0.73%
10	8.00%	60,000	2,000	12	0.61%
Total		600,000	205,000	7,209	3.52%

Figure 12-7   Response Rate by Decile

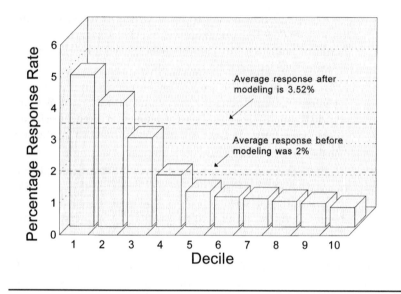

The model score represents the prediction of the model as to relative performance of each decile. 100 percent represents the best possible performance, and 0 percent represents the lowest likelihood of response. In the actual promotion, the records in the best decile—#1—had an average score of 85 percent. The promotion to this decile produced 2,880 sales, which represented a response rate of 4.8 percent.

By mailing only those deciles predicted to be the most responsive, we have reduced our mailing considerably. The result is an overall response rate that jumps from 2 percent to 3.52 percent. The result of modeling is usually referred to as the "lift". In this case, the average lift is 176. The mathematics is:

Lift = 100 x (new response rate) / (old response rate)

Lift = 100 x (3.52 / 2)

Lift = 176

The lift in the top decile is 204—a very substantial lift in terms of demographic based modeling.

The meaning of this change can be shown in the following chart:

Comparison of Promotion to Full File vs. Selected Deciles

	Full File	Model Selects
Number Mailed	600,000	205,000
Cost of Mailing ($0.68)	$408,000	$139,400
Cost of Modeling	$0	$30,000
Cost of Data Appending ($60)	$0	$12,300
Total Promotion Cost	$408,000	$181,700
Response Rate	2.00%	3.52%
Number of Sales	12,000	7,216
Profit from Sales ($28)	$336,000	$202,048
Net Profit from Promotion	($72,000)	$20,348

In this example, the mailing costs $0.68 per piece and the net profit from each successful sale is $28. If the full file were mailed and the response rate were to be the 2 percent which was received on the test, the total mailing would represent a loss of $72,000.

Instead, we have spent $30,000 for a model, and appended data to all 600,000 records (@ $60 per thousand records). Even with these additional costs, by mailing only the most responsive deciles, we have turned a $72,000 loss into a $20,348 profit.

This is the type of result you can get from successful use of a model. But modeling only works in certain limited situations, and usually produces results that are not as exciting as those shown here. Here are some basic guidelines about modeling that you should keep in mind.

- *Appending.* You will find that you cannot append data to many of your records for various reasons. The main reason is that the household cannot be located in the data file you have purchased for appending purposes.

- *Unknown Data.* Do not assume that people for whom you can't get data are just like the people you can get data on. They are probably very different. If you can't append the data, there may be an important reason which can be very powerful. Missing data may be from people with unlisted telephones, from new people who have moved to the area, from new subdivisions, etc. Some of these people may represent a very responsive and useful group for marketing purposes. So don't give up on people for whom you cannot obtain data. They may be a gold mine.

- *Multiple Use Models.* A model only describes who responded to a specific offer at a specific time. It may not be at all accurate for another offer at another time. But, if you have plunked down $30,000 for the model, you will want to use it for several offers. That may be a mistake.

  Jim Wheaton, Vice President of Neodata Services, in Boulder, Colorado, is an expert on modeling. He describes the six basic steps in predictive modeling:

- *Research Design.* Jim points out that you have to begin with a solvable problem. Most direct marketing dilemmas cannot be solved by predictive modeling. Why? Because the answer may not lie in the data at hand. For example, it could be that purchasers of your product cannot be identified by age, income, presence of children, or any standard demographic factors. Why not? Well, suppose you are selling cold remedies, or snow tires, or vacuum cleaners. It is highly possible that these demographic variables will not show a difference between purchasers and non-purchasers. If so, all the modeling in the world won't help. A general rule: if the solution does not seem to make sense to you, then it probably doesn't make sense. Modeling is not magic, it is only a quantification of intuitive logic.

  For the test data, you can use a special test, or you may use past mailing results, which were not originally designed as a test. In such cases, be sure that your past mailings were really representative of the situation you now face. If they weren't they will not be much good as a basis for your model. The time of year, the state of the economy, the group promoted, the product and price all affect the results.

  If available, sales data is preferable to response data. A net sales model is preferable to a gross sales model. If your sales are continuous, long term sales are preferable as a measure to short term response sales.

- *File Creation.* A perfect research design can be ruined by inadequate data. In data processing, it is easy to make a simple mistake that is not noticed, but badly skews the results. For example, people who show up on more than one list are called multi-buyers. They often respond better than other people. Keep this information in your prospect record so that you can use it later. Has your data appending been done correctly?

- *Understanding what you are doing.* Jim points out that:

  — A model is a simulation of reality.

  — Reality cannot be simulated if it is not understood.

  — Reality cannot be understood without human judgment.

  For example, if the distance from the buyer to the store seems not to help in explaining the incidence of purchases, then maybe something is wrong with the data. Perhaps you have calculated the distances wrong. Conclusion: Common sense tells you that people usually shop at nearby stores. If your model says otherwise, it is likely that something is wrong. Find out what it is.

- *Running the Model.* Having cleaned and properly manipulated the underlying data, running the model may be the easiest part. It may take several weeks.

- *Transferring the model to your prospecting universe.* The model is worthless if you can't use it to code your prospects. Be sure that the data available and the format of the data for the prospects is the same as the format of the test data. For example, if the model bases its conclusions on previous sales by department, but there is no such breakdown in the prospect data history, what good is the model for prediction of sales by the prospects?

- *Quality Control Procedures.* The modeling process may last over a couple of years. In most shops, a lot of things change in two years. The data that you started with may be quite different from the data you are working with today. Conclusions reached two years ago, therefore, may not apply. How to guard against this problem?

1) Profile your deciles: find out their demographic makeup. They may be quite different from one another.

2) Store the decile number in each record (they will change over time, and you want to keep track of what decile they were in during your model development.)

3) Every time you do a new mailing, profile your deciles again, scoring the decile number in the records.

4) Compare these new decile numbers to the old deciles to look for consistencies or inconsistencies.

Some of your quality control problems may come about in unexpected places. Most shops, for example, call the best decile in a model "1" and the worst decile "10". Some shops do the opposite. If you tell a service bureau to "mail to the top four deciles," be sure that they know which ones you are talking about. Quality control is needed to catch this.

- *Types of Modeling Chosen.* There are many different types of models in current use. Most common are multivariate models such as CHAID and multiple regressions. A CHAID model is a "tree" algorithm which creates homogeneous segments. For example: 1) women with children who live in single family dwelling units and like to bowl and 2) older single women with no children who live in rented units, and like to bowl with senior citizen groups. A regression tends to create heterogeneous segments which are similar only in their predicted behavior.

Figure 12-8 The Model Is Only 10% of the Job

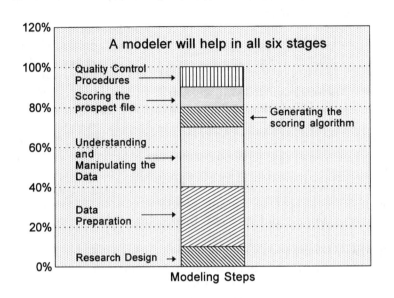

Modeling Steps

USE OF NEURAL NETWORKS IN MODELING

Since 1988, many modelers have been using a new software technique called neural networks. Several vendors, including HNC in San Diego, and Advanced Software Applications in Pittsburgh, sell a software product that can be installed on a very fast PC. Its makers claim that this software package can be used by someone, like myself, who is not a modeler, and has no training in statistics. I tried each of them for very short tests, and I got what I thought were useful results. Neural networks are really the result of linking a bunch of multiple regressions together in an iterative process. You begin by including in your test and control groups (to which you have made an offer) all of the demographic and other data that you can find, which can also be found in the larger prospect universe.

The neural network will crank away for an hour or more, determining the weights to be assigned to each of your variables. The output will be a list of useful variables and weights. If you begin with 40 variables (such as age, income, presence of children, cluster code, etc.) the neural network will tell you, after an hour, that only 6 of them (or some other number) are useful in predicting the results of your test, and each of the 6 has specified weights which can be multiplied by the values in your database records to produce a score for each person. The score represents the likelihood of the person to purchase your product if a similar offer to the test were to be made.

You then test these weights by scoring the control group also stored in your PC. If the scores accurately predict the people in your control group who actually did respond, then you are ready to apply the weights to your large prospect database. The results should be similar to the process shown above.

The reason why neural networks are becoming so popular is that they can be operated by people with only a week or so of training (as opposed to a graduate degree in statistics). You pay $30,000 for the software and a very fast PC, plus $10,000 to train your staff person, and you can do a model for every single marketing promotion which you do from now on. It is much cheaper than hiring an outside modeler. If you do a lot of marketing, your modeling cost per promotion may drop from $20,000 (with an outside source) to $2,000 (with an inside staff person and a neural network).

The alternative, as Jim Wheaton points out, is to have one of your staff trained by an outside professional to use SAS or SPSS (the two most widely used pieces of software for doing regressions). He believes that successful modelers develop a proficiency in doing detective work with their data—really analyzing the data as Sherlock Holmes would do to find out what makes prospects behave the way they do. With "data detective" intensive activity, a marketer can get just as good or better results with SPSS as he could with a neural network.

On the other hand, neural networks are not necessarily any better than the result of hiring a modeler. A lot of the success in modeling results from experience and hunch, which you cannot get from a software package. Your in-house neural network operator may not be as skillful as an outside modeler. As a result, you will save money on the input, but cost yourself big bucks in reduced output savings. What should you do?

CONCLUSION

My advice concerning predictive modeling is this:

1)   *Planning and Data Preparation.* Remember Jim Wheaton's six steps. Be sure that your plan is good and your data clean. Unless these steps are followed, your modeling activities will be wasted.

2)   *Ad-Hoc Queries.* Run a test promotion and use ad-hoc queries on the respondents and non-respondents to see whether any of the appended data which you have or can buy can help you to distinguish respondents from non-respondents. In most cases, you will find that the data is of no value at all. If so, stop there. You cannot use a model. It will be a waste of money. Why? Because the reason why most people buy most products is not a function of their demography.

3)   *Ad-Hoc Trials.* If your ad-hoc query results show that some appended data is useful in separating respondents from non-respondents, on your next promotion, use what you have learned. Separate your marketing universe into three different groups: people who your ad-hoc queries show as being very likely to buy, some who are average, and ones who are unlikely to buy. Mail to all of the first group, half of the second group, and a smaller amount of the third group. See if your hunch pays off, and you increase your profits.

4)   *Modeling Test.* If your ad-hoc trial works, you should seriously consider getting in an outside modeler for your next promotion. She may be able to increase your profits by a significant amount (after subtracting her fees).

5)   *Neural Network Test.* If you have used an outside modeler successfully on several promotions, and feel that modeling works for you, you should then consider assigning the job to a staff

person, and equipping her with neural network software. This is a major commitment, and should not be entered into lightly or unadvisedly. The staff person will have to be trained, and will have to keep at it on a regular basis. The skills grow rusty when not used. Hunch and experience pay off in this business. Too many companies buy the software, train the staff member, and find that six months later the staffer is promoted and the software goes unused thereafter.

BUSINESS-TO-BUSINESS DEMOGRAPHICS

If you have a business-to-business file, the census data will not be useful for you. The census was taken of residential households. No data was complied about the business firms in the area.

There is demographic data that you can use, however. Dun and Bradstreet, TRW, and other firms have spent years in collecting Standard Industrial Classification (SIC) codes for all of the businesses in America. These codes classify businesses by their product or service: rope wholesalers, restaurants, truck rental, steel manufacturing. In many cases, they have done surveys to find out the number of employees in the firm and its annual sales. They have quite a bit of data on executives of the firms, and on the relationships of any particular company to other companies (division, branch, holding company, etc.). You can get that data applied to any business-to-business file—just like household data—and use it in ad-hoc queries and modeling. A caution: the data is much less comprehensive than household survey data, and it is quite often wrong. Companies—particularly small companies—lie about their sales and number of employees. After all, Dun and Bradstreet is not the IRS.

USING NON-RESPONDER DATA

In most direct marketing, a 2 percent response is considered a success. That means that for 100 letters sent out, if 2 people use your coupon, telephone you, or write to you, you have a success. These are your customers. But what do you do with the names and addresses of the 98 people who did not respond? Of what value are they?

A few years ago, many direct marketers threw these names away. No more. Non-respondents are the key to improving your marketing strategy. You must find out *why* they did not respond.

Non-response can be due to an endless list of possible factors:

- bad address

- envelope looked uninteresting

- message did not strike a responsive chord

- product or service too expensive or not wanted

- wrong audience

There are ways of measuring and correcting each of these factors—check and test.

SUMMARY

- Your marketing database file can be *geocoded* to identify the census block in which it is located.

- Private companies can help you to *append* hundreds of items of demographic data to your marketing database records. This data tells you the median household income, education, home value, ethnic makeup, and other attributes of the average family in each block.

- The appended information may be correct, or it may be wrong. In any case, it is not information about *your customer*, only about his or her other *average neighbor*.

- This information is most useful in selecting prospects for new business. You must rent lists of people who have demographic profiles that match those of your best customers.

- It may be that the demography really has nothing to do with predicting behavior in your case. The decision to buy your product may result from some factor in the customer's mind or background which cannot be classified by demographic variables. But demographics have been shown to work in some cases with some types of products.

- Since it is easy to rent lists of prospects by demographic characteristics, you can go out into the market and obtain names of prospects that match the demographic characteristics that your modeling has shown to be best for you. The result should be more successful direct marketing than mere chance, and enough of a "lift" to more than pay the cost of your appending and modeling.

- Geocoding and appending demographic data may not work for your product. You will never know, however, until you experiment and test. It is clearly an area that you should look into once you have established your marketing database. If nothing else, you will learn a little more about your customers than you did before, and this is all to the good.

Chapter 13

Clustering: Short-Cut Modeling

Demographic enhancement of a marketing database and the use of these demographics in modeling is a big leap forward in developing a profile to better understand your customers. To the demographics, you can add lifestyle information, media interests, and even psychological characteristics. Once this information is coded into your customer file, the real modeling can begin. But modeling is difficult and often expensive.

For many database marketers, there is a useful short-cut called clustering. I call it a short-cut because clustering is a technique for classifying your customer file by coding it with external data in which the modeling is already done. Clustering companies have already taken the entire United States population, coded it by hundreds of demographic and lifestyle characteristics, and broken it down into sixty to seventy separate types or clusters. You can have your customer file coded to tell to which cluster each customer belongs. With the cluster comes a wealth of prepackaged information on what type of media the customer responds to, his or her product purchasing behavior and so on.

Some would argue that clustering is not appropriate for database marketing. Robert Smith, President of Focal Point, points out that once you have a customer database, you can learn much more information directly from each customer than you could possibly get from a pre-packaged clustering system. He favors individual marketing with a marketing plan developed for each customer. Myles Megdall of Advanced Information Marketing, Inc., argues that cluster analysis is done for the general case, and almost never with the problem of selling your product in mind. It is no substitute, says Myles, for the hard work of case-by-case modeling. Nevertheless, hundreds of companies have found cluster analysis a useful tool to understanding their customer database and finding clones of their best customers in the outside world. Let's examine how it works.

RESPONSE TO ADVERTISING MESSAGES

For years, direct marketers have pondered the age-old question, "Why do some people react to a message, while others do not?" Part of the answer is mere chance:

- they didn't read the paper or magazine that day;
- they were out of the room while the message was on;
- they were more interested in something else that day.

Part of the answer is psychological:

- some people are psychologically immune to ads;
- some people resent direct mail.

But part of the answer is lifestyle. Research has shown that:

- People in some neighborhoods react better to a certain ad or product than people in other neighborhoods.
- People with certain income levels are more influenced by certain types of appeals (coupons, free samples, better quality, lower prices) than people with other higher or lower incomes.
- Some people's educational level has a direct bearing on their response to certain messages.
- Some people's age bracket (new homeowners, middle age, retirement years) influences their response profile.

- Whether or not they have young children in the home can be a factor with some people.

- In fact, there are dozens of measurable factors which can be used reliably to predict response to advertising messages.

CAN THE RESPONSE BE IMPROVED?

It has long been known that the "country club set" responds differently to certain advertising than blue collar workers or urban ghetto dwellers. These classifications of people are called social groupings or lifestyle descriptors. For many years, using US Census data, subscription lists, catalog response information, and hundreds of other factors, market researchers have been able to identify at least sixty distinct lifestyle clusters which can be used to predict response to advertising.

The central concept in clustering is that "birds of a feather flock together." The country club set lives together in a subdivision out near the country club; blue collar workers live in a moderately priced subdivision on the south side of town.

The US Census has divided the whole population into 7.5 million blocks: areas containing an average of about 14 households. Several commercial statistical analysis firms have classified each of these 7.5 million blocks into one of 60 different lifestyle clusters, each of which has common identifiable characteristics.

CLUSTERING

There are several companies which do a good job of clustering, among them Claritas (whose product is PRIZM), Strategic Mapping (ClusterPlus), Equifax (MicroVision) and CACI (Acorn). The clusters listed in this section are taken from Claritas. The others have very similar systems. Claritas breaks all the millions of blocks listed in the census into 62 cluster groups. These, in turn, are grouped into 12 social groups. The social groups are further classified as (U) Urban, (S) Suburban, (T) Town or (R) Rural.

Claritas Clusters

Cluster	Cluster Name	US Households
1	Blue Blood Estates	757,127
2	Winner's Circle	1,799,826
3	Executive Suites	1,245,372
4	Pools & Patios	1,766,901
5	Kids & Cul-de-Sacs	2,845,802
6	Urban Gold Coast	483,560
7	Money & Brains	1,033,892
8	Young Literati	1,015,481
9	American Dreams	1,356,743
10	Bohemian Mix	1,596,117
11	Second City Elite	1,608,101
12	Upward Bound	1,930,749
13	Gray Power	2,009,840
14	Country Squires	1,063,714
15	God's Country	2,608,305
16	Big Fish, Small Pond	1,911,017
17	Greenbelt Families	912,994
18	Young Influentials	1,146,856
19	New Empty Nests	1,752,973
20	Boomers & Babies	1,208,959
21	Suburban Sprawl	1,731,274
22	Blue Chip Blues	1,991,799
23	Upstarts & Seniors	1,173,601
24	New Beginnings	1,392,855
25	Mobility Blues	1,521,254
26	Gray Collars	2,013,137
27	Urban Achievers	1,518,330
28	Big City Bend	943,340
29	Old Yankee Rows	1,346,092
30	Mid-City Mix	1,203,831
31	Latino America	1,232,421

Cluster	Cluster Name	US Households
32	Middleburg Managers	1,487,183
33	Boomtown Singles	1,174,834
34	Starter Families	1,570,109
35	Sunset City Blues	1,706,722
36	Towns & Gowns	1,340,408
37	New Homesteaders	1,980,974
38	Middle America	1,213,102
39	Red, White & Blues	2,222,682
40	Military Quarters	469,692
41	Big Sky Families	1,398,408
42	New Eco-topia	949,243
43	River City, USA	1,941,863
44	Shotguns & Pickups	1,558,499
45	Single City Blues	1,677,653
46	Hispanic Mix	1,439,421
47	Inner Cities	2,056,436
48	Smalltown Downtown	1,849,277
49	Hometown Retired	1,293,401
50	Family Scramble	1,933,067
51	Southside City	1,918,166
52	Golden Ponds	1,925,383
53	Rural Industria	1,531,564
54	Norma Rae-ville	1,318,804
55	Mines & Mills	1,877,259
56	Agri-Business	1,613,272
57	Grain Belt	1,904,555
58	Blue Highways	2,161,131
59	Rustic Elders	1,832,315
60	Back Country Folks	1,772,932
61	Scrub Pine Flats	1,458,885
62	Hard Scrabble	1,894,589
	Total	96,594,092

Years of research have gone into classifying the lifestyle of each of these 62 clusters. Here are summary descriptions of two of the clusters, as examples:

Blue Blood Estates. These are America's wealthiest suburbs, populated by super-upper established executives, professionals, and heirs to "old money," accustomed to privilege. They live in luxury, supported by servants. One in ten residents is a multi-millionaire. There is a sharp drop from these heights to the next level of affluence. Ranging in age from 35-54, they are predominantly white and high Asian.

God's Country. Educated, upscale, married executives and professionals who choose to raise their many children in the far exurbs of major metros, the outskirts of second cities, and many scenic towns. Their affluence is supported by multiple incomes. Lifestyles are family and outdoor centered.

How the Cluster Indexes Work

Over the years the clusters have been run against a host of lifestyle indicators to further sharpen the image of what the people who live in them like, want, buy, prefer, dislike, vote for and so on. To represent these lifestyle preferences, statisticians use an index.

An index shows whether the cluster is more likely or less likely than the average to have the characteristic. One hundred is average, so an index of 200 shows that the cluster is twice as likely to have the characteristic as the average. An index of 50 is half as likely.

How Can Clustering Be Used to Improve Response?

The concept is simple. For direct mail, you cluster code your outgoing mail and your response. You find that certain clusters respond better than others (see Figure 13-1). The index is computed by dividing the response percentage by the mailed percentage and multiplying by 100.

Figure 13-1   Response vs. Response Index

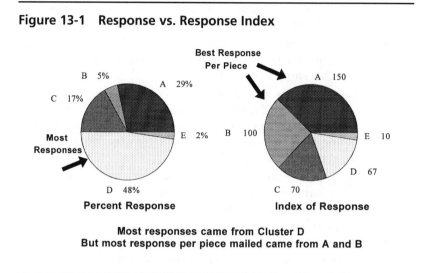

Most responses came from Cluster D
But most response per piece mailed came from A and B

Your greatest number of respondents was in cluster D, which brought you 20 percent of your buyers. But mailing to this cluster was very inefficient as compared with mailing to A or B, where the response per mailed piece was much better. Once you know which clusters respond well and which respond poorly, you can use this information to change your mailing patterns:

- Mail more often to good clusters, less often or not at all to poor clusters.

- Change your message to poor response clusters to try to get their attention.

How Can Clustering Be Used in Direct Mail?

Once the outgoing and incoming direct mail has been coded for lifestyle cluster, here is what can be done:

- For clusters that appear to respond well, try a second or third mailing to all those within the cluster that did not respond.

- To prove your analysis is correct, mail also to a control group from clusters that did not respond well.

- Seek out new prospect lists already coded for clusters responding well. Do not rent names or mail to names from clusters that show a poor response.

- Conduct focus groups from poorly responding clusters that you think should do well: for example, affluent people. Your message to these folks could be wrong. By varying and targeting your message by cluster, you may be able, at low cost, to raise your number of buyers.

- Some people just sample and don't ever buy. Could it be that these samplers-only can be identified in advance by cluster? If so, you can either stop mailing to these people, or make them a different offer.

- There are actually scores of different things that you can do to raise response at low cost once you have the information about the lifestyle cluster of your buyers, samplers, and nonresponders.

How Can Clustering Be Used to Increase Response to Print Ads?

For each identified cluster, you can examine hundreds of different variables that are true of the cluster. You learn not only about their income, age, education, house value, children, automobiles, occupation, and family employment situation; you learn what magazines they read, what type of radio and television programs they tune in to, what hours of the day they are likely to be home. How can you use this in the selection of print ads?

Suppose you have placed advertising in general circulation publications such as *TV Guide* or *Parade*. From the response to these publications, you can learn what clusters respond. But this will also tell you something else very interesting (see Figure 13-2).

This table tells you that cluster B is a sleeper—not many of them read *Parade*, but of those that do the response was phenomenal. Here are folks just waiting to be reached, but probably *Parade* is not the correct vehicle to reach them. What would be a better way?

Figure 13-2   Response to Parade Ad

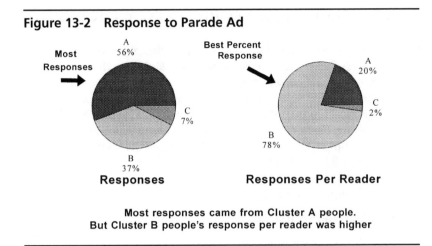

Responses   Responses Per Reader

**Most responses came from Cluster A people.
But Cluster B people's response per reader was higher**

This would suggest that you might try an ad in Publication Y targeted directly at cluster B people. Perhaps try a focus group to design the perfect ad. In any case, you may be able to reach these cluster B people less expensively in Publication Y than you can by scattering your shot in Parade.

Figure 13-3   What Does Cluster B Read?

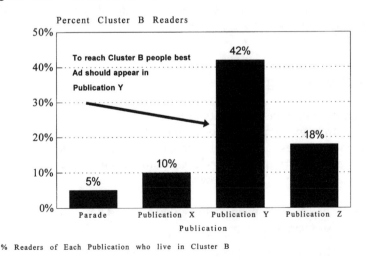

% Readers of Each Publication who live in Cluster B

How Can Clustering Help with Television Advertising?

What station, what hour of the day, what market, what message, how many viewers, how much does the ad cost? These are the factors that go into a normal TV ad selection.

Clustering allows you to add some other important factors. Based on response to TV ads thus far, we can get a good idea of what clusters are responding. From national media surveys we also know what clusters are watching those programs at those times. You know who you want to reach. This can help to:

- Design your message

- Pick your market areas

- Pick your stations

- Pick your hours

Clustering requires a leap of faith on the part of the direct marketer: the assumption that the people in Sacramento who live in a cluster called "Pools & Patios" will react the same way to your message as people in Milwaukee and New Haven who also live in clusters called "Pools & Patios." In some cases this may be true; in other cases it will not be true. The direct marketer has to experiment and test mail to be sure that things are working properly.

Target Grouping

Clustering works because sixty clusters is a much easier number to work with than 7.5 million blocks. But often even sixty are too many different variables to work with for direct marketing. For this reason, most marketers group the sixty clusters into six or eight primary groups which, after analysis, break down into:

- those six or seven clusters who respond best to your product or message;

- the next lower group of six or seven clusters;

- the next lower group, and so on.
- You will normally avoid the bottom groups and concentrate your attention on the top groups.

Each of these groups of clusters is assigned a descriptive name, such as:

- Elite Suburbs
- Urban Uptown
- Second City Society
- Landed Gentry
- The Affluentials
- All Other

Attributing Lifestyle Characteristics

Clustering companies have spent years matching their clusters against scores of national surveys and purchase data. They do this to determine true, or mostly true, statements that can be made about each cluster. As a result of this process, they can determine the likelihood of a particular person having done some of the following things:

- Bought a new imported car
- Bought classical music
- Received a passport
- Took a cruise
- Went downhill skiing
- Played tennis ten times or more in the past year
- Contributed to public TV
- Joined a country club
- Used chewing tobacco
- Owned a pickup truck
- Watched professional wrestling
- Ridden a motorcycle
- Spent $10 or more at a Tupperware® party

- Attended a rodeo

- Went bowling twenty-five times or more in the past year

In terms of media interest, they can attribute likelihood of this behavior to a person:

- Reads the business section of a newspaper

- Reads science or technology magazines

- Reads the editorial sections

- Reads the sports section

- Reads the *Smithsonian*

- Watches C-SPAN

- Reads *Hot Rod*

- Reads the *National Enquirer*

- Reads *Ebony*

- Has a satellite dish

- Watches daytime TV dramas

- Watches college basketball on TV

How Will Clustering Help in Database Marketing?

In theory, clustering is really most useful for direct marketing situations where not much is known about your customers, and you are trying to make sense out of direct response data. But companies properly using marketing databases probably know a great deal more about their customers than they can ever learn from clustering. While doing business, you can ask questions directly and get direct answers that you could only infer indirectly from cluster data. Thus, you may find that clustering is not worth the extra expense in your marketing database.

Where clustering will help you is in prospecting. If you are trying to rent a list of prospects, or to advertise in a magazine, radio, or television station to reach new prospects, clustering can be a great help in making the correct choices. By coding your existing customer database with cluster codes and comparing these codes with the results of your RFM analysis, you can learn in which clusters your best customers live and therefore in which clusters new prospects are likely to live. Armed with this information, you can rent lists loaded with people living in the correct clusters, or advertise in media which people in these clusters read, watch, or listen to. You should markedly improve your response over less sophisticated media selection methods.

As an example of how cluster coding can distinguish the purchasing habits of different social groups, consider the following chart of imported beer drinkers prepared by Claritas and Mediamark Research. It shows the clusters who are most likely to buy imported beer. If you use Neilson data to determine the media habits of each cluster (which can easily be done), you can target your advertising to the correct cluster by careful media buying. If direct mail were appropriate (which is unlikely for a commodity such as beer) you could target your direct mail to the correct cluster, and save yourself a bundle.

Clustering will be more useful for some products than for others. If you have a database of asthmatics, or cat owners, or music lovers, or gamblers, you will find that they don't seem to live in any recognized cluster. Clustering is seldom useful for business-to-business marketing, since the clusters are based on residential households. One company, which was marketing ethical products through pediatricians to the general public, tried to use clustering to categorize the practice base of the physicians in their database. The results were gibberish, since the patients of physicians seldom live within walking distance of their doctors. The cluster code of the block group or zip code of the doctor, therefore, reveals little about the cluster code of the patients. All that glitters is not gold.

Financial Clustering

For businesses in financial services, such as banks, insurance companies, and stockbrokers, clustering has taken one step beyond the simple sixty groups, into lifecycle clusters that include the age of the head of the household in the equation. It makes for a much more interesting targeted segmentation which often works very well for these indus-

Figure 13-4 Imported Beer Drinkers by Cluster

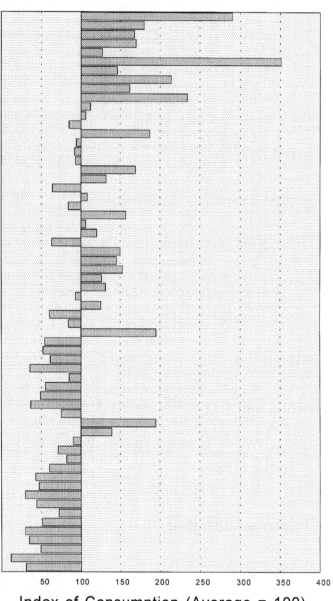

Index of Consumption (Average = 100)

tries. Lifecycle clustering is based on annual surveys done by SRI, Equifax, Accountline, and other companies. SRI, for example, has a national mail panel study of more than 3,000 households representing consumers of all demographic and financial product use categories. The selected families are paid $10 for their completion of the survey. A 70 percent response is achieved in most cases.

The questionnaire is extremely detailed, including such questions as "What was your family income last year? Consult your Federal Income Tax Form in answering this question."

"Think of all the securities your household bought in the last year. What was the approximate amount of securities you purchased from each type of firm?" "How often does your household borrow on margin?" The responses are tracked by cluster *and by age of head of household*. This is because, for financial services, age is one of the most important predictors of purchase behavior. MicroVision, from Equifax Marketing Decision Systems, a leading target marketing and marketing information company in Encinitas, California, divides the households in the country into ten financial groups with details of their predicted financial behavior based on the SRI survey. To illustrate what these groups are designed to predict, descriptions of two of them follow.

Well-Heeled Achievers. This group represents those households at the peak of the financial world. They have the highest incomes and the highest net worth of any financial group. Typically families with heads of households between 40 and 55, the households are heavy users of financial products and services, but also hold high balances. They are five times as likely as the average household to have an asset management account with average balances of $150,000 (they make up 38 percent of all balances).

They are six times as likely to participate in a limited partnership with average values over $70,000 (37 percent of all balances).

They are the lowest users of renter's insurance of all the financial groups.

They are twice as likely as the average household to own investment or vacation real estate with an average value of over $560,000.

Well-Heeled Achievers represent over 3.3 million households and are projected to grow by 55 percent over the next ten years (four times the U.S. growth rate).

Bank Traditionalists. This group is made up mostly of upper middle class families. These are generally larger than average families, with very young or school age children. Mostly homeowners, the heads of household are above average in education and income, and often employed in white collar occupations. The group has the potential for growth, but not all of the households will move into the upper financial groups.

They are less likely than average to participate in a mutual fund.

They are one and a half times as likely as the average household to have a first mortgage with an average balance of $35,000 (22 percent of all balances).

The most likely of all groups to have a retail loan (15 percent of all balances).

They are likely to have life insurance (23 percent of all premiums for universal life).

Bank traditionalists represent almost 12 million households and are projected to grow 32 percent (2.5 times the US rate) over the next ten years.

Using this lifecycle technique, which combines age with demographics and lifestyle, Equifax Marketing Decision Systems, Claritas (using a product they call P$YCLE) and others are able to make what they believe to be far better predictions of purchase behavior for financial services than clusters alone can provide. This information can be coded to a mainframe file and stored in your marketing database, or it can be provided in a PC format on a stand-alone system with mapping capabilities.

KEEPING HOSPITAL BEDS FULL

An interesting example of the practical use of clustering with a marketing database was provided by Anthony Agresta while he was at INFORUM, a healthcare target marketing company based in Nashville, Tennessee. One of INFORUM's targeting techniques is to use patient databases to analyze payor mix. Many hospitals have too many empty beds, and not enough patients with adequate medical insurance. The technique is to set up a database of all past patients, and geocode and cluster code them using their home addresses. The database records show the type of hospital stay, the method of payment, and the amount of revenue. Analysis clearly shows which patients were profitable and which were not. By studying the cluster codes of the profitable and unprofitable patients, the hospital can get a pretty good idea of which neighborhoods within the hospital's service area are providing its principal revenue-producing customers. Once this is known, the hospital can mount an aggressive campaign of direct mail to those profitable areas. Further use of the media preference data linked to the cluster codes can tell the hospital which print media is read by residents of preferred areas. This helps target the advertising to the correct audience.

Figure 13-5   Health Insurance Coverage

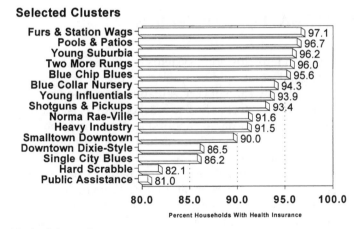

Selected Clusters

A hospital in Dayton, Ohio, had 2,277 inpatients admitted for Major Diagnostic Category 01. They stayed a total of 16,975 days, spending $12,984,477, or $765 per day. But who pays for these days? While 92.2 percent of all households carry health insurance, the percentage insured varies considerably by cluster as shown by INFORUM's Pulse annual survey of 100,000 households nationwide. One of the clusters with the highest percentage of health insurance is Furs and Station Wagons at 97.1 percent. One of the lowest is Public Assistance with only 81 percent insured.

Clearly, Dayton hospitals seeking to improve their bottom line can and do concentrate on attracting patients from heavily insured segments. How is that done? One way is direct mail and advertising. Another is to reach out to physicians, who are usually the ones to designate the hospital where patients will stay. The INFORUM software can locate physician's offices on computer maps, and can calculate which physicians serve patients who are likely to be insured. A direct approach to these physicians can be very fruitful.

CREDIT BASED CLUSTERING

All of the standard clustering systems are based on US Census data. There are good points and bad points to this. It is good, in that the census provides a wealth of very valuable information about the average household in a block. The bad side, of course, is that the average income—and all other data—reported by the census for a block may have nothing at all to do with the actual income or other data of any particular individual in that block.

Trans Union, a national consumer credit information service, headquartered in Chicago, offers an alternative. From their credit reporting system, they have actual age and financial information on about 160 million individuals. Unlike census data which is collected once every ten years, Trans Union credit data is updated every seven days. From the credit data they know how much each of these individuals has borrowed or purchased. They know the amount of available credit, the age and type of account, the amount of credit used. Trans Union has developed an income estimation system called TIE. Trans Union uses TIE to examine the behavioral characteristics which have proved to be predictive in establishing individual income. Using TIE plus age plus 25 other credit characteristics, Trans Union has developed a clustering system called SOLO which classifies people not by where they live (as census related clustering does) but by how they live: what they borrow and spend. SOLO clusters group consumers with similar lifestyles, spending, and payment behaviors.

For particular marketing situations, this type of data about individuals usually proves to be more accurate in predicting response than census data. In one case involving a credit card mailing which was coded by the 40 SOLO clusters, the 25 best clusters represented 60 percent of the mailing, but accounted for 80 percent of the response.

The SOLO clusters are used to group the 160 million individuals on which data is available into nine social groups:

A   Empty Nesters—High income 6 year or more homeowners

B   American Cross-Section—Middle class older home owners

C   Industrial Blue Collar—homeowners with lower incomes

D   Metro Beginners—Younger lower income renters

E   Metropolitan Upscale—Young, high income professionals

F   Young and Rural—Young mobile low income families

G   Suburban Starters—Lots of children, modest homes

H   Mobile Families—Young, mobile, lower income, education

I   Urban Blend—Lower education, income, multi-family homes

The following table shows how SOLO can be used to score a mailing, and predict response.

Figure 13-6 Response by Solo Cluster

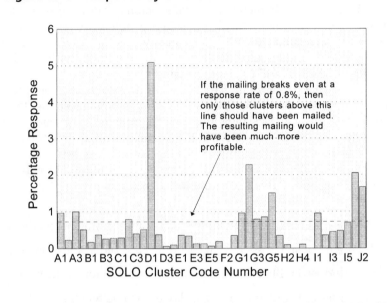

SUMMARY

- Clustering is a way of categorizing the 7.5 million blocks in America into 62 useful types of households based on common neighborhood characteristics such as housing type, demographic similarities, and socioeconomic characteristics which can, in certain cases, make it easier to understand the response to direct marketing efforts.

- Clustering can help you find new prospects by looking for people who live in clusters similar to those in which your best customers live.

- Clustering will not be cost effective in all cases with all products. You should test clustering on a small scale before putting major resources into it.

- For financial services, age of head of household is a very powerful predictor of purchasing behavior. Several companies, such as EMDS, have combined annual financial services questionnaires, such as those prepared by SRI International, with clustering and age to create a very useful and accurate tool for use by database marketers.

- Credit based clustering, such as SOLO from Trans Union, may prove to be even more predictive than census based data for certain products and services.

Chapter 14

Understanding Your Prospects' Lifestyles

You have built a customer marketing database. You have a great many names, and their purchase histories. You have geocoded it so you know where they live, and you know the demographics and lifestyle of their block group. But what are they really like? What motivates them? What do they want? How can you use knowledge about your customers to improve your marketing to non-customers?

SURVEY QUESTIONS

The best single method of getting information is to survey your customers. This is what two-way communication is all about. You use every opportunity to converse with them to ask them a few more questions and tabulate a few more answers. People like to answer questions, particularly if they think that someone is listening to what they are saying.

I have been a member of a Public Radio station for more than ten years. I donate about $200 per year. The station calls me twice a year to participate in a "challenge grant." They announce on one evening during their fund-raising week that Arthur Hughes has agreed to contribute an extra $100 if the number of calls between 9:00 P.M. and 10:00 P.M. exceeds 50, or the dollars pledged in the period exceeds $1000 or some such gimmick. It is flattering to be called, and I always agree. I suppose that the audience always meets the challenge, since they always want my $100. I am sure that they tuck this information about my participation away in some database ready for the next drive, since they always call me again. This is excellent loyalty marketing.

But they have never asked me any questions. They know nothing about me, and have no idea why I listen to the station, what I want to hear, or why I agree to the challenge grant. They have someone call me twice a year and spend time with me on the telephone, but they ask for, and receive, absolutely no information from me at all except my credit card number. They just want the money.

I used to listen to, and contribute to, another Public Radio station in Washington. But this one began to play bluegrass music for more than half of every day, and consumed much of the rest of their programming time with ultra left-wing talk shows. I found little that interested me, and I stopped contributing. They don't know why, and they never asked.

Both stations have missed an opportunity to understand more about their audience, and to use this information in designing their product and sharpening their fund-raising message. This missed opportunity can mean missing out on several million dollars of contributions which they might otherwise get.

Surveys are often easy to organize, if you have set up a database and have some mechanism for a two-way dialog built in, as these stations do. The limiting factor is the creativity of the marketing staff. You have to figure out *what questions to ask* and *what to do with the answers.* One of the biggest problems with survey data is being able to understand, quantify, and apply the results to your particular marketing situation. Some companies are stuck with scores of facts in a database without a useful technique for turning the data into sales. Because this type of research is difficult, many companies are trying shortcuts to understanding their customers, such as using general surveys done by others.

REGISTRATION CARDS

For many years, National Demographics and Lifestyles (NDL) of Denver, Colorado, has been compiling customer information from registration cards packed into more than 100 different consumer products. The makers of these products use a post card, designed by NDL, which asks about the product, its purchase and use, but also asks standard NDL demographics and family lifestyle questions. They have compiled a base of about 20 million respondents, many of whom have bought more than one product and therefore have sent in more than one card. NDL can draw useful conclusions from the resulting consumer file which is available to marketers seeking data about prospects for their products.

To use NDL data, you can have your customer house file overlaid with NDL data. As a result, you can find out whether your customers are more or less likely than the national average to have certain interests or hobbies. Using this data, you can break your customer base into broad categories, such as Athletic, Blue Chip, Cultural, etc. In some cases, this breakdown will help you to predict response to a prospect mailing. For example, if your customers are more likely than the national average (according to NDL data) to be interested in Fitness or Athletics, then you can score your prospects before you mail to them by NDL codes, and mail only to Fitness and Athletics types. You should show a significantly greater profit than you would get by mailing to your entire prospect universe.

For many products and services, NDL data will not provide a "lift" sufficient to overcome the cost of appending the NDL information. It is certainly worth a test, however, to see whether your product is one for which NDL is a profitable route to success.

NICHE MARKETING

Mediamark Research, Inc., is one of the leaders in using segmentation to break down a market into meaningful groups for product targeting. They published a small booklet called *Niche Marketing* which provides an excellent introduction to this technique. The idea is that by seeking out specialized market niches, a marketer can find an area where the competition is less intense and where it is easier to acquire dominance. You identify a narrow and specialized group of consumers with particular needs or desires. You find out just the product or service that appeals to them. You design a product or service for that market alone. Then you find a way to target that segment and tell them about what you have for them. Mediamark has developed a database of 20,000 consumers who are representative of the U.S. market, which they survey extensively once a year. A personal interview is conducted with each respondent in which demographic information and data about exposure to print, radio, broadcast television, and cable media are collected. Data about the use of products, services, and brands are collected in a self-administered questionnaire which the interviewer leaves with the respondent and returns to pick up at a later date. Approximately 450 product categories, 1,900 product types, and 5,700 individual brands are studied and reported. What they have been able to accomplish with their system can be very useful to marketers. For example, in looking at what female housekeepers buy, they have broken this market down into Working Moms, Full-Time Workers, Part-Time Workers, and Not Employed. When you index items like toaster products, Working Moms buy far more than the others.

Figure 14-1   Convenience Foods—Who Buys the Most?

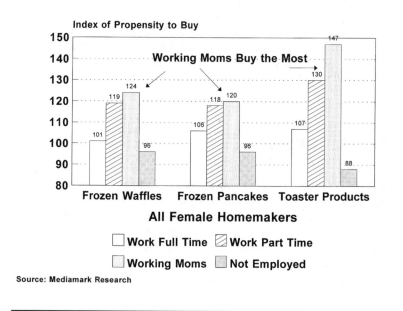

Source: Mediamark Research

As an example of creative segmentation, they did a detailed study of the affluent, defined as the 10 percent of the population with the highest income. Their studies showed that this group can be broken down into five lifestyle segments:

1. **Well-Feathered Nests:** households with at least one high-income earner and children present.

2. **No Strings Attached:** at least one high-income earner and no children.

3. **Nanny's in Charge:** two or more income earners, none high-income, and children present.

4. **Two Careers:** two or more income earners, none high-income, no children.

5. **The Good Life:** high affluence with no one employed, or head of household unemployed.

They back up this segmentation by showing that the spending habits of each of the five groups is very different. Mediamark publishes *Upper Deck Report*, which offers data on purchases by these affluent segments of over 400 categories of consumer products. As they point out, "a good imagination is critical to creating a marketing breakthrough, but only in conjunction with reliable market data. Find out what's really going on in the marketplace and be prepared. Your hunches may be off-base—or brilliant."

Regional Differences

Despite the McDonaldization of America, there are still significant regional differences which you will have to take into account in your marketing, and which, of course, can represent profitable niches for your company if you can recognize them and exploit them. Consider the different sales of salad dressings in the four regions of the U.S. as researched by Mediamark.

Figure 14-2   Regional Preferences in Salad Dressings

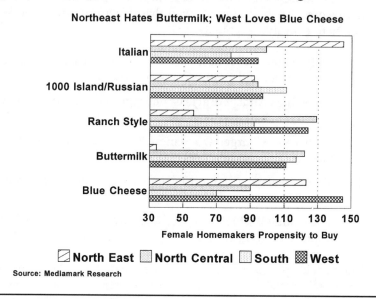

Northeast Hates Buttermilk; West Loves Blue Cheese

Female Homemakers Propensity to Buy

North East North Central South West

Source: Mediamark Research

To take advantage of these differences, you can vary your promotional efforts and product offerings by region. Some food manufacturers, for example, have increased the spiciness of their products in some areas of the country and toned it down in others. To do this, however, you have to know what you are doing. You can get some clues from surveys such as those of Mediamark.

Heavy versus Light Users

It is not enough to know who buys a certain product. Everyone buys soap and electricity. Better to find out who buys a lot of your product, and concentrate on them. Forget the light users. As one example of this type of concentration, consider Mediamark's study of consumers of ground coffee.

Figure 14-3 Ground Coffee Consumption in Average Day

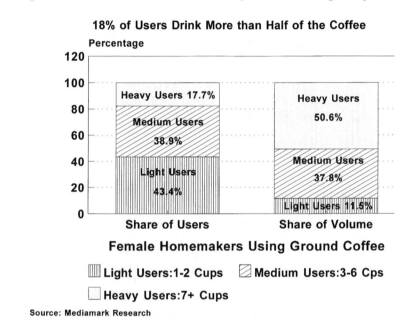

18% of Users Drink More than Half of the Coffee

Female Homemakers Using Ground Coffee

Light Users:1-2 Cups Medium Users:3-6 Cps
Heavy Users:7+ Cups

Source: Mediamark Research

They found that half of all ground coffee bought by female home-makers is bought by only 17.7 percent of the women. The next step was to identify the characteristics of the ground coffee consumer so she can be differentiated from the ordinary female homemaker. Doing modeling analysis, they were able to develop a profile of ground coffee users.

Figure 14-4 Demographics of Coffee Drinkers

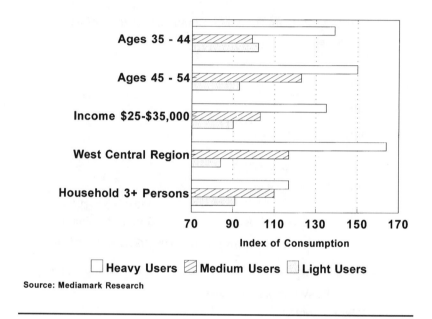

Source: Mediamark Research

This tells you that one of the best places to sell ground coffee is in the West Central region, to female householders from 35-54 with a household income between $25,000 and $35,000 and three or more people in the home—very pinpointed and targeted. This type of analysis can also tell you why you are not succeeding in a market that you think you should be doing better in. Maybe the market just isn't there. There may be many people, but they may be the wrong kind.

Charting Market Growth

Surveys such as Mediamark's can also tell you something about what is happening to your market from year to year. Looking back at their annual survey results from prior years can be very instructive in telling you whether your market is growing or that you may be missing a trend (see the following table).

Table 14-1   Changing Consumption Patterns

	Year1	Year3	Year5
Bought Video Tapes in last twelve months	8.4%	25.5%	38.5%
Bought Microwave Cookware in last twelve months	5.8%	10.4%	10.1%
Bought Chocolate Chip Cookies in last six months	39.9%	37.4%	37.3%
Have MasterCard	17.5%	26.7%	28.5%
Have Visa Card	28.2%	34.1%	37.3%

If you have a consumer product, Mediamark surveys may cover your area. The data can be broken down by geographic area, by cluster or by lifestyle. You may be wondering why business is bad; it may help to know that it is bad all over and that the fault is not yours alone.

COMBINING MARKET RESEARCH AND DATABASE MARKETING

Suppose we are selling a particular brand of luxury automobile. We want to know how big the market is for our type of car and how to target the right customers. How can we figure that out?

From the R. L. Polk Company you can learn how many of each type of automobile is owned in each area of the United States, together with the age of the cars. You can find out how long the average person keeps a particular make of new car before he or she turns it in for a new one. This varies, of course, by lifestyle and by region. Mediamark can help you determine the figure for your region and the purchasing habits of each type of lifestyle group. You can learn, for example, that:

Group A gets a new car every three years

Group B waits until four years

Group C waits five years

Group D waits longer.

Let's say you decided to target a message to Group A. From clustering, you can identify Group A people by their block. From R. L. Polk you can get the actual names and addresses of everyone in your geographic region who is in Group A and who owns a two-and-a-half-year-old model of one of the cars you are targeting. Most of these people will certainly buy some car in the next few months. You can quantify that, and target direct mail to these people.

It is really very simple, yet, even today, few dealers are using this technique. This is because most automobile dealers are really too small to have a marketing staff which is in a position to know these things and to use these techniques. Instead, they have salesmen who sit in the showroom and wait for people to come in response to classified ads.

How can these dealers be helped? Since even the big dealers are too small to have marketing staffs, the automobile manufacturer or distributor should have the database and furnish leads to dealers. A perfect example of the combining of all of these techniques, plus dealer-manufacturer combination. Although it is obvious, there are very few such arrangements in existence today. Targeted direct marketing using a database plus market knowledge and clustering is the exception. Those companies which successfully exploit these techniques could find it profitable.

SUMMARY

- Surveys of your customers are the best way to find out about them. Most companies have simple ways of getting data from their customers.

- The problem with survey data, however, is understanding it, quantifying it, and applying it to your marketing situation. External survey data can help.

- National Demographics and Lifestyles (NDL) maintains a database of 20 million households that have already been surveyed for many types of data that may be interesting and useful to you. You can get your customer or prospect database overlayed with NDL information to improve the profitability of your marketing.

- Mediamark has developed a database of 20,000 consumers which are surveyed annually concerning their purchase habits covering 1,900 product types and 5,700 individual brands. This data is available to subscribers, and can be used in connection with your database.

- Survey results can show regional differences in purchasing behavior for certain products. Perhaps you should not treat customers in Arizona the same as those in Connecticut; they may have very different tastes. Survey results can teach you this.

- Surveys can also help you to pinpoint the heavy users of your product. Normally only 20 percent of your customers account for 80 percent of your sales. Knowing who those 20 percent are *while they are still prospects* can be immensely valuable.

- Many opportunities to exploit these techniques are missed today because the units, such as dealers, are too small to have marketing staffs which understand and make use of the techniques. Manufacturers and distributors are beginning to realize that they must provide assistance if their business is going to grow.

Chapter 15

Getting the Names Right

"Yes, Mr. Hughes" has a nice ring to it, doesn't it? For some strange reason, everyone likes to hear their own name or to see it in print. But the magic doesn't work if you get the name wrong. "Yes, Mr. Hughs" just doesn't do much for me. Getting the name right is crucial to successful database marketing. If you are the manager of a marketing database, you must be sure that every name on your database is:

1. *Correct*—correctly spelled and punctuated, with the correct address. If getting someone's name right is a compliment, what is getting the name wrong?

2. *Unique*—not duplicated somewhere else in the file. If you have duplicates in your database, you cannot develop a valid lifetime relationship with your customers. You will be sending duplicate letters to them, and posting their responses in different records in the database; thus you will never get the whole story when you call up a customer record.

Let us see what the science of direct mail merge/purge can offer to database marketers as we attempt to maintain a clean file of customers and add to it leads that are developed from the outside world.

NAME PROCESSING IS THE LEAST COSTLY PART OF DIRECT MARKETING

John H. Sutton of the Creative Automation Company conducted a small survey of direct mail customers to get an idea of the normal cost distri-

---

Figure 15-1 Direct Mail Costs

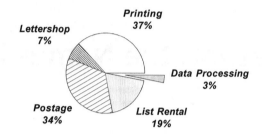

Address Correction Costs Little

Source: John H. Sutton, Creative Automation Company

---

bution of a third-class direct mail package. The results are typical of what seems to be the current trend:

37 percent of the in-the-mail cost was spent on printing

34 percent was spent on postage

19.5 percent was list rental

7 percent was lettershop costs

2.5 percent was computer processing of the names.

This book has emphasized that the correct use of computer technology is one of the most important factors in marketing success. The fact that it is so cheap in relation to other costs makes it practical, and it is imperative to insist that the very best techniques be used.

What techniques can be used today to assure that a mailing database is correctly processed? We will list them here, and then explain some of them in detail. As a marketer you will not be able to do these things yourself, but you must know what they are and see that they are accomplished.

- *Zip Code Correction.* If the zip code is wrong, a third class letter will be *thrown away* by the post office without a word said to the sender. Most modern service bureaus have elaborate software which will compare the city, state, and street address, and correct the zip code, even when the post office has made mass changes to the zip code areas, as they frequently do. You should not pay more than two dollars per thousand for this, and probably much less. If you do not insist on zip code correction, the step may be omitted.

- *Address Correction.* NCOA stands for *National Change of Address*, a system which has been licensed by the Post Office to many large service bureaus throughout the country. They have tapes of address changes registered with the Post Office by people who move. If your correspondent has moved, the service bureaus can automatically update your outgoing mail to the correct new address. When you rent names, you should insist that this be performed before you receive the names. If it is your house file, you will have to do it periodically. Again, you should not pay a service bureau more than about two dollars per thousand for NCOA; and while they are doing this, they should do the zip code correction free of charge.

- *Nixie Elimination.* When you mail specifying *address correction requested* on the envelope, mail that doesn't reach the sender is returned to you. This returned mail (and any other undeliverable mail) is called *nixies*. It has a very important purpose. It should be keypunched and dropped from your database so you don't waste money on a second mailing. On rented lists, the company who rents the lists is supposed to do this.

  If you get many nixies from a rented list, go back to the list source and ask for a substantial rebate. After all, you have paid postage and probably spent considerable sums on the outgoing piece. If it is a new list that you are unsure of, mail a certain randomly selected group first class as a test. If a high percentage come back as nixies, don't mail the rest.

  A second use for nixies is to review the actual appearance of the mail as it looks to the recipient. Study the addresses. Are they correctly spelled and punctuated? Are the names neatly typed? Is the package inside exactly the way you requested it? Did it drop at the post office on the day you were told that it dropped? You should always include "seed names" in any mailing. These are your own names, mixed in with the prospect file. Normally, seed names are your own employees at their homes with disguised names, used to check on the package and delivery. Seed names are useful, but can easily be "fixed up" by the mailshop, while the balance of the job is not done correctly. Nixies tell the real story of what went out and *why it didn't get there*. Insist on studying these things yourself; don't delegate it to someone. And, before you start on any job, ask the list owner what he or she expects in the way of nixies. If the owner is wrong, you may have grounds for a rebate.

- *Special Address Elimination.* Do you want your mail to go to government offices? To overseas military? To federal prisons? To apartment buildings? If you are mailing to consumers, do you want your mail to go to office buildings in downtown areas? Do you want to eliminate people who have specifically asked that they not receive unsolicited "junk mail"? You can have the service bureau find and eliminate all such addresses before you mail for a very modest cost (not over $1 per thousand). Remember, you are running this mailing. Don't just assume that these things will happen without your asking for them—they won't.

WHAT IS MERGE/PURGE?

We come now to the core of this chapter: merge/purge. Duplicate detection and consolidation. A make-or-break process for any marketing database.

We have come a long way in this process in the last twenty years. Service bureaus who are specialists in this business can do wonderful things in finding duplicates from otherwise clean files. Look at some examples:

Mrs. Elizabeth Holbard
4144 Howard Avenue
Kensington,, MD 20895

Betty Holbard
RT 1 Box 378
Kensington,, MD 20895

EA Halbert
4144 Howard
Kens MD 20859

All are the same person. Zip correction will fix the 20859. But will your software catch the Route 1? Will it find that Halbert is really Holbard? These things are being done every day with sophisticated merge/purge software.

Modern software looks for similarity of names, for misplaced digits, for different types of addresses. Look at this example:

Richard Van Dorn
Ridge Road
Haymarket,, VA 22069

Dick Vondorn
RT 3
Haymarket,, VA 22069

R Vandarn
2008 Ridge
Haymarket,, VA

Again, duplicates, and one without a zip code.

Why do these differences exist? Mailing lists are typed by hundreds of different keypunchers from a variety of sources: magazine subscriptions, catalog orders, post office changes of address, membership lists, voter and motor vehicle registrations, coupons, application blanks. There is no similarity in computer record style. Some use separate first name/last name fields. Some have free-form name fields. Some have separate space for titles (Mr., Mrs.) and suffixes (Jr., Sr., MD, PhD); many do not. Some have room for only a middle initial, so Mary Jane becomes Mary J. Many lists are typed overseas by foreigners with only a rudimentary grasp of English, so Mac Laughlin becomes M. Laughlin. In direct mail, you have to take the world as you find it, and make do. This is why merge/purge is so difficult to do correctly.

For a typical large merge/purge job you will have up to forty different input tapes, all in a different format. For some the names will look like this: RITTER/PHILLIP/MARGOLES/III. To do the merge/purge, you first have to translate all forty different tapes into a single format. This can take days, involving the study of the peculiarity of each format. Some (including the Post Office), for example, will put the street number in one field, the street direction in another, the apartment number in a third, the street name in a fourth, and the street type in a fifth:

AV   MAPLE   00003125 E   21B

Which is actually 3125 East Maple Avenue, Apartment 21B.

When all records are in a single format, the various processes begin, including zip and address correction. To find the duplicates, several different approaches are required. First, the file is sorted by zip code, and all similar names within a zip code are compared. Phonetic spelling is often required, with MORE MOORE MOOR MOHR MURE MOUR MUIR all included for comparison. Often it is necessary to compare all names within a state on the ground that zip codes are often wrong, and some escape zip correction.

If software identifies two people:

Ralph Smith   R A Smyth
2235 Willow   235 Willow

The same guy, or two different people? And which is correct: 235 or 2235? And is it Smith or Smyth? Numerous decisions are required, most made by the software, of necessity. Ideally, you should compare every record with every other record to see if you have a duplicate. If you have a million records, this would require more than four hundred billion comparisons. Computers can take on this job readily. It all depends on how much time and money you are willing to spend on the process. One thing to keep in mind: *because of the decisions required, it is absolutely impossible to eliminate all duplicates in a large (100,000+) file.* How can you check whether duplicate elimination has been done correctly?

I have one fairly foolproof method. Tell the service bureau to give you one state: New York, California, or Texas. Sort all records by last name. Then pick a name at random: Jones, Murphy, or Simmons. Ask that the next 200 names and addresses be printed out for you. Study the list. If you can't find a single duplicate in 200 alphabetized names, the job probably has been done correctly. Don't rely on the service bureau to do this final checking. Do it yourself. Duplicate elimination is vital to successful database marketing.

Why Duplicates Must Be Consolidated

Database marketing is really individual, one-on-one relationship marketing. What kind of a corner grocer would keep getting Mrs. Klein mixed up with Mrs. Keene and addressing them both as Miss? There are several vital reasons why this process must be done absolutely correctly:

- If more than one identical letter arrives at a household on the same day, both letters will be thrown in the trash unopened. You will have wasted not only your mailing cost, but your chances of a sale.

- Worse still, your company reputation in the household will suffer. They will realize that when they see something from your company, they are dealing with a computer. The illusion of communication will be shattered before it even has a chance to begin.

- Relationship marketing involves keeping track of what the other person said to you, as well as what you said to them. If you have sent duplicate communications to a household, it means that you have duplicate database records. Responses are unlikely to be posted to the correct names, and gradually confidence within your company in the whole database system will become eroded.

When in doubt, it is better to send no letter at all than to send a duplicate to the same address.

When Duplicates Are Good

In merge/purge, duplicates are usually a very good sign. If you are merging many different lists, and one household shows up on several different lists, you have an ideal correspondent. Here is someone who responds to direct mail. Duplicates should not be *eliminated*, they should be *consolidated*. Leave a space in your record to indicate how many different lists the name appears on. These multi-buyers (as they are called) should receive a second and a third mailing if they don't respond to the first. These are response-prone people. Keep ringing their bell. Eventually they will answer.

Even if the duplicates are already on your house database as a customers, knowing those customers are on many other lists is a useful fact to add to your knowledge of who they are and how to approach them.

Good and Bad Merge/Purge

Look closely into the methods to be used by the service bureau or in-house computer staff when merge/purge is being planned. The fact is that most merge/purge today is badly done. Several inferior methods are widely practiced.

The first is the match-code or keyline process. In this process name and address are combined into a collection of fourteen or sixteen digits, and the resulting match code compared.

Keyline:

Arthur M. Hughes
3014 Ridge Road   22069HGH2A3014R9
Haymarket, VA 22069

Anne Hoghey   22069HGH2A3014R9
3014 Round Robin Road
Haymarket, VA 22069

These are clearly not duplicates, but will show up as such with a match code. The more common error with match codes is that they will identify many duplicates as uniques. As a first cut, match codes are useful, but more sophisticated methods are needed.

It goes without saying that no system is acceptable that looks only for exact duplicates. Because of the many ways that names and streets can be spelled and keypunched, the chance of eliminating many duplicates with an exact match is very remote.

George A. Weller	G Weller
Dr. George Waller	George Weller MD

Four duplicates. How many systems will spot this?

Good software for duplicate elimination is sold by Group 1 software for mainframes. But just buying this software (for about $25,000) does not assure good duplicate elimination—it requires many months and several million names worth of experience before a programming group can really master this art.

An in-house staff will find that it takes specialized manpower, increased disk space, and a very large mainframe to do the job. The process of converting the many unusual tapes you will receive will often require writing ad-hoc software. Unless your staff does this kind of work every day, it will take up to three times as long to do the job in-house (meaning three weeks in-house, versus a week in a service bureau).

Even if you are trying to maintain your marketing database in-house, you should probably insist on the merge/purge being sent to professionals on the outside. What does outside merge/purge cost? For a large job you should expect to spend $2 per thousand records.

How Many Duplicates Will You Find?

As already noted, no large file is ever free of all duplicates. A good individual house file will probably have 2-4 percent duplicates. When you combine many different lists, you should expect to find about one third duplicates (depending on where the lists come from). In many cases, you can buy names from suppliers on a *net name* basis, paying only for the unique new names that they contribute to the job.

HOUSEHOLDING

In most cases in prospecting, and in many cases in a database, you will want to group people by household, so that only one name or telephone call is devoted to a single household. The process is called *householding*.

Mrs. Carol Braemer	Roger Braemer	Julie Braemer
221 Old Post Drive	221 Old Post	221 Old Post Dr.

You clearly want to send only one letter to 221 Old Post Drive, but to whom do you address the letter? If you are like most novice marketers, you probably have never thought about this question. Think about it now. The possibilities:

The Braemer Family	The Braemer Household
Roger Braemer & Family	Roger and Carol Braemer
Roger & Carol & Julie Braemer	Braemer or Current Occupant
Roger Braemer	The Braemer's
Mr. & Mrs. Roger Braemer	Mr. Roger Braemer

I am not going to give you a pat solution. The answer may depend on the file you are using, the product you are selling, the image you want to project. It is preferable that you think this through and discuss it with your service bureau *before* you send the job over. If you don't, the service bureau will pick their own solution, which may be the worst one as far as you are concerned.

Remember, anything is possible. With modern software and a few lines of code, the service bureau can produce any result you are looking for, but you have to know what you want. Remember, this is your mailing. You have paid for the names, the postage, and the mailing piece. Why spoil it all by messing up the householding process?

AUTOSEXING

Insist on sexing a file. The response to:

Mr. Archibald Foster:	*beats*	Archibald Foster:
Dear Mr. Foster:	*beats*	Dear Friend:

Dear Friend is such a weak salutation it is a wonder that anyone uses it. But without knowing that Archibald is a man's name, what else can you say?

Most service bureaus will be able to autosex your file. Some names, of course, cannot be autosexed: Pat, Robin, Chris and Dana are examples. Also, people who use only their initials cannot be sexed. But it is well worth the extra money to pay for autosexing. Many companies throw in sexing free when you do the mailing in their shop—ask about it.

While you do the autosexing, you must consider what to use as a default salutation. Consider the possibilities, when you do not know the sex:

Dear Chris Winger:	Dear Chris:	Dear Winger:
Dear Friend:	Dear Nature Lover:	Dear Winger Household:

Again, there is no really good answer. You must decide what works best. With a large file, test several approaches to see which gets the best response.

THE APPEARANCE OF THE ADDRESS

It should go without saying that all your outgoing correspondence should be properly punctuated and presented. It is so easy to do correctly, yet how much of our mail is sloppily addressed? Consider these names:

WM A MADDOX JR	Mr. William A. Maddox, Jr.
100 MAYFLD BLVD	100 Mayfield Boulevard
W HAMPTON MA 02123	West Hampton, Massachusetts 02123
DEAR WM MADDOX JR:	Dear Mr. Maddox:

Notice that:

WM A becomes Mr. William A.
JR becomes Jr.
MAYFLD BLVD becomes Mayfield Boulevard
W becomes West
MA becomes Massachusetts

Not all service bureaus can do this. Catalog mailers never bother with it. They are sticking labels onto catalogs. Few people look at the label. But if you are sending a letter or a self mailer, the appearance will often determine whether it gets opened or tossed in the trash. It is worth shopping around for a service bureau that can make your output look first class.

Do not accept the excuse that "the keypunching was poor" as the reason why your database records look poor. Modern software can correct almost anything, and you should insist that the service bureau make a flawless presentation.

LASER VERSUS LABEL

The cheapest method of sending anything is to use a cheshire label. Cheshire labels are plain paper, printed four across, which are automatically cut and glued to your letter, catalog, or self mailer in the mailshop. You should probably spend about $1.50 per thousand for labels and another $1 to have them cut and affixed.

But there are times when you want something better. When you have a marketing database and are corresponding with your customers, there are plenty of occasions when a label just won't do. This is the time for a laser letter.

Laser letters can be printed on one side or both sides. They can be letter size, legal size, almost any size that you want. You can have cut sheet lasers (using preprinted stationary or forms) or continuous form lasers (which work with quite complicated and sophisticated forms and letters, such as a four-page personalized letter.)

One of the problems with the way direct marketing agencies are organized is that *production* is a separate function from *creative*. Production people deal with the letter shops and arrange for the labels or the laser letters. They may have become worlds removed from the rest of their organizations. Creative people and database marketers design a nice mailing, oversee the selection of the list, look at the merge/purge, and then assume that production will do the rest.

Big mistake. If you, as a database marketer, are in charge of and worried about customer contact, then production is very much your concern. You want the finished product, as it arrives at your customer's mailbox, to look absolutely stunning. Your whole company image is at stake in every communication—don't blow it.

For example, consider the content of the letter. If you have a laser letter, it should be fully personalized. By that I mean not just the name, address, and salutation; I mean the paragraphs and personal references throughout the body of the letter.

"I know that Mauser has been used to dry dog food. It is easy to prepare, easy to store, and keeps him in top condition. But every once in a while, a dog likes to get a special treat. Last month, we introduced Adult Dog Treats, which have already proved very popular.

"On your next order, which is due there on February 12, may I suggest that we include a one-pound bag of Adult Dog Treats, along with your regular bag of dry formula, Mrs. Warren? If you just give a few of these treats to Mauser whenever he is especially good, you will make him very happy. This bag should last you for a month or more. These treats are scientifically . . ."

This is individualized selling. You recognize the dog's name and sex. You recognize what Mrs. Warren normally buys. Mrs. Warren can easily see that this letter is directed personally to her, and is not general mass-marketing hype.

Of course, the laser letter can go on to get more information from Mrs. Warren. And why not?

"I know that we had a delivery mixup last October. I want to be sure that everything you are receiving now is getting there on time and in good condition. Could you take the time to fill out the little questionnaire at the bottom of the order form to let me know how we are doing in our service to you, Mrs. Warren? It is by helpful comments and suggestions from our best customers, like you, Mrs. Warren, that we can correct whatever is not right, and bring you the kind of responsive service that you want and deserve. Your comments are very valuable to me. Please feel free to call me directly if there is anything that you do not want to write on the form. I am anxious to hear from you.

"Sincerely yours,

"Myron Fuller, Nutrition Specialist."

Why do I introduce this concept in a chapter on getting the names right? Because it is at the service bureau and mailshop level where this type of personalization gets carried out—and gets mixed up. Many service bureaus cannot do a decent job of producing a personalized letter. They may charge you a lot extra. They will say that it will delay the job. They will point out all the problems with the exceptions (no dog name in the record; dog sex not in record; customer's name is S WARREN, so sex is unknown) and try to talk you out of this kind of personalization. If this happens, perhaps it is time to get a new service bureau.

Of course, your database record has gaps in it. For this reason you must prepare defaults. It is complicated, but it is what the corner grocer did which kept him in business. He took an active interest in the lives of his customers. As a database marketer you must take an active interest in the appearance and quality of every communication with every customer. Laser letters are an important example of what you must do to improve communications and maintain a lifetime relationship with your customers.

MERGE/PURGE REPORTS

Most service bureaus can now produce for you, as a standard service at no extra cost, a set of very valuable reports on your merge/purge which will tell you:

- How many names were used from each incoming list. Each list should have its own source code.

- How many bad addresses there were on each list. In general, you should not use lists that are "dirty."

- How many duplicates you had on each incoming list, and how many inter-list duplicates you had. These "multi-buyers" should be specially flagged.

- How your file is broken down by state, by SCF, by zip code, by sex, and by other factors on the file.

Business-to-Business Merge/Purge

When your list is not a consumer list, you have a much bigger problem. Business addresses are very different:

- Whereas 20 percent of all Americans move their residence once a year, about 40 percent of businessmen change their business addresses every year. People are transferred, promoted, fired, and they change jobs. The companies they work for are always changing their locations, internal structure, and even names.

- Decisions need to be made: do you want to mail to a company, or a specific title within the company, or a specific named individual? For a marketing database, the last is clearly the best. But it is the hardest to get.

    a. Arthur Hughes, Exec. VP
        ACS, Inc.
        1807 Michael Faraday Ct.
        Reston, VA 22090

    b. Jim Nathan, Research Div.
        ACS, Inc.
        4011 Sunset Hills Drive
        Reston, VA 22090

    c. Chris Ogden
        ACS, Inc.
        Michael Faraday Court
        Reston, VA 22090

    d. R & D Division
        ACS, Inc.
        1807 Michael Faraday Ct.
        Reston, VA 22090

    e. Director of Research, ACS
        Room 117
        Sunset Hills Drive
        Reston, VA 22090

f.   ACS
1807 Michael Faraday Ct.
Reston, VA 22090

These are all different people. Or are they? Do you want to saturate the company with mail in the hopes of getting to the one person who is interested in your offer, or are you sure you can pinpoint Chris Ogden as your man, even though you are unsure of his title and division?

- In your reformatting of the input names, you should allow separate spaces in your record for specialized business-to-business fields such as:

Last Name

First Name

Title (Mr., Mrs.)

Suffix

Position (Vice President)

Division (Personnel)

Branch (Recruitment and Training)

Company (Denver BioLab Company)

Parent Company (XYZ Drug Industries)

Internal Address

Street Address (2 lines)

City, State, ZIP

And you will want to add such fields as:

SIC Code

Position Code

Division Code (04=Personnel)

- Any software designed for consumer merge/purge *will not work properly* with business-to-business files. Be sure that the software used is specialized for your purpose.

- You must set up some sort of internal coding system which categorizes the types of industries, divisions, and positions you are seeking in your job. A purchasing agent is one code, an end-user is another. A little advance planning and ingenuity here is absolutely essential if the final product is to reach the correct people.

- Be sure that your merge/purge programmers are clear as to who you are seeking and who are duplicates. Are the Vice President for Engineering and the Assistant Vice President for Engineering duplicates or not? If you have the name of the Assistant VP, but no name for the VP, do you drop the VP?

  The best solution is to have a couple of hundred sorted names printed out, study them, and mark who you want in and who out. Then write some rules which explain your decision so that a programmer can use these rules to include and exclude names.

Figure 15-2   Steps in List Processing

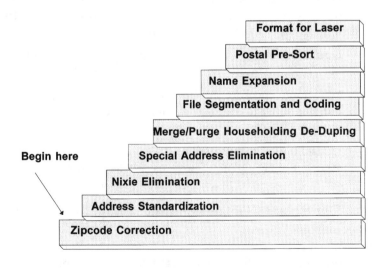

SUMMARY

- Computer processing and correction of names is the least expensive part of any mailing job, but can have a major impact on deliverability and response. Correct processing is very important.

- Service bureaus can correct zip codes and correct the addresses.

- Nixies are non-deliverable returns from previous mailings. They should be studied closely for what they tell you about a mailing.

- All large files contain duplicates. It is hard to find them, but you must do so: duplicate names in a mailing cost money and reduce response.

- Duplicate names in your marketing database will reduce confidence in the database and weaken its impact on the customer.

- Duplicate identification is a specialized art which should be done by professionals with professional software. Don't try it in-house unless you do it on a regular basis.

- Duplicate names occurring on several lists can be very valuable: they are multi-buyers. Mail to them more often.

- You should check for duplicates yourself before any job goes out. It is better to drop some non-duplicates than to mail in a questionable case.

- Householding means mailing only one letter per household. You should get a plan for how to address a household which is consistent with the image of your product.

- Insist on autosexing—determining the sex of your prospect—so you can use a title: Mr. Spaulding, Ms. Rothrock.

- In many cases, the appearance of the address can sour your prospect before the envelope is opened. Service bureaus can do much to make an address look attractive.

- Laser letters look better than labels, and may not cost much more.

- All laser letters can contain many personalized paragraphs and references for little or no additional cost. These can help sell your product.

- Business-to-business merge/purge is specialized and different. Consumer software does not work. Be sure the correct software is used.

Chapter 16

Cloning Your Best Customers

Most marketing databases contain three types of people: customers, prospects, and leads. A *lead* is someone who has responded to one of your offers but has not yet purchased anything. Leads may come to you from many sources: general advertising, direct response advertising, direct mail. One of the best sources of leads is a direct offer to a likely prospect.

A *prospect* is a person who you believe should be buying your product because he has qualities which resemble those of your best customers. He is a "clone" of your best customers.

How do you get the names of prospects to use for your direct marketing effort? Let us assume that you have already profiled your current customers. You have determined some characteristics that distinguish your best customers from your worst, and from non-customers. Once you know that, then you can screen names from outside lists to get people who look like your best current customers. These are your best prospects.

PICKING THE CORRECT AUDIENCE

We are now down to the heart of profiling: finding characteristics of your customers and your non-respondents which will help you to determine which names on an unknown rented list will respond to your next direct marketing program. You want to *predict* your results. For the purpose of this chapter, we will be drawing examples from direct mail, since it is easily the most quantifiable for illustrative purposes. But the principles apply to any type of direct marketing.

It used to be that profiling would consist of finding the characteristics of your customers:

Age: 25-35
Income: $35,000–$70,000
Education: College Graduate

These seem like good criteria, until you profile your non-respondents. Their average profile might be:

Age: 25-35
Income: $35,000–$70,000
Education: College Graduate

In other words, your non-respondents look just like your respondents. This could be because most of the people you mailed to looked like that. More likely, it is because in your profiling, you have not hit on the criteria that separates the sheep from the goats. You must do more research, more modeling. That is why modern database marketers include a vast array of data in their marketing databases. After further research, you may find that the chief difference between your respondents and your non-respondents was something else:

Respondents:
Housing: High-rise and condominiums
Children: Low percentage
Clusters: Pools and Patios, Young Influentials

Non-Respondents:
Housing: Single-family homes
Children: Medium percentage
Clusters: Young Suburbia, Blue Chip Blues

Now that you see the difference, it is much easier to pick the good prospects from the poor prospects. But to get from ignorance to knowledge takes trial and error. Profiling is a hands-on activity in which your marketing staff should participate actively. Profiling is too important to be left to some data processing staff. As a professional database marketer you will want to have database software that permits you to do exhaustive research yourself, with a cost structure in which you don't have to worry how much each iteration of the model will cost. You will also want to have some professional help with what is at all times a complicated process.

In many cases, there will be no discernible difference that you can discover between the respondents and the non-respondents. That is because the factors that cause the difference are not measurable by any data that you have available to you. Suppose, for example, you have no data about pet ownership. You mail an offer for dog food to a list of households. Some respond, and some do not. You look at age, income, type of home, make of automobile—things that you can get appended to your prospect database. Nothing seems to separate buyers from non-buyers. Why not? Because these things are not as important as the one central unknown fact: whether they own a dog or not. In a very large number of cases the purchase decision turns on factors that you cannot possibly know about from public sources. Think about this before you spend a lot of money modeling a database to find the profile of the ideal buyer.

LIST SELECTION

Let us suppose that your marketing database has provided you with a profile which will successfully separate good prospects from the general public. The profile can be used to screen lists for rental, to pick the right publication for advertising, to pick the correct radio or TV show, or even to pick the right time of day. The profile will certainly help you frame your offer by knowing what your preferred respondent looks like. But demography and lifestyle are not enough. They can be outweighed by additional facts that you can discover. You cannot sell pet food to people without pets. You cannot sell software to someone who has no computer. A list taken from subscribers to a pet magazine or a computer magazine should obviously outweigh any results from modeling if your product falls into one of these or similar specialized niches.

Do not automatically assume that there does not exist a list of just the type of prospects that you are looking for. Nowadays if you work with a good list broker there is almost no limit to what can be done. But you yourself must be resourceful. Let us assume that you have done a good job of profiling. The characteristics you have selected are those which are likely to be coded and selectable in outside lists. Thus armed, you venture forth to seek good lists.

Selection of the correct names is probably the single most important factor in any mailing. Ed Burnett developed the following rough statistics on the importance of various factors in the success of a mailing:

Category, Potential Variation in Response

Lists, 300%–1000%
Offer, 50%–200%
Package, 10%
Timing, 10% (Except at Christmas)
Copy, 10%

In most cases, your creative people are involved in designing an attractive piece, and in some cases you might have a modeler who is working on multiple regressions. No one is giving adequate attention to list selection, yet the list is the most important single ingredient in any mailing. We must set about correcting this situation right now.

Figure 16-1   Mailing Response

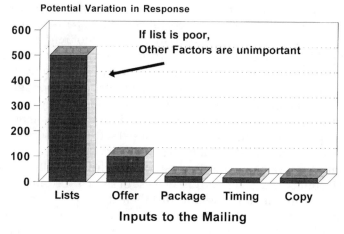

Source: Ed Burnett

OBTAINING PROSPECT NAMES

The United States is a direct marketer's dream. Nowhere else on earth is there such a profusion of available lists of names of prospective buyers and donors. When you first go forth to find the names of people to add to your prospect list, if you are not experienced, you will be overwhelmed by the numbers and seeming quality of the lists available.

There are books available which cover this subject in great detail. The best is *The Complete Direct Mail List Handbook*, by Ed Burnett, one of the most knowledgeable and experienced professionals in the field. Much of what I am outlining here is derived from this excellent book, but my brief extract is no substitute for obtaining a copy of this valuable work for your office bookshelf.

Inside Names

Before you spend money to go outside to find prospect names, you should canvas your internal resources. There are often more names available than you might think. You can start by getting a list of your customers which may be obtained from a variety of sources: warranty registrations, sales slips, credit card charges, checks, order forms. If your system does not provide these names today, perhaps some minor changes in the systems in your company or at the dealer will yield you hundreds or thousands of names at little cost.

The next step is to get your customers to furnish you names. Every time they buy a gift for someone else, you have a very valuable linked pair of names. You should keep both names, and retain the linkage in your database. You can reward customers for recommending your product to others and for supplying you with their names. Again, keep the linkage to use in later correspondence. The telephone is ringing all day at your 800 number with people calling to inquire about something.

Never, never tell anyone anything without first getting their name and address and their phone number. Keep your telemarketers equipped with a list of standard questions they must ask. Are the callers customers? What product did they buy and when? What caused them to buy it? Where did they hear about you? How many other people in the household use the product, or ought to use it? In most companies, if you scratch around enough, you will find a dozen prospect or customer lists being kept by special groups unknown to one another. You may find rebate respondents, sweepstakes entrants, membership lists, upgrade respondents, sales leads and prospects and so on.

Don't forget lists of employees, stockholders, suppliers, and newsletter readers. You may be able to assemble quite a large group of names without spending a cent. If you turn all of these lists over to a service bureau, they can quickly merge them into a single list, eliminating the duplicates and retaining codes that show where each name came from. Don't let them make a major project of it.

If the names are on magnetic tape to start with, you shouldn't have to spend a fortune nor wait more than two weeks to get the job done.

Looking Outside

Once you have exhausted your inside resources, you can begin to explore outside lists for prospects that match your ideal profile. There are about a million mailing lists, of which about 20,000 are commercially available. Many of them are kept in good order with correct addresses (by frequent application of NCOA), and a great many are enhanced with demographics or lifestyle information so that you can select names by criteria that match your preferred customer makeup. New lists are being created every month which list new households, businesses, professionals, graduates, institutions, babies, marriages, credit card holders, automobile registrants. There are twelve major list brokers and hundreds of minor ones. There are six major list compilers who have lists covering almost every household in America, plus most of the businesses.

If you are a newcomer, you should begin by selecting a professional list broker to help you. Unlike real estate, where a broker may know only about property in his immediate neighborhood, any large list broker will be able to find out about and obtain for you names from almost any list in the country.

What the List Broker Can Do for You

If you take the list broker into your confidence, he can be very helpful. Tell him the type of customer that you have now, and the type of prospect that you are seeking to attract. Explain your product and your offer, and how you plan to go about lining up new customers. He has experience. He can help to keep you from making costly mistakes. He may not only find you the right names, he may also help you to structure your offer, to design your tests, to segment your list, and to evaluate your success.

For free—just the cost of the names that you rent through him—your list broker may provide you tens of thousands of dollars worth of valuable consultation. Ed describes several clients who did not put their list broker on their marketing team, and lost big money because of it. The list broker works for you, not for the list owner. He has no vested interest in which list is used. He usually makes very little money on a test. His real return comes on the "continuation" (the large repeat mailing to a list after a successful test). So he is very anxious to find lists that work for you. Here are some of the things that your list broker will insist that you do to craft a successful test by mail or by telemarketing:

- *Use several lists for your test.* You will learn twice as much by mailing to two lists, ten times as much if you select from ten lists. Often the list you thought would not be too useful proves to be the best of the lot.

- *Test different packages, offers, and copy.* While you are testing, test everything. Test your price, your premiums, your envelopes, your sales arguments. While you are doing this, be sure that every variation is tested equally on each list so that you can have a real test. This means nth name segmentation of each list for each test package.

Let's take an example. Suppose you have four lists of 30,000 names each. You have three different offers and two different types of envelopes. That makes twenty-four different segments, six for each of your four lists.

You will have to do a *nth name split* on each of your four lists to split them into six statistically equal parts. Then each of these six parts gets a different offer and envelope. *Put source codes on the response device in your promotion.* A source code is simply a unique combination of letters or numbers that identifies each of the segments that you mailed. The segment source code tells you what list the name came from, what offer, and what envelope (in our present example). In a real life example, we might have many more than twenty-four segments if we were testing more aspects of the promotion.

Be sure that the source codes are captured when the prospects respond to your offer. I have seen mailings where the client developed some excellent source codes, but the letter shop printed them in such a way that they were cut in half when the customer clipped them out to put them in the BRE (business reply envelope). The result was tests with no final scores: wasted effort.

Figure 16-2   All Aspects Are Tested

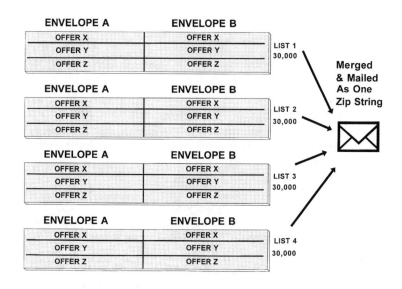

Analyze your results. Again, I have participated in tests where the client developed a grand plan, but didn't take the time to find out what went wrong or right with the final mailing. Back-end analysis is important not just to prove a single mailing, but to prove an entire marketing theory. Let me explain what I mean:

- Most successful test mailings to prospect lists produce a given (and relatively small) percentage response. Depending on your offer, that given percent may make money for you or it may lose money. But either way, you now have the names of customers who have responded and paid money for your product (or provided an inquiry which you later convert to a sale via catalog, telemarketing, or salesman visit).

- Your next step is a *second offer* to those initial respondents. This second offer, if successful, may result in a substantially larger response. You follow that up, right away, with a *third offer* which also should net you a goodly response. We are now getting into "lifetime value."

- However, this is where the ball is usually dropped. How do you determine whether your initial test was successful? By the responses to the first promotion, or to the first plus the second, or to a whole chain of promotions stretching over several months or years? In one project I worked on, we found that TV ads produced excellent responses, but that in the long run people who responded to direct mail bought more (in follow up promotions) than TV respondents. We finally determined that the direct mail respondents were more valuable, even though they were *initially more expensive to acquire.*

- To develop this kind of knowledge requires that you keep track of the initial source codes and all subsequent source codes in a customer's database record. Some companies just keep the *latest* source code, discarding all previous codes. What a mistake! Without these earlier source codes, we would have decided that TV was a better recruiting source than direct mail, whereas the opposite was the case.

Avoid false theories. Mailing list selection is fraught with "old wives' tales" which usually surface as dogmatic statements which may, in fact, be right sometimes and dead wrong other times. A good list broker will help you avoid being mesmerized by these false theories. Let's list a few of them:

- *Direct mail is easy to enter; anyone can make a go of it.* Dead wrong. This is a business for professionals. You can lose your shirt (or your company's shirt) if you are not careful.

- *All lists are pretty much the same.* Completely wrong. The variation on a single large job from best to worst list may be as much as ten to one.

- *For my special situation, there is only one source for my prospect names.* It may be true today, but there is such constant movement in the list business, with new lists coming on the market every month, that you may be missing some very good bets by not constantly testing.

- *All list brokers are the same.* Despite the fact that any list broker can theoretically find for you names from any rental list in the country, the fact is that most brokers specialize in a few of the hundreds of possible areas and are weak in their knowledge of the other areas. A broker who has been finding good names for a non-profit mailer may strike out when seeking customers for a bank or an encyclopedia.

- *Good lists should not be mailed too often.* If the list is working for you, it means that you have developed some synergy with the people on that list. They like what you are selling. If that is so, why would they stop liking it just because you mail to them once a quarter or once a month? This is as true of your customer file as it is of your rented lists. Constant, familiar, friendly, profitable contact is what database marketing is all about.

- *Large lists are better than small lists.* This theory is based on the idea that if a test is successful, but the list is very small, there will be no rollout potential (i.e., the test will have used up all the names). The trouble with this idea is that by selecting only large lists, you may be (and probably are) overlooking gold in a lot of small specialized lists which may give you phenomenal response.

Selecting by Profiled Criteria

How do you, and your broker, decide which will be the best lists for your promotion? Let's assume that you have profiled your best customers, and have arrived at some notion of what makes for a good customer for your particular product or service. You want to find more prospects who match this profile of the good customer. There are several ways you can go:

Find people who are known to need or like your product. Here you can ask for specialized lists:

- A Buick dealer can get a list of owners of three-year-old Buicks.
- A pet food company can get a list of cat or dog owners.
- A bank selling CDs can get a list of affluent older people.
- A cruise line can rent a list of people who have said that they would like to take a cruise (in a national survey).
- An environmental organization can rent a list of people who have responded to some other environmental cause.
- A baby food manufacturer can rent a list of new mothers.
- A furniture company can rent a list of people who have just moved.

Find people with the correct demography. If you are selling a non-specialized product, such as a credit card, a general interest magazine, or lawn care, you may not have any specialized list sources available. For these products, your analysis of your existing customer base might tell you that the ideal customer for your product:

- lives in a single family home;
- has a family income of $40K to $60K;
- has two wage earners in the family;
- has no children;
- is between ages 40 and 60.

Can you rent a list consisting only of people who fit this description? Absolutely.

Find people with the correct lifestyle. At least four large companies specialize in compiling lists of people who have answered survey questions about their lifestyles. "The Lifestyle Selector" has compiled a long list of questions on surveys which are packed into millions of warranty cards of products bought at retail by consumers. About 18 percent of those who "register" their warranty by mailing it in furnish data as to hobbies, interests, reading, mail order purchase, and demographic information. Another service, "The Behavior Bank," asks consumers to indicate their brand usage in coffee, pet food, cereals, milk, coffee creamer, saltines, floor wax, pantyhose, denture cleanser, laxatives, cigarettes, detergents and so on. In addition, they ask about credit cards, mail order buying habits, hobbies, and occupations.

Find people who have bought by mail (or telephone) recently. In many cases, your broker may be able to identify lists of people who have purchased something by mail which is similar to your offering (for instance, in price or in type of product) within a specified period. Recency here is very important. Frequency can also be requested as a discriminant factor. The dollar amount is also a key. If you are selling something that costs $89, a list of proven buyers of some product for $15 may not be very useful.

Find people who live in the right place. Sometimes you want only people who live in your state or city or congressional district. That is very easy to arrange. All lists can be selected by zip code. In most cases, you can also get an overlay for political districts. In some cases, you want *everyone* who lives in a certain area (for cable TV, for example). One of the "big four" list compilers can fix you up with all of the people in Pocatello, Idaho, even including the households ("Current Occupant") where the name of the person living there is as yet unknown.

LIST REFORMATTING

You have selected your lists, and the tapes are beginning to arrive. The first thing you will notice is that some of the tapes are late. It is almost always true that if you order nine different tapes, three will come on time, three will be a week late, and three will be two weeks late. This may delay your drop date, unless you plan in advance. Ask your list broker when the tapes will arrive, and then add two weeks. The merge/ purge process cannot really begin until the last tape has arrived, so the early tapes will just sit. Long before the tapes arrive, you should have made up a list of source codes for your test. On a typical test, you may have 160 different source codes:

> Four different offers
> Four different packages
> Ten different lists
>
> $4 \times 4 \times 10 = 160.$

Assign a different code to each which will help you find out what was working after the test: for example, AA01 AA02, where the first letter is the offer, the second is the package and the next two digits are the list number. Write these codes down in a book or on a PC, and make sure that everyone involved knows what they are and what they mean.

At this point you also will want to give your service bureau a list of seed names. These are names of employees of your company or the creative agency, usually at their home addresses, so that they can receive the package and monitor the mailing to be sure that it has been done correctly and arrives on time. The seeds should be inserted into every package and every offer.

After your service bureau reformats your tapes to a common format, be sure that the job has been done correctly. There are several features to consider.

Appearance. Do the names and addresses look correct and attractive after the reformat? Insist on a dump (legible printout) of at least 300 names, including all lists. To be sure you are getting a random sample, ask for all the names beginning at a certain zip code which you specify. Here is what to look for:

1.   File in upper/lower case, punctuated correctly.

2.   Address correct and standardized.

3.   Names include titles.

Freedom from Duplicates. Read Chapter 15, and follow it.

Complete Statistics. Get the whole story of what happened to every incoming name. How many bad addresses there were; how many were corrected; how many could not be corrected; how many duplicates were found in each list; and how many duplicates there were found against your house file. All new duplicates (appearing on two or more lists, but *not* on your house file) should be set aside in a special file for a follow-up mailing. These are multi-buyers, very powerful names, and should be used in any repeat mailing.

Check the Segmentation. After the list has been corrected and deduped, it should be segmented by package and offer. The tapes already have the original list code in them. They will now get the package and offer letter added. This segmentation should be done on an nth name basis across the file from a zip code standpoint, so that each package and offer will get a proportional number of names, randomly distributed across the entire mailing. The best way to check this is to get a report showing zip codes by package and zip codes by offer, with the zip code being only the first digit of the zip on a large list, or more digits on a smaller list.

PKG/Offer	0	1	2	3	4	5	6	7	8	9
AA	213	423	651	142	91	86	73	76	34	1076
AB	212	420	650	142	92	87	74	77	35	1075
AC, etc.										

Bad Addresses. Some rented lists are loaded with old and incorrect addresses. You can check on this by marking the envelope *ADDRESS CORRECTION REQUESTED,* which alerts the Post Office to return to you all the undelivered mail. These "nixies" cost you money, but it may be well worth it, depending on your program (read Chapter 15).

Improving your Message. There are thousands of different envelopes and millions of different messages and inserts. Something that worked last year may not work this year. The public is fickle, tiring easily of something that once excited it.

Every mailing should be considered as an experiment. Always try something new: different shape envelope, different stamps, varying message. Assign a different source code to each different test, and get prompt reports from your database on which test package pulled the best.

You should also be constantly testing price. It is not necessarily true that lower prices will improve sales. With some products, in certain circumstances, a price increase with appropriate message may position the product in a different "quality niche" which will have it perceived as being better than the other brands, and thus result in increased sales. The only way to know this is to test constantly and produce and study reports. This is a tremendous feature of database marketing: each message stands on its own. If you are selling in a department store, you cannot very well offer an item at one price to one group of shoppers and at another price to others. But in the privacy of one-on-one mailings, every letter you send offers an opportunity for a test, an opportunity which you can exploit.

Figure 16-3   Test Mailings

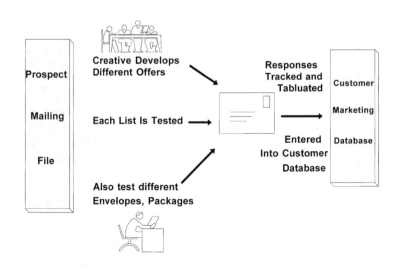

Proper report design and careful study, plus creative imagination in designing test packages, will enable you to get better and better results, and eliminate the envelope and message as a negative factor in your direct mail.

RENTING YOUR OWN LIST

As a direct marketer, you may dread the idea of renting the names of your customers to others. After all, you spent a lot of money acquiring these names; they are *your customers*. They may resent being *shopped around* to every vendor in the country.

But consider what we have been saying in this chapter. We have been advising you on how to find prospects by renting names from other companies. If they all felt the way you feel about renting, then why are they renting names? Do they know something that you don't know? Probably. Let's consider some of the advantages of renting out your names.

Lists get stale. Twenty percent of Americans move every year. If you sit on a list for two or three years without using it, it will become almost worthless. If you have a valuable list, consider it as a rapidly depreciating asset. Get value out of it before it is too late.

Renting can rejuvenate a list. If you develop a cooperative relationship with another company that is using your list, you can agree jointly that they will share with you the results of their mailing: the nixies, the changes of address, the households that responded and how much they bought. After all, you are in the driver's seat. You can insist on anything you want. When they give you their results, you enter the data into your database. You have a better list after each mailing.

Some people like receiving mail. My wife Helena is a confirmed catalog shopper. She gets an average of about twelve catalogs *a day* all year round. She buys most of our Christmas presents and a good amount of her wardrobe by mail. She looks forward to seeing new catalogs. She scans every page eagerly for new ideas. She is aware that, because of her activity, her name is being actively traded. She is a multi-buyer. She loves it. Renting the names of people like Helena is a favor to them. There are millions like her.

Database marketing permits "No Rental" flags. If you are worried that some of your customers will be turned off by having their names shopped around, ask them. They won't mind at all telling you their preference. When they do, code their answer in a "No Rental" flag in the database, and don't rent names that don't want to be rented. Many of your customers will appreciate your surveying them on this question, no matter what their preference, and this survey is just one more little dialog which helps maintain the relationship with them. Incidentally, seldom more than 2 percent of customers ever request that their names not be rented. In other words, it doesn't cost much to ask, and you won't lose many names by doing it. Another case where good customer service is profitable for both parties.

Renting names is profitable. Depending on the value of your list, you should be able to realize from 20 cents to one dollar per name per year after all expenses and broker's fees are paid. This means that if you have a customer database of 500,000 names, you should be taking in $100,000 or more in list rental fees. This revenue could be enough to pay a lot of the expenses of your marketing database. This is not insignificant revenue for most marketing staffs. It should permit you to do a lot more experimentation, enhancement, modeling, surveys, NCOA, and other activities which you otherwise might not be able to afford.

Exchanges can be even more profitable. Here is a chance for you to become a creative database marketer. Who has a list that you could use in your business? Who would like to use the list that you have? If you sell nuts and bolts by mail, wouldn't the Black and Decker mailing list be ideal for you? And wouldn't your list be ideal for them? Two possibilities open up: you can exchange lists, or you can go in for a cooperative mailing and share the costs. You will not only share the costs, you will share the benefits. Even if the other company makes more sales than you do, you should still come out ahead: your database will be bigger, your customer names will be refreshed, another chance for dialog with your customers has occurred. Remember, the fact that you have a marketing database has made this all possible.

SUMMARY

- Picking the correct names is the most important single factor in the success of any direct mail effort.

- Before you look outside to rent prospects, explore your own company. There may be, and probably are, many useful lists of customers or prospects resident in different branches of your organization. Consider in particular people who are calling in on your customer service hotline.

- If you decide to go outside, the first step is to find a good list broker and take him fully into your confidence.

- Always test several lists at once. At the same time, test variations of your offer, price, package, premiums, and copy. Test these variations equally across all lists.

- Use a different source code for every different offer, package, or what have you, in each list so you can do sophisticated back-end analysis of your success.

- Be sure that your source codes are captured when the responses come in.

- Keep track of source codes for the life of the customer, not just during the response period. The success of a list may be finally known only after several repeat promotions, not just after the first response.

- Avoid false theories or rules of thumb, such as "Good lists should not be mailed too often," or "Large lists are better than small lists."

- In finding people who match your customer profile, you may find a list that is tailor-made for your situation (such as a list of new mothers for a diaper manufacturer).

- You can also find lists that match your sought-after demographic factors.

- There are four major compilers who specialize in "Lifestyle Selection," including information on what brands of hundreds of products they currently buy.

- Allow enough time for proper reformatting and merge/purge of your list. Oversee the process yourself.

- Test different envelopes, packages, offers. Test, test, test. Count, and learn.

- Rent your own list to others. Work out intelligent exchanges and profitable cooperative arrangements.

Chapter 17

Telephone Technology

On Monday nights a large section of the American public is glued to television watching "Monday Night Football." During halftime, viewers participate in an innovative audience opinion poll which takes place before their eyes. They watch a series of the best plays in the twenty-year history of the series in different categories: running, passing, tackling. Viewers vote to select the winners by calling a 900 telephone number. When they call, they hear a digitally recorded commentator greeting them and explaining how to vote for their favorite plays. ABC Sports then tells the viewers how the vote is going throughout the second half of the game.

The product of *Call Interactive*, a joint venture of AT&T and American Express Information Services Corporation, the technology makes the event possible because it can process 10,000 calls in ninety seconds, 450,000 calls in one hour.

In one ABC broadcast of the Sugar Bowl using this system, ABC received 110,000 calls during the broadcast. Before this venture began, it was not possible to receive this many calls in 90 seconds in any place in the world. The automatic machinery which they used to handle the calls, therefore, was in fact the only way that the calls could have been handled. The interactive poll would have been impossible without the machines.

This is an illustration of one of the principles of database marketing: modern technology is not only making it easier for us to keep up with customer demand at lower and lower cost, but it is creating new customer demand by providing new services that could not exist without the technology.

Why did the promoters decide on such a football poll? Let's analyze some of the possible reasons:

- Since calls came in on a 900 number, they undoubtedly made a profit on the poll itself, while costing each caller only a nominal sum.

- ABC Sports management can use the results of this poll to demonstrate to advertisers how many people were really watching, from what parts of the country, and how responsive they were to the right message. The poll will help to sell other advertising.

- The service is tailor-made for automatic order entry. To facilitate this, *Call Interactive* is tied to a fulfillment operation which can verify credit cards, prepare mailing lists and labels, print shipping instructions and invoices, and deliver a product.

Organizing the equipment to put on such an event is no small feat. But it is only a little more complicated than what the average company must go through to set up a modern telephone call center. Without a functioning telephone call center, you cannot conduct effective database marketing today. That is what this chapter is about—what telephone technology is needed to support effective database marketing, and what new marketing opportunities are presented by modern telephone technology.

THE GROWTH IN TELEPHONE TECHNOLOGY

We have all seen amazing changes in telephones in our lifetimes. I grew up in New Canaan, Connecticut, a bedroom community for New York City. All during the Thirties, our telephone number was 87 Ring 5, which meant that we were on a party line. All the families on our line had to count the rings to know if the call was for them or for someone else. When you picked up the telephone, you didn't get a dial tone, you got an operator who said "Number please." It wasn't until the eve of World War II that we got a dial telephone. Of course, that was followed thirty years later by touch tone phones, and ten years after that by modems that enable us to connect our PCs by phone, and by the ubiquitous fax, which has made it so easy to exchange contracts and data across the country. The real advances in telephone technology are still to come. They will greatly affect database marketing.

There is hardly any company today which does not expect to do some portion of its sales and a large portion of its customer service by telephone. But many of them do not yet realize how to organize around the new technology to get the most out of their new system. Consider the cost of acquiring a new customer.

Every year the cost of acquiring a new customer by direct sales visits increases. Business-to-business direct sales calls average more than $350 by the mid-1990s. Using the telephone, acquisition of a residential customer often is computed at between $15 and $25 for each new customer. A breakdown of that $25 (Figure 17-1) is provided by Andrew J. Waite, publisher of *Inbound Outbound* and author of *The Inbound Telephone Call Center,* published by the Telecom Library. Andrew Waite is the source for much of the information in this chapter, as well as being a leader in the telephone marketing industry.

Figure 17-1   Cost of Acquiring a Customer

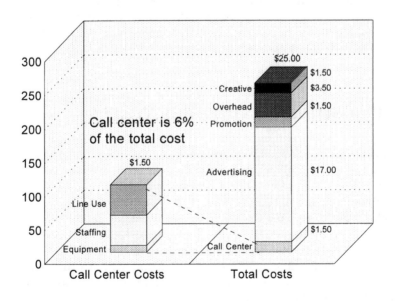

This shows that a call center costs only $1.50 of the total of $25 to acquire a customer. Yet, if the call center does not have proper equipment or properly trained staff, their mismanagement of the incoming call can defeat the rest of the marketing effort and expense. In fact, the more effective a campaign is (unanticipated huge volume of calls), the greater the potential of the incoming call center to destroy it by failure to react promptly and effectively.

Good marketing and good products put heavy inbound call volume demand on your lines, your equipment, and your people. Your callers get busy signals. They get put on "Eternity Hold." They are forced to listen to boring music (often on your expensive INWATS lines), and they hang up ("Call Abandonment"). At this point they may never call back. They become lost as a prospective customer, despite your elegant, expensive marketing and your beautiful new product.

Waite, in his book, quotes a nice example of a failure of communication between a marketing staff and the call center. The case involved the call center at a bus line. One morning, the center was swamped with inbound calls. Not until the morning break, when an employee got a chance to read the morning paper, was it discovered that the company had run a huge advertisement pushing a new, low fare. The call center was totally unaware of the promotion and of the anticipated increase in customer calls. It was understaffed to meet the demand. It dulled a potentially good ad campaign, not to mention wasting valuable advertising dollars.

SUPPORTING EXISTING CUSTOMERS

Any call from a prospect or a customer usually involves more than the business at hand, which may be a simple inquiry or a service request. The call may be to buy a ticket, to request help for a complex piece of software leading to the purchase of the latest release, an emergency call for help, or an inquiry about an invoice discrepancy. Whatever it is, it can be and should be a part of a larger business transaction which concerns the lifetime value of this customer to your company. The call center can determine, in one short interaction, whether this customer will be with you for years buying again and again, or leave you forever in disgust and anger.

Lets look at a few of the ways in which call centers are being used today:

Reservation sales and service are not only common telephone applications, they are the reason for the current technology. Most of the existing call equipment was designed first for the travel industry, and has spread from there to other uses.

Catalog Sales. More and more companies are discovering that catalog sales cannot only supplement their retail business, but can actually result in *bringing more people into their stores.* A major computer company started an experiment to see if selling small items and supplies by catalog and telephone was a viable business. Five years later, its two call centers were responsible for 10 percent of its total revenue.

Dispatch of taxis, delivery service, police, ambulances, fire departments, and repair crews.

Claims processing by telephone is growing in the insurance industry. It speeds up service, reduces cost for the company, and helps to serve an aging population which cannot get around very well. The Social Security Administration now does a significant portion of their application and claims work by telephone without the need for senior citizens to stir outside of their homes.

Contrast that with the long waiting lines usually associated with any governmental service office. The beauty of the Social Security system is that the government service worker has the senior citizen's entire contribution and claims history available on a terminal connected to the SSA database, and can thus talk knowledgeably with the applicant about eligibility. In earlier days, a clerk at a window would merely receive paper application forms which would have to be checked weeks later against the claimant's paper dossier in a subsequent, labor intensive operation—the outcome of which might be a letter to the applicant informing him or her of ineligibility because of an improperly completed form.

Stockholder Relations. The junk bond raiders of the '80s led management in many companies to realize that cultivation of the stockholder can be as vital to survival as the retention of the customer. American Transtech, a call center service agency, is an AT&T unit that began life in the early 1980s, consoling widows and orphans who held stock in the about-to-be dismembered AT&T. Transtech was so successful that they have continued as a profitable strategic unit within AT&T.

Technical Services and Software Support, otherwise known as Help Desks. Effective management of calls in this type of service is particularly important because the personnel involved are, of necessity, highly trained and expensive. Every unnecessary minute they spend on the telephone is quite costly.

Registration by telephone is growing in community colleges, hospitals, and motor vehicle agencies. Volume in such cases is often concentrated in a few days every quarter or year. The equipment has to be efficient.

HOW A CALL CENTER IS ORGANIZED

A modern call center is designed to efficiently handle a large volume of calls with minimum personnel. There are many different aspects of the center. They include:

- the Automatic Call Distributor (ACD);
- Interactive Voice Response Units (IVR);
- DNIS and ANI telephone features which detect the number dialed (DNIS) and the calling number (ANI);
- the agents (your operators who talk in the telephone);
- the economics of the center.

The Automatic Call Distributor (ACD)

This vital device does several important things:

- It manages the incoming calls automatically, taking the one that has been waiting longest first.

- It places the call automatically with an agent who is free to talk. If there is more than one free, it gives the call to the one who has been idle longest.

- It gives calls to those agents designated to handle the calls. In busy times, it can give calls to overflow agents or supervisors, or route them over to entirely different departments, depending on your instructions.

- Using Automatic Number Identification (ANI), it can tell who is calling you, and automatically signal your marketing database to retrieve the customer record of the agent with whom it has placed the call.

- Also using ANI, if the caller is not on your database, it can trigger Donnelley FastData to display the name and address of the caller automatically on the agent's screen. The agent does not need to waste valuable telephone time typing in a name and address. The agent can get right down to taking the sales call and providing service.

- Also using ANI, it can automatically route the call to the dealer who handles the incoming caller's area code, rather than wasting the caller's time while the agent asks the address. Your dealers can be located in every state of the union, but they can all be reached by calling a single 800 number.

- Using Dialed Number Identification (DNIS), the ACD can know what incoming number was dialed. Depending on your setup, this number could trigger a different routing. For example, one number could be for encyclopedia sales, another for country-western records, another for health insurance. All these calls might be fielded by the same call center with many incoming lines. The ACD can alert your agent to the type of call to expect. The computer screen will already be displaying health insurance questions when the caller comes on the line.

- Of crucial importance, the ACD contains a computer with extensive memory. It uses this computer to monitor what is happening in your call center all day long, providing up-to-the-minute reports to your call center supervision and post-call printed reports to your management. The ACD permits you to manage your agent resources effectively.

Interactive Voice Response Units (IVR)

Interactive Voice Response Units permit the incoming caller to determine his or her own routing within the company. "Thank you for calling Wearever Windows. For Sales, push '1'; for Service, push '2'; for Information or an operator, push '3'." This unit can save you the cost of one or several operators, and get the customer connected to the right party faster than most other methods. Why faster? Because often with human operators, what you get is, "All Wearever Windows agents are currently busy. Please stay on the line and your call will be answered in turn." When you finally do get to talk to an operator, he or she will just switch you to Service, where your wait starts all over again.

Another feature of voice response units is that you can ask the customer to enter some meaningful number such as a personal ID, social security or account number, or telephone number. This number, rather than ANI, can be the trigger to bring the customer's database record up on the screen. Using such a number eliminates the "privacy" issues surrounding ANI.

Figure 17-2   The Automatic Call Distributor

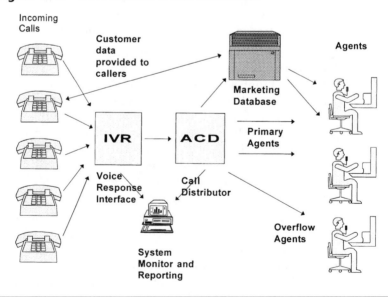

Available Agents

It is not easy to find enough people to handle your telephone calls. If you visit a large mail order catalog company, you will often see rows upon rows of empty telephone representative positions, ready to be used at the slightest uptick in business. Expensive telephone lines and switching facilities lie idle waiting for the next catalog mailing drop or the onset of the Christmas buying season. This idleness and under-utilization is the way of life of the call center manager. No call center can ever afford to be equipped to handle the *average* capacity; it must be equipped for the *peak*. Call centers typically grow beyond reasonable expectations at unanticipated rates. Once your customers know that they can get you on the telephone whenever they want, and that you will provide helpful service, they will call you constantly. Your business may grow at frightening speed. Where will you find all the agents you will need to meet peak loads? This will normally be your biggest problem. You can buy equipment and have it installed anywhere, but agents must be found where they live. For this reason, call centers are not necessarily located where your company is. You may find it more economical and practical to locate your call center in Nebraska or Utah or Colorado, when your company is in Chicago or New York, simply because you will be unable to find the full-time and part-time agents needed in the area where your company is located.

For that reason also, you may find that it is more practical to contract out your call center function to a telemarketing firm. Let them have the problem of finding agents, training them, laying them off in slow periods, and motivating them to come in on Saturday and Sunday when you have peak calling times.

When you have over 150 agent positions, a call center becomes unwieldy to manage. It is very hard to maintain a full complement of staff. Industry sources have estimated that during the '90s, 8 million new jobs will be created in telemarketing and call centers. Many call centers in the Northeast have experienced high abandonment rates (incoming callers hanging up because of too long waiting on hold) due to lack of staff. One solution has been to establish a secondary center in other parts of the country.

Part-time employees are a vital resource for any call center, but it is not economical for most of them to drive for an hour to reach a three- or four-hour part-time job. A partial solution to this problem is to build decentralized call centers, close to the workers, with calls switched easily and transparently from the central ACD unit.

There are many communities dependent on some seasonal business, such as fishing or winter or summer tourists. Many of these communities have a steady core of well-educated labor looking for the steady schedule offered by a call center. Today's technology makes the promise of this decentralized siting a viable alternative.

How Much Do Call Centers Cost?

A telephone center with thirty telephone representatives will cost you approximately $1,500,000 per year. Here is the breakdown:

Thirty Representatives @ $7 per hour plus benefits	$550,000
Two Supervisors @ $9 per hour plus benefits	$ 50,000
192 hours per day of WATS service @ $16 per hour	$775,000
Telephone equipment @ $3,500 per position	$100,000
Total cost for one year	$1,475,000

How many calls can a thirty-agent system handle in a year? I can answer that with a question: "What are you trying to accomplish with your calls?" Telephone directory service calls average fifteen seconds per call. A "Help Desk" information service may average twenty minutes per call. But most sales and support transactions average about three to four minutes per call. Depending on the time of day, you can expect your agents to be talking on the telephone about forty minutes out of the average hour.

If your call center is working a normal business day, forty hours a week, your thirty agents will be taking about 2,400 four minute calls a day. Using our figure of $1,500,000 per year, your typical day will cost you $6,000. Your 2400 calls, thus, will average you about $2.50 each. This price includes everything: WATS charges, labor, supervision, and equipment.

WHEN TO ANSWER THE TELEPHONE

In normal telephone work, the call begins when you answer it. But with ACD, your equipment can sense a call even before it has started ringing and begin to process it *before the call is answered*. The standard

North American ring cycle is two seconds of ringing and four seconds of silence, for a total of six seconds. A caller, calling a business, will typically accept hearing a ring tone from two to seven times, or twelve to forty-two seconds. An intelligent inbound call phone system can use this time to its advantage in busy times. A careful management of delay and abandoned call statistics will allow a call center manager to determine the actual "threshold of pain" that callers are willing to accept. The logic is that it's cheaper to let the phone ring than to answer it and put the caller on hold on your expensive 800 number circuit. In non-busy times, the ACD could pick up the incoming call at electronic speeds, before it has even had a chance to ring. But experience shows that this does not really save the time per call that you might think. The reason is that our phone conditioning causes us to expect some amount of ringing when we make a call. By eliminating all ringing, the inbound caller becomes disoriented and uses up more than six seconds trying to figure out what happened. Any saving is thus offset.

The delay before answering can serve even more useful purposes for a call center. Using ANI, the ACD system can determine who is calling you before the call is answered. That means that if your system involves switching certain incoming calls to certain agents or dealers or salesmen, depending on the location or identity of the caller, all this decision making and switching can take place before the call is actually answered.

For example, let us suppose that you have determined who your best customers are by RFM analysis. You want to give these customers "gold card" treatment with special agents. When any call comes in, your ACD determines from ANI what the caller's number is. This number is checked against a table of "gold card" customer numbers. If it is there, the call is automatically switched to the "gold card" agents *before the telephone is answered*. This is more efficient for you and much more satisfying to your callers, who don't have to wait to be rerouted after they first reach an agent.

When to Hang Up

In most telephone service, the caller controls the length of the call. Your call center is thus at the mercy of your customers. If they take a while hanging up after their call, your call center is still connected. You may lose several seconds at the end of each call while your equipment is waiting for your callers to disconnect. This wait is billed at 800 number rates, and ties up your call center which could be using the time to talk to someone else. Modern ACD equipment will cut the circuit as soon as the agent has disconnected, not waiting for the caller. Over a year, this feature could save you a hundred times its cost.

Delay Announcements

You place a call and the Voice Response Unit tells you that all available agents are busy. You have to wait. Experience shows that people wait longer if they have something to listen to. What will it be? What are the options?

- Music.

- Silence, broken by constant repeat announcements: "All available agents are still busy. Stay on the line and your call will be answered in turn."

- An intelligent speaker providing useful information about your company, products, and services.

Clearly the last option is the best. Whoever is calling you is interested in your company, or they wouldn't have called. Movie theatres have learned this. They know that 99 percent of all calls are from people who want to know what's playing and when, so they tell you that in a recorded announcement up front. The best announcements also tell you that there are long lines for a particular movie so you had better get there early.

Despite the last option being the best, few companies are doing it yet. Why? Because it is a lot of work figuring out what to say and getting someone to record it. Customer service is not yet an important enough function in most companies to command the resources necessary to create and present an imaginative and helpful recorded message. As database marketers we know how important this is. We will see that something is done about it.

HOW DO CALL CENTERS HELP BUSINESS?

Twenty-eight million grapefruits are processed annually by the Crest Fruit Company of Alamo, Texas. Originally, they spent $6.62 to process each telephone order. Three years later, after installation of ACD equipment, their cost was down to 75 cents per order. Crest employs twenty-eight order takers and two customer inquiry reps in four user groups. Crest operates a grapefruit club that ships produce to its members each month. Keeping track on their database of who buys seasonally helps them target customers who might be interested in buying year round. Since Crest installed its ACD system, its operations have grown by 30 percent.

Rogers Cable TV Ltd, Canada's largest cable provider with 1,580,000 subscribers, created a regional call center to improve subscriber service. The first result of the new center was to cut the call abandonment rate from 16 percent during peak periods to 2 to 5 percent. After the center was operating, they were able to answer 95 percent of their calls within 15 seconds with an average wait time of 7 seconds. The modern ACD equipment helped not only customers but also the staff. Turnover is down among the 125 customer service reps from an attrition rate of 60 per year before to 15 or less per year.

Carnival Cruise Lines maintained 142 reservation agents in their call center handling calls from travel agencies. Shortening the time a caller spends waiting is essential. The average time that a travel agent spends waiting before a disconnect is just 15 seconds. There are a lot of cruise lines out there.

Carnival installed an ACD called Infoswitch by Teknekron, in Fort Worth, Texas. Next, they organized their agents into groups of twelve, each with a supervisor. The ACD gives each of these supervisors a color-coded real-time display console showing what each agent is doing at any given moment. A supervisor can easily find out how much time agents spend on calls, how much time they spend working after each call, and how many calls each agent handles in a period. The support to supervisors is revolutionary. The colored screen takes on an overall hue based on the various levels of business. A roving supervisor can see this overall color from a distance and react if critical thresholds are reached.

Howard Savings Bank in Livingstone, New Jersey, installed an ACD with 78 incoming lines to process calls from its 350,000 customers. Previously, the calls had gone to 75 different branches. With the new call center, call volume has gone up by 14 percent per year. The number of call abandonments has declined dramatically. On one typical busy day, more than 2,500 calls came in and only two were abandoned.

SUMMARY

- Database marketing means a lot of customer contact. One of the most effective means of contact is the telephone. Customer contact by telephone is growing faster than any other method. For successful database marketing, the telephone call center must be state-of-the-art. Why?

  — Telephone calls are expensive. You should be as efficient at handling them as possible to reduce your costs.

  — Your call center, to your customer, is your company. What your agents say and do on the telephone will determine whether the customer stays with you for a lifetime or abandons you in disgust.

  — Proper, modern equipment can help you to process more calls per hour, make your customers happier, and boost your sales and service.

- You will need an Automatic Call Distributor (ACD) which unclogs the telephone lifelines that stand between you and your customers. It distributes incoming calls among available telephone agents, and provides efficient reporting systems so that you can manage your agents and calls effectively.

- You will probably need Automatic Number Identification (ANI) and Dialed Number Identification (DNIS). You will also probably need automatic attendants that ask your callers to select the department they want to speak to by pushing buttons.

- Finding good agents is always a problem. There are three solutions: 1) Locate your call center where the agents are, rather than where you are. This may mean Utah or Nebraska. 2) You may try splitting your call center up into several de-centralized centers linked by switching equipment. 3) You may find it more practical to contract with a telemarketing firm to staff and manage a call center for you.

- Call centers will cost you about a half a million dollars per year for every ten agents. Depending on what you are selling and how you manage, that translates into about $2.50 per incoming call.

- ACD units should be used to route your calls, even before answering them. Using ANI and DNIS you can figure out who the caller should be talking to, and put the call through directly to the salesman, dealer, service unit, or Gold Card Response Unit, rather than making the caller tell you that after you have answered.

Chapter 18

"In Six to Eight Weeks"

The ultimate test of the usefulness of any marketing database from the customer's point of view is the fulfillment system. How fast can you respond to a telephone call or letter with the catalog, the sample, or the product that is ordered? In your customers' eyes, all your computers, software, soft-talking sales representatives, and personalized direct mail are worthless if you cannot deliver what they want when they want it.

General Electric is one of the leaders in this field. In 1980, they decided to set up a customer service operation that would be second to none. They tackled a field which is one of the most difficult to deal with in any industry: spare parts for appliances. You know how tough this is. Something breaks on your refrigerator, washing machine, or dryer. You need a part. You cannot describe it properly, and you have no idea of where to go for it. The dealer you bought it from is probably a discount house which no longer stocks the model you bought, and doesn't keep spare parts anyway—that is why he can afford to discount. You are on your own.

If you look in the yellow pages and are lucky enough to live in a major metropolitan area, you will probably find an appliance parts warehouse on the other side of town. Their hours are from 7:00 A.M. to 3:30 P.M. Monday through Friday. They don't deliver and they don't take phone orders. You take a day off from work, travel across town, wait in line, work with an employee who peers at a dozen microfiche transparencies, and finally tells you that the part you want is probably a GGH223-033YY-3310, which costs $26.30 and will have to be special-ordered. You can pick it up here in six to eight weeks; you'll get a post card when it arrives.

The alternative is to take a couple of days off from work to wait at home for a repairman who, when he comes, has to special-order the same part for you with the same six- to eight-week delay, charging you $26.30 plus $120 for his two visits.

How did GE tackle this seemingly impossible problem? With a parts database and a super customer service attitude. They built the GE Answer Center at Louisville, Kentucky, where a well-trained staff of 250 answer 3 million telephone calls a year from people who are considering buying a GE product, or who have already bought one and need a part or information. When you call their nationwide 800 number, you get an intelligent sounding operator who has at hand the diagrams and parts lists of everything that GE has ever made. The part number and price is quickly determined. The operator takes your name and address and credit card number, then tells you that your part will be delivered to you by UPS within three days. The operator is electronically connected with four GE parts warehouses throughout the country.

To make such service effective, GE has unusually good software and unusually well-trained employees. Each of their candidates has to memorize 120 product lines and over 8,500 models. A college degree is mandatory. After five weeks of training, they begin work. They receive 100 hours of additional refresher training every year. Turnover is very low, and GE Answer Center employees stay in 'the family' for many years.

The GE Answer Center is the brainchild of N. Powell Taylor, who has managed it since its doors opened. He figures that each call costs an average of $4, but that the center generates multiple times that in sales, profits, and savings, since the calls help the company avoid service calls for products under warranty. Their trained employees can often explain to people over the telephone how to operate their new appliances and how to make simple repairs.

Pre-purchase inquiries represent 25 percent of the calls. The center knows the complete GE line with colors, sizes, and specifications. They can also direct the caller to the nearest GE dealers.

You may be wondering what they do with these 3 million names per year. In the many years they have been operating, they could have built up a tremendous database of people owning or interested in GE products. Actually, there is no database. Names are retained only long enough to assure that the parts are delivered on time, or that the complaint is resolved. N. Powell Taylor says that GE is interested in using the center only to provide information, parts, and service to customers and would-be customers. "We don't believe in sending junk mail to the people who call us," he explains. So callers do not receive anything beyond what they have requested—no catalogs, no promotional literature. And the names are not turned over to GE dealers. Whether this is sound marketing policy, I will let the reader judge. There is no question, however, that GE is providing probably the best customer service of any major corporation in America.

HOW DO THEY DO IT?

Rapid fulfillment of orders which may seem from the outside like a fairly simple and straightforward process is really quite complicated. The secret of success is tight system integration. In any database operation, there are at least a dozen separate functions that have to be closely linked together electronically to make things happen fast. The way MCRB, a leading fulfillment house with warehouses on both coasts, fills their orders illustrates the complexity of the operation.

MCRB guarantees 48 hours order processing, or the order is free. Customer orders are received either by mail, by the client's 800 customer service, by MCRB's telemarketers, or by an outside telemarketing company. Orders have to be processed electronically: the items are called up on the screen and orders are entered directly into the computer along with the customer's name, address, and credit card number. All these services must be linked electronically with MCRB.

In the event of mail orders which may include cash, checks, or money orders, MCRB has to check the order, collect and deposit the remittance, and enter the order into the computer within a matter of hours after opening the mail each day.

Credit cards are verified and automatic deposits made to the client's accounts by an outside credit card authorization company in another state, with the action taking place at electronic speed. Several quality control steps take place during the first day to assure that the customer is actually getting what he or she ordered, and that the amount remitted or charged is the correct amount.

All during this process there are decision branches (not enough remittance, incorrect item number, incorrect quantity, bad credit card). These errors are flagged to customer service for prompt follow-up with the customer to explain why the order cannot be filled as promised.

Day Two: Processing the Qualified Orders

At the end of the first twenty-four hours, the order has been qualified. That means that the payment has been assured, the item number is correct, the ship-to address is confirmed. The second day is equally hectic.

MCRB has two fulfillment centers, one in California, one in Maryland. Each must be stocked with inventory from the client. The computer will decide which center ships the item: the one closest to the customer, unless that center is out of stock.

Shipping labels and packing slips are automatically generated. The inventory system must be posted to show the drawdown of items. And even at that stage the customer could call up and cancel the order, or ask for a change in the quantity or color. The system has to be responsive up to the last minute. The warehouse must stock both client's products and packing materials. The labeling system, therefore, must be so designed to tell the packers what type of carton or bag or envelope to ship the item in—and this brings up a whole new database function: multi-pack.

Packing Several Items to a Box

You can order one item or a dozen. They can be the same, or all different shapes, sizes, and weights. No matter what you order, to save shipping costs, they should all go out in the same UPS box, if possible. To assure that this happens, the computer should store the dimensions and weights of all products in the warehouse, plus the capacities of all containers. The computer determines which container to use, and what goes in it. A label is generated for each container. If what you ordered won't fit in one box, the computer will select two appropriately sized boxes, and generate labels and packing slips for each.

The last step is the UPS manifest. This is a computer-generated report that tells UPS every day all the items that they are to pick up, where they are to go, how much they weigh, and what UPS zone the customers lie in, in relation to the warehouse.

Once or twice or several times a day, UPS trucks back up to the loading ramp and take on hundreds or thousands of packages. Some items go by U.S. mail. Others go by Federal Express. The customers, the client, or the product may determine the routing.

But shipment is not the end of the process. Daily reports must be run: back order reports, inventory reports, status reports, banking reports (credit cards, checks, returns, bad checks and so on), order activity reports, and source code reports (which media ad or type of customer call produced which orders). These daily reports are vital to let both the client and the fulfillment house know exactly what is happening: where things need improvement, where the problems are, where the profit is.

How Things Are Usually Done

Most fulfillment operations are not like GE or MCRB. Most of them are really pretty sloppy, and heedless of their impact on customers. We did business with one fulfillment house that was supposed to send out samples to people calling an 800 number. Two months after the program started, we visited their warehouse to fix a printer connection. We noticed stacks of labels that had been Federal Expressed to them every day since the program began. There were thousands of them. Some were covered with a little layer of dust.

"What are all those labels doing there?" we asked.

"Those are just for samples. We thought that the priority was to get out the paid orders. So we have concentrated on that. Paid orders go out within a couple of days."

Eye-balling the samples, we could see that there were about 100,000 sample orders sitting there. A part of our direct marketing test program was designed to determine how many people who received samples converted to paid products and how long it took. Of course, our statistics were worthless since most people ordering samples either never got them or got them two to three months late. We fired the fulfillment house, but the test was ruined.

How common is this experience? Consider these statistics (collected by Ray O'Brien for Inquiry Systems and Analysis, a Boston fulfillment bureau, and reported in *Inbound Outbound*):

20% of inquirers never receive information.

40% of inquirers receive information too late to use it.

70% of inquirers are never contacted by a sales representative.

Why is this so? Part of the answer is sloppy fulfillment. The rest is due to the attitude of the sales staff towards DM-generated sales leads: they don't think that most leads are worth the effort. But consider these further statistics (from Ray O'Brien):

60% of all inquirers purchase something within a year.
20% of inquirers have an immediate need.
10% are hot leads.
60% of inquirers also contact your competitors.
50% of all new business starts as an inquiry.

Conclusion: If you don't react immediately, you will lose sales.

When we recently needed an exhibition booth for a convention, I replied to two ads from an in-flight magazine, both of which advertised the type of booth required. One company contacted me within a week. A saleswoman from the company visited us very soon thereafter. Three weeks later we bought her booth. The week after we had signed a contract I got a catalog from the second company. We filed it. A month after that, an executive from the second company called me on the phone to learn of my reaction to their catalog. I told the executive that I had already bought from a competitor, and that he was much too late with his response. He had wasted the money he spent on the in-flight advertisement and had the wrong fulfillment house.

What Should You Do?

Fulfillment is often the weak link in your database marketing system. If you can't fulfill a customer's request rapidly, all the rest of your database system is really wasted effort. To make database marketing a reality, you must set standards for fulfillment and live up to them. What should those standards be? As far as I can see, you should have your response (product, sample, catalog, letter) out the door in 48 hours or less. This is an achievable goal. Many companies are living up to it today. In our program for fulfillment of pet food, we achieved a 24-hour out-the-door record on a sustained basis, so I know it can be done.

The Very Thing in Salem, NH ships women's clothing the same day by Federal Express. My wife, Helena, has bought from them several times, and is thrilled with the service. Yet many companies still advertise shipment in six to eight weeks, and are content with it.

What does it take to assure 48-hour out-the-door fulfillment?

1. *Set the standard.* Let everyone in your organization know what your standard is. Get daily reports and circulate them. Give awards for timesaving ideas. Make everyone time conscious.

2. *Get a rapid data-entry system.* Study your data capture methods. Most of them can be improved.

    Some companies send their inquiries to Jamaica or India for keypunching, thus cutting the data entry costs by 50 percent or more. Of course, the time consumed may be more than a month. To decide whether the delay is significant, you should analyze how much business is generated from these inquiries and how much business is lost through late fulfillment. It could be that the dollars saved through offshore data entry are dwarfed by the cost to you of lost sales.

    Some companies have developed creative solutions to the data entry problem. A major software house uses order forms designed for the Tartan X-80, a scanning machine created by Recognition Equipment, Inc. of Dallas, Texas. The order forms are printed on 8 1/2 by 11 inch paper with light colored blue squares for the customer to fill in name, address, and other information. The Tartan X-80 has the capability of reading handwriting in pen or pencil. The mailshop opens envelopes and feeds forms into the hopper of the X-80, which reads at a constant rate of sixty forms a minute.

    It takes an electronic picture of the form as it reads it. If there is any letter or number on the input form that the machine cannot read, it flashes an alert to the two or three data entry clerks located in offices adjacent to the machine. The clerk sees the photograph of the form which the machine could not read, together with a little arrow pointing to the blue square with the questionable letter. The clerk enters the correct number, and the machine speeds on.

    Delays by the data entry clerks do not slow down the X-80: it keeps reading at a constant speed. The errors accumulate on a disk, waiting for the clerks to correct them.

    Why this system? Because it is a very cost effective way of getting product out the door in twenty-four hours. And twenty-four hour service is vital to maintaining the validity of database marketing.

If you study data entry techniques needed to achieve forty-eight hour fulfillment, you will probably conclude that you will be successful only with an outside service bureau or telemarketer who can handle your peak loads, has a lower wage scale, and has the experience to move as fast as you need to move.

3. *Tie your data entry to your payment system electronically.* There are several services nationwide that will give you instant turn-around on credit card authorization and posting. All you have to do is write the software to link up with them, and make the link an automatic part of your ordering system.

4. *Use an outside fulfillment bureau.* There are two reasons why you should go outside rather than use your own company warehouse: time and money. If you are a large package goods company, most of your current business comes from servicing large distributors and retail stores. Your warehouse operates in carloads or skids. The minimum order is a carton. Your employees are well paid. But database marketing involves, typically, sending single orders to individual customers. The whole pace of the operation is different. You will need a different type of employee with a different concept of the job. Trying to introduce this type of operation into your company warehouse may be difficult and costly. Better to go to one of the hundreds of professional fulfillment houses that are used to single orders, fast service, and low-wage employees. You will get the orders out faster and keep your costs down.

5. *Spend the money on good computer software.* Fast turnaround is the result of streamlined operations where computers do most of the thinking and most of the work. Try to keep paper flow to an absolute minimum. Use an outside service bureau to write the software, and run your system on their equipment.

6. *Keep your eye on the ball.* Getting literature, samples, or products out the door in 24 hours is only one objective of fulfillment. The other objective is sales: converting samples and literature into orders, and converting product shipments into

repeat business. In many cases, the "Constructors" who are busy setting up a super fulfillment operation lose sight of the objective of the operation: to make a profit.

Making a profit requires closing the loop: every outgoing communication has to have a planned incoming response, preferably an order. How is this accomplished?

- Make sure that every outgoing product or sample package contains literature and an order form. Put source codes on the order forms so that you know which orders resulted from "bounce backs."

- Build in an automatic follow-up system for all outgoing goods and messages which invites customers to tell you how they liked the service, and asks them for additional orders. Your computer must be programmed to know when to drop that follow-up message. Again, code the order forms.

- Spot-check your system with telemarketing follow-up in such a way that you can find out what you do well, and what you do poorly.

We set up a fulfillment system for one client which did result in 24-hour turnaround. But for the first six months, he didn't get around to designing any order forms to accompany his outgoing products and samples. By the time the order forms were printed, the client's management was ready to scrap the program because of the failure of repeat orders. Only by pointing out that repeat business had not yet really been given a chance were we able to keep the program going long enough for it to prove itself (which it did).

SUMMARY

- Fulfillment is the most important part of database marketing from the customer's point of view. To be successful, you must get catalogs, literature, samples, and products out the door in 48 hours or less.

- To accomplish this, you must set up an integrated system that links electronically:

  — cashiering (opening envelopes and extracting orders and remittances)

  — telemarketing sales and customer service calls

  — data entry of orders, names, addresses, credit card numbers

  — authorization and deposit of credit card accounts

  — verifying and posting inventory

  — creating packing slips, labels, shipping manifests

  — determining what type of packing materials to use

  — warehouse fulfillment operations

  — daily reports on your operations.

- To achieve 48-hour fulfillment you will need to:

  — set high standards and stick to them

  — get a rapid data-entry system, probably at a service bureau

  — get automatic credit card verification

  — use an outside fulfillment bureau

  — use an outside database management service bureau.

- To make your operation profitable, you need to close the loop: make every fulfillment action the beginning of another order cycle by including literature and order forms in with the outgoing fulfillment. Keep track of source codes, and report on every action that you take.

Part V:

Database Marketing Applications

Chapter 19

Rewarding Newspaper Customers

This is the information age. More people have access to more inexpensive information than ever before in the history of the world—and the pace is accelerating. By the late 1990s, 99 percent of households had television, 95 percent had radio, 94 percent had telephone, 65 percent had VCRs, 65 percent had cable TV, and more than 30 percent had a computer or fax machine in their home. The information available on these systems is growing even faster: more channels on cable TV, more databases available to computer users, more fax-on-demand. Today, you can sit at home with a telephone, PC, and fax machine, and find out almost anything you need to know from anywhere in the world.

NEWSPAPERS ARE LOSING OUT

If this is the information age, why aren't newspapers prospering? As the chart below shows, newspapers are losing out to other media any way you look at it. There are fewer papers printed per 100 people every year, there are fewer papers in total, and the newspapers' share of the advertising dollar continues to decline. What can papers do to survive?

Figure 19-1 Newspaper Market Share

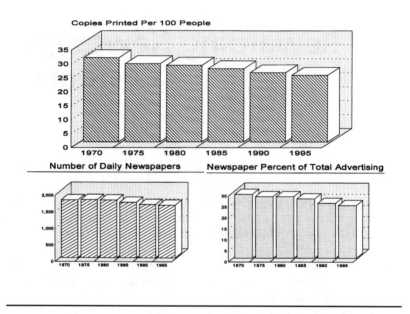

While the overall picture looks bleak, a number of papers are prospering. What is their secret of success? Let's look at one large newspaper for some clues.

The Globe and Mail is Canada's national newspaper, the most prestigious newspaper in Canada. Like other papers, 75 percent of its revenue comes from advertising. The other 25 percent comes from readers, but there is a catch. The circulation to readers is essential to attract the advertisers. To advertisers, not all readers are alike. Most advertisers prefer middle class city dwellers to rural blue collar subscribers. To increase its advertising revenue, therefore, which was the lifeblood of the paper, The Globe and Mail had to increase the number of middle class urban subscribers. How to do that?

Early in the 1980s the circulation department fell into a trap. They began to offer a trial 3, 6, or 12 month subscription at a 50 percent discount from the regular price. They couldn't advertise this discount, or their regular subscribers would feel like chumps and stop paying full price. The deal had to be made under the table. The method: telemarketing to non-subscribing selected householders in the right neighborhoods.

The scheme worked. The Globe and Mail boosted its circulation. But there was a heavy price. Eighty-eight percent of all new subscribers dropped their subscription after the discount period was over. Investigation showed that many of these lapsed subscribers liked the paper, but found that they could get it without paying the full price. They reverted to single copy purchases until the telemarketers got around to calling them again for another shot at a 50 percent-off deal.

The net result: it was costing The Globe and Mail $7 million per year for telemarketing expenses, while losing $3 million per year in 50 percent discounts. It was really a trap.

At this point, Nigel Pleasants was appointed Director of Readership Development, which included establishing the circulation marketing strategy. After some experimentation, he evolved a solution to the problem which completely revolutionized the relationship between The Globe and Mail and its readers. He solved the circulation problem, and saved millions of dollars per year. In retrospect, what he did seems fairly straightforward. In reality, however, it was not that simple. He had to feel his way along, step by step, learning more and more, until he produced the winning combination.

BUILDING A CUSTOMER DATABASE

His first move was to build a marketing database of prospective subscribers. The names of existing subscribers were known to The Globe as all subscribers paid at The Globe office, not to their carriers. He took the existing subscriber list and had the data enhanced with Canadian cluster codes and demographic data provided by Compusearch. When he analyzed the data, he began to see that in some postal walks (the Canadian equivalent of the US Zip+4), there were no paid subscribers. In others there was a high penetration. How to account for the difference? By looking at the cluster codes, he was able to find reasons: The Globe and Mail really appealed only to Canadians with certain lifestyles, and not to others. Armed with this information, he could do a much better job of building the prospect database at which to target his telemarketing and direct mail efforts.

The existing telemarketing program that he inherited dialed most numbers in the telephone book. It was costly and unproductive. Each three-month half-price subscription obtained by the system cost The Globe and Mail about $40 in telemarketing and processing costs. The subscriber paid about $30 for the three months and only about 12 percent renewed at the end of the period. It was a losing proposition—except that it was necessary to keep the advertising revenue.

Nigel decided to increase the efficiency of the telemarketing effort. He purchased predictive dialing equipment, which doubled the number of contacts per hour and, using the prospect database, dialed homes which research showed were most likely to subscribe, and contained people most likely to buy from advertisers. The resulting system worked very well indeed. He cut more than three million dollars per year off the telemarketing costs. But he hadn't gone far enough.

BOLD MOVES

Then Nigel did something quite radical. He abolished discounts entirely. The only way to subscribe to The Globe and Mail was to pay full price. No exceptions. People should take the paper because it was the best one in the country, not because it was cheap. You might expect the result: it was much harder to get people to subscribe. But those who did, tended to renew much more easily. His retention rate for new subscribers went from about 12 percent to 45 percent in a matter of two years. The no discount policy was perfect database marketing strategy: focus the customer on the product and the relationship, and forget about the money. It is worth noting that at $200 per year, The Globe has one of the highest subscription rates in North America.

His final innovation, however, was his most important one. With the help of an outside marketing consulting firm, Geoffrey Bailey & Associates, he established a "Til Forbid" system of automatic monthly payments for the paper. When the telemarketers called, the only option that they offered to subscribers was an automatic monthly payment program: we will keep sending you the paper month in and month out with the cost charged to your credit card each month, until you forbid us to continue. By training his telemarketers to use this approach—and only this approach—he was able to get 90 percent of all new subscribers on the "Til Forbid" plan. The retention rate of new subscribers after a year went up from 45 percent to 69 percent. The Toronto Star instituted the same plan in the early 1990s and soon had 80,000 subscribers on automatic payment. Two years later, the Vancouver Sun increased its paid-in-advance subscribers from 30 percent to 93 percent and also adopted the automatic payment plan.

At the Vancouver Sun, subscribers who opt for automatic payment receive a bag of grocery and household items, and are eligible to participate in a monthly contest. Winners get their previous month's VISA or Master Card bill paid by the newspaper company, up to $1,000. For winners without credit cards, the company will deposit $250 in their checking account.

At The Globe and Mail, the four changes introduced by Nigel Pleasants reduced the costs of their circulation department by $3 million per year, increased revenue by $3 million per year and also built customer loyalty. Scores of other papers have adopted similar programs with varied amounts of success.

A Customer Focused Approach

Nigel Pleasants' circulation innovations, while successful, were simply an implementation of the standard benefits that come naturally to well-planned database marketing programs. An even broader gain to newspapers can come from asking some fundamental questions, such as "Who are our customers?" and "How can we build a relationship with them to promote loyalty and increased profits for both?"

An answer to the first question has to be: newspaper customers are both advertisers and readers. Since advertisers represent about 75 percent of newspaper revenue, a focus on readers alone misses the main show. One reason why newspapers have failed to look squarely at their customer focus is their historical role as information providers. A paper that caters to their advertisers, the conventional wisdom dictates, is no longer an objective news source. Reporters and editors should be shielded from the advertisers organizationally so that they can report the news objectively. Reporters covering a major corporation are not supposed to even be aware that the organization they are trashing in their news stories is also a major supporter of the paper.

This is well and good for the reporters and editors, but it need not apply to the marketing department. Advertisers, after all, are very important customers. We may not let them in the newsroom, but why make them come to the tradesman's entrance when they want to deal with the paper?

How to Treat the Advertiser as a Customer

How can you build a relationship with advertisers? Treat them as any good business treats its business-to-business customers. Recognize them as people: give them special services, information, helpfulness. Solicit their opinions, and act on their suggestions.

The first step is to build an advertiser database. After solving their readership problems, The Globe and Mail did that. Using the advertiser database, they identified three main advertiser groups:

Figure 19-2   Advertiser Groups

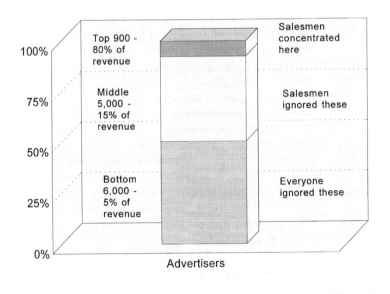

The top 900 (7.5 percent) of advertisers accounted for 80 percent of the advertising revenue. It was this group that the sales staff concentrated on. The second tier of 5,000 advertisers brought in about $25 million in 1992. What the database revealed was that 2,900 of these advertisers, who had spent $14.7 million with The Globe in 1992, did not spend any money on advertising with The Globe in 1993. Yet most of them were not visited or called on by the sales staff. Why not? Because the sales staff, working on commission, felt that they could maximize their take home pay by concentrating on the top 900. And, they were correct.

Applying the principles of database marketing, Nigel Pleasants began a program to reach these 2,900 lapsed advertisers directly. Each one was called to determine the reason why the advertising in The Globe was dropped, the name of the decision maker, and other information, which was tucked into the database. Then he began a systematic effort to win back their business through direct mail and telemarketing using an external sales company. Within nine months, he had brought in $2.1 million from these lapsed advertisers.

His success brought on problems. The newspaper sales reps resented the loss of the commissions from these customers which they had previously written off and correctly chosen not to call. The sales reps insisted that the telemarketing effort be brought in-house. This is, actually, a rather common problem whenever database marketing is introduced into an entrenched unionized sales force situation.

TREATING ADVERTISERS AS CUSTOMERS

Paying attention to lapsed advertisers is only a beginning of what can be done. It still does not establish the kind of relationship that really pays off—that would have prevented the advertisers from lapsing in the first place. What should a paper do?

Experience in other industries suggests that advertisers can be retained best by treating them well. That means not just siccing the sales force on them. It means recognition, privileges, services. And how can a newspaper do that?

- *Segmentation.* Figure out, as The Globe and Mail did, who your best customers are, and who your worst ones are. Develop programs to keep the best; design programs to encourage the leavers to stay; and ignore the worthless ones.

- *Recognition and rewards.* Create a preferred customer club. What can a newspaper do for its advertisers? Plenty. A newspaper lives in a stratified world. Newspapers have access to celebrities in the world of sports, entertainment, and politics. Throw a party at the country club when big names come to town. Invite the big names and your preferred advertisers. Let your advertisers know that they have entered an elite world when they advertise with "The Haymarket Register."

- *Personal correspondence.* Remember that your advertising customer is not "The Fisher Hardware Depot." It is really Eliza Hughes, Advertising Manager for Fisher. Eliza is a real person, with individuality, interests, questions, a husband, children, and an ego. Use your database to find out about Eliza, and what she likes and doesn't like. Treat her like an individual. Write to her and call her. Not just about her daily ads, but to get her opinion on a new Style Section, or to ask her to speak at the next Business Forum.

BRINGING BOTH WORLDS TOGETHER

Your two customer groups, then, are advertisers and readers. You need both. They both need each other. They have interests in common. You are the intermediary that brings them together. You can help them both, and do yourself a favor at the same time.

Many newspapers have established a preferred readers' club. Subscribers pay a fee to get a preferred reader card which opens up a whole new world for them. They receive discounts at restaurants and stores. They receive free gifts. They are invited to events.

Initially, most newspapers created their club to boost retention and loyalty. By giving their readers something more than a newspaper, they hoped to reduce their rate of churn. In many cases it worked, but only when the club was really valuable for the readers. In some cases the discounts offered were meager. The merchants did not cooperate enthusiastically. Result: the readers soon found the cards were essentially worthless, and the scheme failed. Why did they fail?

All database marketing ventures have to be profitable for all parties, or they will fail. Readers will not be interested in a club that has nothing in it for them. Merchants will not cooperate if there is nothing in it for them. To be successful, everyone has to win. To succeed, therefore, newspapers have to combine the reader club with their advertiser database, giving special recognition and benefits to advertisers who offer their readers something extra. In turn, the advertisers give something useful to the readers who participate. The newspaper marketers have to be extremely active in rewarding the merchants who reward their readers. When done correctly, such a club is valuable for everyone. Done in a pro-forma or half-hearted way, the club is a waste of money and time.

Essentially, such a club will work only when the paper has created an advertiser database and built a lasting relationship with its best advertisers. Once a cooperative relationship is established with the advertisers, it is a simple step to get their cooperation in building a preferred readers club that will benefit readers, advertisers, and the paper. Without the advertiser cooperation, the project will fail.

Getting on the Highway

Reader and advertiser clubs are just the beginning. If newspapers are going to survive into the twenty-first century, they are going to have to get with it. Newsprint and ink will not be enough. Some newspapers have already moved on to the information superhighway.

The Washington Post classified section includes a section called PersonalsPlus. You might place an ad like this:

"Orange Line 2:30 P.M. Our eyes spoke, we exchanged smiles, waves. I got off at Ballston, but left my heart with you. I wore a gray suit with briefcase and glasses. Please reunite me with my heart."

When you call the Post to place your ad, you receive a mail confirmation with instructions on making a voice recording and activating your PersonalsPlus service. Responders pay $5 for a secret pass code. Using that code, they can browse to listen to the recorded messages for $1.99 per minute, and leave their own recorded message in response to any ad. All calls are billed to a credit card.

In this way, the Post is serving as a community mailbox in a new way that goes far beyond an ordinary classified. It is a highly popular and profitable service.

Another Washington Post service is Post-Haste: a free telephone information service. Readers can call the Post-Haste line to hear recorded election returns, stock quotes, sports news, lottery numbers, soap opera summaries, and weather reports. How can they afford to offer this free service? It is paid for by the twenty-four banks and mortgage companies that offer the Mortgage Rate Hotline. In this service, the Post is expanding on its role as an information service—not just a newsprint deliverer.

The Los Angeles Times has pioneered with TimesLink, an online interactive news, information, and transaction service. Written by a team of 25 journalists, artists, advertising, marketing, and production experts using material from wire services and the LA Times newsroom. TimesLink is delivered via the Prodigy Network, features comprehensive news, and complete archives of the LA Times going back to 1985. It includes movie and restaurant reviews, entertainment calendars, and an e-mail bulletin board so that readers can talk to LA Times reporters and editors, give their opinions to political leaders, and swap information with other readers.

For advertisers, TimesLink Ads appear on screen throughout the service. Readers can interact with ads, clicking any ad for more information, and talking directly to any advertiser about his products or services. Advertisers can use the service to build lasting relationships, generate databases, test new products and prices, and learn more about their customers and prospects. Typical users of the service are 25-44 years old with a household income of $70,000 or more, college educated, owning a home worth more than $200,000, and typically health and fitness oriented.

How to Figure Lifetime Value

Newspapers can calculate customer lifetime value in a unique way. If they were to calculate subscription fees alone, all customers would have a negative lifetime value: the subscription payments represent only about 25 percent of the cost of the delivered product, with the other 75 percent provided by advertisers. But these advertisers will place ads only if they are assured that the paper has enough of the right kind of readers. Each reader, therefore, is responsible for bringing in a certain number of advertising dollars. A newspaper lifetime value chart, therefore, should look something like this:

Haymarket Free Press Subscriber Lifetime Value

Revenue	Year1	Year2	Year3
R1 Subscribers	1000	150	23
R2 Retention Rate	15.00%	15.00%	15.00%
R3 Subscription Revenue	$120.00	$120.00	$120.00
R4 Subscription Discount - $50	($50.00)	($50.00)	($50.00)
R5 Ad Revenue	$120.00	$120.00	$120.00
R6 Total Revenue	$190,000	$28,500	$4,370
Costs			
C1 Variable Cost Percentage	70%	70%	70%
C2 Variable Costs	$133,000	$19,950	$3,059
C3 Acquisition/ Renewal - $40	$40,000	$4,500	$690
C4 Total Costs	$173,000	$24,450	$3,749
Profits			
P1 Gross Profit	$17,000	$4,050	$621
P2 Discount Rate	1.00	1.20	1.44
P3 NPV Profit	$17,000	$3,375	$431
P4 Cumulative NPV Profit	$17,000	$20,375	$20,806
L1 Subscriber Lifetime Value	$17.00	$20.38	$20.81

A modern newspaper will incorporate many, if not all of the reader and advertiser service strategies outlined in this chapter. If so, their lifetime value table might look something like this:

Haymarket Free Press Lifetime Value

With Database Marketing Programs

Revenue	Year1	Year2	Year3
R1 Referral Rate	5%	6%	7%
R2 Referred Subscribers	0	50	33
R3 Retention Rate	50%	60%	70%
R4 Retained Subscribers	1000	500	330
R5 Total Subscribers	1000	550	363
R6 Subscription Revenue	$120.00	$120.00	$120.00
R7 Ad Revenue	$140.00	$140.00	$140.00
R8 On-Line, Voice Mail	$10.00	$10.00	$10.00
R9 Total Revenue	$270,000	$148,500	$98,010

Costs

C1 Variable Cost Percentage	70%	70%	70%
C2 Variable Costs	$189,000	$103,950	$68,607
C3 Acquisition Cost—$40	$40,000	$0	$0
C4 Reader Database—$2	$2,000	$1,000	$0
C5 Preferred Reader Club—$1	$1,000	$550	$363
C6 Advertiser Database—$4	$4,000	$2,200	$1,452
C7 Advertiser Elite Club—$3	$3,000	$1,650	$1,089
C8 Referral Incentives—$10	$0	$500	$330
C9 Total Costs	$239,000	$109,850	$71,841

Profits

P1 Gross Profit	$31,000	$38,650	$26,169
P2 Discount Rate	1.00	1.20	1.44
P3 NPV Profit	$31,000	$32,208	$18,173
P4 Cumulative NPV Profit	$31,000	$63,208	$81,381
L1 Subscriber Lifetime Value	$31.00	$63.21	$81.38

Each of the database marketing strategies is included here to show the total effect on lifetime value. By eliminating discounts, subscription revenue ends up being $50 more per year. Ad revenue goes from $120 to $140 per reader by virtue of the advertiser's elite club and retention efforts. The Preferred Readers' Club increases retention and referral, at a cost of $1 per year. Online and voice mail services bring in $10 per year.

Overall, the lifetime value after three years goes from $20.81 to over $81 dollars. Is this realistic? Who knows? Each newspaper will have to estimate the benefits and costs of each strategy and include it in their own lifetime value table. The numbers, however, are reasonably conservative. They can be tested to see if they work. They illustrate the potentialities which may be available to those marketers who look for them.

SUMMARY

- Newspapers are having a tough time surviving in the information age. Their numbers are declining, as is the number of papers printed per 100 people. Some papers, however, have been able to change and grow in this climate.

- Using database marketing principles, papers are abandoning discounts in favor of negative option monthly billing. The result is more satisfying for the readers, and more profitable for the paper.

- Profiling a newspaper readership can disclose who the subscribers are and where they live. This permits more economical targeting of subscription efforts.

- Newspapers should build an advertiser database. Using this system they can learn more about their advertisers, and boost retention and sales. The best advertisers can be formed into an elite club with special privileges and benefits.

- Once advertisers are in the club, they can help the paper to boost readership through assistance with a Preferred Readers' Club, offering discounts to regular subscribers. The combination of advertisers with readers is a win-win proposition for the paper.

- The role of newspapers is changing. They used to deliver news printed on paper. They are becoming an information source using fax, telephone, and computers in addition to paper.

Chapter 20

Frequent Banker

If you were to list the attributes to look for in the ideal customer marketing database, it might include these things:

- *Loyalty*. Customers are rewarded for staying with you—and they do.

- *Increased Sales*. Customers are rewarded for increasing the level of their purchases, and they respond to the rewards.

- *Referrals*. Customers are incentivised to enlist their friends and relatives as customers; and they actively and enthusiastically respond to your incentives.

- *Equity*. Over time, customers are conscious of a build up in a tangible equity in their relationship with you so that they are unwilling to leave you, despite the blandishments of the competition.

- *Focus on Relationship and Service rather than Price*. Discounting is the least desirable way to attract and keep customers. Why? Because anyone can do it. Your product or service becomes a commodity which is easily compared with others by using a rate chart. Instead, you want your customer to focus on the super service that they get, the nice people that they deal with, and the idea that your company is a family friend. They may know that they could save a penny by going elsewhere, but they don't want to do that.

A program that has all of these attributes can be found in the Frequent Banker program designed and supplied by Emanacom Data Services in Dover, New Hampshire, headed by Ted Amazeen, President.

This chapter provides a picture of what they did for the Wilmington Savings Fund Society (WSFS) in Wilmington, Delaware.

WHY WSFS TURNED TO DATABASE MARKETING

In 1990, WSFS, a 160-year-old savings institution, was in deep trouble. Mistakes in real estate financing in the 1980s forced the institution to write off $96 million of its $100 million in capital. The publicity caused depositor confidence to evaporate amid rumors that the bank was about to be seized by the RTC. Panic losses shrank deposits from $1.1 billion in 1990 to only $600 million at the end of 1993. The bank was only saved from extinction by two successful waves of recapitalization.

The bank faced a basic dilemma in their core business: consumer banking. In the 1980s real estate loans had been highly profitable. WSFS attracted cash by paying the highest rates on CDs. At the same time, they offered the lowest rates on consumer loans. These were not good strategies to succeed in the 1990s. As a result, they had two serious difficulties as they faced the new 1990s marketplace:

- *Price conscious consumers:* Most of their customers had been attracted by the bank's low rates. They had been trained to focus strictly on price. This type of customer tends to defect as soon as the customer sees lower rates elsewhere.

- *No competitive differentiation:* By basing their entire strategy on price alone, WSFS had made their products seem to be commodities. The bank had an insufficient reputation for service, helpfulness, or friendship to fall back on to maintain their customer relationships.

To turn things around, under the leadership of Robin Williams, Senior Vice President for business planning and marketing, WSFS instituted a new program called "MVP," billed as "The More Value Program for our Most Valued People." Designed to copy the success of the airlines frequent flyer programs, the objective was to encourage people to stay with WSFS by allowing customers, by their use of WSFS services, to earn points towards meaningful and desirable specially awarded benefits. The points could be earned quarterly by a variety of customer behaviors:

- Level of average deposit balances
- Balance increases during the quarter
- New loans and mortgages settled during the quarter
- New customer referrals

Depending on the number of points earned, a customer could fall into one of four classes: Non qualifiers, and qualifiers in Tier 1, Tier 2, and Tier 3. Each qualifier received a quarterly statement providing the calculation of his points. Depending on the points achieved, he was also notified of the awards he was eligible for. The awards included special offers of bank services plus goods and services at local merchants. The higher the tier, the more valuable the rewards. MVP points were accumulated quarter after quarter, and could be redeemed for "Something Extra" awards which included merchandise, free memberships, and travel and entertainment prizes.

The "Something Extra" points were designed as "golden handcuffs," which became stronger each quarter. As the points accumulated and the redemption awards sought attained greater and greater value, there was a higher and higher cost to defection from the bank. Customers found themselves able to tolerate less advantageous pricing in favor of continuing to build their "Something Extra" points. By the end of the first year, MVP customers were holding points worth over $80,000 in redemption value.

The bank competes for credit card business with national issuers such as MBNA Corp. of Delaware and First USA, Inc. in Dallas. These two companies run very aggressive promotions in the WSFS area. The bank also must compete with large traditional institutions such as PNC National Bank, Meridian Bank, and the Mellon Bank. "All of these institutions have powerful regional offers and deep pockets for their advertising budgets," according to Robin Williams. In the face of this competition, the bank had to stop the erosion of its business and go on to win new accounts.

HOW CUSTOMERS WERE SEGMENTED

The 15,000 customers originally qualifying for the program (Tiers 1, 2, and 3) represented only 30 percent of the bank's customer base of 50,000. But these 30 percent held 94 percent of the bank's total deposit balances. The remaining 70 percent of the bank's customers, which held only 6 percent of the deposits, did not make sufficient use of bank services to become eligible. They represented no cost to the MVP program. By segmenting customers in this way, WSFS put their emphasis, and marketing dollars, where they could do the most good. The cost of the program to WSFS for one year was $60,000 paid to Emanacom, plus $80,000 in award liabilities. This worked out to about $9.30 per qualified customer per year. Let's see what WSFS got for their $9.30 investment.

- *Increased Deposits.* In the first two quarters, the average deposit balances held by MVP participants increased by $21 million, or $1,400 per participant. To put this in perspective, in the previous year WSFS deposits fell by $19 million. This was a real turnaround.

- *Increased Qualifiers.* In the first six months, 3,363 non-qualifiers raised their balances by $15.2 million (an average of $4,519) and became qualified. Sixty-six percent of the original "charter" qualifiers also raised their balances during the same period.

- *Reduced Price Sensitivity.* As the program began, WSFS fell behind its competitors in the rates that it was able to offer to its depositors. In previous years, this would have signaled a substantial loss of deposits. Due to the MVP program, WSFS was able to hold its own—and actually increase the level of deposits. Because of the rising interest rates, of course, WSFS had to make some increases in the rates it paid to its holders of $230 million in time deposits. Had it increased the rates offered to the same level as its strongest competition, in keeping with prior year practices, it would have had to pay out $805,000 more in interest payments than it actually did pay. Contrast this saving of $805,000 with the total cost of the MVP program of $140,000, and you will get an idea of the return from a well designed database marketing program.

- *Cross Selling.* In the first six months, WSFS MVP qualifying customers took out 624 new loans totaling $12.5 million. These qualifying members also enrolled in 892 new banking services during this period.

- *Referrals.* MVP customers referred a total of 108 new households who became customers during the first six months of the program.

SOPHISTICATED ANALYSIS

Once you have a database which segments customers into useful categories, it is possible to do a great deal of refined and profitable analysis which helps both the customers and the bank.

For example, using their Insight database system, provided by the Customer Insight Company, WSFS was able to predict potential defections by MVP program members who experienced a balance decrease over a certain "harmless" threshold. Since defecting customers would forfeit their "Something Extra" points if they failed to qualify for at least Tier 1 for two consecutive quarters, WSFS was able to remind these customers of the accrued value of their points with letters and phone calls, thereby heading off a loss both to the bank and to the customers involved.

Some bank branches did better than others. Where a branch had a high concentration of non-qualifiers, WSFS was able to funnel additional MVP Point of Sale materials to the branch. In branches with a high movement of qualified MVP customers to higher tiers, WSFS emphasized their referral programs. MVP reports were used to influence branch sales goals and branch staffing.

What the Customer Sees

Every quarter, all qualifying MVP members receive a statement package consisting of:

- Personalized Statement similar to the frequent flyer statements provided by airlines. This details the points earned in the current quarter, and their accumulated "Something Extra" points.

- Award Certificates
- Referral Forms
- A catalog of "Something Extra" rewards

For those customers who qualify, the benefits are quite real. Qualified customers, for example, receive a 5 percent discount on fares for an unlimited number of trips with American, Delta, or Northwest during the next quarter. At a participating supermarket, qualified members receive coupons for $5 off a single purchase of $25 or more every two weeks for the entire quarter. Members receive installment loans which are priced 1/2 percent below those available to other bank customers. These are only a few of the benefits made available to qualifiers.

The MVP program was well advertised within the bank. There were ceiling mobiles, teller counter sliders, take-ones, and sweatshirts worn by associates on designated MVP days. Bank merchant customers were solicited for participation in the awards programs. Merchants selected were those who had less than desired market share plus excess capacity or excessive "spoilage." Spoilage is defined as a lost opportunity to sell a service or product—examples being airlines or cruise lines with vacant seats or cabins. The solicited business gained significant targeted advertising to a high-wealth group of consumers in exchange for providing these consumers with a high-value single use or evergreen offer.

HOW THE PROGRAM DATABASE WORKS

The Customer Insight Company helped WSFS create and household their customer database. To collect data to calculate the MVP points, the name, address, quarter average deposit balance, social security number, and new accounts opened information is sent quarterly to Emanacom in New Hampshire. Emanacom programmers then processed the data, applying the WSFS MVP point formulas, and produced and mailed the MVP statements, stuffed with special offer certificates for tier qualifiers.

Once this was completed, Emanacom sent a disk to WSFS which was used to append the MVP tier number to each bank customer's record, using the social security number.

As soon as a customer qualifies for MVP, he receives a welcome letter and booklet of smaller value certificates good for bank services and local merchant goods. Calling lists, sorted by type of sales opportunity within branch, are generated for branch telemarketing.

Product Holes

After the MVP statement was generated, WSFS used Insight to generate personalized letters to MVP customers with a "product hole" (absence or inadequate utilization of a bank service expected of members with corresponding balances). For example, Tier 3 customers were qualified for the premier packaged checking program, free of all pricing requirements for as long as they remained in Tier 3. For those who were in this tier, who don't have a checking account, for example, a letter was sent enumerating in detail the extraordinary value of the offer, and providing a simplified method of opening the new account.

For those who still had not snapped at the bait, WSFS furnished each branch with a calling list, identifying the qualifying members. Sales representatives at each branch called the customer to close the cross-sale. Appended demographics in the database make it easier for the telemarketers to position their discussions.

PROGRAM DESIGN

It took a full year to put the entire program together. Included in the advance planning was the design of the database, computation of the elasticity of demand for time deposits, and an estimate of the value of the benefits needed to provide to MVP members to get them to keep and increase their use of bank products. Much thought went into the questions of the monetary value required for each MVP "Something Extra" point. The process involved a three-way collaboration among Emanacom, Customer Insight Company, and WSFS. Within WSFS, marketing had to get the support of top management not just for the database activities, which were relatively modest in cost, but for inclusion of branch personnel in program promotion and administration. For a program like this to work properly, everyone in the bank has to be conscious of its objectives, and working to make it a success. That is what the Wilmington Savings Fund Society was able to do.

CONCLUSION

"This program has paid for itself many times over by our ability to price less aggressively," said Robin Williams. "For example, the bank does not now have to compete for Certificate of Deposit customers on the basis of interest rates alone, because WSFS customers are finding that their having a CD balance with the bank can bring them other value. The great thing about this system is that it's extremely flexible. We can use it to encourage behavior in whatever fashion we want."

Other banks instituting similar programs include The Republic National Bank in New York, and the Metropolitan Credit Union in Chelsea, Mass. This credit union, with $250 million in assets, had a similar experience to that of WSFS. Because the company's research indicated that its 12,000 customers generally favored cash back bonuses, Metropolitan rewards customer credit card usage not with points, but with checks at the end of the year. As reported by Candace Doucette, Vice President and Director of Marketing, "Transaction volumes have increased and the company has been able to retain its card base in a highly competitive market. It's a great card enhancement." In the first year of operation, Metropolitan increased its balances by $1 million and added 2,300 new accounts. Against these gains, the program cost the credit union only $40,000 per year for Emanacom, plus the credits earned by customers.

Loyalty Building at Central Bank

Central Bank in Jefferson City, Missouri, has pioneered with a loyalty banking program which offers bonus rates on deposits, discount rates on loans and other valuable offers to customers who qualify based on accumulating loyalty points. Customers are allowed to compute their own loyalty points by filling out a simple scorecard. Here are the things that earn points:

- Years of continuous banking
- Members of family with accounts at the bank
- Customers referred to the bank
- Number of checking accounts at the bank
- Not requiring canceled checks returned
- Gold Accounts and CDs
- Personal loans, mortgage loans and home equity loans
- Automatic loan payments add two points
- Cash reserve lines of credit
- Credit cards and ATM cards
- Business accounts
- Direct deposit services (payroll, social security, etc.)
- Automatic monthly transfers
- Services on One Statement Banking
- Safe deposit box
- Classic Club Member
- IRA or an annuity
- Use bank Discount Brokerage or Marketline Service
- Use bank trust or pension plan services

Depending on the number of points that the customer accumulates, he can get a discount of up to 0.6 percent on a personal loan, or additional interest of up to 0.3 percent on a qualifying CD, plus other special benefits. Once a customer has enrolled, his accumulated points show up on his monthly statement, and he receives special offers throughout the year.

How successful has the program been for the bank? In the first year, according to Marketing Officer Nancy Dreisinger, the bank increased its checking account balances by 13 percent, savings balances by 14 percent, money market accounts by 23 percent and CDs by 11 percent. Total asset gains from the program in the year were over $6 million, for a total cost of $116,000. The net profit from the program in the year was $96,332.

The program was organized and run by The Harrison Company of Aurora, Colorado. Harrison has run such programs for 65 banks in the United States. Widely publicized in the bank to its customers, the ongoing Harrison loyalty programs include annual loyalty awards banquets and picnics for the bank's most loyal customers. Each new customer who registers receives a book of eight Reward Certificates and another new book each year. Banks provide an ongoing cash reward to employees of $5 for each Loyalty Registration secured.

Most banks accomplish a minimum of 70 percent registration of their customer family within four years, 40 percent of which is achieved in the first year. Once registered, all CD customers are called by phone to tell them that their CDs will be adjusted to a new higher rate based on their earned loyalty status at the time of renewal.

The way the system is set up, it pays for a household to consolidate their services to maximize the number of loyalty points. The program is unique in that business services for which the household is owner can be consolidated with personal services to accumulate points. The bank appoints a Loyalty Banking Manager whose job is to oversee the program, to train bank staff, manage the software system, and report to management.

Central Bank uses the Okra system (Tampa, Florida) to create its Customer Information File and keep track of the earned loyalty points. Nancy Dreisinger, the Loyalty Banking Manager, has arranged for all of the scorecard information to be displayed on each Customer Service Terminal so that all bank personnel can use this information when dealing with customers who call on the telephone or visit the bank. The system has been highly successful for Central.

SUMMARY

Bankers are increasingly making use of database marketing to retain their customers and expand sales. The goals, which are not difficult to achieve, are:

- *Retention:* By helping customers to build equity in remaining with the bank, customers are less likely to drift away.

- *Cross Sales:* "Holes" in a customer's portfolio can be identified. The customer can be encouraged to plug the holes by pointing out that increased use of bank services can increase his equity without cost to him.

- *Reduction in price sensitivity:* One continuing goal of database marketing is to get customers to think about the value of the product and the service, and to forget about the price. Database marketing helps wonderfully in this objective, particularly in a banking situation in which service can be meaningful, and price competition is always a threat.

- *Referrals:* Word of mouth works well in financial services. If customers have an incentive to refer their friends and relatives, they will do so, as MCI has proved to the world.

The cost of such a system is really quite modest, in relation to the possible increased profits. What are the secrets of success that will make such a program flourish or founder?

First, and foremost, is conducting a close calculation of the possible benefits to the customer. Customers are ultimately interested in making a personal profit from their patronage with any institution. What they consider a profit is what the bank will have to discover. For some airline passengers, for example, frequent flyer points may be desired because they provide the ability to travel first class. For others they may be valued because they provide free transportation. Likewise in a banking situation, giving some customers free trips may be more meaningful to them than reducing their loan rates by 1/2 percent. If you are planning to set up such a system, spend as much of your planning time in designing the benefits for the customers—and in building in variations for different types of customers—as you do in laying out the mechanics of the database. If the benefits for customers are wrong, the rest of the program is just a waste of your money and time.

Second, and related to the previous point, is the cultivation of merchant bank customers who provide the premiums for your consumer customers. Enthusiastic participation by these merchants is essential for your success. At the same time, the program itself can be a godsend for the merchants by introducing them to wealthy bank customers that they might otherwise be unaware of. In setting up the program, the bank becomes an intermediary which benefits both parties and at the same time helps the bank. Invest enough resources in merchant re-cruitment to make the system pay off. The experience of banks in this field is quite similar to that of newspapers who also try to enlist mer-chant cooperation (see previous chapter).

The *third secret*, it seems to me, is outsourcing your system to someone who has experience in the field. WSFS picked Emanacom as a provider. There are others, of course, who can provide this type of service. Outsourcing permits a bank to get up and running in less time and at far less cost than trying to do the entire project in-house. When you look at the figures for WSFS in the first year: $60,000 to Emanacom versus $800,000 in interest savings, there is just no question that outsourcing is the way to go.

Chapter 21

How Database Marketing Saved a Company

Database marketing is in a bit of a rut. Few of the triumphs extend into mainstream marketing as full-blown marketing database applications; most examples of database marketing involve tactical execution rather than the use of strategic resources. Completely missing are the concepts of relationship building, creating dialogue, maximizing customer profit over time, etc. and those of us that educate are still pointing to the same few good examples of database marketing we were using as case histories in earlier years.

> It's not easy to explain this, but a lot of the blame has to go to poor salesmanship—the failure, in many instances, to make management understand that a solid database program takes not only a hefty investment in time, money, and manpower, it also takes patience. The "sell" is flawed if management gives the go-ahead for the program's development and then expects results overnight.
>
> —Rob Jackson, Donnelley Marketing, Inc.

> Every direct marketing function I participate in inevitably has a session on database marketing. These sessions focus on computer techniques and how to create a database but spend almost no time on how to develop, build and enhance the relationship between your company and its customers.
>
> —Bernie Goldberg, Direct Marketing Publishers

In this chapter, we are going to look at a marketing case study about a company, TROY-BILT, which had a perfect product, but failed to reach out to their customers. After going bankrupt, the reorganized company adopted a new policy based on direct marketing, database marketing, and customer service. The change rescued the company from bankruptcy and made it an international success.

THE PERFECT PRODUCT

Everyone has at some time in their life experienced the wonderful thrill that comes with owning a perfect product. It may be your first car, first house, first cocktail dress, first computer, piano, or encyclopedia. Whatever it is, you feel that you share with the maker of this wonderful masterpiece the joy of its creation.

In an earlier day when products were made by a single craftsman you could go personally and congratulate the person who made your dining room table or your suit of clothes. Today, such products are made by a great many employees collaborating together in an organized production process. That fact does not reduce the feeling of awe and appreciation that people experience in those moments when they realize the wonder of what mankind can fashion with his hands and his brain and his machines.

A few years ago, I was overcome by the perfection of a book— *Jacobean Pageant: The Court of King James I* by G. P. V. Akrigg. It is history at its best. The book was published thirty years before. In a surge of enthusiasm, hoping that he was still alive, I wrote to the author, in care of the publisher in New York. After some time, my letter reached him, a retired college professor in his country home in Vancouver. He wrote back, thanking me for my interest, and telling me of the pride of accomplishment he felt in having written the book, and his happiness in knowing that it was still being read and appreciated after all these years.

Building a Relationship

What has this to do with database marketing? Everything. In playing a role in the production of products and services for customers we are, in many cases, helping to create works of functional art. We are bringing comfort and joy to millions who could not afford these things without the competitive mass production system that brings forth this stream of constantly new and improved products. Through building one-on-one relationships with customers, we are reestablishing the link between the creators and those who benefit by the process. This relationship enriches both parties.

For more than forty years I used a Remington electric razor. As each new model came out, I bought it, happy with the constant improvements year after year. Remington, however, has no database. They seem to have no interest in their customers. There is no one to talk to except the constantly changing local service personnel who don't remember their customers from day to day. When I bought the latest model, it failed after a week. I took it back. They said I would have to leave it for a few days since there were others ahead of me. I bought a Norelco, and have never been back. Norelco, incidentally, has a customer database, created by National Demographics and Lifestyles. They offered me a chance to earn $1,000 for becoming a registered customer. What they do with their database I have yet to learn.

When Helena and I visited Guilford, Connecticut, we visited an art gallery and bought our first genuine piece of art—a lovely oil painting of a Cape Cod house by a Massachusetts artist. We hang it proudly in our front hall. We like it so much that we wanted to know something about the man who painted it. We identify with him because he has captured in his painting the spirit of a New England village that makes us love the area. At our request, the gallery tracked him down and sent us his biography.

Customer Advocates

The point: Many people feel a real attachment to some of the products that they acquire. They identify themselves with these creations. In many cases, they would like to establish a relationship with the company or individuals who made the product that they value so much. By building a database and setting up the one-on-one communications that the database makes possible, we are doing these people a real service.

This service, like any free market transaction, profits both parties. By providing a conduit for customers to contact you, you are increasing their loyalty to your company and your products. This will result in increased sales, reduction in attrition, and adoption of new products when they come out. The identification that people feel with you can be converted into advocacy and referrals.

THE TROY-BILT STORY

TROY-BILT Manufacturing Company was originally organized around an idea: to build a new and better kind of gardening power tool. The focus was on the product. The company struggled for thirty years making excellent products that did not find a wide audience. After the entrepreneur who founded it and kept it going all those years retired, it foundered and was sold. It almost died.

At that moment, a creative genius in marketing was asked to help the company. He had an idea: make the customer the center of the strategy, and provide the customer with a vision, a concept of what could be done with the product. By redirecting TROY-BILT as Garden Way, Lyman Wood, a genuine marketing folk hero, pioneered in direct marketing, followed by database marketing, and made a tremendous success out of a failed business.

The Early Years of Rototiller

Rototiller, Inc. was founded in New York City in 1930 to exploit a better method of tilling the soil. Imported originally from Germany, the idea was to churn up the earth in a single pass by a rear mounted rotary wheel with metal tines, instead of the more cumbersome three pass method of plowing, disking and harrowing. An American engineer and entrepreneur, Carl Kelsey, formed the company and ran it for twenty-six years, producing a succession of small gasoline-powered cultivators from a factory in Troy, New York.

During these years, the focus was always on the machine: how to make it better, more versatile, lighter in weight. A new model was produced every year. Each year new attachments were created to widen its versatility. The advertising during the early years was always on the product.

The machines were excellent, and well liked by those who used them, but the sales through dealers throughout the country were insufficient to maintain the business. Always suffering from slow sales, after Kelsey retired in 1956 the company went down hill and was sold in 1959 to a series of owners, eventually ending up in 1962 as a company called Watco, headed by George Done, an engineer who had been with Kelsey since the beginning. Trying to solve the marketing problem, George turned to Lyman Wood, a direct marketer who had a successful career in mail order sales with Noroton Publishing in Connecticut and Farm and Garden Research Associates in Vermont.

Wood saw the limitations in marketing the Watco product, The Trojan Horse, exclusively through a dealer system. The company could sell only as many machines as the dealers ordered and only at one time of the year. Wood proposed that the company use direct marketing techniques to sell the 400-pound $350 Trojan Horse through the mail. With today's hindsight, and the experience of Dell Computer, it does not seem so revolutionary. But at the time, it was.

Most people were skeptical that anyone would buy such a large item through the mail. Wood, however, felt that mail order would benefit gardeners who had no access to a dealer. Since there would be no middleman, the price could be kept low. Wood was so enthusiastic that he offered to pay all the marketing expenses out of his own pocket, being reimbursed only if the technique worked.

Early in 1963 ads were placed in national gardening magazines encouraging readers to write for information. Likely buyers were sent a brochure and the name of the nearest dealer. Those too far from the dealer could order from the factory. While sales went up by 1965, they were not sufficient, and the plant was again faced with bankruptcy. A post mortem of the sales showed, however, that the direct marketing campaign was the only part of the sales program that was really working.

Encouraged by this discovery, the team of Done and Wood decided to attract additional operating capital to exploit the direct marketing idea. Most of the new stockholders were friends of Lyman Wood. They were marketers. They formed Precision Marketing Associates (PMA) in Norwalk, Connecticut to fill Watco's needs for advertising, printing, and mailing.

PMA was more than simply a service agency for the tiller business, however. Its importance in the successful selling of Watco's machines was crucial, as they supplied both organizational direction and creative expertise to the company. Tillers were manufactured in Troy, but tiller sales were manufactured in Norwalk.

How Direct Marketing for Rototiller Began

Lyman Wood got his start in the advertising business working for J. Walter Thompson from 1936 to 1940. Leaving it to found the Life-Study Fellowship, in a few years he established the Noroton Publishing Company. In 1944, the company published a booklet by Ed Robinson, called the "Have More Plan," a detailed explanation showing how a family could produce most of their food on a couple of acres of land and a few hours of labor per week.

The Have More Plan became an overnight classic. Hundreds of thousands of copies were purchased. It led Lyman Wood to establish The Country Bookstore which distributed it and offered other gardening and self-sufficiency books through the mail. One of the products that caught Wood's attention was the Rototiller, which he felt fitted in well with the needs of the small farmer.

In the 1950s and 1960s the advancement of self-sufficiency through gardening became something of a crusade for Lyman Wood. He wanted to see his personal philosophy become a way of life for hundreds of thousands of gardeners. When George Done asked him for help with Rototiller in 1962, he took it as a challenge to his marketing skills. He felt that with the right formula, nearly anything could be sold through the mail. He also believed in the product. He felt that the Trojan Horse would help people get "back to the land" by enabling them to grow more of their own food with less work.

As Lyman Wood's direct marketing techniques began to pay off, Dean Leith, Jr. was added in 1966 as the first full-time advertising and sales manager. He brought his own touch to the company, personally answering questions from Tiller owners and prospective buyers. He also wrote to customers after each sale making sure that they received top notch service.

By 1968, the direct marketing program was becoming quite successful. Sales were higher than at any time in the company's history. The Trojan Horse name was changed to TROY-BILT, and Watco was renamed the Garden Way Manufacturing Company to better reflect the philosophy that gardening was a way of life which was the centerpiece of the marketing strategy.

Lyman Wood added a gardening consultant to the staff, Dick Raymond, who was a firm advocate of turning under cover crops to enrich the soil. As a result of his suggestions, the product was modified to add self-cleaning tines which assisted in the "green manuring" process. Raymond wrote several books on gardening advice which were published by the company.

Adding to the gardening philosophy, Wood established Garden Way Research in 1969 to manufacture and market his Garden Way Cart (a two-wheeled gardener's cart), and introduced other products including cider presses, home workbenches, home generators, and solar greenhouses. In 1970 he founded Garden Way Publishing to print books on gardening and self sufficient living.

In 1972 Garden Way funded a national non-profit organization Gardens for All, to encourage food gardening by providing information and advice to anyone interested. At the same time, providing access to both equipment and information became the primary thrust of the profit-making business. In 1973 the first Garden Way Living Center was opened in Burlington, Vermont. Under one roof were collected thousands of books and tools needed for gardening, cooking, home food preservation, and alternate energy sources. Soon, living centers were opened in many other states from Oregon and Washington to Georgia.

For many years, The Garden Way Catalog offered these same products by mail. In the early 1980s, building on the success of the previous decade, the company underwent a major reorganization. All operations were consolidated in Troy under the TROY-BILT name. Reflecting the changed consumer approach of the 1980s, the manufacturing operations were separated from the Garden Way philosophy. Lyman Wood retired to Vermont, but his legacy to the company lives on today.

As a part of the reorganization, the company organized and trained their 150 Regional Key Dealers to supply the full line of TROY-BILT products, with factory trained service. Seven TROY-BILT factory stores from coast to coast round out the distribution system. The bulk of the sales which used to come from direct response to TV ads, print, direct mail, and customers on their database during the 1970s now come increasingly from the dealer network—although direct is still a vital part of the mix.

The Growth of Database Marketing

Under Dean's leadership the company began to publish a tabloid sized TROY-BILT OWNER NEWS which has grown to twenty pages and now comes to owners free four times per year.

The subscription list, built from TROY-BILT owner registrations, totals more than 700,000. The OWNER NEWS provides part of what is called a "continuing free course in gardening" which goes with the purchase of TROY-BILT machines. The News gives gardening information, tiller maintenance and service tips, recipes and food preservation hints, and the latest news from the factory.

A sample of the articles in one issue includes:

- Management options for your yard materials

- Zucchini apple pie

- Tips, tricks and suggestions on gardening from readers

- A versatile compost bin

- Weed control hints

- Create a time-saving landscape

- Summer salads

The TROY-BILT OWNER NEWS forms an important part of the good feeling between company and customers which holds them together. An inspiration by an editor of the NEWS led a few customers spontaneously to organize a Good Neighbor Gardening Club. The idea caught on. There are more than 600 clubs, with chapters in each of the 50 states, and in Canada.

The Good Neighbor Gardening Clubs are not official company sponsored organizations. They are simply a product of the enthusiasm that comes from getting customers and suppliers together in an information-sharing system. Owners are encouraged to write to the factory with anything that is on their minds. A special toll free Hot Line was established in the 1970s which has survived for a quarter of a century.

In 1985, Jairo Estrada became Chairman of the Board and CEO of Garden Way. He provided the leadership for a major expansion and change in direction for the company as a whole. The direction changed from a focus on the use of the company's products for the production of food, to their use for suburban lawn and gardening. In keeping with the new focus, the product line was expanded. They now make large chipper machines and mulching mowers. All of these products are sold by direct response advertising, and by catalogs sent to existing customers as a central part of the TROY-BILT OWNER NEWS. By the mid 1990s they had 1,600 employees and annual sales of $310 million.

Customer Service

The best part of the entire customer focus, however, is the customer service. TROY-BILT provides four different 800 numbers for customer service, free technical advice, spare parts, and help in selecting a model. To illustrate the kind of service that TROY-BILT gives, consider this letter from a reader and the editor's response:

> *"This is just a quick note to express my gratitude to the representatives of your company. I recently purchased a ten-year-old Horse Model, which is in fine working condition. I've been on the phone a few times for parts, and to Technical Service for information. I am impressed with the quality of support provided and the kind, helpful attitude of your representatives.*
>
> *To me, this aspect of TROY-BILT Manufacturing Co. is as important as the superb quality of the machine produced, if not more so. Thanks!"*
>
> *_____, Patuxent River, Md.*

> *Thank you, ___, and a word to folks who sell their TROY-BILT machines: Please be sure to include the Manual, Parts Catalog, and Warranty Transfer Card, so the buyer can get off to a good start as an owner. If you no longer have the paperwork for the equipment, tell the buyer to call 1-800-*

833-6990 and give the machine's serial number so we can provide the right information.

Editor

On the face of it, this is an amazing letter. How many companies provide technical support to people who bought their product used from some third party? How many will register such people in their database, and provide them with the same benefits as owners of new products? Damn few.

Yet, Lyman Wood and Dean Leith saw the concept: everyone in the database is a potential purchaser of a new machine or other related product. Being in the database provides benefits to both parties. The bigger the database, the greater the repeat sales, cross sales, and long term support.

Why has TROY-BILT succeeded when so many other database marketing programs have failed? There are a number of reasons:

- *Top quality.* The machines themselves are top-of-the-line products built to last for years. Parts are maintained for all the early models so that the machines, if well maintained, will never wear out. They sell for enough so that the margin covers the cost of the database.

- *Focus on the customer.* Since its reorganization under Lyman Wood's marketing leadership, TROY-BILT focused on the customer, rather than the product. The reason for providing free technical advice to people who have bought their machines used from some third party is that they are looking at the lifetime value of each gardener on their database, rather than the profit from selling their current stock. They have devoted a considerable part of their marketing budget to database marketing, year after year.

- *Selling direct.* TROY-BILT sells through dealers, from official factory stores, and direct. The fact that they have been able to bridge the gap between direct sales and dealer sales—and make both of them work—shows a sophistication in marketing that few corporations have managed.

- *Rebuilding.* TROY-BILT has an active rebuilding program, inviting customers to have their old machines rebuilt for half the price of a new model. These used machines are reconditioned and are returned with the same warranty and 30-Day

Trial Offer as new equipment. Spare parts are stocked for all models from the beginning of the company. The rebuilding program is not actually used that much. Its significance, however, is that it says to every customer: "Your Roto-Tiller will last a lifetime. We will help you maintain it. We are your friends, not a supplier trying to force new models on you." Psychologically, the rebuilding program is dynamite database marketing.

- *The TROY-BILT OWNER NEWS.* The focus of the 20-page TROY-BILT OWNER NEWS is not primarily on the product, but on gardening, cooking, recycling, yard care, safety, composting, landscaping, plus tips from owners. The newspaper is interesting and informative. It contains information that most people would willingly pay for if it were a regular magazine. It is part of the extra profit which customers want today from their suppliers—beyond an excellent product.

- *Identification.* The database—and the company—were built around an idea: the value of self-reliance and home gardening. The idea was communicated to the customers in a dozen different ways. The customer can identify with the idea and, hence, with the company. In the past decade, reflecting a changed and more affluent suburban consumer, the stress is no longer on self-reliance (Garden Way). The group identification, however, lives on in the faith that customers have in the products and the company that makes them. TROY-BILT is truly building a relationship.

- *Customer organization.* The fact that hundreds of garden clubs have come into being spontaneously throughout the country shows that TROY-BILT is reaching customers with more than just good products. The customers and TROY-BILT are concentrating on what can be done with the products. The company is built around an idea.

RECAPITULATION

The TROY-BILT story is database marketing at its very best. It contains all the elements essential to a winning strategy:

- A vision of what you want to accomplish through your business: not just make a profit, but to improve the world. In this case, under Lyman Wood's leadership it was to sell the vision of self-sufficient gardening. Today it is refocused on customers' responsible use and enjoyment of their yards and gardens.

- A sufficient margin on the sale price to afford the customer service and other relationship building programs.

- A core strategy: sell direct.

- A long term commitment to making the customer the focus of the marketing program.

- The spontaneous organization by the customers into clubs.

- Regular communication with customers, free customer service, free technical support, spare parts information.

- Enrollment of buyers of used machines from third parties the same free customer service, free technical support, free enrollment in clubs and services as is provided to buyers of new products.

CAN YOUR COMPANY USE THE TROY-BILT STRATEGY?

Database marketing is difficult because each successful program requires very creative strategic ideas, such as those of Lyman Wood, plus years of follow-through. Looking back at twenty years of success with Lyman Wood, and the subsequent years, it looks easy and obvious. It was not easy or obvious in 1962 when Wood started marketing for a bankrupt company with a new and untried marketing plan.

Are there other Lyman Woods out there today? Yes there are. Most of them are the unrecognized heroes of tomorrow. It is possible to speculate on where they will arise:

A piano maker who provides instruments to piano teachers, organizes piano competitions, recitals, clubs; focus on the customer and what you can do with the piano.

An automobile manufacturer like Land Rover who provides super customer service, organizes customers into clubs, sponsors events; focuses on the customer, and what you can do with the car.

A movie maker, like Disney, who takes the vision of their films, and builds theme parks, organizes fan clubs, and provides an institution that their customers can identify with.

An appliance manufacturer, like General Electric, that provides super customer service, spare parts, and a vision of what the company stands for that makes customers say "That is my company".

A software or computer manufacturer that provides a vision of what they are trying to create, and organizes their customers into user groups focused on what you can do with their product.

The Kool Aid Wacky Warehouse, the Burger King Kids Club, the Crystal Lite Club are pale imitations, but are surviving specimens of the breed.

Where does this leave most packaged goods? Out; unless they can get up interest in some idea beyond the product itself. Low markup commodity package goods are unlikely database candidates.

Database marketing is not for everyone, sad to say. But for those with the right product, a genius with a vision like Lyman Wood, and the ability to think long term, database marketing can be very profitable.

SUMMARY

- People like to identify with the products that they buy, and with the people and companies that make them. Manufacturers can do their customers a favor by assisting in this process, and at the same time be rewarded by loyalty, reduction in attrition, and repeat sales.

- Lyman Wood showed that direct sales of heavy expensive products like Rototillers is possible, and compatible with the maintenance of a dealer network.

- He showed that a company and customers can be motivated and organized around a strategic concept like self sufficient gardening—i.e. what you can do with the product. The strategic vision, plus the quality of the product, permitted customers to identify with the company, and built loyalty.

- Companies can benefit from the spontaneous organization of hundreds of thousands of their customers into groups which not only help the customers, but also build knowledge of and support for the company's products.

- TROY-BILT showed how free customer service and technical support after the sale could be extended to purchasers of used products from third parties, benefiting the company in the long run, and building loyalty and repeat sales.

- TROY-BILT shows how the strategic vision that surrounds a core product could be extended to hundreds of other related products in a program that supports the vision and goals of the customers and the company.

- TROY-BILT's reorganization in the 1980s to reflect a changed consumer base shows the adaptability possible with true consumer focused marketing. Yet they manage to have generated a group feeling among their hundreds of thousands of loyal customers. The group feeling is expressed in the TROY-BILT OWNER NEWS.

- TROY-BILT has created a huge customer database from owner registrations and maintains communications with them four times a year in a very interesting tabloid newspaper that is devoted to the vision of what can be done with the products, not just to the product itself.

- Many other companies can use the Lyman Wood approach to marketing. It takes the right combination of circumstances: a sufficient margin in the selling price, and a great strategic idea, plus a genius with the drive to sell the idea for a long term.

Chapter 22

Promoting Trial in Packaged Goods

The vast majority of packaged goods are sold through a combination of four methods: awareness advertising, every day low price (EDLP), price-discount sales to retailers, and massive doses of free standing insert (FSI) coupons. These methods work. Packaged goods manufacturers and their agencies are organized around these methods. Retailers understand and accept them. So where does database marketing fit in?

The short answer is: "Almost nowhere, right now." The long answer is: "There are some new profitable possibilities which are being actively explored." To understand the role of database marketing in packaged goods, we have to go back to some basic principles and facts.

- There is such a thing as brand loyalty.

- It is, in general, easier to sell to loyal and occasional customers than to beat the bushes for new ones.

- Ninety-six percent of FSI coupons are not redeemed by anybody. Of those that are redeemed, a great many of the coupons are redeemed by regular users who would have bought the product without the coupon. People who actually redeem most coupons are the heaviest coupon-using segments of the population; they tend to be extremely price sensitive and the biggest brand switchers. They are amongst the worst loyalty prospects.

- Although FSI coupons can induce trial in a competitive brand user, they do not build brand loyalty on the part of loyal or occasional users. Coupons focus attention on price, not on the quality of the product.

- On the other hand, FSI coupons do influence occasional users to make that purchase now (and of your brand) when they might have waited, or bought some other brand. These occasional user purchases are why FSIs work, despite their imperfections, and will probably continue far into the future.

- The fact that most coupons are redeemed by regular or occasional users forces manufacturers to offer relatively modest "cents off" coupons, rather than premiums sufficiently valuable to induce trial by a high percentage of competitive brand users.

- Packaged goods are sold through retailers who, in many cases, have private label products that compete with manufacturers. Rather than cooperating with manufacturers, they are often in competition with them.

WHAT CAN DATABASE MARKETING DO?

Given the above, what can database marketing contribute? While there are all sorts of claims for packaged goods database programs, there really are only three practical things that can be accomplished through database marketing. They are:

- *Promote Retention, Referral, and Cross Sales:* Build brand loyalty on the part of existing brand users, a loyalty which can be immune to competitors' discounts. Examples include affinity groups, niche market clubs, and newsletters.

- *Sell Direct:* Sell products directly to large volume consumer users. Examples include pet foods, baby diapers, specialty coffees.

- *Induce Trial:* Target new consumers or competitive brand users with high premium offers that result in significant trial and conversion. Examples include new baby programs, and programs like Target Mail (see below).

PROMOTING RETENTION AND CROSS SALES

Kraft General Foods has blazed a trail in this area. Working from their massive 30 million name database, they pioneered with the Crystal Lite Lightstyle Club, which offers 1 million diet-conscious customers an interesting newsletter on diet and fitness, discount coupons on Kraft General Foods products, a cover letter, and a catalog. The catalog is part of the club image, because it offers watches, mugs, jogging suits, and other gear that bears the Crystal Light emblem. This highly successful club has been going for several years, maintaining the loyalty of medium to heavy users of the product, and promoting related KGF low fat/low calorie foods of interest to this special niche market.

A similar effort has been used by Kraft to promote Kool Aid sales. The Wacky Warehouse newsletter is mailed to a large group of pre-teens. It has successfully kept its database of 4 million children drinking Kool Aid for many years.

Carnation, along with a half dozen other companies, has concentrated database marketing attention on parents of new babies. Working from a database of expectant parents, The Carnation Special Delivery Club mails helpful information about child nutrition and baby care beginning as early as eight months before the birth. These mailings promote use of their baby products, building a base for introduction to other related products. Concentrating on this special niche market of baby parents, the redemption rate of coupons runs more than 24 percent as opposed to 4 percent or less for FSIs. The baby mailings both promote trial (through high value initial coupons) and retention (through very creative and useful baby care information delivered along with the coupons). There is a referral program, a sweepstakes, an educational booklet, *Pregnancy, Nutrition and You* and an 800 number baby hot line with experts that can answer questions.

In all of these efforts, the success comes from one simple principle: offering information, assistance, helpfulness, and reassurance. The coupons (and in some cases checks) simply serve as a communications vehicle, rather than being the central focus of the outreach program.

They are building loyalty to Carnation, rather than building up the expectation of getting something for nothing.

Where Retention Promotion Fails

Not all efforts at retention building for packaged goods are successful. One noted failure was The Society To End Dull Meals Forever promoted by McCormick-Shilling. A quarterly newsletter was mailed to 200,000 customers interested in cooking. The idea was to teach people something that most of them did not know: how to use spices in cooking. The program was designed to build loyalty to McCormick and increase the sales of their bottles of lemon and pepper and other spices. The creative was very well done. The response from the public was excellent. They correctly targeted a niche market (people who like to cook using spices). They forgot only one thing: the economics.

Spices sell for $2.50 in the supermarket. The retailer gets about half of that, and McCormick probably nets $0.20 out of the remainder. So for each additional bottle sold, McCormick makes 20 cents incremental profit. The problem: how many additional bottles of spice can the average family on the database buy in a year? Six perhaps? Remember that bottles of marjoram, thyme, sage, and curry tend to last a long time—perhaps several years—and take up space in the average kitchen. Six extra bottles per customer per year is $1.20 in incremental profit per year.

How much does it cost to maintain a database, and to design, print, and mail a quarterly newsletter to their customers? It is unlikely that you can do this for less than $1.50 per year. Result: Despite increased sales, McCormick was losing at least $0.30 per year for every customer that signed up for the free newsletter. They eventually realized this, and canned the entire program.

Conclusion: Packaged goods margins are very thin. Even successful efforts aimed at niche markets will fail if the incremental increase in retention and cross sales cannot pay for the cost of the database and customer communications. Parents of babies, pre-teens, serious dieters, ethnic cooks, and pet owners represent valid niche markets. Whether cultivating them will pay off depends on the economics of the products being promoted.

PROMOTING REFERRAL

In cruise lines, long distance services, restaurants, medical services, or software, for example, the recommendation of a friend or colleague is often the most important factor in the decision-making process. How important this can be in packaged goods is often overlooked. Carnation found that it was very powerful when they introduced Perform, a premium pet food delivered direct to the consumer. They introduced a referral program (similar to the highly successful MCI Friends and Family Program) whereby customers could recommend other customers and receive a reduction in price on their next offer if the referral became a customer.

On-pack offers in products at retail can be used to provide customers and the people they recommend with coupons which exceed the value of the FSIs appearing in the Sunday newspapers. In the process, the manufacturer can build his database of loyal users. To get the high value coupons, the householder needs to persuade someone else to buy, and has to fill out a survey. Will such a program work for all products? Absolutely not. There has to be a high enough margin, and sufficient annual purchases of the product by each customer to justify the costs. The beauty of such a program, however, is that the costs of an on-pack offer of this kind are relatively low, in comparison with solo mailings or mass FSI distribution. The manufacturer gets value for the redemption in the form of two customer's names and survey data. These names, of course, have no value at all unless the manufacturer has figured out a way to make use of these names in subsequent profitable marketing activities.

PROMOTING TRIAL

One of the best methods of using database marketing in the field of packaged goods lies in promoting trial of your product to heavy users of competitive brands. As already pointed out, this is hard to do through FSIs because the vast majority are redeemed by existing brand users. How can you single out only the competitive brand users, giving them an offer that they can't refuse: a free large size box of your product? There is a way.

Target Mail, in Scarborough, Canada has been pioneering a method which successfully identifies the heavy users of packaged goods products. Their unique method of selective insertion puts very high value coupons into the hands of heavy users of competitive brands in Canada and the United States at a very modest mailing cost. Their redemption rates are extremely high.

How the Process Works

In Canada, for example, Target Mail sends a large questionnaire to all 10 million Canadian households in four waves of 2,500,000 each over a two year period. With the offer of a sweepstakes and a package of significant valuable coupons, they achieve a consistent response rate of 22 percent. Their resulting database of 2,200,000 households is representative of the broad scope of the Canadian buying public, and not just coupon clippers. Target Mail grew and prospered while most of their competition in Canada and the US (Computerized Marketing Technologies, JFY Audit America and others) went out of business. Carol Wright is the only surviving competitor which mails a household survey. One reason why the other companies have failed is that the quality of their data was poor.

With a response rate in the 2 percent–4 percent range, offering mainly medium value coupons as a reward, these competitors garnered mainly that portion of the buying public keenly interested in acquiring and using coupons.

To keep their costs down, Target Mail developed their own scanning system which focuses twelve digital cameras at each side of a 14 by 17 inch survey form containing 1000 bytes of demographic data and answers to product use questions provided by a maximum of 51 different brand sponsors. The demographic questions ask about infants, children, adults, grandchildren, pets, employment, dwelling type, income, home businesses, and hobbies. They ask whether people normally use coupons, and about their grocery shopping habits. The sponsored questions deal with product use, travel habits, investments, reading and sporting interests, and medical problems. Using their scanning system, they capture this information about each household with better than 99 percent accuracy, charging their manufacturing clients about 10 cents per completed survey. Each participating manufacturer is taught to use a decision tree that looks something like this:

Figure 22-1 Decision Tree

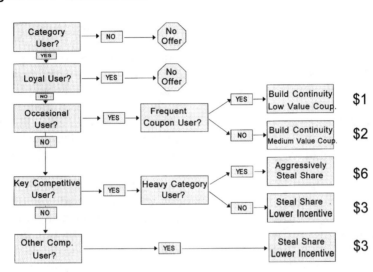

To "aggressively steal share" the manufacturer offers an extremely valuable coupon, amounting in some cases to a free large size product. You will notice that loyal users receive no offer at all. The frequent coupon users and the light category users receive lower value coupons. This clever targeting method makes optimum use of the marketer's dollar.

To deliver the coupons, Target Mail feeds the results of each of the 51 manufacturer's "decision trees" into computer software that runs a complex insertion process. Each envelope is run through a 24 pocket selective inserter eight times before it is ready to be mailed. The result of this process is that every one of the targeted households receives a packet whose contents differ from that sent to every other household. This extremely selective system puts each manufacturer's coupon in the mail (along with others) for about $0.02 per household, including postage.

How do the economics of such targeting work?

In the first place, the goal of the program is conversion of incremental purchases—getting heavy users of competitive brands to switch some or all of their purchases to your brand, and getting the less-loyal occasional users of your brand to increase the percentage of times they buy from you.

To determine what value to assign to the offer, the manufacturer is assisted by Target Mail to use a formula which calculates the conversion rate they will need to achieve if the promotion is going to payout in 12 months. If the conversion rated needed is absurdly high or low in their experience, then the decisions concerning "if" and "how" to target the groups in question are relatively clear. If the conversion rates are in the gray zone (maybe we can achieve them, maybe not) then the client can adjust the design by altering the definition of the target group or changing the value of the offer to see if a more achievable conversion rate can be produced.

Once the buying and coupon using habits of each household are known, the value of each coupon necessary to assure redemption by a desired percentage of households can be determined with scientific accuracy. These rates can run from 5 percent to more than 50 percent, depending on coupon value, and targeting of households. As an example of how this works, picture four possible target groups which may be targeted using a decision tree:

	Number Household	Coupon Face Value	Percent Redeemed	Coupons Redeemed	Variable[1] Costs
Group A					
Occasional Light Users	50,000	$0.75	15.0%	7,500	$9,555
Group B					
High Users					
Comp. Brand	75,000	$1.00	20.0%	15,000	$21,458
Freq. Coupons					

	Number Household	Coupon Face Value	Percent Redeemed	Coupons Redeemed	Variable[1] Costs
Group C					
High Users Comp. Brand Infreq. Coup.	75,000	$2.00	15.0%	11,250	$28,395
Group D Light Users Comp. Brand	100,000	$1.00	5.0%	5,000	$11,360

[1]Variable costs shown here include more than face value redemption. They also cover printing costs, distribution costs, and coupon handling fees.

Looking at these four groups, the manufacturer decides on the value of the coupons to send to each group. The percent redeemed is simply a function of the type of household targeted and the value of the coupon. This can be tested and adjusted, and therefore, predicted with some accuracy.

The variable costs derived from this chart are used as input to another chart which computes the conversion rate required to pay back the variable promotion costs in one year.

	Number Households	Variable Costs	Margin From Coupon Redemption	Costs Less Redemption Revenue	Incremental Potential Revenue	Conversion Percentage Required
Group A Occasional Light Users	50,000	$9,555	$6,188	$3,367	$24,750	13.6%
Group B High Users Comp. Brand Freq. Coupons	75,000	$21,458	$18,750	$2,708	$112,500	2.4%
Group C High Users Comp. Brand Infreq. Coup.	75,000	$28,395	$14,063	$14,332	$84,375	17.0%
Group D Light Users Comp. Brand	100,000	$11,360	$6,250	$5,110	$18,750	27.3%

In fact, few manufacturers want to go to the trouble and pay the costs to determine the actual rate at which the target audience is converting to their brand. What they can see from this formula is that Group B looks like a very worthwhile target, and Group D looks like a long shot. Whether Groups A and C are worthwhile depends on the manufacturer's perception. They may want to tinker with the offer to bring the conversion percentage down a little more for Group A, and skip Group C altogether.

OTHER DATABASE SOURCES

There are few competitors to Target Mail in North America. Larry Tucker specializes in demographic targeting, seniors, households with children, etc. Their data does not provide brand-use, volume of consumption, and coupon using habits. Carol Wright has surveys aimed at these brand-use questions, but their response rates are quite different. Catalina and Advanced Promotion Technologies (APT) coordinate access to retailer scanner data for packaged goods brands, and make it possible to deliver targeted coupons that are printed at the checkout counter. The data which they release to manufacturers is cumulated at the store level, and not attached to individual shoppers. Their data, therefore is not available to clients that want to build their own databases.

RETAILER CARD DATA

Some retailers may make household scanner data (see Chapter 24) available to manufacturers on reasonable terms in the future. Household scanner data (data from households that show their shopping card at checkout time) suffers from several serious limitations: not everyone who buys has a card, and not everyone who has a card uses it every time they shop. People shop at more than one store, which means you cannot be sure that the data you have is all the important data on the household. Finally, there is the volume problem.

The amount of data generated at the cash registers in a supermarket is so gigantic that even the largest chains find it almost impossible to keep track of household purchases by SKU (product and brand). The volume chokes even the largest computers. They tend to accumulate information by department (meat, grocery) by month, rather than keeping track of every tube of toothpaste bought by each household. The problem is that the tube of toothpaste data is precisely what the manufacturers want to know. Summarizing scanner data has been compared to "trying to sip from a fire hose". Citicorp's Reward America program (see Chapter 24) went broke for several reasons, one of the most important being that they underestimated the complexity of processing and summarizing the data generated from the hundreds of stores involved.

Use of household scanner data is becoming more common as the public becomes more aware of the value of such shopping cards, and as retailers and manufacturers provide more benefits to those who use them. As household scanner data increases in accuracy (if it does), however, it may offer real competition to the Target Mail approach. Knowing what each household actually buys every week certainly has the potential, one day, to beat asking them what they remember buying.

WHAT THE FUTURE HOLDS

The possibility for database marketing in packaged goods is wide open. There are serious barriers to immediate expansion because of the slim margins, and the lack of contact between the manufacturer and the customer. The expansion of niche marketing and scanner data plus innovative methods pioneered by companies like Target Mail offer great opportunities for the future.

SUMMARY

- Mass marketing is what packaged goods are all about. Mass marketing brought prices down, and created much of today's prosperity. It is used to sell packaged goods today, and will be so used for the foreseeable future.

- Database marketing cannot work for most packaged goods for a number of reasons: You can find out who your customers are, but you can't keep track of their purchases. The margins on such products are very thin.

- Database marketing in packaged goods works well with niche products: baby products, pet food, gourmet diners, diet products, kids products. FSI coupons maintain sales, but most coupons are redeemed by current users, so the coupon value has to be kept low.

- One avenue for database marketing with packaged goods is in promoting trial. Household surveys can tell you several things: who is loyal, a switcher, or a competitive brand user. They can tell you if the household is a frequent coupon user, and much else about the household. Armed with this information, a marketer can build a decision tree to send a large value coupon to a competitive brand user, no coupon to a loyalist, and a medium value coupon to a frequent coupon redeemer. As a result, such a system can be used to promote trial and conversion.

Chapter 23

Your Sales Staff and Your Dealers

One obstacle to successful database marketing is often overlooked: the vice president for sales. Why is it that sales almost always tries to fight the installation of a marketing database system? There are several reasons. Let's begin the discussion by listing some of them.

WHY SALESPEOPLE FIGHT MARKETING DATABASES

- A marketing database implies direct sales, which means that no salespeople will be needed. Sales will be cut out of the loop and the commissions. Salespeople are usually asked to provide the database with a list of their contacts. Salespeople live by their contacts. To surrender them is to give up their livelihood. Once the names are in the database you will write letters to them and call them; the next thing you know, your telemarketers will be selling to them, not the salesman. Goodbye, commissions.

- One of the main functions of a marketing system is to develop leads. These leads are usually turned over to salespeople for action. But with a functioning database system, complete with telemarketers, you may decide to pursue the lead yourself. What happens to the salespeople?

- Even worse, you may supply all your leads to sales. In the past, salespeople have ignored the leads that they didn't think were worth bothering with. But now your database has a lead tracking system which asks for reports on the status of each lead. The salesperson feels Big Brother breathing down his or her neck.

- In fact, the database can become a management tool for evaluating the effectiveness of each salesperson. Whereas in the past a salesperson could say that sales were poor because the market was not good, today, with a steady flow of leads, the salesperson will have to hustle and dance to someone else's tune. The database may actually reduce commissions. In the cable TV industry, for example, individual cable services are often paid a bonus for the percentage of coverage that they can achieve. For example, if the cables have been run past 100,000 houses in a city, the goal is to have 100,000 subscribers. There are bonuses for 80 percent, 85 percent and so on.

  Along comes the marketing database, and through close study of the service area it may be possible to discover that the cables actually are serving 120,000 possible homes, not 100,000. What was 80 percent now becomes 66 percent overnight. Goodbye, bonus.

- Look at it from the salespeople's point of view. They are out on the firing line, trying to find leads, win them over, make sales, and get commissions. Marketing people think that they can do the same thing by direct mail and telemarketing. This is threatening. Suppose they are correct? They will force salespeople out of their jobs. Even if the marketers are not correct, they will waste a lot of time, get credit for half of the sales, and cut into salespeoples' opportunities to make commissions. What good can possibly come out of cooperating with them?

- To top it off, marketing departments are often staffed by MBAs who have learned all the theory, but have never, in fact, closed on a sale themselves. They consider themselves above the crass business of asking for a sale. They want to conduct marketing with computers, producing reams of fine reports and statistics.

You may smile at these differences, but they are real differences in most companies, and unless you recognize the problems and deal with them *your marketing database will be a failure.* Janet Park, President of Marketing Frontiers, tells an interesting story which illustrates this point. "I was having lunch one day with several executives from a leading business-to-business list compiler. They were describing to me in detail the intricacies of their three-year database research project for one of the largest and most sophisticated marketing companies in the United States. Millions of dollars had been spent on surveys, data overlays, and analytical models to refine the 'perfect' business list for supporting their brokers in the field offices.

"That same afternoon, I had a meeting with a friend of mine who just happened to be a broker for the same sophisticated marketing company mentioned above. I asked him how he got his leads.

'Yellow Pages,' he said. 'I look in the Yellow Pages and call them up. Sometimes,' he added guiltily, 'I just resort to smokestacking. If I see an interesting looking building while driving around, I'll just stop and make a cold call to see if there's anything worth pursuing.'

"It seemed ironic to me that the sophisticated results of the home office database marketing projects had not yet 'trickled down' to benefit the street soldiers of sales. Smokestacking, not linear regression, was still the default method of research in the field. And this happened quite recently." The problem is a natural one. The salesman thinks to himself: As long as marketing people are thinking up new types of direct-mail pieces to generate new leads, their activities are not threatening.

But when they try to include *my* customers on their marketing database, I can see the handwriting on the wall, and I am going to fight it.

Remember: the database aims at the lifetime value of a customer. Repeat sales, cross-selling, upselling, referrals — these are the lifeblood of a marketing database, but they are also the meat and potatoes of the sales staff. Who wants constantly to hunt down new customers when the old customers are so much easier to service? Salespeople will see the database as a threat to force them into the harder work of new customer acquisition, while the marketing database gets all the credit and honors for the easy work of servicing existing customers.

CHANGING CUSTOMER ATTITUDES

The attitude of the business customer towards your sales staff has been changing over the past several decades as database marketing has grown in sophistication. Arthur Andersen did a series of surveys of what business customers wanted most from their suppliers over three decades. The results are quite surprising:

Customer Interest	Ranking in Various Years		
	1970	*1980*	*1990*
Contact with outside salespeople	1st	3rd	5th
Fast Delivery	2nd	1st	2nd
Low Price	3rd	2nd	4th
Wide range of products	4th	5th	3rd
Capable inside sales person	5th	4th	1st

In 1970 business customers wanted to be called on by a live salesperson. They wanted that human contact more than anything else. By 1990, their desires had changed completely. They most wanted contact with an inside salesperson who could get them what they wanted. What is the reason for the shift in customer attitude? I think that several factors are at work:

- People are busier today than they used to be. They just don't have time to entertain and make pleasantries with a salesman in their office. They would much rather pick up the phone and talk directly to someone who can fill their needs—and then hang up and go on to other work.

- Suppliers have reorganized internally. They now have competent inside sales people who know the merchandise, know the customers, and can get things done faster and more efficiently than a salesman on the road.

SALES AND MARKETING COLLABORATION

In most companies sales is strong, marketing weak. In a head-to-head contest, the marketing database will lose. So if you can't beat them, join them. Let's start with the theory, then proceed to practice. What you want to achieve is a system in which the salespeople feel comfortable with your database.

They feel that it is their baby; that they can play with it, feed it, get information out of it, and *get credit for its success.* The main concern will be the threat to their compensation method.

This means that if you have a strong salesforce that works on commission, you have to see that they continue to get their commissions once the database is installed. This may be tricky to do with a telemarketing and direct mail program cross-selling and upselling to customers directly. If you have to pay a salesperson a commission on sales he or she did not make, the economics of the database may come into question. Where is the money for the telemarketing and direct mail programs? Some companies have solved that problem by installing the telemarketers right in the sales divisional headquarters. The commissions earned go partly to the telemarketers and partly to the salesperson of record for the account. The telemarketers are under the supervision of the division sales manager, and come to all the meetings with the salesforce. The salesperson is encouraged to feed the telemarketers work since, in many cases, they can cover more ground in a day than salespeople can cover in a week.

In this arrangement, the telemarketer talks first to any new lead and qualifies it before it is given to a salesperson. Meanwhile, the salespeople are handling the big accounts which need their special attention and clinching ability. The telemarketer handles the less likely accounts, the smaller ones, the long shots. Direct mail is used for the cold calling, followed up by telemarketing. If an account looks really promising, it is then turned over to a salesperson.

Working thus as a team, salespeople can accept and work well with a marketing database. Somewhere in the background is the marketing manager, who is still in charge of the database and is directing the effort from the sidelines. The manager is the coach; the sales division manager is the quarterback. The salespeople are the running and passing backs and the ends; while the marketing database serves as guard, tackle, and center: fighting off the unqualified leads and passing the ball to the quarterback for the scoring plays.

HEWLETT-PACKARD EXPERIENCE

Here's how Karen Blue, President of Advanced Marketing Solutions in Oakland, California, went about successfully solving this problem at the Hewlett-Packard Company. It is a wonderful example of marketing and sales working as a team. A few years ago Hewlett-Packard, facing a tough competitive situation, created a new Customer Information Center to improve customer satisfaction and increase field productivity. The Center was intended to handle the entire Hewlett-Packard line of computers and electronic equipment. Ms. Blue was Direct Marketing Manager for the new center. She established three objectives:

- to fill the sales funnel with timely, qualified leads;
- to integrate and improve the productivity of all direct marketing activities; and
- to automate the feedback and promotion evaluation process.

The internal customer lists that they started with were difficult to use. They were designed for sales analysis and order processing, not marketing. They contained account numbers, order statistics, and invoice addresses, not user names, shipping locations, or the profile information they needed for an effective marketing program. The salespeople initially were very resistant. They didn't think that a marketing unit could effectively qualify leads. They especially didn't want anyone else to contact their accounts —through mail or telephone. To turn things around Ms. Blue directed two important steps:

- She set up a training program to educate the marketing and sales managers to show them how they would benefit from proper use of marketing tools. She used an outside consultant who had helped to set up the marketing database: Victor Hunter of Hunter Business Direct of Milwaukee.

- The Customer Information Center, when set up, would support the company's sales and marketing strategy with five components:

  1. Lead generation.

  2. Inquiry management.

  3. Lead qualification.

  4. Lead distribution and feedback.

  5. Promotion campaign measurement and market analysis.

Lead Generation and Inquiry Management

Lead generation became the responsibility of the direct marketing program managers in each of six marketplaces. They reported both to national field management and to the marketing communications manager in their respective sections. Inquiries were centralized. There were previously more than fifty toll-free numbers to handle customer inquiries. The center began to handle all of these on a single inbound toll-free number that fulfills all requests for both mail-in and telemarketing literature.

Figure 23-1   Changing Sales Force Time Allocation

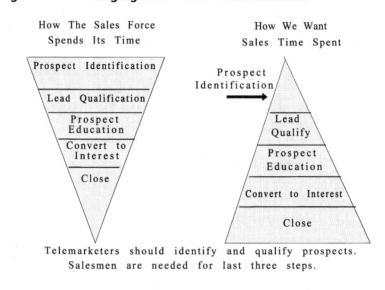

Telemarketers should identify and qualify prospects. Salesmen are needed for last three steps.

All inquiries, plus additional profile and qualification information, are stored in the inquiry management database. Customer support, telemarketing, and sales reps all have direct access to this database.

Customers were encouraged to call, rather than to write in with their inquiries. They found it was less expensive to have customers call on a toll-free number than to try to reach them with outbound calls as a result of a mail-in.

Lead Qualification

A key to Ms. Blue's success in this area was the direct involvement of salespeople in the process. They contributed to telemarketer training; they defined what constituted a qualified lead; and they helped in designing the feedback and analysis loop.

The salesforce began to believe that trained professional telemarketers could evaluate sales opportunities properly and save field reps much time in the qualification process. Here is what some of them said:

"I really was concerned about someone else getting involved in my selling relationship, but in four of the six qualified leads I received in the pilot program, it looks like I will close sales for more than $600,000."

"With the telemarketer's comments on one of my leads, I was able to go in prepared to talk about a leasing option and save myself an additional visit."

The telemarketers are well-educated, service oriented communicators. Their job is to identify real sales opportunities, and free up the salesforce for its primary job: selling.

Figure 23-2   Lowering Sales Costs

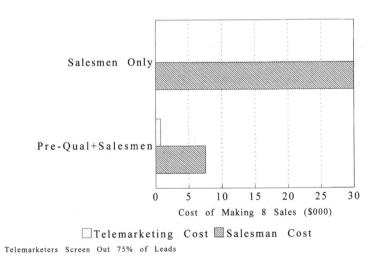

Cost of Making 8 Sales ($000)

☐ Telemarketing Cost ▧ Salesman Cost

Telemarketers Screen Out 75% of Leads

Keeping the Leads Hot

A frequent complaint of salespeople is that leads are "cold" by the time they get to them. To solve this problem, the Hewlett-Packard Customer Information Center developed a Qualified Lead Tracking System (QUILTS) that electronically sent inquiries to telemarketers in the Midwest. The telemarketers qualified, ranked, and electronically returned leads to the appropriate sales office. QUILTS reduced turnaround time from as much as 14 weeks to 48 hours. Hot leads were telephoned directly to the sales office.

A pilot program was developed to tie this system into the portable PCs of some sales managers, which were integrated into the QUILTS system with leads being transferred electronically every evening.

Feedback

A strong selling point of the new system from the field point of view was its capability to feed back quantitative information to product divisions on win/loss statistics. Previously, when a sales rep called a research and development manager to point out a missing feature on a product or complain about the pricing, his or her views were set aside. Now they were entered into the database, which later reported back percentages of wins and losses from field-generated ideas. The feedback system helped the product divisions to respond better to customer ideas and helped sales reps beat the competition.

Results

How well did the Hewlett-Packard system perform? Some answers were provided by Russell McBrien, Application Marketing Manager at Hewlett-Packard. He pointed out that before the new system, studies had shown that salespeople were with customers only about 26 percent of their average day. Using laptop portables, with 130 reps participating and logging over 8,000 hours in a test, they were able to increase customer contact to 33 percent, a gain of 27 percent in selling time due to the new system. Why did this work?

The database information kept the reps on the road and out of the office. Remote access to the database meant fewer trips back and forth to the office and less time lost in ad-hoc meetings or chitchat. Before the system, responses to ads in magazines had taken six weeks to arrive at Hewlett-Packard, and another eight weeks before they got to a sales rep. Most of the leads were thrown away as being too old. The ratio of good leads to bad was about one to twenty-five. With the new system, qualified leads are distributed overnight to the sales reps. Customer satisfaction had measurably increased, with inquiry fulfillment being completed in one week rather than six. Over 90 percent of questions are resolved over the phone from the Center, since the 800 number was a gateway to the entire HP Installed Base Center.

INSTALLED BASE CENTER

While the Information Center primarily deals with prospects, Installed Base Center is the Hewlett-Packard name for their marketing database of existing customers. Data collected on these customers includes:

- inventory
- contacts
- buying plans, cycles, and habits
- call patterns
- account history
- response to product information and promotions
- contracts
- competitive information provided by the customer

Customers are identified by name, title, buying power, and sales history. Such customer knowledge helps to target direct mail programs usually announcing new products or promotions. After the mailings, telemarketers call customers to check their response to the mailing and to learn if they are ready to buy. These "tele-sales reps" are assigned to specific accounts, therefore giving the customer a regional contact if questions arise. This sales team works together closely to be aware of customer needs, and only when the customer has been qualified is the field sales rep sent to call, making the sales reps' time more productive. The goals of the Installed Base Center database system are to increase sales volume by 15 percent, increase the number of contacts per account by 50 percent, reduce the cost per order dollar by 10 percent and the number of field sales calls per order by 25 percent while increasing customer satisfaction and creating a customer profile on the database. Another goal of the Installed Base Center is to reduce the new product introduction cycle time by 67 percent. Using this new system, Hewlett-Packard freed itself from the MIS-generated static reports which proved untimely and inflexible in their search criteria. Product managers using the database and laptops could get win/loss reports, customer histories, sales analyses and forecasts, product profitability, and information about the competition.

MANAGING YOUR DEALERS

Cyndi Greenglass of Smith Lask Associates in Chicago suggests a program for integrating your dealer with your database system in ten steps:

- Identify successful dealers. Find out which are your most successful dealers, and find out why. Study them to learn their secrets: their sales structure, marketing methods, and financial resources.

- Identify your customers. Which are your most profitable products? Who is buying them? Make a profile of the ultimate consumer.

- Quantify your market potential. Compare your database with the market to decide whether you have underpenetrated market segments. Figure out which dealers' markets have the greatest potential.

- Create a customer and prospect database. Invite dealers to contribute to it, and to receive data from it.

- Protect territorial rights. Establish district territories for your dealers. Let them know you are looking out for them.

- Set up a central point for dealer marketing. Provide an 800 number for your dealers to reach the database. Provide someone knowledgeable who can help dealers get prospects and leads.

- Create a marketing program that's simple to use. The objective is to help your dealers get out there and sell, instead of filling out forms and providing reports. Set up a program that generates a consistent base of useful leads. Make it easy for the dealers.

- Share the costs with your dealers. They will use it if they fund it. You must provide some funding to maintain control.

- Brag about your success. If it works, tell everyone about it. Find a few successful dealers, and tell everyone about them.

- Learn from experience. Designing a database driven dealer program is a complex task. Build in some early successes, and let the dealer grapevine do the rest.

INTEGRATED MARKETING AT AMOCO TBA

In the Eighties, full service gas stations faced some disturbing new competition. Muffler shops, quick lube stations, discount tire stores, and "mini-marts" combined to rob stations of their "back end" sales, while "Gas & Go" stations put increasing pressure on their core business. In a few years, Amoco lost more than half of their 10,000 full service stations. The picture was bleak.

Faced with this situation, Henry Hart, head of research at Amoco TBA (Tires, Batteries, and Accessories) came up with a unique solution using database marketing which not only helped to bolster their core gasoline and oil business, but built their TBA sales as well. His goal was to keep the remaining Amoco dealers loyal. He wanted to find a way to cut Amoco TBA costs while increasing service to dealers.

The core idea was one central to database marketing: give customers some reason other than low prices to remain loyal to their local Amoco dealer. That reason was service. Bring your car to the man who will take care of both you and your car. To realize this objective, Amoco had to train their dealers to provide the right kind of service and to manage their stations efficiently. They had to start by building a bond between Amoco and the dealers by helping them to manage their businesses better so they could retain their customers.

As a first step, Hart sought someone who could help Amoco design a marketing database that would coordinate all sales and marketing activities. His search led to Vic Hunter, President of Hunter Business Direct, Inc. of Milwaukee. Vic's idea was to establish Integrated Account Management—to pull together all dealer contact media: mail, phone, and field personnel, into a strategic tool that would improve customer (dealer) relationships at a greatly reduced cost.

The remaining Amoco dealers were a mixed bag of privately owned, company owned, franchised, and independent jobber businesses. The database that Hunter built was designed to create an integrated account management system which would record everything known about each dealer: his sales, phone calls, mail, and personal contacts. Contact and sales history on the database were kept for at least three years. The database included hardware and software to handle all customer contacts and services, and a sales plan plus a system to measure the ongoing success of the plan.

For many years, Amoco had placed almost total reliance on about 70 sales representatives to handle their dealers. The system was high in cost. Hunter changed this. The field sales force was cut in half and changed in function. The new sales force was integrated with a low-cost, high-volume phone and mail contact system. As time went on, central telemarketers wrote a greater and greater share of the orders—from a small percentage at first to over 70 percent when in full operation. The field sales reps shifted from being order takers to being management consultants. They helped dealers to manage their businesses better so as to sell more TBA.

Figure 23-3   Percent of Revenue by Telemarketers

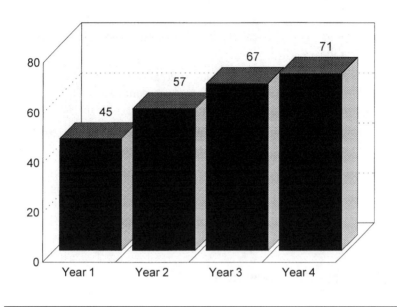

As the system operated once Hunter was providing full service, there were 37 Amoco sales reps. Each Hunter telemarketer was assigned five or six territories, each of which had one Amoco sales rep. The Amoco sales reps were hired from college directly for this job. On a regular basis, normally weekly, each dealer was called by a telemarketer to ask how they were doing, to take orders for TBA, to solve problems, and to schedule a visit for the assigned sales rep. Under the new system, dealers had one number to call to place orders, to check on deliveries, or to solve any problem. Hunter maintained a 24-hour-a-day customer service operation which "took charge" of any problem from call to resolution.

The telemarketers have a dealer profile on the screen in front of them when talking on the phone. The profile includes a sales potential forecast and the expectations for each dealer. Central to the philosophy of Hunter's system were five key ideas:

- One location: Operations were consolidated in a single location.

- Integrated software: The software integrated telemarketing and customer service operations with dealer and product databases.

- Classification: Criteria classified and graded each dealer. Not all were equal. This concept was central to effective use of resources.

- Individualized marketing: The marketing programs, based on Amoco strategic goals, were customized to meet the needs and expectations of each dealer.

- Measurement: Automated reporting systems measured the productivity of telemarketers, field sales personnel, individual dealers, and individual product programs.

Sales Force Compensation

Virtually all business-to-business database systems run into the compensation problem: how to integrate the activities of inside telemarketers with outside salesmen so that each was compensated in the most effective way. Salesmen normally work on commission. Commissions are their reward for activity. Anything or anyone who "robs" them of their commissions will be opposed. Such problems have plagued hundreds of marketing programs—see the Globe and Mail story in Chapter 19.

Amoco and Hunter solved this problem in an unusual and successful way: They compensated everyone in a territory for successful sales. In this way, whether the order was taken by the field sales rep or the inside telemarketer, both receive the commission. This encouraged the field sales reps to concentrate on offering consultation, marketing, and management advice to dealers, knowing that the resulting orders—taken by the Hunter telemarketers—would result in commissions for themselves.

To get the new system accepted, joint meetings were held in which the Amoco TBA customer retention strategy and the role of Integrated

Account Management was explained in detail. The strategy dictated that each contact with a dealer was to be viewed as an opportunity to add value to the relationship with the dealer—regardless of whether or not it resulted in a sale. As the field sales force started to appreciate the value—and success—of the telephone sales representatives, more and more the two began to work as a team.

What the Database Contained

The TBA database was more than just a record for each dealer. It contained:

- A TBA Price Master which provided master product information with prices, cost by vendor, adjustment costs, taxes, and suggested retail prices.

- Standard Codes to link the database with Amoco's corporate information system.

- An Order Processing System for all TBA products.

- Telephone Marketing Software—both inbound and outbound—to maintain personal contact with the dealer.

- Vendor-driven promotion programs.

- Warehouse coordination. Each vendor warehouse was linked to the database so that they could process packing, shipping, confirmation, and adjustments.

Dealer Budget Planning

Ultimately there were 2,000 full service dealers on the system, and another 6,500 who were supplied by jobbers. Hunter and Amoco worked jointly with each of the 2,000 full service dealers to develop an annual sales plan. This plan showed how much each dealer plans to sell of gas, oil, service, and TBA products. The pricing of products was partially driven by this plan. The database monitors each plan on a regular basis. If a particular dealer had an annual plan for selling 300 tires, and, when June arrived, for example, he had sold only 50 tires, the telemarketer would see that on her screen. She would work with the field sales rep to develop a program to solve that problem. Either she or the sales rep would then call on the dealer to see what could be done to pep up tire sales for the balance of the year. Many opportunities existed to turn things around. The sales rep could suggest special coop advertising to promote tire sales, point of purchase displays, etc.

One year, they used the database to develop a special offer to 600 dealers who did not carry Amoco tires. A direct mail offer was launched, followed by telephone calls, followed by a sales rep visit, and more calls. This proved to be a most successful program. During the year, they picked up 77 new tire dealers who bought 10,000 tires for $500,000 in business. The following year, those same 77 dealers sold more than $1,000,000 worth of tires. The tire consumers, of course, returned to get their tires rotated, leading to further service opportunities, etc., so that the tire sales were only the beginning of a continuing marketing success for the dealers and for Amoco TBA.

Dealer Consulting

The field reps, therefore, were no longer salesmen, they were business consultants. They were supposed to be counseling the dealers on their training, merchandising, advertising, and setting up commission programs for their employees. In this way the field rep could make the dealer more successful, and sell more TBA. By the same token, the field sales reps were not problem solvers, either. Problems were solved by customer service. The field sales rep was truly a management consultant, not burdened with sales or problems.

What they helped dealers with was business management. For example, it was important to control dealer inventory. There were over 600 TBA parts. One small dealership cannot stock a large number of each part. Which one should he stock, and how many of each? To answer that question, the sales rep had to study each dealer to learn what his business was. What type of cars did he service—new cars or old cars? Was he located on a busy highway, or a back street? Does he get a lot of repair business or mainly fill-ups and lubrication? All of this information was maintained in the database, and used in developing the sales plan.

Amoco dealers have an edge over muffler or quick lube stations, because the national gasoline advertising brings in the business. In the average busy station, 10,000 cars a week drive in to the station to buy gas. It was up to the dealer, the TBA rep, and the Hunter telemarketers to see that the people driving those cars also buy tires, batteries, accessories, service, inspections, etc., while they were there. They did this through providing the dealer with window displays, print advertising, point of purchase flyers and displays, and such things as employee incentive programs. It was possible to take a service station operator with two or three service bays that earns $8,000 a week from those bays, and show him how he could earn $20,000 or $30,000 a week from those same bays by using the right techniques. The business was out there, it was just a matter of proper marketing techniques.

Training the Telemarketing Rep

Telemarketers had to know the products as well as the sales reps. As a part of their training, telemarketers spent time traveling with sales reps visiting service stations and handling problems directly. After training, the telephone sales representatives assumed greater and greater responsibility of creating the total sales effort, staying ahead of dealer demand. Instead of being order takers, they assumed an active sales role, calling dealers every week, and working to achieve the annual sales plan.

Customer service was a function separate from telephone sales. There was one number for all Amoco dealers to call. The rep answers, "Amoco TBA customer service. How may I help you?" Drawing on the information contained in the database in front of her, the Customer Service Rep lets the customer know immediately that they have reached the right number for help. If the call is to place an order, the dealer was transferred directly to the appropriate sales representative. If the call was a problem, the Customer Service Reps were "empowered" to take ownership of every problem they received from a customer. It was their responsibility to find the answer and tell the customer when the problem had been solved. Customer service received more than 5,000 customer service calls every month. They provided information, security, and real assistance to Amoco dealers. Feedback from this dialogue went into the database and was used to inform all concerned about the dealer's interests.

Figure 23-4   Customer Service Calls per $1,000 of Total Revenue

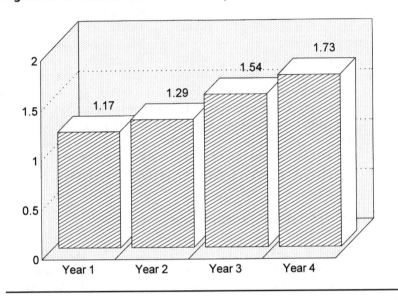

The Amoco TBA database was not just a repository of information. It was a tool that was used to help thousands of dealers to manage their businesses better by assisting them to achieve mutually developed sales plans, and by solving their problems as they arose. The system was a combination of computer assisted telemarketing, database management, account management, sales planning, and detailed reporting.

All information in the database had just one purpose: contributing to the goal of customer (dealer) satisfaction. Acting as a central nervous system, the database handled sales and fulfillment, facilitated customer service, generated management reports, provided quantitative research data, selected customers for subsequent contact, automatically initiated invoicing and adjustments, derived inventory control and material handling requirements, generated customer profiling and histories, and played an instrumental role in assisting strategic planning.

- Call Planner: When a tactical sales contact plan was developed for individual dealers, a Call Planner was generated automatically. This planner gave the field sales rep the specific data he needed for each dealer prior to making a call. This information included order history, sales by product versus plan, and other information needed to make the call a success.

- Shipping Tickets: Once an order was entered, a shipping ticket was generated and inventory was automatically allocated at the warehouse where the inventory was located. Warehouse replenishment and drop-ship vendor orders were also automatically generated.

- Follow-Up Calls: The computer automatically flags the customer service rep when a follow-up call was due to resolve a customer service call.

- Measurement Reports were automatically generated from data gathered by sales and customer service representatives. These reports monitored dealer responsiveness, attainment of goals, program effectiveness, regional disparities, and other evaluation criteria.

Results of the Amoco TBA Database Program

- Sales per dealer increased by an average of 28 percent over the first four years of the program. The average dealer now sells $2 million per year. Seventy percent of those sales were taken by telephone sales representatives. Dealers have been trained to realize that they have to be managers, not workers. They now use computers to manage their dealerships.

- Dealer loss was ended. The erosion of the dealer base which was the main reason for setting up the program in the first place came to an end. There was actually an increase in dealers in the later years.

- Costs stayed fixed, while revenue gained. The first year, the system cost 5.18 percent of the total revenue. Four years later the identical system costs represented only 2.84 percent of a revenue that totaled over $50 million dollars.

Figure 23-5 Database Programs Cost as a Percent of Revenue

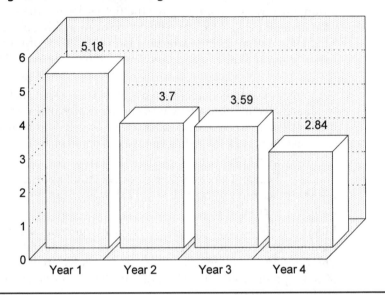

- Dealer loyalty increased. A permanent bond was built between Amoco and their dealers which inoculated them from competitive offers. This gain was shown in retention, plus in surveys which showed an increasing number (22 percent more) of dealers agreed that Amoco was headed in the right direction—as compared with similar survey results when the plan began.

SUMMARY

- In many companies, the salesforce will oppose a marketing database as a threat to their commissions.
- The salesforce may look on a lead tracking system as a management intrusion into their business.

- To have a successful marketing database in a company with a large salesforce, you have to find a compromise which brings sales and the database together in the same organization.

- One method is to locate the telemarketers working with the database right in the sales division, under the supervision of the regional sales director.

- Telemarketers pre-qualify leads, passing on only those which sales has agreed are qualified. Sales should train the telemarketers and develop the qualification criteria.

- As a part of the system, the database should be used to track leads, and speed them through qualification to a salesperson for action. No time should be lost.

- Hewlett-Packard's experience shows how a sales staff can work closely with a marketing database and telemarketers in an integrated system which can pre-qualify leads, increase salesperson contact time with customers, and improve sales productivity.

- Amoco TBA experience showed that telemarketers can profitably take over 70 percent of the sales force's order taking and problem solving work, cutting the field sales force in half, while retaining a valid compensation structure for both, and providing better service to the customer (the dealers).

Chapter 24

Database Marketing in Retail Stores

"Why should I be loyal to any one supermarket? They do nothing differ-ent for me after shopping there for several years than for someone com-ing in off the street and shopping there for the first time! They still don't even know my name!"

—Shopper quoted in Measured Marketing by Brian Woolf

Retailers were not first in line to adopt database marketing. Retailing has been in a wild state of flux for several decades. With intense com-petition from malls, discount stores, and catalogs, many large chains have been in deep trouble. Many have gone out of business altogether. In recent years, an increasing number of department stores, specialty stores, and supermarkets have begun to look at database marketing as a way of building and maintaining customer loyalty—something desperately needed in the intensely competitive retail scene.

Lets take a look at some of the problems which have led to the current focus on database marketing. Then we will concentrate on the methods and results of these methods.

A SATURATED MARKET

For two decades, the retail industry has been on a building spree. From 1970 to 1990 retail square footage increased from 1.5 billion to 4.4 billion, according to Harris Gordon of EDS Management in Cambridge, Mass, a real expert in this field. Harris was one of the principal authors of *Profitable Retailing using Relationship and Database Marketing,* commissioned by the Direct Marketing Association (212-492-7277 ext 356). Much of the interesting detail concerning retailing in this chapter stems from this extremely valuable report.

The result has been an increase in square feet per capita from 8 in 1972 to more than 18 in the mid-1990s. Unfortunately, sales have not kept up with the growth in floor space. Sales per square foot declined from $185 to $162 in constant 1990 dollars from 1972 to 1992.

One reason for the decline in sales per square foot has been the growth of shopping through alternate channels. The number of people shopping by catalog increased by 100 percent from 1982 to 1992. During this same period, the average time spent by a typical shopper in a mall declined by 20 percent, and the number of individual stores visited fell by 28 percent. Clearly, busy people were shopping more by mail and phone, and had less time available for visiting the gigantic structures which the retailers had erected.

The effect of this change in shopping habits could be read in growth rates of various industries. In the decade following 1985, the retail sector as a whole gained 5.7 percent per year. The big winners were Warehouse Clubs which grew by more than 30 percent, and discount stores which grew at a 10 percent rate. Falling below average were Grocery Stores, Department Stores, Women's Ready to Wear, and Furniture Stores. At the same time, direct marketing was gaining by an average of 15 percent per year.

WHY DATABASE MARKETING IS TOUGH IN RETAIL STORES

The central idea of database marketing is that you identify specific people, remember what they buy and prefer, and build a relationship with them which is profitable for both parties. This idea works wonderfully in such fields as travel and recreation. There are problems in retailing, however, as Harris Gordon points out:

- The majority of purchases are not made using the store's proprietary card, so in most cases you cannot really identify who is buying what. This means that even your best customers may be shopping anonymously, as far as you can tell.

- There is little opportunity to enhance each transaction, since identification of the purchaser usually occurs at the conclusion of the product selection process, not at the beginning. The customer has arrived at a checkout stand with the merchandise in her hand or her shopping cart. There are others waiting. You can't really have a leisurely discussion of the customer's needs, leading to assistance in finding out exactly what the customer wants, which could build a relationship and produce additional sales plus retention.

- In direct marketing, you can manage classes of customers. Gold card holders get treated better. In a retail store, this is difficult or impossible to do.

The method for building a relationship with customers, however, has arrived. It consists of three vital techniques:

- Bar Code Scanning: Every item purchased in a retail store today is scanned into a computer. The bar code, incidentally, is part of the reason for the whole retail crisis. The bar code has permitted every store to know every day exactly what is selling and when. It enables them to keep very accurate control of inventory, ordering more of the necessary items when they run low.

  The bar code, as much as anything else, has put the corner grocers out of business. In any large institution, the law of diminishing returns threatens efficiency. A corner grocer can know what is in his store, what the customer is buying, and what he should order. A large store cannot do that—or could not do it until the bar code system came along. Now, thanks to the scanning system, any store can have access to far more data than they can make profitable use of. The corner grocer, meanwhile, was forced out. He could have installed a scanner, but he could not afford to install and learn the software, and use his computer to analyze the scanner data. His costs would be too high. His intuitive methods, which served him well for centuries, put him at a disadvantage today. He is out of business.

Probably the ultimate in scanning use is Wal-Mart, for whom the scanner has been vital to their success. Wal-Mart does not own the products on its shelves. They are left there on consignment by the manufacturers. But due to the scanning system, Wal-Mart knows what is there, what is selling, and what needs replenishment every day. The scanner has pushed back the law of diminishing returns, and made it possible to build and manage larger inventories than would have been possible a short time ago.

- Customer Cards: The same equipment that scans SKUs can also scan a bar-coded customer card so as to associate the customer and her purchases in the computer. This process can take only a second or two per transaction, and requires only that the customer produce her card at purchase time. Customer cards are becoming more and more ubiquitous, but have run into serious problems in their ability to generate profits, as we will see later in the chapter.

- Large Scale Databases: The database required to capture purchases by household is very large indeed. It is so large that companies which have attempted this process have been forced to make all sorts of compromises in terms of what data they retain. The cost of databases is still falling year by year as computers become more powerful and less expensive. It will soon be possible to retain, economically, whatever data is necessary to build a lasting relationship with each customer.

DATABASE MARKETING IN DEPARTMENT STORES

Department stores in the 1990s began to create preferred customer clubs. Some examples include:

- Bloomingdale's "Premier Gold" program is given to their best spending customers. The program provides a branded charge card, a quarterly newsletter, and a customer hotline. Participants get free local delivery, free alterations, private sales and events, and free shipping of catalog items. It is designed to recognize and reward high spenders.

- Macy's "Frequent Shopper Program" provides certificates giving points for purchases. Members get a newsletter, free alternations, delivery and gift wrap, plus valet parking at the stores.

- Neiman Marcus "InCircle" provides most of the above benefits plus complementary magazine subscriptions, travel certificates, fee credit card protection, and special "InCircle Nights".

  The Neiman Marcus InCircle points program is reserved for credit card holders who spend more than $3,000 annually. This amount is adjusted annually for inflation. Customers can cash in their points for rewards as simple as a vase or expensive as a Caribbean vacation. InCircle members enjoy twice yearly private shopping nights which include live music, wine, champagne, and hors d'oeuvres. They also receive vendor giveaways, offers for drawings, and invitations to designer personal appearances.

  An invitation to have lunch at the store for the customer and a few friends, hosted by the store manager and complete with a private fashion show, was one of the most popular items redeemed early in the programs life cycle. All rewards do not have to be discount or merchandise oriented.

  For those that did not qualify for the InCircle program, Neiman has a NM+ preferred customer program which requires a payment of $50 to join. The members get advance notification of sales, discount coupons, perfume samples, and other gifts. If their purchases reach $3,000 per year, they are automatically enrolled in InCircle.

  The InCircle program enabled Neiman Marcus to gradually reduce their expenditures on mass advertising. It now represents a minority of the company's marketing budget. The program is more than ten years old and, as one of the first such programs, it gained many advantages over its competition who were not even collecting data.

- Saks Fifth Avenue "Saks First" and Dayton Hudson "Regards" are similar to other programs but add welcome gifts, and merchandise locators.

None of these programs offer discounts. The preferred program members are, after all, big spenders. They have money and don't need discounts. What these programs offer is recognition, convenience, service, helpfulness: they make the members feel "special".

A program aimed at the regular shopper is Zellers' Club Z. Club Z at Zellers in Canada offers 100 points for every Canadian dollar spent. Members choose rewards from a 156-page magazine format catalog. Members may mix cash and points to redeem their rewards. The program is so popular that out of a total of 11.2 million Canadian households, the 276 store chain has signed up about seven million members.

There are, of course, two basic types of customers: transaction buyers and relationship buyers. By emphasizing price, discount, sales, two for one, a merchant is training his customer to be a transaction buyer: to think only of the price of his goods and not about their quality or the benefits of having a relationship with his institution.

Relationship buyers, on the other hand, are not so much concerned with getting a bargain with each transaction. They are looking at a long term relationship with someone like Bloomingdale's or Neiman Marcus. They would like to be thought of as "special", given recognition, service, helpfulness. In return, they will reward the stores with loyalty, repeat sales, referrals, and increased spending levels.

These stores recognize that 80 percent of their revenue comes from 20 percent of their customers (or some similar figures). They want to cultivate these 20 percent. Member clubs offering recognition are a way of doing that. Such stores create lifetime value tables for the members of their preferred customer clubs. They can test the value of each new strategy by measuring its effect on the customer lifetime value. To obtain the recognition and services available to members, and, indeed, to remain in the club, the customer has to continue to use her preferred buyer card. The use of that card enables the store to track her purchases, maintain their database, and prove that their efforts are paying off.

HOW TO SET UP A PREFERRED BUYER CLUB

For a chain that has not yet instituted such a program, there are a series of simple steps that they can go through to determine who to nominate, and what to do for them.

- Issue cards, and get them used. To know who are the preferred buyers, you need first to be able to track everyone's purchases. Issue cards to all store shoppers, and encourage their use by providing some benefits to the card holder. If there are no benefits, the card holder will leave the card at home and not use it. She may be a loyal and profitable customer, but you will never know it.

    The Incredible Universe requires every shopper to have a shopping card that is issued after the customer fills out an application card with demographics. A purchase cannot be made without this card, and it is scanned when they enter the store. This method enables the Incredible Universe to know what each individual buys, but also to track people who come in and buy nothing. Understanding the rate and trends of not-purchasing can be as revealing as knowing what is purchased.

- Build a database. Build a database from the card application forms. You will want to know the age of the person, the income level, presence of children in the home, whether they use the store to shop for themselves only or to buy presents for children or grandchildren—lots of important data. Set up software to capture use of the cards at point of sale. Poll the POS terminals every night. In addition to everything else, store three vital pieces of information in everyone's database record:

    — the date of the most recent purchase
    — the total number of purchases (trips to the store)
    — the total dollars spent since the database began

- Identify your best customers. Using RFM (Recency, Frequency, Monetary) analysis (see Chapter 7), pick out your best customers. Design your preferred customer club only for these best customers. Don't make the mistake of including too many people in your club. If you do, you will find that to be cost effective, you will have to water down the benefits so that they are meaningless. Your best customers will leave their cards at home. Wrong thinking. Keep the club small so that you can afford to provide benefits that are generous and meaningful.

One female customer spent more than $15,000 per year on menswear for her husband and their two sons, but was unknown to the salespeople and managers. When they identified her, they sent her flowers and chocolates and offered her special discounts on accessories such as underwear and socks when she asked for them.

A southern specialty menswear retailer uses its database to make high-ticket buyers feel important. It sends a letter, signed by both the CEO and the chairman of the board, to each customer who spends more than $1,500 in a single visit. Without the database, this practice would take too much clerical work to be profitable.

- Create Great Benefits. Say to yourself, "What would I want as a really honored guest in my store? What would be really meaningful to me?" Remember Richard Gere in Pretty Woman who encouraged the store employees to engage in "major sucking up" to Julia Roberts when she was shopping. The success of your club will be in direct proportion to the recognition and benefits provided. Be sure that your benefits are so generous that you could not possibly afford to give them to the average shopper.

  A regional department store sends boxes of chocolates each Valentine's day to the top 10 percent of its customer base.

- Create a team and train your staff. Preferred buyer clubs should not just be the responsibility of the marketing staff. If they are to work, everyone in the store will have to know about them, will have to recognize the gold card holders, and give them special treatment. The special treatment is given not just by the sales staff, but also by the gift wrap department, the credit department, the delivery staff, the coat and package checkers, the parking staff, the special events planners. You will need a team to coordinate what you are doing to make sure that it all works efficiently and seamlessly.

  Any successful database marketing plan needs employee enthusiasm, which can be generated by having them play a role in designing the program, and commissions if it succeeds.

  Employees should be able to enter information into the system including:

— Birthdays and anniversaries

— Customers' preferences in styles—notify them when they come in

— Customers who return merchandise or have a service call

— Promotions on a specific item that would interest certain customers

You can provide each sales associate with the details on the top 20 customers in their department, as well as the store overall retention rate and LTV compared to other stores in the chain.

- Use the database. Consider the possibilities:

— A menswear retailer had an excessive inventory of size 42-regular suits. From the database, they identified all size 42-regular customers. The names were furnished to the sales associates who called them. Fifty percent of those called purchased one of the overstocked suits. This not only sold suits, it helped develop customer relationships by initiating personalized contacts.

— A marketer at a New York retailer challenged the CEO's idea that the store customers were very loyal. From the database he produced a list of several thousand former loyal customers who no longer shopped at the store. The sales manager divided these names among the sales assistants and provided an additional commission if they could get these customers back. The sales assistants were able to reactivate nearly half of these lapsed customers after making personal calls to each customer.

— One retail chain identified the shopping habits of "strivers"—young women who wanted to dress like more affluent women. The database showed that these women only bought items on sale, but that they often did not hear of the sale until the third or fourth round of markdowns. Using the database, they targeted these women with flyers as soon as the sales began, thus prompting them to visit the store sooner in the markdown cycle. They got better merchandise and the store profited from the exercise.

— Seeking women to target for a promotion involving fragrances, a store did not find enough women on its database. Using demographic data in the database, the marketing manager selected shoppers from other departments that matched the purchase and demographic pattern of the fragrance buyers. The augmented list was promoted, and resulted in a higher response rate than any previous promotion by the store or the chain.

INVITATIONAL MARKETING

Max Grassfield is the owner of a successful menswear store in Denver. He created a customer retention technique that he calls Invitational Marketing™. The core is this thought: "If there were just some way to insure that every customer received a periodic, well-written, personalized note, hand-signed by their salesperson, surely it would pay handsome dividends." Max used his store data to build a customer database, complete with such information as what they purchased and when, whether their wife accompanied them on their purchasing trip, their birthday, sizes, product preferences, lifestyle, and the name of their sales associate. Once his database was up and running, he put it to active use.

All new customers receive a personal letter, brochure, and the business card of their personal sales associate. The wives who visit the store also receive a welcoming letter which says, in part:

> We've recently had the privilege of welcoming your husband to Grassfield's family of customers and I'd like to extend a special welcome to you . . .
> After helping your husband with his selection, we now have all of his sizes on file. You might find this information useful when you want help selecting a gift for those special occasions . . . birthdays, holidays, anniversaries. And surprise gifts are always a success when they're a perfect fit.
> Knowing that your husband values your opinion, we'd also like to determine the extent of your participation in his wardrobe selections. I

would sincerely appreciate you taking one minute to complete the enclosed survey. It's self addressed and pre-stamped. In return for your time, please accept the attached ten dollar gift certificate. Just detach it from the survey and spend it in our store as if it were cash.

Thank you for your response. And again, welcome.

Cordially,

Max Grassfield

P.S. You are welcome to take advantage of our secure, covered parking next to our store. We'll give you two hours of free validated parking.

Invitational Marketing is based on the idea "Business goes where business is invited." Max sends out lots of personal notes, written on a laser printer, hand signed by the sales associate, and bearing a commemorative issue stamp. "We planned three different notes: one to our primary (active) customers, one to our secondary customers (defined as anyone who had not made a purchase in a year or more) and one to all the wives in our customer files, regardless of whether or not her husband had been active." In addition, he sent three four-color oversized post cards to portray a new fashion look for the store. These were sent bulk rate to the entire list.

The note to the wives was particularly interesting:

November 2, 19..

Dear Debbie:

It's hard to believe . . . the holiday season will soon be upon us.

I would like to call your attention to two special services available to you. First, for your convenience, we are happy to open a special charge account in your name. Second, any gift charged to your account will not be billed to you until after December 25th . . . interest free.

Also, I want to remind you that I have all of Glen's sizes on file. And, of course, we'll gift wrap any selection you make without charge.

When you come in, please ask for me by name. I'll be happy to serve you.

John Jordan

P.S. By making your selections early, before December 4th, we'll honor the enclosed $20 certificate for any one-day shopping spree of $100 or more.

Results: "We mailed 3,115 notes. Only 154 wives responded or about 5 percent. The average sale, however, was $392, resulting in total volume of in excess of $60,000 . . . all on a $20 gift certificate.

"The last fashion card was mailed the first week in December. In return for a purchase of $100 or more, it offered a free lunch (not to exceed $30) at any one of three well-known Cherry Creek North restaurants . . . We arranged to pay the restaurants $20 for each certificate redeemed. The restaurants were delighted with both the advertising value and the fiduciary arrangement. Based on the average sale, we found the $20 certificate to be well under an equivalent 10 percent markdown.

"An integral part of our fall plan was to ascertain if, through Invitational Marketing, we could significantly change the ratio between active and inactive customers." The reactivation letter read:

October 10, 19..

Dear Ray:

I was catching up on some of my customers the other day when it occurred to me that I haven't seen you in the store in some time. I hope you're well and that life is treating you kindly.

Next time you're in Cherry Creek North, why don't you drop by? It would be great to get caught up with you, and I could show you some of our new arrivals. We have some wonderful items this season that I think you would really like.

Looking forward to seeing you,

Rick McGowen

P.S. Max told me to tell you that through October 20th, he'll give you $25 off your first $100 purchase. What a guy!

Results: "On July 1, our ratio was 37 percent active, 63 percent inactive. To our astonishment, when we ran the comparison at the end of December, we found a new gain of 271 customers. If you multiply the gain by our year-to-date average sale of $232, we're looking at nearly $63,000 of regular price (highly profitable) business. Not bad for a one-to-one half-sheet note and a first-class stamp. Our new ratio was 44 percent active, 56 percent inactive...

"We must make our customers feel so appreciated, so valued, so listened to, so respected that they develop a proprietary sense about our stores. Because what we're all hoping for is that the next time our customers go shopping, they'll say, 'Guess I'll start at Grassfield's.' Why? Because 'sometimes you want to go where everybody knows your name'."

CREATING LIFETIME VALUE TABLES

Too many programs of this sort are launched without anyone knowing how to measure whether they are worth the effort and money expended. There is a method, and it is quite accountable. It is sufficiently rigorous that you can take it to your CFO and get a budget to fund your program. There are two steps (as outlined in Chapter 10): build a base lifetime value, and then create a second table which shows the benefits and costs of your club. What would such tables look like?

Preferred Customer Base Lifetime Value Table

Revenue	Year1	Year2	Year3
A Customers	1000	300	105
B Retention Rate	30%	35%	40%
C Spending Rate	$450.00	$450.00	$450.00
D Total Revenue	$450,000	$135,000	$47,250
Variable Costs			
E Cost Percent	50	50	50
F Total Costs	$225,000	$67,500	$23,625
Profits			
G Gross Profit	$225,000	$67,500	$23,625
H Discount Rate	1	1.2	1.44
I NPV Profit	$225,000	$56,250	$16,406
J Cumulative NPV Profit	$225,000	$281,250	$297,656
K Lifetime Value (NPV)	$225.00	$281.25	$297.66

The details of this table are explained in Chapter 10. This assumes that for the preferred club, you have selected people whose annual purchases exceed $400. The average spending of the people selected is $450. You are tracking these people over three years since they first took out the store proprietary card.

Their retention rate is 30 percent—meaning that only 300 of 1,000 of Year1 people are still shopping with you in Year2. Based on these numbers, you can calculate that the lifetime value of the average preferred customer after three years is $297. This number is based on their retention rate and their spending rate.

The second step is to figure out what the advantage for you would be if you were to provide these valuable customers with special privileges and benefits for using their card. We will assume that the benefits would be similar to those shown above for Saks, Macy's, Bloomingdale's, etc.

Let's assume that we spend $50 per customer per year to make these top customers feel extra special. This $50 includes the gold cards, the training of employees, the valet service, gift wrapping, gifts, thank you letters, newsletters, member nights, etc. You have to figure out what all of these good things would do for the preferred members. Here is a suggested table:

Preferred Buyers with Database Marketing Programs

Revenue	Year1	Year2	Year3
A Referral Rate	8%	8%	8%
B Referred Customers		80	46
C Total Customers	1000	580	394
D Retention Rate	50%	60%	70%
E Spending Rate	$550.00	$600.00	$650.00
F Total Revenue	$550,000	$348,000	$256,100
Variable Costs			
G Cost Percent	50	50	50
H Variable Direct Costs	$275,000	$174,000	$128,050
I Database Activities $50	$50,000	$29,000	$19,700
J Referral Incentives $50	$0	$4,000	$2,300
K Total Costs	$325,000	$207,000	$150,050

Preferred Buyers with Database Marketing Programs *(continued)*

Profits	Year1	Year2	Year3
L Gross Profit	$225,000	$141,000	$106,050
M Discount Rate	1.00	1.20	1.44
N NPV Profit	$225,000	$117,500	$73,646
O Cumulative NPV Profit	$225,000	$342,500	$416,146
P Lifetime Value (NPV)	$225.00	$342.50	$416.15

The first assumption is that the retention rate will rise. It is shown here going from 30 percent to 50 percent. Will it actually rise that much? It depends on the success of your program. If you really do provide attractive services and recognition it is possible to get that kind of a lift from a well designed program. The figure, while only a guess in the beginning, is completely testable. At the end of Year2 you will know whether it is real or not, and will know what the figure actually is. All these numbers are measurable and provable.

The second assumption here is that the spending rate will rise. We are assuming that the average preferred buyer, subjected to this recognition and service, will spend $100 more per year, so that the average spending moves to $550 per year. This again can be proved by experience.

Finally, we are assuming that you can install an incentive system whereby satisfied customers refer their big spending friends and relatives to your preferred buyer club. The number estimated here is 8 percent: you can get 8 out of 100 people to sign up a friend or relative who has their same spending habits.

In terms of cost, in addition to the $50 per member that you spend for your database and the associated benefits, we are assuming that you will reward those who recommend others who become high spenders with some sort of gift or recognition worth an average of $50 per referred member.

What does this all add up to? Here is a table:

Lifetime Value Change Due to Database Programs

	Year1	Year2	Year3
Without DB			
Programs	$225.00	$281.25	$297.66
With Database			
Programs	$225.00	$342.50	$416.15
Increase	$0.00	$61.25	$118.49
50,000 Customers	$0	$3,062,500	$5,924,500

These numbers are instructive. In the first year, your database has yielded you absolutely nothing. The benefits have just exactly paid for the costs. This is typical of any new database program. There are startup costs which will very likely eat up any profits which customers give you in the first year. Building up loyalty (retention), spending, and referral rates take time. You will need a long range budget and top level support.

Look, however, at what has happened in Year3. The real benefits of your activities show up in terms of a $6 million dollar profit—if you have 50,000 preferred customers.

These are real numbers, folks. They can be tested. If the referrals are only 4 percent, change the table. If the new spending rate is only $502, put that in: but when you have done this, you will have solid experience which will help you know what to add and what to leave out of future programs so as to maximize the satisfaction of your customers, and profit to your company.

DATABASE MARKETING IN SUPERMARKETS

Thousands of supermarkets have issued shopper cards to their customers to help keep track of what they are buying, so as to influence their behavior and make them more loyal to the store. A detailed study of such programs was made by Brian Woolf, President of the Retail Strategy Center in Greenville, SC, for the Coca-Cola Retailing Research Council. He found that there were many unrealistic expectations about what such card programs would accomplish. There are two common myths:

- Manufacturers will pay handsomely for use of the names of their consumers. False. Most manufacturers of packaged goods won't pay for the names because they don't know what to do with the names they already have. Thinking up profitable database marketing strategies for most packaged goods is quite difficult. Citicorp's $200 million dollar Reward America program, which signed up a large number of supermarkets in shopper card programs, was based on the premise that profits could be made by selling packaged goods consumer names to manufacturers. It was a false premise. Citicorp lost their $200 million.

- You can find out and store information on what every household buys. Wrong. You can't afford to keep all of that information. There are four possible levels of data you can keep on supermarket customers:

    1. Total spent per visit. The customer record includes the date and time of each visit and the amount spent, without breaking it down further. This minimum data provides supermarkets with an enormous amount of valuable information. It can be used to promote customer retention, and to determine the most profitable customers.

    2. Total at the departmental level. Stores typically have ten to twenty departments. If a store can afford to keep this information, it can help in targeting newsletters and promotions to people which reflects what they have purchased.

    3. Total at the category level. This finer breakdown enables stores to find dieters, health food nuts, beer and wine drinkers, and to share information with manufacturers of certain specialty products like Italian food or frozen pizza.

    4. Total at the SKU level. This is the ultimate in information. We keep track of absolutely everything that everyone has ever bought: the stock keeping unit (SKU), the time of day, the other items purchased with it, etc. I can safely say, in a book that I hope will be read well

> into the next century, that no one will ever keep information at this level. Why not? Because the cost of keeping such data—even with drastically reduced computer prices—will always exceed the profits you can make by keeping and making use of the data. There is no way that anyone can ever make money by knowing that on August 27th at 3:12 PM, Arthur Hughes bought ten pounds of potatoes and a box of Kellogg's Apple Jacks.

Most stores keep information only at Level 1. They find that this data gives them enough for relationship building activities. Data at lower levels costs much more. The profits from detailed data are hard to come by.

Costs of a Supermarket Card System

Brian Woolf's study shows that it costs between $14,000 to $20,000 for the first year per store to install a basic card-based program. These figures assume a store doing $200,000 per week with 10,000 transactions. About half of the first year sign-ups for the card will occur in the first month. Cards cost between $0.20 to $0.35 depending on the quality of the card.

Other costs involved in the first year include:

- A welcome letter to new customers at $0.40 per letter.
- $2,600 for maintenance and transmission of data.

What Can Such a Program Accomplish?

Many stores introduced electronic marketing programs, but let the programs die after a few months. For those that stuck with them and used them as an important part of their marketing strategy, they found:

- Increased Sales and profits from the system.
- Few additional costs since it was paid for by reduced mass media advertising.
- Better service to and communications with customers.

- Integrated benefits if the cards were also used for check cashing, video rentals, and other programs.
- A wealth of information about customers and their purchasing habits.

Some of the surprising information learned included:

- Shopping habits: Over 80 percent of supermarket customers shop there less than once a week.
- Retention Rate typically is between 50 to 75 percent.
- The top decile of customers visits the store 1.78 times per week, spends $40 per visit, and buys $3,674 (in 1993 dollars) each year. This top 10 percent accounts for almost 43 percent of the total store sales.
- Card holding customers spend more. The average customer who uses a frequent shopper card buys four times as much as a non-card using customer.

The lifetime value of a typical supermarket customer is $1,067 after three years:

Typical Supermarket Customer Lifetime Value

Revenue	Year1	Year2	Year3
A Customers	1000	700	490
B Retention Rate	70%	70%	70%
C Spending Rate	$2,500.00	$2,500.00	2,500.00
D Total Revenue	$2,500,000	$1,750,000	$1,225,000
Variable Costs			
E Cost Percent	77.80%	77.80%	77.80%
F Total Costs	$1,945,000	$1,361,500	$953,050
Profits			
G Gross Profit	$555,000	$388,500	$271,950
H Discount Rate	1	1.2	1.44
I NPV Profit	$555,000	$323,750	$188,854
J Cumulative NPV Profit	$555,000	$878,750	$1,067,604
K Lifetime Value (NPV)	$555.00	$878.75	$1,067.60

This table is based on Brian Woolf's study "Measured Marketing." It shows that the average retention rate is about 70 percent and the average spending rate for a shopping card holder is $2,500. The typical cost percentage is 77.8 percent.

With a database, supermarkets can compute these numbers for each group of card holders, enabling them to provide special benefits for their best customers to improve their retention rate and boost their spending rate.

MAKING MEASURED MARKETING WORK

As already noted, many stores tried out shopper's cards and then gave it up. Others have used them successfully for years. Why are there these differences? Brian Woolf defines measured marketing:

The purpose of measured marketing is to capture the majority of customer transactions and sales, through electronic marketing and other means, with the goal of measuring and monitoring existing and new customer activity, and using this information to improve the company's marketing strategy, tactics, and results.

The goals of measured marketing are:

- *Retention.* To improve the retention rate.
- *Frequency.* To improve the frequency of store visits.
- *Acquisition.* To add new customers who want the benefits of frequent shopper cards.
- *Lifetime Value.* To improve customer lifetime value.

There are some techniques which appear to work better than others in achieving these goals. Stores which failed to make measured marketing pay off did not succeed in using these techniques profitably. They are:

- Give shoppers a good reason to use their cards. This reason comes in two parts: provide deep discounts on a few items for card holders only. This gives people a sense of immediate gratification from shopping visits that include those items.

Deep discounts on a few items has proven to be more effective than minor discounts on a great many items.

The second reason to use the cards is to build up equity. Some stores offer gift certificates when the customer's cumulative spending reaches certain milestones such as $2,500, $5,000, $10,000, etc. This not only encourages customers to come back but discourages them from splitting their visits between your store and some other store.

- Spend money on value, not tinsel. The budget should be spent on markdowns, not on expensive cards and welcome kits. Limiting the number of discounted items that can be purchased on a single visit saves money (permits deeper discounts) and increases the frequency of visits.

- Festoon the store with reminders of the program. Measured marketing can be and, to be successful, should be the center of the store's marketing program. Special value products for preferred customers should be pivotally placed through the aisles rather than being bunched together in clusters. Special offers, tied to the program, should be visible in every aisle.

- Employee Training. Constant training of employees is necessary, because of turnover problems. Involve employees in the testing of the program, and provide a special discount to employees who use their cards. Provide "Ask me about the program" buttons. Give employees regular feedback on the success of the program. Compare each store's percentage of card members with that of other stores, and reward the winning store's employees. Post the names of the 20 top customers in each store's break room, so that employees can learn who they are, and help to greet them by name. This is database marketing!

- Make joining the program easy. Have application forms constantly available. Don't ask for too much information on the initial application. More data can be obtained later in a satisfaction survey. Give out a plastic card immediately in the store, rather than having them wait weeks for mail delivery.

- Welcome the newcomers with a letter and a reason to return: a questionnaire which when filled in can be redeemed for a gift.

- Cater to customer's ego. Examples of methods include giving your best customers a gold card, which will be recognized and honored by clerks when the customer arrives at checkout. Seek customer's advice. Put top customers on advisory panels that meet periodically to advise the store on new products and policies.

- Add value to the cards by getting non-competing retailers and services to accept the card, giving a 10 percent discount. The more valuable your card is perceived as being, the more it will be used, and the more loyal your card holders will be to you.

- Don't offer gifts for signups. Signing up should be considered something similar to establishing credit, or beginning a relationship. The card itself should be perceived as having value. If you give someone a gift for signing up, they then have the gift, and what was the value of the card?

SUMMARY

- Retailers are late getting into the database game. One problem they have is keeping track of their customers' purchases. Bar code scanners make it possible only if customers will use a store identification card. To get them to use the card, the store must provide benefits for card use. This can be expensive.

- Major department store chains have established preferred buyer programs which offer recognition and special services to their best customers. To reach this stage a store must first go through several steps:

  — Issue store cards and get customers to use them.

  — Build a database from the application forms.

  — Track customer purchases and feed them into the database.

- — Identify your best customers; give them a special card.

- — Create great benefits for these best customers.

- — Create lifetime value tables to determine whether your member club is paying off.

- If your program is working, it will affect the retention rate, the referral rate, and the spending rate. You can prove whether the benefits are greater than the costs.

- Supermarkets have been using shopper cards for some time. There is a limit to the amount of data that a store should store on supermarket purchases. In general, the less information kept the better. Keep only that information that you can use to build a relationship.

- Product manufacturers, in general, are not interested in buying data from retail stores about the ultimate consumers.

- Many supermarket card programs have failed. Those that succeed have these features:

  - — Shoppers have a good reason to use their cards.

  - — Money should be spent on discounts, not frills.

  - — The store should be papered with references to the program.

  - — Employees should be trained to support the program.

  - — Joining the program should be easy for customers.

  - — Newcomers should receive a welcome letter.

  - — The program should cater to the ego of their best customers.

Part VI:

Economics and Corporate Relationships

Chapter 25

Why Database Marketing Works

Anyone can compile a list of customer names, and call it a marketing database. A list of names, however, will not earn any money—it will cost you money to maintain it. What makes it into a profit center is using it to implement a marketing strategy which will boost spending, retention, and referrals, and cut direct and marketing costs. In this chapter, we are going to cover how you go about that process, and provide an illustration of how it works. First, let's ask why database marketing is so much in the news today. What makes it so special?

MASS MARKETING

To answer this question, we have to go back a few decades. Before and during World War II, groceries, hardware, and other consumer products were generally sold by proprietors of small stores (old corner grocers) who knew their customers by name, did special services and favors for them, and built up customer loyalty that kept them coming back for a lifetime. The coming of the war brought massive changes in America and its marketing system. During the war the government shut down the production of consumer durable goods (cars, washing machines, etc.) in favor of military production. Many items were rationed. Civilians were encouraged to save their money and buy war bonds. Military service and war production activities moved millions of men and women to new locations and gave them new skills. Marriages and families were postponed.

When the war ended, the newly skilled and relocated men and women who had worked in the factories or the military went to college using the G.I. bill, and began to form families at an unprecedented rate. Using their war bonds, they had the cash to buy houses, cars, and appliances. Banks extended credit for housing, automobile finance, and consumer loans. A mass market was created overnight. National radio advertising expanded as never before.

The marketing industry grabbed at this opportunity. Here was a new market with cash to spend and, furthermore, everyone wanted the same things: housing, cars, washers, dryers, radios, phonographs, clothing. By the 1950s television came along and everyone wanted that. But television brought something else: a means of mass communication that could show the product as well as talk about it. Everyone watched, absorbed the message, and spent their money. It was like shooting fish in a barrel.

At the same time, supermarkets expanded nationwide putting the old corner grocers out of business. Displaying an average of 10,000 different products (SKUs) in the Seventies, 20,000 SKUs in the Eighties, and 30,000 in the Nineties, these retailers, and their counterparts, huge national department store chains, home repair chains, electronic chains, and shopping malls, made mass marketing a reality.

TARGET MARKETING

During this period, marketers began to forget about customers as human beings. Customers became targets. The language of warfare was adopted to describe the customer relationship. Since everyone wanted the same things, "market share" became a method of comparing how you were doing in dividing up this lucrative national customer pie. New products—color TVs, VCRs, cameras, microwave ovens, cellular phones, computers—quickly became commodities with similar features where price became the principal criterion.

MARKET SATURATION

Beginning in the 1990s, a new trend appeared. The post-war mass market had become saturated. Everyone had the basics. While the media tended to focus on the plight of the poor, the great mass of the population became relatively affluent. Real disposable per capita income increased steadily year by year for 85 percent of the population. By the end of the millennium, there were 80 million affluent households who already owned a car, telephone, several TVs, VCRs, cameras, washers, dryers, and microwave ovens, and who no longer had to spend the bulk of their income on the products sold by mass marketing. In the 1950s, for example, the average household spent 31 percent of their income on food. By the late 1990s this was down to 12 percent and falling—even though the quantity and quality of food consumed per person was considerably greater. Per capita consumption of fresh fruits and vegetables, for example, gained 26 percent from 1970 to 1990. People ate better, were healthier, and lived longer.

The rate of growth of the population came down. There were fewer new families being formed, and those that were formed had a higher disposable income than those in earlier generations. More than 60 percent of adult women were working, meaning that in most households there was no one at home during the day: no one to listen to the soap operas, to take care of the children, to let the plumber in to do repairs. Leisure time became scarcer and had a higher perceived value.

In the free market, both parties to a transaction always make a profit: both the consumer and the supplier. Consumers' profits during the mass marketing heydays were measured in dollars: how much cheaper could you rent a car from Avis than from Hertz? By the late 1990s the consumer rated his profits differently: how much more convenient was it to rent a car from Hertz than from their competitors? How much more recognition and service did you receive by being a Hertz Number One Club Gold Member, than being an ordinary person waiting in line at a Hertz counter?

Instead of continuing to use mass marketing to acquire and reacquire the same customers over and over again, the marketing objective began to shift to retention. Since there were less and less new customers (because of slower family formation and market saturation) it was vital (and less expensive) to work hard to keep the customers you already had acquired, than to keep beating the bushes for new ones.

DATABASE MARKETING

Database marketing arrived, therefore, at the ideal time. By keeping track of customer information: purchases, demographics, lifestyle, preferences, attitudes, it was possible to recreate the friendly helpfulness, recognition, and service provided by the old corner grocer, but on a national scale.

I do a lot of traveling. Recently, I became a Hertz Number One Club Gold Member. They had me fill out a form asking my preferences in car rental, my credit card number, license number, etc. My travel agent has my Hertz Gold number on her database. When I travel, she automatically gets me a Hertz car with four doors, using my number. When I arrive at an airport, I board a Hertz bus and give the driver my name: Arthur Hughes—that is all. He drives me to a covered walkway where there is an 18-inch-high sign in bright lights that says "Hughes, A". There is an arrow on the sign which points to a car.

The trunk of the car is open, the key is in the ignition, and the motor is running. If it is winter, the heater is on, and the car is warm. If it is summer, the AC is on, and the car is cool. I put my bags in the trunk, slide behind the wheel and drive out. At the gate I show my driver's license, get directions, and go. No forms to fill out. No lines to wait in. Nothing to sign. This is service. This is recognition. This is convenience. This is database marketing.

There is no discount with the Hertz Number One Club. I pay full price. I could, of course, shop around each time I rent a car to find the best deal in each city. But the money I would save would not pay my company back for the time I would have to spend getting comparable rates and haggling. I have looked them all over, and settled on one company. I identify with Hertz.

Of course, there are side benefits, besides super service. I automatically get 500 American Airlines Advantage Miles when I use Hertz with an AA trip. Helena and I travel to Chile every two years. We have already taken two free trips to Chile using American Airlines miles. How typical am I of Hertz customers? I don't know. I am probably not typical. I am sure that many other Hertz customers are looking for the lowest priced rental car, and are willing to stand in line to get it. The beauty of database marketing is that Hertz can use the database to figure out what each individual customer prefers, and give them that. It is no longer "one size fits all".

How did Hertz get me as a Number One Club member? They used a partner. I am a member of the British Airways Executive Club. British Airways ran a joint promotion with Hertz which offered a Gold membership with Hertz as a benefit to British Airways Executive Club members. Hertz probably paid a handsome sum for the mailing which ended up in acquiring me. Getting people to join your database is not necessarily inexpensive. But they got me, and now I am hooked.

Database marketing has been theoretically possible for decades, but it wasn't economically practical until quite recently. By the 1990s computers became so inexpensive and speedy that you could capture and store vast amounts of information provided by customers, and retrieve and use that information to provide better service to customers, and have the cost of doing this be less than the net additional profits realized.

AVIS and National also provide super services to their business customers. I could use them, but I now have a vested interest in Hertz. Hertz is now getting all of my rental car business, whereas a few years ago, they only got 20 percent of it. The benefits to me of Hertz Gold membership have increased my loyalty to Hertz. That increased loyalty (read: "increased retention" and "increased spending rate") is also worth money to Hertz. It costs money to keep track of which flight I am coming in on, remember when it lands, put my name up in lights at the proper moment, and have the car motor running and the AC on while I take the bus from the airport to the Hertz lot. The database costs money. The bottom line: does Arthur Hughes's increased retention and spending provide enough additional revenue to pay for all of these extra services?

How can Hertz, or anyone, figure that out? They can use a simple lifetime value table. Here is what it might look like:

Hertz Business Non-Gold Customers *

Revenue	Year1	Year2	Year3
R1 Customers	100,000	50,000	30,000
R2 Retention Rate	50.00%	60.00%	70.00%
R3 Spending Rate	$160.00	$200.00	$240.00
R4 Total			
Revenue	$16,000,000	$10,000,000	$7,200,000
Variable Costs			
C1 Direct Percent	60.00%	60.00%	60.00%
C2 Variable			
Direct Costs	$9,600,000	$6,000,000	$4,320,000
C3 Total Costs	$9,600,000	$6,000,000	$4,320,000
Profits			
P1 Gross Profit	$6,400,000	$4,000,000	$2,880,000
P2 Discount Rate	1.00	.20	1.44
P3 NPV Profit	$6,400,000	$3,333,333	$2,000,000
P4 Cumulative			
NPV Profit	$6,400,000	$9,733,333	$11,733,333
L1 Customer			
Lifetime Value	$64.00	$97.33	$117.33

*Illustrative figures only. Not based on Hertz information or data.

We are looking at 100,000 regular business customers who are acquired by Hertz. For these charts, I am using illustrative (made up) figures not based on any contacts or information whatsoever from Hertz. The real Hertz data may be quite different from what is shown here—and would certainly not be available for publication so that it could be studied by Avis, National, Budget, etc. I am using Hertz as an example, because it is a very good and well known company which illustrates the points that I am trying to make in this chapter. I am assuming that the average new Hertz business customer does about $400 per year in rental cars, of which about 40 percent is from Hertz. Hertz retains about half of these customers after one year. This retention percentage grows for those who do come back to 70 percent in the third year. The lifetime value of a Hertz business customer after three years is about $117.

Let's look at what could happen to the lifetime value of Hertz Number One Club Gold members. The picture is quite different:

Hertz Number One Club Gold Customer Lifetime Value*

Revenue	*Year1*	*Year2*	*Year3*
R1 Referral Rate	8.00%	10.00%	12.00%
R2 Referred			
Customers	0	8000	8800
R3 Total Customers	100,000	88,000	79,200
R4 Retention Rate	80.00%	80.00%	80.00%
R5 Spending Rate	$400.00	$400.00	$400.00
R6 Total Revenue	$40,000,000	$35,200,000	$31,680,000
Variable Costs			
C1 Direct Percent	60.00%	60.00%	60.00%
C2 Variable Direct			
Costs	$24,000,000	$21,120,000	$19,008,000
C3 Club Acquisi-			
tion Costs $50	$5,000,000	$0	$0
C4 Database			
Costs $5	$500,000	$440,000	$396,000
C5 Special			
Services $40	$4,000,000	$3,520,000	$3,168,000
C6 Referral			
Incentives $20	$0	$160,000	$176,000
C7 Total Costs	$33,500,000	$25,240,000	$22,748,000
Profits			
P1 Gross Profit	$6,500,000	$9,960,000	$8,932,000
P2 Discount Rate	1.00	1.20	1.44
P3 NPV Profit	$6,500,000	$8,300,000	$6,202,778
P4 Cumulative			
NPV Profit	$6,500,000	$14,800,000	$21,002,778
L1 Customer			
Lifetime Value	$65.00	$148.00	$210.03

* Illustrative figures only, not based on Hertz information or data.

The club is expensive. It costs $50 to acquire each new club member, and then $5 per year for the database, and $40 per year for special services for club members. The benefits for Hertz, however, are substantial. The spending rate goes from $160 per year (25 percent of member's business) to $400 per year—all of their rental business. The retention rate also increases. In addition, satisfied Hertz Club members can be incentivized to suggest other people who become customers. These referred customers add to the bottom line due to database marketing.

The net effect of getting people to join the Number One Club could be to raise the three year lifetime value from $117 to $210. What does this mean for the Hertz bottom line?

It means that if Hertz were to convert 100,000 regular business customers to Hertz Number One Club Gold Customers, their profits from these customers could increase by $9 million dollars.

Comparison of Lifetime Value Gain

	Year1	Year2	Year3
Value Without Database	$64.00	$97.33	$117.33
Value With Database	$ 65.00	$148.00	$210.03
Difference	$ 1.00	$ 50.67	$ 92.70
100,000 Members	$ 100,000	$ 5,067,000	$ 9,270,000

Is this a fact? Are you sure? Of course not. I have no inside information on Hertz. What I am illustrating here is how Hertz or anyone can go about the job of determining the value of a club strategy. The fact is that in some situations, building a database, and using it to provide recognition, helpfulness, special services, and convenience to customers can be very profitable for both the customer and the provider. Furthermore, if it is not profitable for the customer, they won't cooperate, and it won't end up being profitable for the provider.

RELATIONSHIP VS. TRANSACTION BUYERS

Professor Paul Wang of Northwestern University has drawn a very useful and valid distinction between two types of buyers: relationship buyers and transaction buyers. As he defines it:

- A relationship buyer is a person who buys from you because you have developed a satisfactory relationship. Price is not the primary consideration. Instead, the relationship buyer trusts you, and accepts your brand or your company as being the one he prefers to deal with. He doesn't have to shop around all the time. He is happy with the long term decision he has made.

- A transaction buyer is a person who is always looking for the best price. He concentrates on the transaction at hand. He may have bought from you a hundred times, but each time his decision is made after checking your price against the competition.

Some people are born to be transaction buyers, and some are naturally loyal relationship types. But most people are not necessarily one or the other. We, the suppliers, train these people to become a relationship or a transaction buyer. If our advertising and promotion is concentrated on price, if we are always having sales and discounts, we focus the customer on the price he is paying. Wal-Mart does this. Coupons do this. Cash back does this. Soon the customer becomes accustomed to thinking of your product as a commodity whose sole quality is price.

The problem with transaction buyers is that they have no loyalty at all. They are trained to seek the lowest price. They will jump to your competitor as soon as he announces a new low price offer. You can't make much money with transaction buyers. Better wish them on your competition.

Relationship buyers are much more profitable. We can train these people to appreciate the quality of the product or service that we provide. We get them to appreciate the recognition we accord them, the personal service, the convenience, the helpfulness of our customer service personnel, the security which our company provides. By focusing on these things, we inoculate these buyers from the price cutting of our competitors.

Once you start database marketing, you have embarked on a program of customer training. From that moment on, you should banish from your lexicon the words sale, discount, free, cash back, half off, and two for one. These are transaction words, not relationship words.

If you have a friend, do you think about how much your friendship is worth in terms of dollars? How much money you save by having someone next door who watches your kids when you have to run an errand? Would you offer your neighbor a $5 bill for helping you to carry a heavy table up your stairs? He would be insulted. It would change your entire relationship. The association you have is friendship, which has no dollar price. That is what you want to have with your relationship buyers.

WHERE DATABASE MARKETING DOESN'T WORK

Of course, database marketing will not work with every product and service. It won't really work well with a great many packaged goods—unless you can identify a special niche market like pet owners, parents of babies, dieters, Italian food lovers, gourmands, etc. Even with these groups, you can't really build a database that has purchase history, since there doesn't seem to be any economic way to keep track of your customer's purchases of individual items. Many companies, however, are doing quite well marketing to the parents of new babies and selling them diapers and baby food. There are pet databases, and dieter databases that work very well.

But there are thousands of products where a database is not going to work at all. Can you create a profitable marketing database of consumers who use toilet paper? diskettes? shoe polish? nails? light bulbs? furniture? picture frames? I think not. For some of these products, the margin is so slim that personalized marketing would eat up all the potential increased profits. In other cases (furniture or picture frames) the purchase is so seldom for a given household that you simply could not identify consumers who would be likely to purchase your product in the near future.

If you had a database of new movers, you could sell them furniture or picture frames (perhaps). If you had a database of large institutions that are open at night, you might get a lightbulb database going, but it seems like a long shot.

In short, database marketing will not always work. There are thousands of products and services for which it won't work, and existing methods of marketing (awareness ads, shelf space, coupons, yellow pages) may be the best solution.

WHY IT WORKS

So why does it work? Because the customers want it to work. They get some personal subjective benefit from it. The benefit is not low price. You can cut your price without a database. Relationship buyers pay full price. The benefit is something else: it is recognition, convenience, helpfulness, service, information, and identification. Before you rush into database marketing, therefore, think to yourself: "Why would I want to be on this database? What would be in it for me? What do I want that the database could help me to get?"

If you can't come up with a good answer to that question, you do not have a valid database program. It will fail because the customers will see no value in it for them. If they see no value in it, they will chuck out your newsletters, leave your gold cards in their bureau drawers, and never call your 800 number. As a result, you won't be able to increase your retention rate, or spending rate. You won't be able to generate referral business. It's as simple as that.

SUMMARY

The question we started with was, "What is so special about database marketing that makes it so effective today?" can now be answered.

Database marketing is effective today because of:

- *Economics.* Computers, which are essential to database marketing, are now able to store vast amounts of customer data at a very reasonable cost.

- *Affluence.* There are many more affluent customers who prefer service and convenience over discounts, and are willing to pay full price if they can be given the services that they want.

- *Busy Consumers.* Most adult family members are now working. They have less time during the day. Their leisure time is more valuable to them. They are willing to pay a little more for helpfulness and convenience. Databases can aid manufacturers and retailers in providing this helpfulness.

- *Loyalty.* Customers will be loyal to you, if you can give them a reason for doing so. Database marketing helps you to maintain contact with them in ways that will build their loyalty.

- *Customer Profits.* Customers will only do business if it is profitable for them. What they consider profitable is not necessarily a cheap price. It may be recognition, reduced inconvenience, increased leisure time, or secondary benefits (such as airmiles or status). Database marketing is a method of providing those benefits.

There are two types of buyers: Relationship Buyers (who are loyal to one supplier) and Transaction Buyers (who tend to shop around for the best price every time.) You can train your customers through your actions. By concentrating on price, discounts, sales, and coupons, you train your customers to think of your product as a commodity. Such transaction buyers are easy for your competitor to steal. By training customers to be relationship buyers, you inoculate them against the competitors sales and discounts.

Database marketing works because the customer wants it to work. She gets something valuable to her out of the relationship. If you can't come up with some benefit for the customer out of your database, it will fail and waste your company's money.

Chapter 26

Using the Database for Media Selection

What is the best medium to use when seeking new customers? The answer to this question varies widely with the product and the industry. Popular packaged goods like foods, beverages, soap, and clothing often rely on awareness advertising through television. Automobile manufacturers, airlines, and department stores also use this same medium. Since TV is so ubiquitous, many people are surprised to learn that less than a quarter of all advertising dollars actually goes into TV ads, as compared to other media.

With such a wide variety of possible media available, what is the most effective use of your dollar to produce the best return? There was one answer before database marketing, and there is quite a different answer today with advertisers able to use extensive customer data to guide their decisions.

To see the changes, let's explore the marketing decisions which can be made by the supplier of a continuity product or service where it is possible to track customer performance. Examples would be department stores, financial services, travel and leisure, gasoline, cellular phones, magazine and newspaper subscriptions. In each of these situations, it is feasible to use any or all of the media shown in the chart above. It is also possible to keep track of customers' purchases from month to month, and record them on a database.

This chapter stems from an article originally written jointly with Prof. Paul Wang of Northwestern University. The article appeared in the *Journal of Database Marketing* in 1995.

Figure 26-1 Advertising Spending Ratios

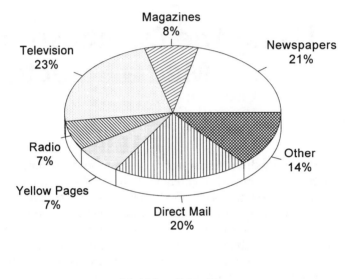

Robert J. Coen, McCann-Erickson

THE TARGET MARKETING APPROACH

If we go back to the 1980s, some advertisers had become quite sophisticated in their measurement of customer acquisition costs and benefits. As we emerged from our preoccupation with mass awareness advertising, and moved into more reliance on targeted marketing, savvy media buyers began by defining their desired prospect universe by analyzing the characteristics of their existing customers. A financial services marketer, for example, might target people over forty with a household income of more than $50,000 for a particular product. Census data projected to census tract made targeting quite precise. To reach these prospects, the media buyer evaluated each medium by its ability to reach the desired prospect segment, and the cost per thousand (CPM) exposures of that segment. Market penetration ratios were established.

Following the rules of target marketing, a smart media buyer's calculations might look something like this:

Media	CPM Exposures	Penetration of Target Audience	CPM of Target Audience
Magazine A	$8	8%	$100
Magazine B	$12	16%	$75
Magazine C	$15	10%	$150

The data for this chart can be obtained from rate cards and ABC circulation data, projected against the known customer base and desired prospect audience. Magazine A provides more exposures per dollar invested than either of the other two magazines. However, when the target audience is considered, it has a penetration ratio of only about 8 percent. The effective cost per thousand exposures of the target group is thus much higher than the reach of magazine B which costs more, but penetrates into more of the desired prospect base. Magazine C is out on all counts.

THE DIRECT MARKETING APPROACH

Of course, exposures are not sales. The proof of the pudding is in the eating. Direct marketers, therefore, would take this same picture one step further, and ask how many of the target audience actually made a purchase. The conversion ratio might also vary by media. Whereas CPM and penetration ratios can be learned by detailed study of available data, conversion rates can be learned only by testing. With any test, there are many variables which can prejudice the results such as differing months, seasons, copy, offer, etc. As a result, precise calculations are very difficult. However, if the advertiser is persistent, has a multi-year program, and a sufficient budget, it is possible to come up with a table that looks something like this:

Media	CPM of Target Audience	Buyers per 1000 Exposures	Cost Per Customer
Magazine A	$100	2	$50.00
Magazine B	$75	2	$37.50
Magazine C	$150	5	$30.00

Awareness advertising criteria, therefore, would dictate choice of Magazine B, since it has the lowest cost per thousand exposures in the target audience. Direct marketing criteria would point to Magazine C, since the cost to acquire a buyer is the lowest. Why should the buyers vary with the magazine? That depends on the magazine and the product. If I were to suggest that the product is a mutual fund, and magazines A, B, and C are *Parade*, *Newsweek* and *Money* magazine respectively, the picture may become a little clearer.

THE IMPORTANCE OF THE RETENTION RATE

With database marketing, we have a new way of looking at the same data. With a database, you can keep track of the source of the customer and his subsequent purchases. In many product situations, the profit is not in the initial sale, but in the repeat purchases made in subsequent periods. To acquire a credit card customer, for example, costs an average of $80 per card holder. If that card holder were to drop the card immediately, the bank would have lost $80, and have nothing to show for it. It may take a year before that card holder has earned back the $80 and two years before he returns a profit. The same situation may be true in hundreds of other products: life insurance, cellular phone service, newspaper subscriptions. The real test of success, therefore, is not customer acquisition, but customer retention. The measurement method is lifetime value. Lets look, for example, at the lifetime value of a credit card holder after three years:

Lifetime Value of Credit Card Customers

Revenue	Year1	Year2	Year3
Customers	1000	800	640
Retention Rate	80.00%	80.00%	80.00%
Spending Rate	$120.00	$120.00	$120.00
Total Revenue	$120,000	$96,000	$76,800

Costs			
Cost Percent	25.00%	25.00%	25.00%
Direct Costs	$30,000	$24,000	$19,200
Marketing Costs	$80,000	$4,000	$3,200
Total Costs	$110,000	$28,000	$22,400

Profits			
Gross Profit	$10,000	$68,000	$54,400
Discount Rate	1.00	1.20	1.44
NPV Profit	$10,000	$56,667	$37,778
Cumulative NPV Profit	$10,000	$66,667	$104,444
Lifetime Value (NPV)	$10.00	$66.67	$104.44

At the end of the first year, the spending rate has just barely kept even with the high acquisition cost of $80 per card holder. By Year2, however, the card holder's lifetime value has paid off the acquisition cost and earned a tidy profit which is increased in future years. The important factor in this chart is the retention rate, which is shown here as 80 percent. Were that rate to fall substantially, to 60 percent or 40 percent for example, the lifetime value would change dramatically.

Lifetime Value with Lower Retention Rate

Revenue	Year1	Year2	Year3
Customers	1000	400	160
Retention Rate	40.00%	40.00%	40.00%
Spending Rate	$120.00	$120.00	$120.00
Total Revenue	$120,000	$48,000	$19,200
Costs			
Cost Percent	25.00%	25.00%	25.00%
Direct Costs	$30,000	$12,000	$4,800
Marketing Costs	$80,000	$4,000	$3,200
Total Costs	$110,000	$16,000	$8,000
Profits			
Gross Profit	$10,000	$32,000	$11,200
Discount Rate	1.00	1.20	.44
NPV Profit	$10,000	$26,667	$7,778
Cumulative NPV Profit	$10,000	$36,667	$44,444
Lifetime Value (NPV)	$10.00	$36.67	$44.44

The substantial profits anticipated by Year3 have evaporated. The return on investment has fallen off dramatically.

The purpose of these charts is to illustrate that marketers today have to calculate future profits, rather than simple awareness, or direct response to promotion.

RETENTION RATE BY PROFILE

The lifetime value charts shown here are the result of averaging all customers together. In fact, however, customer behavior varies considerably from profile to profile. If one were to break customers down into Recency Frequency Monetary (RFM) cells (see Chapter 7), it would be possible to see wide variations in the retention rate of different customers. Some groups keep making purchases for years. Others abandon ship after a few months. Being able to distinguish these groups, and treating them differently, can make a big difference in the total profit picture.

Based on past experience, therefore, we might be able to break our new customers down into three (or more) broad profiles:

Profile Customers	Percent	Lifetime Value	Retention Rate
Loyalists	30%	$200	90%
Average	50%	$100	70%
Bargain Hunters	20%	$10	10%

Knowing which customer is in which profile enables the marketer to focus his retention building programs on the Average group, ignoring both the Loyalists and the Bargain Hunters: the first because they don't need stroking, and the second because the stroking is probably not worth the effort.

FOCUS ON THE ACQUISITION MEDIA

Creating these profiles has a second, and even more interesting use. It is possible to trace each customer back to his source: the media that caused his acquisition in the first place. This media source can then be compared with his current retention profile. While this analysis may not show any significant variation in some product situations, there are cases in which the results can be quite striking.

We had experience with one client who was selling a premium pet food on a continuity program: it came monthly, charged to the customer's credit card automatically. When we compared the retention rates of customers by media, we discovered a major difference in the results. Buyers acquired by television ads were by far the more numerous, and had a lower cost of acquisition per customer. They tended to have a very low retention rate, however. After one year, more than half of them were gone. Buyers acquired by direct mail, on the other hand, had a retention rate of more than 80 percent. The difference led us to reconsider the media selection program. Media selection in the past had been based on CPM and cost of acquisition. With lifetime value in view, we switched to considering the cost per active customer in Year2. The profit picture changed dramatically.

Here, using illustrative figures, is the type of thing that we discovered:

Media Cost Calculation Sheet for Lifetime Value Maximization

A	B	C	D	E	F	G
Media	Average CPM Exposures	Startup Media Budget	Thousands of Exposures	Buyers Per 1,000 Exposures	Customers In Year1	Acq. Cost Per/Cust Year1
TV 30	$5.40	$200,000	37,037	0.30	11,111	$18.00
Infomercials	$10.00	$200,000	20,000	0.50	10,000	$20.00
Newspaper	$16.00	$200,000	12,500	0.70	8,750	$22.86
Magazines	$24.00	$200,000	8,333	1.00	8,333	$24.00
Specialty Mags.	$26.00	$200,000	7,692	1.10	8,461	$23.64
Radio	$5.00	$100,000	20,000	0.20	4,000	$25.00
Direct Mail	$350.00	$400,000	1,143	16.00	18,288	$21.87
Total		$1,500,000	106,705	6.46	68,943	$21.76

In this chart, the media buyer obtained CPM costs from each media, and from tests was able to calculate the buyers per 1000 exposures for each type of media. The acquisition cost varied from $18.00 to $25.00 with 30 second TV commercials producing the best value per dollar spent.

Subsequent tracking of buyer's performance based on acquisition method can show a very different picture. The following chart takes up where the previous chart left off. It uses the retention rate calculated based on the performance of buyers acquired from each media source.

Acquisition Cost of Buyers Who Remain after Two Years

A	F	G	H	I	J
	Customers In	Acq. Cost Per/Cust	Reten.	Customers In	Acq. Cost Per/Cust
Media	Year1	Year1	Rate	Year2	Year2
TV 30	11,111	$18.00	10.00%	1,111	$180.00
Infomercials	10,000	$20.00	12.00%	1,200	$166.67
Newspaper	8,750	$22.86	30.00%	2,625	$76.19
Magazines	8,333	$24.00	30.00%	2,500	$80.00
Specialty Mags.	8,461	$23.64	40.00%	3,384	$59.09
Radio	4,000	$25.00	15.00%	600	$166.67
Direct Mail	18,288	$21.87	50.00%	9,144	$43.74
Total	68,943	$21.76	29.83%	20,564	$72.94

In this chart, the differing retention rates of buyers acquired from different media are factored in. The result is that the cheapest way to acquire buyers who remain for two years is direct mail. Television, which was the winner based on immediate acquisition, falls seriously short when the retention rate is used.

The actual numbers which can be obtained in each situation may differ considerably from those used in these illustrations. What is shown here, however, is a fairly universal method for determining the best media mix for customer acquisition based on long term retention. Any marketer who has built a customer database, and has a method for capturing long term purchasing behavior can, and should, measure the retention rates based on the media. In some cases, the result can be a radical shift in acquisition media choices and a significant improvement in the bottom line.

CAN YOU DO THIS?

Fine tuning the media selection program is an untapped profit opportunity in most companies. The reason is that media buying is usually done by specialists in an advertising agency whose knowledge and understanding of the principles outlined in this chapter is exactly zero.

What they usually know about are rates, schedules, coop deals, seasons of the year, etc. They measure their success by awareness tests, recall ability, focus groups, and similar criteria. They seek to help their agency win design awards. To get them to think about buyers per 1000 exposures, for example, is a giant forward step which few companies have even explored. But, after all, it's your money they are spending. Once you have a database, you can begin to collect data to see if there are some hard headed criteria for measuring success.

Most companies are light years away from being able to create the charts shown in this chapter. If you have built a customer database, and are able to keep track of customer purchases (which is true in utilities, financial services, travel, and most business-to-business products) you can, and should, begin to collect the data necessary to measuring your media success.

To start with, be sure to keep the media source of every new customer. To the list above, you should add such sources as referrals from existing customers, dealers, trade shows, etc. With two years worth of data at your fingertips, it should be possible to begin to flesh out these tables with real experience. You may be amazed at what you find. How many trade show customers are still with you after two years, as opposed to yellow page or print ad acquisitions?

We are just scratching the surface in exploring the potentials of database marketing for building profits. The sky is the limit.

SUMMARY

- Target marketing helps media buyers to use penetration ratios to measure the cost per thousand exposures (CPM) of people in the correct target audience. This is much more valuable than the traditional cost per thousand people exposed.

- Direct marketing measures buyers per thousand exposures. This gives you a cost per customer acquired. This is much more useful than the standard CPM.

- Database marketing takes you one step further. In many product and service situations you are looking at long-term retention rather than one-shot sales. By keeping track of the source of all new customers, you can measure the cost of acquiring customers who remain buyers into the second or subsequent years. This cost is much more valuable than any of the foregoing. By tracing second year customers back to their original source, you can make much more useful decisions on media selection than can be made in any other way.

- Few companies are in a position to do this type of sophisticated analysis at present. Once they have built their customer databases, they will be able to do this, and can use the technique to build their profits. The beauty of this type of analysis is that it is so inexpensive. The database provides all of the data. No expensive consultants or external resources are needed.

Chapter 27

The Privacy Issue— and Other Philosophical Problems

"Modern civilization has given man undreamt of powers largely because, without understanding it, he has developed methods of utilizing more knowledge and resources than any one mind is aware of." (F. A. Hayek, *New Studies*, University of Chicago Press, 1978.)

Database marketing is one of those methods. Proponents of database marketing are advocating a revolution in marketing technique. It goes by many names: individual marketing, relationship marketing, database marketing. The concept is that you try to learn more about your customers, to become friendly with them, to understand them, to develop two-way communications, to remember what they say, and to use it in building rapport.

As a result, the theory goes, you can build a lifetime relationship with these customers instead of just making a sale or two. Compared to other methods of marketing, such as mass marketing and direct marketing, database marketing represents the development of a new philosophy of marketing. As with any philosophy it is partly faith and partly reasoning. In any case, if it is a valid philosophy it must stand up to rigorous scrutiny. Let's look at it and raise some fundamental questions.

Question: Isn't database marketing really phony or fake? A computer doesn't care about customers. Building a database system which seems to care, complete with personalized letters, is really a fraud on the consumer, right?

Answer: It can be. If all a company does is collect information from consumers and feed it back to them without modifying behavior in the company, then it is a fraud.

I visited the offices of a major non-profit corporation one spring. The organization had modified their renewal forms to include a space for members to indicate their preferred program activities. Hundreds of thousands were completed and mailed in to the group together with their membership contributions. Unfortunately, the corporation had not done its homework. They had not modified their database to receive and report on contributor preferences. Their database programmers were way behind on their software development and simply could not fit this new information into the database. They were in fact throwing away the contribution forms after depositing the money and recording the name and address. The favorite program information was not recorded or tabulated. Did the failure to capture this information and use it bother management? No one seemed much concerned. In fact, some expressed the belief that the very act of having an opportunity to tell the group what programs they preferred probably made the contributors feel better about the organization and helped contributions. The fact that their responses were thrown away would not be known and was unimportant.

Some even expressed a worry to me about what to do with the information if they did actually capture and record these preferences. Suppose, for example, that the survey showed that a majority of contributors were opposed to some activity favored by the board of directors. Should they take that into consideration in their program decisions? Some said that that idea would be contrary to the whole philosophy of a public interest group, which should be run for the public good, not for the *contributors*, who, after all, make up only a small faction of the general public who would receive the benefits.

We must leave this controversy to the high-minded public interest sector, and worry here about the reaction of a profit-making company to customer views and desires. Here the objective is clear: giving people exactly what they want should be good for both the business and the customers. The company that discovers what its customers are thinking and then *modifies its behavior* as a result, gives these customers better service and, in the long run, has more sales and more profits.

The only fraud, it seems to me, is in collecting quantities of information and then not acting on it. Successful database marketing will change the behavior of a company. It will have to grant a higher status to customer services. It will have to figure out how to include customer preferences and customer profiles in the design of products and services, the design of advertising, the marketing strategy, the pricing policy, the design of manuals and packages, the billing and delivery methods, the repair and replacement policies, the colors, shapes, sizes, fragrances, and weights.

Conclusion: It is true that a computer doesn't care about anyone. But a company can, and should. The database is an information gathering and processing device. The information that it collects and serves up to marketing management should be acted upon. This information tells what the customer wants in the way of products and services. Acting on this information to modify the products and procedures of the company is not a fraud. It is in the highest interests of both the consumer and the producer.

Question: Isn't database marketing really advocating a return to older methods of marketing which the public has already rejected?

Answer: In this book there are constant references to bringing back the old corner grocer. Why are we trying to bring him back? After all, in 1950 there were tens of thousands of them all over America. Today they are virtually extinct. There was a free marketplace, and they lost out. They were swept aside by the supermarkets. Doesn't that tell us something? If he lost out in the market once, why do we think that we can bring him back now?

Let us see why he lost out. He was not economically viable. His small store was labor intensive. Besides the grocer, there were many clerks waiting on customers. There were stock boys and delivery boys. The selection in his small store was limited. He could not buy in bulk, so his prices were high. One could argue that he lost out not because people didn't like his personal friendly style, but because they did not want to pay high prices at a store with a very limited choice of items.

I am reminded of the look on the faces of visitors from Eastern Europe who get their first experience in a modern American supermarket. Row after row of fruits and vegetables piled high in the middle of winter; an endless variety of meats, fish, bakery goods, dairy products, canned and dry foods. It is overwhelming, even for an American used to such things. You wheel an immense shopping cart down aisle after aisle, taking things from the racks as if you already owned them and piling your cart high with wonderful looking, clean, wholesome food and household products.

There is no way that the corner grocer could compete with that. He lost; he is gone. But with his departure we lost something that many of us miss. We lost the warmth and friendship which he provided. When you are in a supermarket or any large discount, department, or hardware store and need help, it is usually very hard to find any employees, other than the overworked cashiers facing lines of people trying to get out. When you ask employees for assistance, you always feel that you are interrupting their regular work. They are there to replenish stock or do something else, not to answer your questions. And they may not know anything about the merchandise you are asking about. In any event, they are strangers who you may never see again. They don't know who you are, and they don't care. You are an anonymous shopper alone in a warehouse.

What database marketing promises to do is to retain the efficiency, low prices, and tremendously wide variety of the modern product delivery service, but to add to it some of the warmth, individual concern, and understanding that was provided by the old corner grocer. This is possible because the dramatic drop in the price of computer storage has made it possible to retain hundreds of facts about each customer, and to call them up to use in communicating with them on a daily basis. It is possible to recreate by computer some of the thoughtfulness of the old corner grocer without having also to recreate his inefficiency, high prices, and poor variety of stock.

Conclusion: Yes, we are advocating bringing back something good from the past, but we are bringing it back in an entirely new, contemporary way which builds on modern marketing methods and practices that the public wants to retain.

Question: Aren't there some people who will be turned off by database marketing? Do people really want to become buddies with their suppliers? Don't people just want to be left alone?

Answer: A valid question. Certainly, back in the heyday of the corner grocer, there were plenty of people who resented his commercial heartiness. They just wanted to slip into a store, buy what they wanted, and get out without a lot of conversation. Those people were thrilled when the impersonal supermarket came along. They don't want to go back to the old days. They resent today's telemarketers, who interrupt their evening meal with importunate demands. Can database marketing accommodate these people?

It can, and it must. Some people don't want a lot of mail or telephone calls. They will tell you that. This is information that you must tuck away in their record in the database. Every customer record should have a place for a "No mail," "No phone," and "No visit" code. Listen to what people say, accept it graciously, and respect their wishes. Thereafter, don't bother your customer with unwanted messages. The beauty of database marketing is that you can treat everyone differently, individually, as they want to be treated. The public is no longer at the mercy of a computer-driven mass marketing machine.

Conclusion: Yes, some people will be turned off by too much togetherness with vendors. Database marketing is ideally suited to recognize this and to respect it better than any other system.

Question: Isn't database marketing an invasion of privacy?

Answer: In America, everyone is free to be against everything. No sooner does a manufacturer come out with a great new product or process than some group springs up to point out that the innovation might damage the environment or could kill mice if they consumed megadoses of it. Database marketing is new, but already has its opponents. The question is: do we want private commercial concerns to be building up huge dossiers on us which can, in the future, be used to take away our privacy?

The average corner grocer was, essentially, harmless. We told him things about ourselves, and he acted like a friend. But not all of them were saints. Some were gossips. They chatted with the banker about people's overdrafts and bad debts. They discussed medical problems with the doctor, and asked the bartender and the policeman about people's drinking habits or police records. Such gossip in a small town could be dangerous. Database marketing is a powerful tool which, in the wrong hands, could seriously invade people's private lives. How do you, as the designer and proponent, guard against that?

First, you should steer clear of building up secondary data in customer's records. Keep facts that your customers have told you about themselves, but not what you have learned about them from others. If they have passed you a bad check, you are entitled to remember it. If you are thinking of making them a big loan, you should request their permission to consult their credit references. If you are selling insurance, a physical examination is in order. But you should not store external data (like credit information, medical problems, or arrest records) in a marketing database. If you do, you are laying the groundwork for a future legal challenge that could seriously damage the whole marketing industry.

Second, you should think twice about exchanging sensitive information with other companies. Elsewhere in this book I have advocated the renting of customer names as a valuable way to keep a customer list clean and useful. But watch what you are renting. If you are the keeper of credit information or medical histories, you have a responsibility to be sure that the people who use your data are doing so in a responsible way. If industry does not regulate itself, government will step in and spoil the party for everyone.

Third, you should set up an ombudsman for your database. It is easy for proponents of a database to build in everything that can be learned about prospects and customers which could conceivably help in the marketing process, but the company needs to think of broader issues. Just as the corner grocer had to watch his mouth if he wanted to stay in business, you have to watch your database. One way of doing that is to have someone within the company who is not actively involved in marketing who reviews, periodically, the information being kept on customers and how it is being used. This person should have a pipeline to the top of the company, and the responsibility to assure that the marketing database does not end up being like the CIA. The ombudsman needs to be on board from the beginning, with a definite charter and recognized status. Database marketing is too important to be left to the marketers.

Conclusion: Yes, database marketing can easily become an invasion of personal privacy. You as a database marketer have a responsibility and a civic duty to see that that does not happen. You must take active steps to prevent it.

Question: How do we know that database marketing will actually increase sales?

Answer: Any new technique has to prove itself in dollars and cents. You begin database marketing because of a hunch, but that hunch can be and must be tested before you throw millions of dollars into it.

From the start, you need to do two things: create a lifetime value table and engage in a series of well planned tests. The lifetime value table should be a base line against which you measure all strategies before they are executed. Marketing strategies have benefits and costs. The benefits are improvements in customer retention, referrals, spending rate, reduced marketing costs, and reduced direct costs. The costs of database marketing are usually in the building and maintenance of the database, but also in the communications needed to maintain a dialogue with your customers, and to act on that dialogue to modify your behavior. After you have dreamed up a new strategy—such as a preferred customer club—and before you order the cards and begin the creative, you should ask yourself: "How will this club improve retention, referrals, etc.?" Build that into your lifetime value table. Then compute your costs of establishing and maintaining the club. Build those costs in.

When you finish your table, you will be able to see whether your club will increase or decrease customer lifetime value—and by how much. You as a database marketer are way ahead of the advertising staff of your company which has no way of proving whether the funds they spend do any good at all.

The second thing you must do is to constantly run tests. This is an area in which most database marketers fall down on the job. You get a great creative idea which you are sure will work. The spring (let us say) is the ideal time to run it. How can you let the spring go by with just a little test? Let's roll out the whole thing now, and capture the right moment. Millions of dollars are wasted in just that way. Let me give you a recent example.

A national chain of restaurants wanted to get into database marketing. They got a great idea. They designed a frequent diner card which they promoted by FSIs in print ads, in-store displays, and direct mail to a database they had compiled. Diners who used the card ten times in a two month period would get a free movie ticket to a movie theater of their choice. The card would capture the name and address of the diner. Great thought?

Actually, it might have been. But in the rush to get the idea going, they forgot some basic principles. The cards did not request any information from their customers other than name and address. What was the family composition? Age? Income? How often did they eat out? Did they visit the chain from home or from the office? Did they eat alone, or in groups? Did they visit the chain daily, weekly, monthly, or almost never? Did they visit more because of the club? What kind of movies did they want to see? The chain learned almost nothing from this expensive national effort.

Better: do a small test, where the problems would have been obvious, followed by a larger national rollout which would really produce valuable results. The final mistake was this: the chain had no plans whatsoever as to what to do with the names once they had acquired them. Such a club seldom pays for itself in the first instance. The payoff is in intelligent use of the database to boost retention, referrals, and spending rates in subsequent marketing strategies. But unless you have thought through these next steps, you may fail to capture the information you need for these next steps. That was what happened in the case cited here.

Some people argue that database marketing is too expensive: millions of dollars must be spent building up the database before you know if it works. That is not necessary. Start small—use it for your best customers only. Test and sharpen your techniques before you spend big money. Do not embark on a five-year plan to build up a database, embark on a one-year plan. In that one year, build in several tests. All during the year, review the results of the tests before going on to bigger and better things.

Database marketing is one-on-one; you and your customer alone together. You can try one thing with one customer and something entirely different with another customer. That is OK—it is one of the beauties of database marketing. Every customer can be a test. But be sure that you really are testing and counting. If you are not consciously trying to learn something from your database, you will learn nothing, and you will be swept aside by competitors who are learning more.

Some techniques will work better than others. Some will not work at all. Database marketing does not guarantee results. It is a technique which you can use to get results, but it requires creative imagination, innovative experimentation, rigorous analysis of the results, and modification of your approach based on your analysis.

Conclusion: Database marketing is one of the most verifiable techniques in any company's marketing arsenal. Unlike general advertising or direct marketing, you can audit your results and validate your techniques with rigorous scientific accuracy. If you are having an effect on sales, you will be able to prove it.

Question: What will happen when everyone has a marketing database? Won't the selling advantages cancel each other out?

Answer: Cash back. Coupons. Green Stamps. Four-page ads. Once one company uses them, the others have to follow suit. Soon you find yourself spending a fortune just to maintain market share, with no hope of increasing it. Philosopher Immanuel Kant foresaw it all in 1770 in his *Critique of Pure Reason*: "Always act so that you can will that everybody shall follow the principle of your action." He developed the concept of the *categorical imperative* which commands that "every rational being ought to act as if he were by his principles a legislating member of a universal kingdom of ends." He foresaw a perfect society conducted by rational spirits. Following Kant's idea, cash back as a universal principle becomes absurd. If everyone offers cash back it will lose its punch as an inducement and become an accounting nuisance.

What Kant's categorical imperative means for us is that we should not start an expensive innovation, like database marketing, unless we have looked ahead to see what will happen when everyone has adopted it. Is it just another cash back trap? Database marketing may have little impact on the first sale. You may still have to offer some dramatic gimmick to get the public's attention in the first place. All gimmicks are easily copied. The public becomes bored with them. You will have to constantly come up with new ones to attract new customers.

Database marketing aims not at that first sale, but at the second, the third, and the following sales. It aims at building up a lifetime relationship with a customer. It aims at establishing a mutually profitable dialog in which customers tell you what they want, and you modify your behavior *towards them* to give them what they want. It involves modifying your products and services, your delivery methods and billing practices, your customer support and your prices. If you follow it rigorously, it will involve everyone in your company in some way. It will transform the way you create and deliver products and services.

Suppose everyone had a marketing database? Would that be good or bad? If we follow the logic of Kant's categorical imperative, it seems to me that it would be ideal. Every company would be trying to give their customers the particular kind of individual service and attention that they ask for. People would stick with your company not because of the wonderful advertisements, the deep discounts, or the celebrity endorsements, but because you are giving them real service, personalized attention, responsive performance. It is much cheaper to sell to existing customers than to beat the bushes to find new ones. If all companies had a larger repeat business, and could count on it, prices could come down.

For more than ten years, I bought Subaru station wagons. I love the color gold, and all of mine were gold. When I came to buy my third wagon, I asked for gold. "Oh, they don't make gold Subarus any more," the sales lady told me.

"Weren't they popular?" I asked.

"Oh, yes. We sold a lot of them. But this year we have a new designer and a whole new line of colors." This was my third visit to Stohlman Subaru to buy a car in ten years. I was dealing with a new salesperson. In each of the previous visits I had new salespersons, since the old ones no longer worked there. That is the nature of the business. I had had all my required servicing done at Stohlman. But no one there knew me or remembered me. I had driven to the lot in my gold Subaru, which I parked out in front. As the salesperson walked me to a new station wagon for a test drive, she said, "I can't let you drive it off the lot. Subarus are a different driving experience. I will drive it out into the country, and then you can take over."

Needless to say, I bought a gold Dodge Colt Vista that year, and have never gone back to Subaru. Would a marketing database have helped Stohlman keep me as a customer, despite their constantly changing salesforce? I don't know, but I think so. Whatever feeling of loyalty I had towards the brand was dissipated by the attitude of the staff towards me. This was many years ago, before the computer revolution.

Today it would be fairly easy to keep track of Arthur Hughes and to give him the recognition he wanted and felt he deserved when he came in to buy his third Subaru. Yet few companies today are doing anything about this. The database marketing revolution is still in the future. But it is coming, and companies that have it should see a measurable increase in repeat business. When all companies have it, it will provide all consumers with a higher level of recognition, service, and ability to influence the providers of products and services to give them what they want.

Conclusion: If every company had marketing databases it would help them to keep customers, and it would provide to all their customers better service than they would otherwise get. It would probably reduce prices. Universalizing database marketing would probably help both companies and customers.

SUMMARY

- Database marketing is fraudulent if the company that practices it does not listen to its customers and act on their suggestions. If used to find out what customers want, and give it to them, database marketing is wholly meritorious.

- Does database marketing involve returning to a rejected method of marketing—the old corner grocer? Yes. What was rejected was his inefficiency, high prices, and poor selection. Database marketing brings back his service, recognition, friendship, and loyalty, while retaining modern efficiency, low prices, and wide variety.

- Won't some people be turned off by database marketing? Yes. Code into the database not to telephone them or otherwise intrude in a manner offensive to them. Database marketing is ideally suited to respect customers' wishes.

- Isn't database marketing an invasion of privacy? It can be. Companies setting up databases must take steps to see that they are used for marketing and not for snooping.

- How do you know that database marketing will actually increase sales? Database marketing lives by counting and reports. If it increases sales, you will be able to prove it. If it doesn't, you should cut it back.

- If every company had a marketing database, would that not tend to cancel out the advantages? Not at all. A successful marketing database increases repeat sales and customer loyalty. It should improve service to customers and reduce costs and prices. If every company had such a database, it would improve overall customer satisfaction and reduce the general level of prices.

Chapter 28

Selling Your Database to Top Management

The hardest thing in database marketing is getting the budget and top level approval necessary to undertake programs that may require three or more years for ultimate success. Explored in this chapter are five methods of selling your database programs to top management. They are:

- Convince yourself first.

- Deal with the lost advertising argument.

- Find allies.

- Create some early successes.

- Become an information powerhouse.

CONVINCING YOURSELF

Let's face it, database marketing is usually a hard sell. In theory it should be easy. Every entrepreneur realizes that pleasing customers is what business is all about. Making customers happy, getting them to stay with you, keeping them buying, buying more, recommending your business to their friends—that has always been the formula for long term success.

Unfortunately, in most businesses the entrepreneurs have lost control to the established bureaucracy. The interests of the customers have been completely buried in a tangle of competing managers with inconsistent objectives, including those of:

Brand managers

Advertising managers

Product developers

Sales managers

Dealer Support managers

Regional managers

Sales Promotion specialists

Finance managers

Branch managers

Quality Control managers

The main reason why customers are overlooked is that the compensation scheme for most managers in most businesses is not tied to overall customer satisfaction or sales. Instead, it is tied to the performance of a small part of the business, and competes with other parts of the business. The person in charge of home equity loan promotion is not compensated when some of his prospects take out automobile loans from the bank. The brand manager for pet food does not gain if some of his customers start buying the company's instant coffee. In short, the database marketing manager faces a perverse internal compensation system which does not reward success in building overall customer loyalty and increased company-wide sales. As a marketer, you are seldom in a position to change the compensation system.

Database marketing really represents a return to the approach of the old corner grocer. He measured his success in customer retention and increased sales. He didn't gauge his achievements on how much ice cream or chicken he sold, but on his ability to retain and sell more and more products to his regular customers. When it snowed, he laid in a supply of snow shovels and car window scrapers—not as a new profit center, but because people asked for them, and found it handy to pick them up while they were shopping for groceries. These seasonal items made his store more satisfying to the customers, and kept them from going elsewhere. He was thinking lifetime value, not a quick buck.

As businesses have grown and become more specialized, we have so subdivided the work and compensation system that the focus on overall customer retention, which is the goal of database marketing, often just doesn't fit. So this is your first problem that you will need to address when trying to sell database marketing.

When Database Marketing Will Not Work

There are other reasons why database marketing may not sell. It may not be right for your company or your product at all. A product or dealer focus, instead of an ultimate customer focus, may well be the most profitable strategy for many companies. There are tens of thousands of products, particularly packaged goods, where database marketing aimed at the consumer will not work at all. I cannot see how you can sell Ivory soap, pencils, dental floss, or brass door knockers with a database. Retail stores that sell these items may profitably maintain customer marketing databases. The manufacturers may profitably maintain databases of retail outlets for their products. But the manufacturers cannot profit by keeping a database of the ultimate consumers. The economics are just not there.

So, before you think about selling your database to top management, first sell it to yourself. Assure yourself that you have a product or service that can benefit from a database. How can you do that? It seems to me that there are several basic analytical concepts you have to use in your justification. They are:

- Incremental Profit

- Increased Retention, Referrals, and Spending

- Reduced Direct Costs and Marketing Costs

Let's consider these one at a time.

Incremental Profit. There must be enough margin in the profit on the sale to fund database marketing activity. The margin may be in a single sale (like a set of golf clubs, or an encyclopedia), or a continuing string of sales (like baby diapers, insurance, securities, oil changes for your car, pizza deliveries). There is a certain minimum cost in building a database and communicating with customers which has to be paid for by the incremental profit.

Many people don't understand the concept of incremental profit. Here it is in a nutshell: the vast majority of all products and services are being sold today without a database. Salesmen, awareness advertising, shelf space, yellow pages, store fronts are working. For you to suggest that database marketing is appropriate for your situation, you must argue that the extra profit you can realize from extra sales generated by database marketing activities will be greater than the extra costs of the database marketing activities.

To be specific: suppose you are selling $20 million worth of lift tickets, food, and lodging per year to your ski resort patrons using your current methods. Suppose that using database marketing, you can sell $24 million worth. Your incremental sales are $4 million. The incremental profit from these extra sales is (let us say) 20 percent, or $800,000. If the database software, surveys, data entry, letters, telephone calls, and other database activities come to more than $800,000, your database marketing program is a loser. You cannot, in other words, justify your database program against the $24 million in sales, or the $4 million in increased sales, but only against the $800,000 in incremental profit.

Of course, many people come skiing once, and never return. It is possible through database based customer relationships to build the retention rate. If that is so, then you can measure your database budget not just against the $4 million in incremental sales, but also against some other additional revenue generated by attrition reduction in the entire $24 million. In such case, your database can pay for itself.

How do you do the computations? With a lifetime value table. (See chapter 10.) Build a table that represents the present situation, and a second one that represents what benefits you will get from the database (increased sales, increased retention, increased referrals, etc.) and the cost of the database activities. See if the lifetime value goes up or down. If it goes up, you have a winning proposal for top management.

Increased Retention and Referrals. When you calculate the customer retention rate using your database, it will probably be a shock to everyone in the company. The only companies that really know retention rates are those who receive monthly payments like utilities or financial service companies. Retailers and manufacturers usually have very hazy ideas about retention rates. If database marketing does anything well, it boosts retention rates. You will be the first one in your company to understand this, and to point out the long term profits which can result.

If you build in an active referral program, you can also point to real profits. MCI's Friends and Family program—probably the most outstanding referral program ever up to that time—was such a success that AT&T and Sprint spent a good part of their advertising budgets trying to counteract it.

So how do you use the database to increase retention and referrals? There is only one answer: think up and implement some strategy that will get the customers to feel an increased loyalty to your company. It should not involve a discount. Discounts do not increase customer loyalty. They help to train customers to think only about price, and not about quality and service.

What you have to think up are things that will provide customers information, convenience, and helpfulness. Ask their advice, act on it, and tell 'em what you did. Provide recognition to your top quintile by issuing them gold cards. But, before you do this, be sure that the card provides some valuable benefits other than a discount. Give them free parking, gift wrapping, sneak previews, executive reports; something that they will value, and that clearly sets them apart from the less profitable customers. People love to be recognized and rewarded for good behavior. Just like dogs that have been praised and patted, they will lick your hand.

Once customers are loyal, they will be quite willing to listen to you discussing other products that you sell. Loyalty is defined as retention. But, once you have retained them, you are then in an excellent position to sell them additional products. If you're in, you're in.

Reduced Direct and Marketing Costs. Once you have a working customer marketing database, you can sometimes change your selling methods. Software companies realized this immediately. As soon as you buy their product, they force you to register, promising free support, information, etc. Once you have registered, it will not be long before you receive a letter describing an exciting new upgrade or a companion product. These upgrades and cross-sales are made direct, not through a retail store or mail order house. Their direct costs are lower. Can you use direct in your business? Think about it. In the database you now have your customers' address, phone number, fax number, and probably their e-mail address. Experiment. Think big.

Marketing costs, of course, can be brought way down once you have a database. RFM directed sales to existing customers can be vastly more profitable than almost any other type of offer. Your database will tell you a lot about your customers. You can learn what they read, watch, and listen to. You know that some of them will respond to a personal e-mail message, and others to a discreet fax. How do you know? You asked them, and then you tested it.

In summary, your first job, therefore, is to explore the methods listed above, and determine for yourself whether database marketing is going to work in your company. Once you have convinced yourself, it will be much easier to win over top management.

LOST ADVERTISING

Where does a company get the money to pay for database marketing? There may be many sources, but most likely it is from the advertising budget. If your company, for example, has an annual advertising budget of $10 million, your management might consider devoting $1 million of that amount to database marketing activities. What is the purpose of advertising? To produce sales. It attracts new customers, and reminds existing customers that you are still there. It informs the public about new products, services, and sales. Advertising is usually measured by awareness. Few advertising managers like to be measured by immediate response. They argue, correctly, that having their message before the public day after day has a cumulative effect.

If you plan to use $1 million—10 percent—of this advertising budget for database marketing, it means that you are saying that you can make better use of this $1 million than the advertising manager would have made of it. By promoting customer loyalty, retention, referrals, reactivations, and cross sales, you can bring in more profits than $1 million spent on regular ads. You will have to use lifetime value tables to show what you can do with this $1 million.

Before you get too cocky, however, you will have to deal with the advertising manager's argument. Let's say that your company spends $10 million on advertising which supports $100 million worth of business. The advertising manager will argue—with some justification—that by cutting her budget by 10 percent, the company will lose some sales. How much? She may say that the loss could be as much as $10 million. Of course, she is wrong. If all advertising ended tomorrow, your company would still have sales as a result of continued customer loyalty, salesmen's activities, etc. But, at the same time, you cannot argue that a 10 percent reduction in the ad budget will not affect sales at all. To justify your database programs, you have to make some assumption about the lost revenue from lost advertising. Your database benefits therefore have to overcome this loss in addition to any potential gains.

How would you go about doing this? There is a way, using lifetime value analysis. Let's first start out by conceding that cutting the advertising budget will reduce the number of new acquisitions. The advertising manager can't prove that, but you can't prove that it won't, so give her her assumption. If your database marketing program is a strong one, you can accept that loss, and still show that your company will come out ahead. Why?

Because the gains that you create by your activities will apply to the entire customer base. You are going to affect overall retention, referrals, and spending rate. The cut in the ad budget will affect only one thing: the acquisition rate. Let's show this by a practical example.

Preferred Customer Base Lifetime Value Table

Revenue	Year1	Year2	Year3	Year4	Year5
A Customers	1000	300	105	42	19
B Retention Rate	30%	35%	40%	45%	50%
C Spending Rate	$450.00	$450.00	$450.00	$450.00	$450.00
D Total Revenue	$450,000	$135,000	$47,250	$18,900	$8,550
Variable Costs					
E Cost Percent	50	50	50	50	50
F Total Costs	$225,000	$67,500	$23,625	$9,450	$4,275
Profits					
G Gross Profit	$225,000	$67,500	$23,625	$9,450	$4,275
H Discount Rate	1	1.2	1.44	1.73	2.07
I NPV Profit	$225,000	$56,250	$16,406	$5,462	$2,065
J Cumulative NPV Profit	$225,000	$281,250	$297,656	$303,119	$305,184
K Lifetime Value (NPV)	$225.00	$281.25	$297.66	$303.12	$305.18

In this situation, you have a relatively low retention rate: 30 percent. Most people buy once and disappear. The spending rate is flat at $450 per year. Five year lifetime value is $305.

Now let's see what an aggressive database marketing program might accomplish if we pulled out all the stops.

Preferred Buyers with Database Marketing Programs

	Revenue	Year1	Year2	Year3	Year4	Year5
A	Referral Rate	8%	8%	8%	8%	8%
B	Referred Customers	80	46	32	25	
C	Total Customers	1000	580	394	308	256
D	Retention Rate	50%	60%	70%	75%	80%
E	Spending Rate	$550.00	$600.00	$650.00	$700	$750
F	Total Revenue	$550,000	$348,000	$256,100	$215,600	$192,000
G	Cost Percent	50	50	50	50	50
H	Variable Direct Costs	$275,000	$174,000	$128,050	$107,800	$96,000
I	Database Activities $50	$50,000	$29,000	$19,700	$15,400	$12,800
J	Referral Incentives $50	$0	$4,000	$2,300	$1,600	$1,250
K	Total Costs	$325,000	$207,000	$150,050	$124,800	$110,050
L	Gross Profit	$225,000	$141,000	$106,050	$90,800	$81,950
M	Discount Rate	1.00	1.20	1.44	1.73	2.07
N	NPV Profit	$225,000	$117,500	$73,646	$52,486	$39,589
O	Cumulative NPV Profit	$225,000	$342,500	$416,146	$468,632	$508,221
P	Lifetime Value (NPV)	$225.00	$342.50	$416.15	$468.63	$508.22

Building a relationship with customers has boosted the retention rate from 30 percent to 50 percent—a tremendous achievement—but not unusual with well designed database marketing strategies. Second, you have an aggressive referral program, resulting in 8 percent of your customers bringing in new customers every year. These referred customers cost you $50 each in incentives, but this is probably much less than you are now spending to acquire a customer. Finally, your activities have increased the overall spending rate from $450 to $550, a significant jump.

Unfortunately, these gains have come at a definite cost. The aggressive database marketing activities cost you $50 per person per year, in addition to the $50 per referred customer. The database, of course is only a tiny fraction of that amount—maybe $1 or $2 per person per year. The rest of the increased cost lies in increased customer services, benefits, and communications, which serve to build the relationship. The result, of course, is that in Year1 your lifetime value has stayed flat at $225—just what it was before you inaugurated your new program.

The gains from database marketing come, as they always do, in the future. Lifetime value in Year3 goes from $297 to $416. Lifetime value in Year5 goes up from $305 to $508.

If you have done your homework and you can show a lifetime value gain from database marketing after three years from $297 without the database programs to $416 with the programs, let's see if this can make up for the lost advertising.

Assume your company has 200,000 customers. Your database budget is $1 million, which is carved out of an advertising budget of $10 million—a 10 percent cut. Lets assume that this 10 percent cut reduces customer acquisition by 10 percent or 20,000 customers—an unfair assumption from your standpoint, but the type of argument you can expect to hear from the advertising manager. If your database marketing programs are strong enough, you can show that the resulting 180,000 customers will bring in more profits after three years than the 200,000 would have produced without the database.

Here are the numbers in black and white:

Database Marketing Gain, Adjusting for Advertising Acquisition Loss

	Year1	Year2	Year3
Lifetime Value w/o database	$225.00	$281.25	$297.66
Lifetime Value with database	$225.00	$342.50	$416.15
W/o DB 200,000 Customers	$45,000,000	$56,250,000	$59,532,000
With DB 180,000 Customers	$40,500,000	$61,650,000	$74,907,000
Profit shift from DB	($4,500,000)	$5,400,000	$15,375,000

Give the ad manager her 10 percent cut in acquisitions. The first year, it will cut into profits. Less customers is less profits in the short run. But as time goes on, the improvements in profits are dramatic. How can that be? Because you are squeezing more sales not just out of the new customers but also out of the customers that you already have. You are getting them to be more loyal and to bring in their friends and relatives. Advertising can't do that.

Look at it another way. Which is better, 100,000 customers who spend $100 each for sales of $1 million, or 10,000 customers who spend

$1,000 each for sales of $1 million? Clearly it will be easier to make a profit by servicing only 10,000 customers and getting all of their business, than having to service ten times that many for the same revenue which represents only a part of their total purchases in your category. More customers are not necessarily profitable. More profitable customers are what affect the bottom line.

I am suggesting that you become a little aggressive about your job. Remember, for many products and services, database marketing does not work. It will never work. But for the remainder, it can often work like gangbusters. If you are selling one of these products, and do your job right, the profits are real, provable, measurable, dramatic. Don't be shy about it. Do your homework. Draw up lifetime value tables, and sell your ideas to the top brass. Don't waste your time on the ad manager. You can never sell her. Her whole compensation scheme is based, not on sales, but on the size of her budget. Make yours dependent on lifetime value.

Let's show how these profit gains look graphed over five years:

Figure 28-1   Gains from Database Marketing

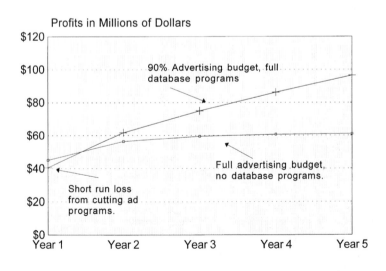

FINDING ALLIES

OK. You have sold yourself. You know that database marketing will work in your company, and you have the figures to prove it. You have dealt with the lost advertising problem. To sell top management, however, you will probably need more than great figures. You need friends.

Look around. When you propose database marketing, who are the people who are likely to support you, and who will oppose you? Here is a little list, based on what has happened in scores of other companies:

- *Top Level Supporters.* You can't be successful unless someone high up is in favor of database marketing. Why? Because the budget for your activities has to come from somewhere—most likely out of the advertising budget. The advertising manager won't give you part of her budget out of the goodness of her heart. You need a champion.

  How do you go about converting someone high up to your cause? You must begin with education. Get a few copies of this book and spread them around. Get someone high up to go to the National Center for Database Marketing conferences. They are held twice a year: in Chicago in July and in Orlando in December. This is the best type of education. Work out a strategy for a winning database program and try to sell it to someone up on top. If they like the idea, then you can work on other people in the organization.

- *MIS.* Information Services people may be very nice, but normally they are not enthusiastic about database marketing. They may be enemies. No matter how nice they seem, they will end up trying to torpedo your database plans. Be particularly cautious if they want to put your customer database into a data warehouse (see Chapter 5).

  Why are they not friends? Because in most cases, successful marketing databases are not built in-house. MIS operations are run in a certain way. There is always a queue of jobs that need to be programmed. The queue is always at least six months long. That means that any changes you want to make in your database will take six months to carry out.

You simply cannot do dynamic database marketing on a schedule like that.

MIS departments do not have the software you need for database marketing, and will resist buying and installing it. I am talking about merge/purge, ad-hoc query, postal presort, householding, data overlay, event driven communications, and segmentation software. They will try to modify their existing database to make it serve marketing purposes. Wrong thinking. It won't work. Once MIS has control of your database, you will have lost the ability to do what you want.

After a while, you will realize that you simply cannot do database marketing if it is under the control of MIS. You will want to go to an outside service bureau. MIS will probably not permit this to happen. To do database marketing with a database of any size (over 100,000 records) you really must outsource it to a responsive service bureau that has experience in database marketing, and operates under a contract that you control. You must be able to fire them. You can't fire MIS.

- *Sales.* At first, sales managers will not be friends either. Why? Because sales fears that you will steal their commissions. With your database, you will be setting up telemarketers who will call customers and get them to buy more. What happens to the commissions? Don't underestimate the power of sales in your organization. If they are strong, you will have to find a system, in the beginning, that assures them of commissions. Read the Amoco story in Chapter 23 and use some of those techniques.

- *Advertising.* The advertising staff may seem like friends, but are probably not. Why? Because it is their money that you will need to build your database. Winning them over will be a hard sell.

- *The Advertising Agency.* These guys may or may not be helpful. If they are an old line agency, they will fight you every step of the way, and probably will win. If you are lucky and have an agency that is skilled in direct, and understands database marketing, you may be able to get some support there. Test the waters carefully.

Some of the most successful database marketing programs have actually been dreamed up in direct response agencies. If you can find one with experience in database marketing and some winning ideas on how it would work in your company, you should engage them fast. They will often be able to gain the entre to the top levels of your company that you need to have.

- *Customer Service.* These folks are more than likely to be friends. Almost anything that you do will boost the role of customer service in the company. Your database can be used by customer service, and customer service calls will be used to update your records. Cultivate them.

- *Service Bureau.* If you treat a service bureau as a vendor, you will not get much help. If you treat them like a partner, and tell them that they will succeed only if you succeed, then you may get a big boost from them (if they are any good). Pick only a service bureau that has built marketing databases before. Examine what they have done. Ask them questions like this: "How do you think that we will be able to improve our retention rate and spending rate with this database? What are the steps that will get us from here to there? How long will it take, and how will we measure our progress?" If they don't have many good ideas, look for someone else.

- *Product Managers.* These managers are probably not going to be much help to you, unless the compensation system is changed. The VP in charge of sporting goods does not get a boost if customers buy more men's furnishings. He sees the men's furnishings VP as a rival. To make database marketing work, the compensation system has to change. You need a VP for Senior Citizens, and a VP for Working Consumers, and a VP for Business Customers. These people will be allies. They will help you to set up your database.

After studying all of these people, seek out the friends, and work to convince the others. Build an action team. Get some outside experts in to help you convince doubters.

EARLY SUCCESSES

If you have reached the point where you have been able to build a database, but do not have a budget for building relationships with it, there is a two step formula for getting that crucial three year budget. It is this:

- Develop your budget supported by lifetime value tables.
- Prove your point with early successes.

    What are early successes? Simple pilot demonstrations of the power of database marketing. These pilot demonstrations are really more like tricks than real database marketing, because you can't demonstrate relationship building in a few months. But you have to show something to get top management attention. That is why I recommend that you scratch your brain and come up with some early successes. Here are some ideas:

- *RFM Rollout.* If you have data on customer purchases in your database, score the file by RFM cell (see Chapter 7). Make an offer to an Nth (a statistically representative sample) of your customer base, and note the response rate by RFM cell. For the rollout, mail only those RFM cells whose test rates showed break even or better. You can't lose. You will be an instant winner.

- *Locating the top quintile.* Rank all of your customers by annual purchases and find out who are the top 20 percent. Add up their total sales, compared to everyone else, so you can say, "Our top 20 percent customers are responsible for XX percent of our total business." It should be between 60 percent and 80 percent. This will be of interest to everyone. Next step: do the same thing for the customers who were buying from you last year. See how many of the top 20 percent disappeared from last year to this year. Survey these high spending dropouts to find out why. Develop two programs: a) reactivate your lapsed top quintile. b) find a way to lavish attention on this year's top quintile to make sure they will not defect.

    By focusing on a small number of high spenders, you are quite likely to score some early and profitable successes at relatively low cost.

- *Syndicated Mailing.* You can demonstrate the power of your database at very little cost with the help of a syndicator. Find someone who wants to market some product or service to your customer base. It should be some non-competing product which is relevant to your customers. Let the external marketer (the syndicator) put up all the money, design, print, and mail the offer in envelopes and stationary with your company's logo, and first class postage. You supply the appropriate names from your database, and review and approve the mailing. The responses come in to you. You collect the money. The syndicator does the fulfillment. If done right, it should earn a handsome profit for your company with no investment at all. If it fails, you may still win something. Since it was sent first class, with the returned envelopes, you will test your database, find out who responds and who doesn't, and locate people who have moved or died so you can update your database. You will know a lot more about your customers than you did.

- *Lapsed Spenders.* From your database produce a list of several thousand very profitable customers who are no longer buying from you. Challenge the sales staff to find out why they left. Develop a reactivation program.

- *Big Spenders.* Make up a list of the top 20 customers in each department of the company. Furnish this list to the department heads. Ask them whether they know these people, and what they can do to reward them for their patronage. Try a thank you letter from the president of the company.

BECOME AN INFORMATION POWERHOUSE

In any business, information is power. Once you have built your database and used it, you will begin to know things that no one else in the company does. In most companies, the CFO has real power because his analysis of the financial situation gives him clout with the top brass. They consult him before taking any major step. You can achieve the same situation with the data that comes out of your database. You can know:

- Customer lifetime value
- The retention rate and the referral rate
- Who the top customers are and how much they are worth
- What customers are thinking and planning to do
- Survey results

Consciously develop your database as an information powerhouse. It will get you noticed, and help you get your budget approved. Remember, top management are customers too. Find out what they want, and sell them that. One thing that you have to sell is information. Develop it and sell it.

SUMMARY

- Selling database marketing to top management is difficult. Gains are long term, but in the short term you need funding to set up your database and associated programs.

- Database marketing aims at keeping customers, whereas most other parts of your company are compensated for doing something else. You may have to recommend a reorganization and change in the compensation scheme.

- Your first step in winning over management is to sell yourself. You do that in three ways: a) demonstrate incremental profit, b) demonstrate increased retention, referrals, and spending, c) demonstrate reduced direct and marketing costs.

- Deal with the lost advertising problem: the argument that database money comes out of the advertising budget, and will therefore reduce the acquisition rate. If you can't overcome that argument, your database selling program is doomed.

- Find allies and build a database team composed of people inside and outside of your company. You can't win without allies.

- Become an information powerhouse in your company. Knowledge is power. You have, or can develop, some unique information that no one else in the company can have. Use it.

Part VII:

Concluding Words

Chapter 29

The Future of Database Marketing

Someone reading this chapter years from now may smile and say, "How naive he was. He was way off the mark." I'll accept that. Virtually no one in the world correctly predicted the collapse of Communism, yet this massive structure virtually disintegrated before our eyes within one year.

With this as a humbling backdrop, I don't want to presume to tell you that database marketing will be everywhere in 10 years. It probably won't. But it seems clear to me from the intense interest in this subject, and the number of companies that are experimenting with it, that it will grow a great deal and will change the way business is conducted in many fields. Someone was giving advice to economists on forecasting. He said, "By all means, specify a figure. By all means, specify a date. But never specify both." Rather than giving you a set of numbers that will probably be proved to be wrong, I will list those things that have to happen in industry for database marketing to become pervasive.

THE IMPORTANCE OF GENIUS

As I have already said, a marketing database by itself will not accomplish anything. It won't make money or increase sales. It can waste a lot of resources. For it to be successful, it must be part of an ongoing program with a viable marketing concept. Behind that concept is an idea person who dreams it up and sells it to whoever needs to be sold.

Unfortunately, there are few people who have the imagination and drive to dream up such ideas and to push them through. The growth of database marketing will definitely be limited by the number of creative leaders in advertising and industry. What has made America a beacon to the world is that we have provided opportunity for people of vision to rise to positions of power so that they can realize their dreams. The top managements of most companies are looking for such people, even though the bureaucratic structure within the companies is constantly impeding their rise. The opportunity is here; we will just have to wait to see what happens.

THE IMPORTANCE OF RISK TAKING

Not all creative ideas will ultimately be successful. Many of them will fail. When this happens we write them off and go on to the next thing. Database marketing is new. It represents a shakeup in the relationships inside a company, and often a change in selling methods. With all that against it, success depends on a company management willing to experiment and take a few risks. Many will say, "We are content with a 28 percent market share. Let's not rock the boat." Database marketing may be tried by those who have only a 3 percent market share or those who see their market share eroding. For this new selling medium to work, management has to budget funds for a couple of years at least, and be willing to accept the internal shifts and disruption that it is likely to produce. Top management really has to get religion about a new relationship with customers; and then put their money where their mouth is. Unless someone high up is interested and willing to take the risk, forget database marketing for that company. It cannot come about as a result of the committee system or a branch manager's initiative.

THE ROLE OF THE SERVICE BUREAU

As you know well by now, marketing databases are seldom successfully mounted on in-house MIS computers. They should be set up on outside service bureau computers, using the most modern relational database software, on-line access, and custom reporting. How many service bureaus are capable of providing that type of support? There are scores of them. The number is growing. I see no impediment to this happening. The opportunities are there. Service bureau owners are beginning to open their eyes, acquire larger computers, hire systems engineers, attend the right conferences, and read books like this one. They will be ready when the clients are ready.

THE ROLE OF CUSTOMER SERVICE

When a company installs an 800 number and begins to listen to what the customer is saying for the first time, something can happen. Reports can filter up. The possibility of using this information function as a direct sales support vehicle may occur to someone, and the germ of an idea for a marketing database may take root. It seems clear to me that customer service today is a growth industry. More and more, management is beginning to understand just how significant a development it is. It could be that the database marketing revolution will ride on the back of an expanding customer service explosion.

A CHECKLIST FOR LAUNCHING A MARKETING DATABASE

A marketing database, by itself, will do nothing good for the bottom line. To be successful in bolstering customer loyalty, reducing attrition, creating repeat sales, and building profits, the database must be constructed properly and combined with a comprehensive marketing program which extends throughout the entire company. The following list presents most of the elements necessary for a successful, functioning marketing database. If you leave too many of these elements out of your design, you will not be successful.

Not all databases will require everything on the list, but all of them will probably need most of what is listed. You will have to judge for yourself which features are required on your database.

1. Database Management

Database Administrator. There is a DBA on the marketing or product management side of your company who has the authority and the resources to make central decisions concerning the database.

Marketing Team. The DBA has created a marketing team which oversees the operations of the database. The team includes personnel from sales, dealer support, customer service, the creative agency, product management, marketing, the telemarketing agency, the outside service bureau, MIS, and any other part of your company which has customer contact (delivery, technical support, billing). On the team are represented both "constructors" (people who like to build databases) and "creators" (people who like to design marketing plans using databases). The importance of both functions is understood.

Construction Time. The process of designing and building the database takes place in *one year or less.* If the scope of the total project requires a longer time frame, the scope should be scaled back so that an active, functioning database can be created in one year. Your learning curve and return on investment begin *after the database is up and running,* not during the planning phase.

Database Size. If this is your first marketing database, it should not be too big. Make a small one as a test from which you can learn; make your grand database later, after you have made all your serious mistakes.

2. The Database Location

Service Bureau. The database is resident on a powerful computer at an outside service bureau with relational software which permits two simultaneous functions:

- batch updating; and
- on-line ad-hoc counting and reporting.

Stand Alone. The marketing database is separate from any general ledger, operational database or data warehouse. It is periodically updated from the company database on a regular planned basis.

Programming Staff. There is a programming staff that understands that it will have to make rapid changes in the database structure and software as marketing strategy evolves. This staff should be experienced in database marketing, have a significant array of relevant software, and be able to be expanded on short notice to meet marketing deadlines. They must be responsive to the DBA.

3. Customer Information

Duplicate Elimination. All customer records have had the names and addresses cleaned and corrected. Duplicates have been eliminated, and an ongoing duplicate detection program has been set up.

Edit Checks. There are software edit checks built-in to assure that all new data going into the system is correct.

Database Captures All Relevant Data. The system captures all relevant information about all customers: their product registrations, purchases, coupon redemptions, letters and telephone calls, complaints, returns, and survey results.

Universal Access. All customer information is available to everyone in the company and to dealers with a need to know. This includes both individual customer records and standard reports on the database as a whole (how many responded to offer X, who are our "Gold Card" customers).

Record Enhancement. Customer records have been enhanced, as appropriate, with demographics, cluster coding, modeling results, and RFM analysis to identify the best and the not-so-good customers. These data enhancements are used as a basis for active programs for interaction with customers and for developing a customer profile for acquiring new customers.

Protecting Customer Privacy. In all that you set up, you are conscious of and aware of the problems of *invasion of privacy.* You build in steps to assure that the database does not become the CIA. You make sure that the database contains "don't mail" and "don't telephone" flags, and that everyone knows how to set the flags on and how to assure that they are adhered to.

4. The Marketing Program

A Creative Leader. Somewhere in the company or the creative agency, there is a man or woman of genius who is masterminding the marketing activities developed for the database. This person has not only the creative ideas to launch the database, but the follow-through to stay with it during the first two years overseeing operations, correcting the embarrassing mistakes, and making the dynamic shifts which will be necessary due to actual hands-on experience.

Learning from Customers. There is a clear understanding throughout the company that the database marketing program is a responsive system. That means that it involves finding out from customers what they want, and changing company programs and policies as a result of what is learned.

Compensation System. Marketers will be compensated based on customer purchases, not on product sales. Managers will be responsible for groups of customers and not particular products.

First Two-Year Funding Assured. When the database is launched, there is a dynamic marketing program approved and funded for at least the first two years of operations. This program includes plans and dates for all mailings and customer responses, for surveys, for telephone calls.

Lifetime Value Analysis. Work has begun on analysis to determine the lifetime value of groups of customers, together with efforts to act on this information to improve acquisition, attrition reduction, loyalty programs and so on. Lifetime value is used to predict the success of new strategies before serious money is expended on them.

Your Own Satisfied Customers Are Your Best Prospects for Future Sales. This is the guiding principle of your database and its associated marketing plan. This may require a review and modification of your existing program of general advertising, coupons, rebates, cash back, owner registration, order forms and such. The database anticipates when customers are due for a refill, a new model, an upgrade, an update, and reminds them and your dealers or your salespeople.

You are aware of the difference between Transaction Buyers and Relationship Buyers. You have designed your entire advertising message to train your customers to be relationship buyers: to think of the quality of your product and service rather than its price alone.

5. Interactions with Customers

Two-Way Communication. There is a recognition throughout the company of the value of two-way communication with customers. This means that your company uses customer contacts both to *provide helpful information* to the customer and to *receive helpful information* back from the customers. Methods are set up for all employees involved in customer contact enabling them to enter the results of their contact into the database.

Needed Information Has Been Planned in Advance. The information you want to capture from customers has been determined, and space has been set aside in the database for it. Surveys are designed, and telemarketers have been given scripts which ask for the needed information.

Information Is Collected. Every contact with a customer has been thought through, and has been designed to gather more information. Each outgoing letter, newsletter, product delivery, service, or telephone call, is matched by an incoming survey, response, or order. All existing order forms, monthly statements, catalogs, registration forms and such have been reviewed and modified to play a role in building the database.

6. Customer Service and Direct Sales

Incoming Lines. Customers can call an 800 or 900 number where your agents capture their names, addresses, and phone numbers. The agents have a checklist of information that you want to obtain from customers for the database.

Database Access by Telephone Agents. The agents have access to a database (not necessarily the marketing database) and can retrieve a customer's record while on the telephone; the agents can enter information directly into the database while talking. The agents have the ability to get information from technical people within the company, if necessary.

Follow-Up Correspondence. There is a planned and automatic system for follow-up letters to every person who calls, thanking them for the call and requesting additional information from them (a simple survey— Were we helpful? Did we give you what you wanted?).

Sales by Customer Service. Customer service has a philosophy of selling! They have been trained to know what you sell, and how to go about it. They have all the information they need on your dealers, your salesmen, your products, the good and bad features, what new products are coming.

Modern Equipment. Your call center (which may be at an outside telemarketing bureau) has an ACD telephone system so that callers are quickly routed to the proper people. If callers must be put on hold, they listen to something useful about your product or company. You have arranged for enough equipment and enough agents so that customers can get through to you in busy times.

7. Rewarding Loyal Customers

Recognition. The database has been set up to provide recognition and special services to your best customers. A method for identifying them has been developed. They receive a special card or other token so that *they know* that they are special. All your employees with customer contact are aware of who these special customers are.

8. Acquiring New Customers

Customer Referral Program. The database is seen as a method for acquiring new customers. One important method is asking customers to recommend other customers. The database is set up to keep track of who recommended whom, and to provide suitable thank-yous and later activities.

Customer Profiling. The database is used to build a profile of your customers which is used to determine criteria for finding new customers. These criteria may include demographics, cluster coding, geographic areas, age, automobiles, responsiveness to direct marketing and so on. In the case of business customers, the criteria can include line of business, products, number of employees, sales and such.

Lead-Tracking System. The database has been designed as a lead-tracking vehicle. All leads from prospecting are monitored to make sure that timely and appropriate responses follow each lead identification through to rejection or closing.

9. Salespeople and Dealers

Salespeople Are Included. Company salespeople are part of the database system. It is not a threat to their commissions. They feel that it is "theirs." Telemarketers whom they train are used to qualify leads before the salespeople get them. Salespeople can access the database and use it in their work to acquire new customers and service existing ones.

Dealers Are Part of Your Team. Dealers play a role in the database system. They may have PCs, reports, and lead cards permitting them direct access to customer information. They provide information to the system and get information out. Dealers feel that the database *helps them to get more business,* that it does not compete with them.

10. Quality Control

Direct Mail. A system has been set up to monitor quality on a regular basis. This means that there is a review of the quality of all outgoing mail, including the appearance of the name and address, the correctness of the information, the proper selection of the list, the proper placement of items within the envelope.

Personal Contacts. A system exists to monitor the quality of telephone and personal contacts with customers, including such methods as surveys back from customers which are read and entered into the database and rewards to employees for especially good jobs of customer contact and sales. Employees include delivery and service personnel, accounts receivable and complaint department employees—everyone gets into the act.

Teamwork. The database has created a community of users who are interested and concerned with making the whole process work. A method has been set up whereby all users can make suggestions on how to improve customer contact, service and sales. Suggestions and ideas are encouraged, welcomed, and rewarded.

11. Reports

A Constant Information Stream. A dynamic set of reports is designed and programmed to provide periodic feedback for marketing, sales, product management, top management, dealers, customer service, and everyone else, on how they are doing, what the customers are thinking, buying, rejecting. These reports are printed and distributed by the database service bureau, but are also available to everyone in the company who has a PC.

Ad-hoc Reports Generated Easily. A method has been set up to generate Ad-hoc reports on data in the database. Such reports can be entered by marketing planners with one minute response time. Everyone with a need-to-know should be able to get information out of the database without getting permission or asking anyone else to do anything. Everyone who needs training should have received it.

12. Return on Investment

Keeping Your Eye on the Bottom Line. The purpose of a marketing database is to make money. At the time the database is launched, there is a definite plan for how you will use it to increase profits and how you will *demonstrate and prove* that you are generating profits. There is a clear statement of goals and objectives, and benchmark milestones at definite points of time where you can measure your progress. The database is quantifiable.

A TEST FOR THE READER

Let's try an experiment. You have finished this book; you have learned much about database marketing. I will describe a great creative concept; see if you can find the potential flaws in it.

A successful candy company had always sold through stores. It had a substantial national reputation through its line of higher priced collections of hard candy and chocolate. It had never sold direct. The vice president for marketing had a great creative idea: sell direct to consumers with this gimmick—the candy company would help each household to compile a "Family Register," a list of birthdays and anniversaries of everyone in the household and all their relations, including all the parents, aunts, uncles, nieces, nephews, grandparents, children, and grandchildren.

To compile the register, customers call an 800 number and, free of charge, the candy company's gift counselors would take information from them. Every quarter, customers are sent a printed list of all the birthdays and anniversaries coming up, together with addresses and telephone numbers. For most of these birthdays, the candy company would automatically send an attractive gift of candy on the correct day, charging the gift to the credit card of the householder.

If the prospect is a business, the recipients would be clients who would receive their candy at Christmas or on some other suitable occasion. In addition to gifts, customers could have candy shipped to themselves once a month.

You can call the 800 number at any time to add or delete or cancel gifts, or just to find out what birthdays are coming up in the next few weeks. With any luck, the Register could produce an average of ten or more sales per year for several years in a row. At an average sale of $15 per box plus delivery, the average total sales over a year might be $150, with total per household over three years averaging perhaps $250, considering attrition and cancellations.

The vice president for marketing sent the proposal up the line for approval. Is this a workable idea? Should the candy company risk a few million dollars on developing the idea? Let's now use some of the concepts in this book to analyze it and see what the vice president has left out of his plan that could cause it to fail.

What the Vice President Forgot

1. *The Direct Agency.* The company has a history of sales through stores only. No company should try to shift to direct without some outside help from a creative direct agency with experience. Before the VP goes up the line with his idea, he needs to find the right agency and get their help and advice.

    The agency will discuss his concept, and if it makes sense, will develop some creative ideas and copy to go with it. They will help him to decide just who he is going to target with this concept: people in their 30s, 50s, or 70s? People making $40K, $60K, or $80K? Focus groups may be needed, and tests, tests, tests. What media is he going to use? Where can he find lists of candy lovers? Of gift givers? Are there really several markets out there? What about the corporate market?

All these things will be the province of the direct agency. The agency will also have to write the script for the telemarketers. What you say when people call can make all the difference in a single sale, or multiple sales, or no sale. Agencies should know how to write the script.

2.   *The Telemarketers.* No one who has not done it can appreciate the impact on an organization of 1,000 telephone calls a day. How many people does it take to handle that number? How many lines? What training is needed for the staff? The vice president really needs to find an outside telemarketer who can staff up an operation to receive the calls; expecting the company's employees to man the phones spells disaster.

The VP will need very skillful telemarketers trained as gift counselors who are adept at extracting birthdays, telephone numbers, addresses, and other information over the telephone, and who are good at selling candy as the ideal solution to the birthday and holiday gift problem. Can you find and train such telemarketers, and can they do the job at a reasonable price?

3.   *The Warehouse.* Warehouses accustomed to shipping in skid lots cannot be converted overnight to shipping one box of candy at a time. Your costs will go through the roof. No one will know how to handle these little shipments efficiently. What kind of packages are available that will arrive undamaged after delivery? Will the product spoil if left out in the sun all day? What about rain or freezing? How much will the shipping and packing cost? How does that enter into the profit picture? Before the VP goes further, he has to talk things over with the warehouse manager or an outside fulfillment staff.

4.   *The Sales Staff and the Dealers.* How will stores take to the idea of the company selling direct? There is a lot of competition in the candy business. It is not that hard to get into it. If a store thinks that the national ads that they see for the candy will help total sales, but possibly hurt theirs, they may drop the line. Your sales staff will be quick to spot that. Unless you get their cooperation, they may fight the VP's plan from the be-

ginning. What can be done? One possible solution is a gift certificate for candy good at any retailer who carries the company's products. Printed on the back of the certificate would be the addresses of the stores in the vicinity of the recipient. The VP had better talk to sales before he goes too far.

5. *The Service Bureau.* Who is going to set up this system for automatic delivery of candy all throughout the year? Who is going to generate the orders, the shipping documents? Who is going to provide the equipment and screens for the telemarketers to enter, change, and cancel orders? Before the VP goes much further, he should contact some service bureaus to find one that has the experience and the creative drive to put his idea into operation quickly. He will need an on-line marketing database which permits telemarketers to call up any household instantly on the screen so that they can read off and change information on birthdays and gifts. The database has also to generate the automatic orders, credit card charges, and shipments on the correct days; handle bad cards, cancellations, out-of-stock items and so on. While he is at it, he will have to steel himself against the possible opposition of MIS to his building a computer database outside the organization.

6. *Economic Analysis.* The VP needs to think the project through for the first two years and get top management used to the idea that it won't pay off in the beginning. He has to calculate the lifetime value of his customers and balance that off against the acquisition cost. He has to set up some goals and benchmarks for himself so that he can determine when the program is a success or when it is a failure and losses had better be cut.

The message from this exercise is this: successful marketing databases will evolve as a result of little brainstorms like the one the VP had. A creative agency, telemarketers, a service bureau, and inside staff—that is the only way that database marketing is going to move ahead.

A FAREWELL TO THE READER

You have now graduated. You are ready to go forth into the world to make customers happy and your company profitable. As we part, recall the words that we began with: Database marketing offers us a chance to make America a better place to live. It is not just a better way to sell products and services. It is a way of bringing back something that we have lost during the mass marketing fervor of the last thirty years. It is a way of restoring the personal contact with customers that we all enjoyed in the early years of America when you knew your merchants, and they knew you, recognized you, appreciated you, and did personal favors and services for you on a regular basis. Database marketing, when done properly, will bring back loyalty and personal recognition as an important part of the business relationships which we all will come to experience and enjoy.

SUMMARY

- Marketing databases don't accomplish anything unless they are a part of an ongoing program with a viable marketing concept.

- The growth of marketing databases will be limited to the availability of men and women with ideas and leadership capability either in advertising or marketing.

- Marketing databases involve risk. They will flower only in companies that are willing to take a chance on something new and potentially risky.

- No marketing database can succeed without the support of an effective creative direct advertising agency.

- An outside service bureau is essential for a successful marketing database. There are not enough such service bureaus with experience today, but their number will grow.

- Outside telemarketers are another vital ingredient of successful database marketing.

- The database marketing revolution will make America a better place to live. It will bring back loyalty and personal recognition as an important part of business relationships in the years to come.

Appendix

How to Keep Up with Database Marketing

Database marketing is new. Most people don't even know what it is. To keep up with the many new innovations and developments in this field, you will have to read books, magazines, and newsletters, talk to people and attend conferences. This appendix points you in the right direction:

PUBLICATIONS

Periodicals that you should subscribe to:

- *The Cowles Report on Database Marketing,* Laurie Petersen, Editor in Chief, 470 Park Avenue South, New York, NY 10016 (800) 775-3777

- *DM News,* Mill Hollow Corporation, 19 West 21st Street, New York, NY 10010 (212) 741-2095, FAX (212) 633-9367

- *Target Marketing,* 401 North Broad Street, Philadelphia, PA 19108 (215) 238-5300

- *Canadian Direct Marketing News,* 1200 Markham Road, Scarborough, Ontario M1H 3C3 (416) 439-4083

- *Direct,* Six River Bend Center, Stamford, CT 06907 (203) 358-9900

- *Direct Marketing,* 224 Seventh Street, Garden City, New York, 11530 (800) 229-6700

- *American Demographics,* PO Box 68, Ithaca, New York 14851 (800) 828-1133

- *Marketing Tools,* PO Box 68, Ithaca, New York 14851 (607) 273-6343

Books you should read:

- *Strategic Database Marketing—The Masterplan for Starting and Managing a Profitable Customer-Based Marketing Program,* by Arthur M. Hughes. Chicago: Probus Publishing Company 1994. 354 pp. Call (703) 644-4830 to order.

- *The One to One Future Building Relationships One Customer at a Time,* by Don Peppers and Martha Rogers. New York: Currency Doubleday 1993. 443 pp.

- *After Marketing,* by Terry Vavra, Homewood, IL: Business One Irwin 1992. 292 pp.

- *The Great Marketing Turnaround,* by Stan Rapp and Thomas L. Collins, Prentice-Hall, 1990.

SOFTWARE

There are too many software packages available for database marketing, and they are modified and superseded by competition too rapidly to recommend any in a permanent volume such as this. Shop around and call some of the companies listed in this book for suggestions.

For construction of lifetime value and RFM tables, I recommend a *Lifetime Value Diskette* used with Excel or Lotus spreadsheets. Obtained from the Database Marketing Institute, (703) 644-4830 ($36 plus $4 shipping).

CONFERENCES AND TRAINING

Conventions you should attend:

The following convention is probably the best two days you could possibly spend on learning about database marketing. The sessions are held every six months in Chicago and Orlando. Attended by over 1,000 people each time, with about seventy speakers, they will give you a chance to hear about new things, and to meet all sorts of people in the business:

- National Center for Database Marketing, 911 Hope Street, Box 4232, Stamford, CT 06907-0232 (800) 927-5007

The following conferences are also of great interest to database marketers in the business-to-business arena:

- Direct Marketing to Business and Industry National Conference sponsored by Federal Express and Dun's Marketing Services. PO Box 1161, Ridgefield CT 06877 (203) 438-2318

- Direct Marketing Association. Several conferences and exhibitions each year, at least one of which features Database Marketing. 11 West 42nd Street, New York, NY 10036, (212) 972-2410

There are also other valuable database marketing conferences called from time to time by such institutions as Canadian Direct Marketing News and Target Marketing (see magazines).

HANDS-ON TRAINING IN DATABASE MARKETING

An institution provides two days of intensive hands-on training in database marketing four times a year. The seminars are designed for marketers, rather than for computer types. They are limited to less than

50 people each time, and deal with advanced marketing strategy, lifetime value, RFM, modeling, testing and controls, profiling, and selling the database to top management. The seminars include competitive exercises in which you match wits with senior marketing staff members from major corporations.

- The Database Marketing Institute, Arlington, Virginia (703) 908-9309. Two day sessions held four times a year in Washington, D. C., led by Paul Wang and Arthur Hughes.

HOW TO SPREAD THE WORD

A great deal of the information in this second edition has come from readers of the earlier edition and *Strategic Database Marketing* who have called or written to tell me of their successes in database marketing. I was able to use their stories in this book. If you also have had successes (or failures!) in database marketing, I would be delighted to hear from you. With your permission, and providing you credit, I will include your ideas in a forthcoming book or article, so that others can share your insights. You can reach me at:

ACS, Inc. 1807 Michael Faraday Court, Reston, VA 22203
Telephone 703 742 9798
Fax 703 351 7417
E-Mail ArthurMH@aol.com

Glossary

Abandonment As in the phrase "call abandonment." This refers to people who, being placed on hold in an incoming call, elect to hang up ("abandon") the call. Call centers monitor closely the "abandonment rate" as a measure of their inefficiency.

ACD Automatic Call Distributor. A complex machine used in modern call centers for incoming calls. It routes calls to available agents, holds overflow calls, gives and takes messages, provides reports. A must for modern database marketing.

Acquisition Cost The cost of signing up a new customer. Lifetime Value is often used to compute the maximum allowable acquisition cost.

Address A computer term for the location on a disk or in memory of a piece of information. Addresses help the computer to find things rapidly, and to store them for later retrieval.

Ad-hoc Report A reporting method which permits you to ask questions like: How may women over 60 have bought more than $200 from us in the last 4 months?

Affinity People who are similar in lifestyle.

Affinity Analysis A process of finding relationships between customer purchases. People who buy skis buy snow tires.

Affinity Matrix A cross tab showing cross buying patterns by customers who did or did not buy Products A, B, C, and D.

Affluents Households with 30 percent or more than the cost of living plus taxes. 25 million (out of 87 million) households.

Agent The word for a telephone operator in a modern inbound call center in a company that takes a lot of customer service and sales calls.

Analog Regular telephone service comes over analog lines. Modern improved service (often used for data lines) comes over Digital lines in which all the sounds are converted to 1s and 0s. For database marketing computer communications, digital is better.

ANI Automatic Number Identification. A system whereby you can learn the number of a person who is calling you on the telephone. Can be linked to a database to find the person's name and address.

Appended Data A process whereby a customer file has data appended to it (such as age, income, home value) from some external data file. See overlay.

ASCII American Standard format for data storage on magnetic media (tape or disk).

Attrition Model A model that predicts which customers are most likely to leave. Usually expressed as a percentage of likelihood.

Attrition Rate The opposite of retention rate. The percentage of customers this year who are no longer buying next year.

Autosexing A computer process for finding the sex and appending titles (Mr., Ms.) to a file of names.

Back End As in phrase "back end analysis" refers to the results of actions with people who have responded to your initial offer.

Batch Mode If you have received 10,000 replies to a mailing, you can update your master file with these replies in one batch. This is the fastest and cheapest way to update records. The opposite is On-Line updating.

Baud Rate A measure of line transmission speed—9,600 Baud is a good speed for terminals and PCs connected to a marketing database. Speeds can go up to 56,000 or more.

Bits If a byte is like an atom in computer language, a bit is like an electron. A bit is either on or off. It is either a 1 or a zero. Eight bits make up one byte.

Block The smallest reported unit in the 1990 Census. About 14 households in a block.

Block Group The smallest reported unit in the 1980 Census. About 340 households on average.

Bounce Back The practice of sending another identical (or similar) catalog back to someone who has just ordered something from one of your catalogs.

Brand Managers Most packaged goods companies organize themselves by brand. The brand manager is responsible for advertising, marketing, and sales of the product. The brand manager is typically the main obstacle to database marketing which is customer focused rather than product focused.

BRC or BRE Business Reply Card or Business Reply Envelope.

Brokerage Commission The commission (usually 20 percent) paid by a list owner to a broker to handle the rental of a list.

Bugs Errors that crop up in software. Caused by inability of programmers to predict all possible ways that the code in their programs will be needed to process data.

Byte A unit of computer memory. One letter or number is a byte. A byte is usually composed of eight bits.

Call Center The word for an inbound telephone division in a company. The operators are called Agents. The call center uses an ACD (automatic call distributor) to manage the calls efficiently.

Call Tracking Keeping track of what happened to customer calls.

CD A banking term for certificate of deposit. Also: a compact disk, a form of digitized data storage (as in CD-ROM).

Cell Code After completing RFM analysis, every customer is assigned a cell code which identifies her recency frequency and monetary level of buying. The cell code is often used in mailing. Sometimes used interchangeably with the term Source Code.

CFO Chief financial officer. The person in charge of budgets.

Channel (1) An input-output device as part of a mainframe computer. (2) A means of distributing product to the market. For example, dealers, retail stores, direct marketing.

Cheshire Label A type of plain paper label used in mailing. Requires a Cheshire machine to affix to mailing material. The most common computer label.

Chip The thing in the center of a computer that makes it work. On a PC a 486 chip is a fast chip. A Pentium is faster. Faster and faster chips keep coming out. Chips are the size of your fingernail, and hold millions of circuits shrunk by photographic methods to tiny size.

Churning The practice of customers switching to another supplier based on special discount offers. Particularly used in the cellular telephone industry.

Chutzpah What the Presidents of direct response agencies need to have to be successful at database marketing. Audacity, Guts, Boldness, Willpower.

CIF Customer Information File, usually in banks and financial institutions. A consolidation of many different accounts held by a household or individual, used for marketing purposes.

Cleaning Names A process whereby names and addresses on a customer or prospect list are corrected (addresses standardized, zips corrected, spelling and punctuation corrected, duplicates consolidated, etc.)

Cluster A way of dividing all households in the country into about forty different types, such as "Blue Blood Estates" and "Shotguns and Pickups." Usually called lifestyle groups. Useful for file segmentation. Clustering systems are provided by Claritas, Equifax, Donnelley, CACI.

Compiled List Names and addresses taken from directories, newspapers, public records. People who have something in common.

Computation Period The number of years from now that you can safely project customer lifetime value. The period is short for products that soon become obsolete.

Confidentiality Agreement An agreement which precedes any contract with an outsourcing agency. It says that your secrets will not be revealed to others.

Continuity Products or services bought as a series of small purchases, rather than all at one time. Book of The Month Club, or other products shipped on a regular schedule.

Continuation A mailing to the same list following a successful test of a portion of the list. A continuation becomes a "rollout" when the entire list is mailed.

Control Group Every database promotion should include a control group of customers who are not exposed to the promotion. The success of the promotion is measured by the difference in response of the promoted group compared to the control group (after subtracting the cost of the promotion).

Controller A device for managing the data input and output from several devices which are connected with a mainframe. These devices can include terminals or disks or tape drives. Controllers usually have a small computer inside them which permits them to manage the flow of instructions from the computer to the units in an organized way. They make the computer more powerful.

Conversion Rate The percentage of responders who become customers.

Coop Mailing A mailing in which two or more offers—usually from different companies—are included in the same envelope, and share the costs.

Copy The text of your direct mail piece.

CPI Cost per inquiry.

CPO Cost per order.

CPU Central Processing Unit. The heart of a mainframe.

Cross-Selling Encouraging customers to buy products from other departments or categories.

Custom Report A database report designed by the marketing staff which exactly meets the marketing needs of the company. Once programmed, it can be run daily or weekly for very little cost.

Database Marketing Collecting data on customers and using it to provide recognition and services to customers, resulting in increased customer loyalty and repeat sales.

Data Enhancement A process whereby a customer file has data appended to it (such as age, income, home value) from some external data file. See overlay.

Data entry Also called Keypunching. Entering names and addresses and other data into magnetic media such as tape.

DBA Database Administrator. A person who controls a marketing database. The DBA should be someone from marketing or sales who has the budget for the database.

DDA A banking term for checking account balances.

Dealer Training A process whereby dealers are trained to handle your product.

Decile One-tenth of a mailing, usually divided by percentage of response.

Decoy A unique name added to a mailing list used to spot unauthorized use of the list.

De-Dupe Identifying and consolidating duplicate names usually done in a merge/purge operation.

Demographics Demographic data usually refers to the data which the Census Bureau collects on a neighborhood such as income, education level, etc. This data can be appended to a household record. It isn't necessarily accurate for any particular household since it is the average for households in that block. But it is usually the only data available.

Digital Line A type of telephone transmission service that is much more reliable than the normal analog line. All data is converted into bits before it is transmitted. A regular telephone line is called an Analog Line.

Direct Access A disk is a direct access device. Tape drives are not direct access because to find data on them, you have to read all the way through thousands of records to find the one you want. With direct access, you have all data stored at particular addresses. You can access each piece of data directly.

Direct Cost Percent The percentage of revenue that is applied to the cost of the product plus overhead, fixed costs, etc.

Direct Marketing Interactive marketing that produces a measurable response or purchase. The data is stored on a database. Direct Response Advertising or promotion that seeks not just to provide information, but to generate an inquiry, order, or visit.

Discount Rate The amount by which any future dollar amount must divided to produce the net present value of the amount. The formula is $DR = (1 + i)n$ where i = market rate of interest and n = number of years. The interest rate is usually doubled in the formula to account for risk.

Disk Magnetic disks are attached to computers. They hold information (records) which can be retrieved very rapidly if the computer knows the address of the information on the disk (Direct Access). In relational databases, the address of records and information within records are kept on indexes which make access to the records very rapid.

DNIS   Dialed Number Identification System. A system whereby you can learn in a call center what number the incoming callers dialed to reach you. Important because many call centers handle calls from many incoming numbers for many purposes, but use the same bank of agents to take the calls. They have to know what number people were dialing so they can react properly to the call.

Downsizing   Moving a function from a mainframe computer to a smaller computer such as a Mini, a LAN, or a PC.

Dump   Printed display of the contents of a tape or data file. You should look at a dump of some records in your customer database to check accuracy.

Duplicate   The same name occurring twice or more on the same file. All very large databases contain duplicates because name or address spelling may vary slightly. Good service bureaus can reduce but never totally eliminate duplicates.

Duplication   The percent of names on one list that are also on another Factor list. It is a measure of affinity in the lists.

EBCDIC   A protocol for putting data on a tape. All IBM mainframes use EBCDIC. Most others use ASCII.

Edit Check   A software process whereby data to be entered into a marketing database is checked for logic before it goes into the database.

Enhancement   Appending demographic or lifestyle data to a list.

Event Driven Programs   Database programs which are triggered to produce output (usually communications) based on events: a birthday letter, anniversary letter, thank you letter, etc.

Extract   A system for creating a sequential file from a relational marketing database. The extract can be used for preparing reports, or for sending data to other companies for their use.

Fixed Field Organization of a tape or data file in which each group of data (such as name, address, city, zip) has a fixed location and length within the file.

Flat File Another name for a sequential name file. Contrasted with a database file (not flat because of the indexes).

Focus Group A group of customers who are assembled together by an advertising agency in a conference room to discuss a particular product. Useful for learning what the public thinks of your product or message or company.

Format The way data (name and address) is organized on a disk or tape. There is no standard format. Every company has their own.

Frequency A term for how many times a person buys from you.

FSI Free Standing Insert. Usually a coupon or other promotion found in a magazine or newspaper. The least expensive way to distribute coupons.

Fulfillment The process of responding to a customer request with literature or product. Fulfillment us usually outsourced to a fulfillment house.

Geocoding A system for assigning a census code to any name and address. Once a file is geocoded, you can append census data (income, race, etc.) to the records and assign cluster codes.

Geodemographics Census data that can be appended to a household file once it has been geocoded. Includes such factors as income, education, home type, etc. Derived from the neighborhood of the household. Same as Demographics.

Geographic Information System (GIS) Software that displays data on a computer generated map.

Gigabyte A billion bytes (characters). A measure of the size of mainframe disk storage. A typical mainframe shop will have 100 gigabytes or more. "Her database used over 35 gig!"

Graphical User Interface (GUI)   Software that permits users to access their data by manipulating a mouse.

Hardware   Computers and disks, tape drives, printers, and other gear that are plugged into computers.

Hawthorne Effect   A psychological phenomenon whereby people (customers) act differently when they are being studied.

Hidden Layer   A group of internal nodes inside of a Neural Network which it uses to build a model. The less known about hidden layers by non-statisticians, the better.

House File   The organization's own file of active and former customers.

Householding   A process in which all people and their accounts are grouped by the house that they live in so that they only get one letter per house in a promotion.

ID Number   A number assigned to a record to help to relate it to other records in the computer which have the same ID.

Identification   The process whereby a customer identifies himself with the company which provides him with products or services.

Index   1) Used in relational databases to help to find common data in thousands of records. An index for income could help find all the customers whose income was between $25K and $35K. Using an index you can query a file of 10 million customers and find out how many women aged 60+ bought more than $200 in the last 6 months, and do it in 5 seconds. 2) A statistical term for relating the value of two sets of numbers. If one group had a response index of 100 and another had 120, the second group had 20 percent more replies than the first one. The average of any group always has an index of 100.

Influentials   In business-to-business, executives who have the authority to make or influence a purchase.

Infrastructure The process of maintaining a database: nightly backup, cleaning, merge/purge, deduplication, update, etc.

IS Information Systems (Also MIS) - the part of the company responsible for the central data processing operations.

IVR Interactive Voice Response a piece of equipment connected with an ACD which permits inbound callers to a call center to choose their own routing of the call ("Push 1 for Sales, Push 2 for Service . . .")

Keyline or Match Key A combination of numbers and letters usually beginning with the zip code, which is used as a rough household duplicate eliminator.

Keypunching The process whereby someone enters names and addresses and other data from hard copy (paper forms) onto a computer tape or disk. It is done on a typewriter-like keyboard into a small computer. Same as Data Entry.

LAN Local Area Network. A system for linking several PCs into a single system with a File Server PC that keeps a central database. Some databases are located on LANs.

Laser Letter A letter produced on a laser printer. Very clean and neat looking. Possible to have unlimited personalization of the text of the letter.

Lead A prospect who has responded.

Lead Conversion Rate The percentage of leads which become customers.

Lead Tracking The process of keeping up with what has happened to a lead (prospect who has expressed an interest in your product or service). Lead tracking is very difficult because salesmen hate to report on the status of leads.

Lettershop An independent company that handles all the details of printing and mailing letters.

Lifestyle Lifestyle data about a neighborhood comes from clustering. If a significant number of people in a given cluster have taken a foreign trip, it is assumed that all similar households have done this. It is a lifestyle attribute. Included are magazines read, TV programs watched, etc.

Lifetime Value (LTV) The contribution to overhead and profit made by a customer during her total relationship with your company.

Lift The improvement in response from a mailing due to modeling and segmentation. Divide the response from a segment by the overall response, subtract 1, and multiply by 100.

List Broker A service which brings list owners and prospective list renters (users) together.

List Maintenance Keeping a mailing list current through correcting and updating the addresses and other data.

List Rental The process of renting (for one time use, or other periods) a list of names of customers owned by some other organization for an agreed upon cost per thousand.

Loss Leader A product sold at a loss to get customers to begin buying.

Loyalty Customer loyalty is measured as Retention. A loyal customer is one who keeps buying from you.

Loyalty Programs Rewards that encourage customers to keep being customers longer, or to purchase more.

Mailing List A list of customers or prospects used to mail catalogs or sale announcements. It is not a marketing database because it does not provide for a two-way communication with customers.

Mail Shop An independent company which specializes in preparing materials for mailing. They affix labels, sort for bulk rates, prepare bagtags, insert in postal bags.

Mainframe The largest computers used in business applications. They require raised floors and special air conditioning. Mainframes are recommended for marketing databases because of their power, input-output capability and speed measured in MIPS.

MAND Money, Authority, Need and Desire The requisites of a qualified lead.

Market Penetration The percentage of buyers you have as compared with the total households or businesses in the area you have selected as your market.

Market Rate of Interest The cost of borrowing money by your company from banks or other institutions. In discount rate computations, this amount is usually doubled to account for risk.

Market Research Statistical analysis of customer data to draw overall conclusions as a basis for action.

MarketVision A mainframe software product of ACS, Inc. which permits users at a PC to do ad-hoc counts from large customer databases.

Mass Marketing Selling to everyone through mass media such as radio, TV, or a newspaper, as opposed to database marketing which is aimed at a small selected audience.

Match Code A keyline. An extract of the name and address used to identify a specific record. Used in de-duping.

Media Communications channels that convey messages, such as radio, TV, magazines, direct mail.

Megabyte A million bytes. Disks are rated in megabytes.

Memory The amount of information that a computer can hold in its head while it is doing work. The more memory, the faster a computer can work, and the more complicated programs it can handle. New computers today have 8 megabytes of memory, which can be expanded.

Merge/Purge A software system used to merge many different input tapes in differing formats and put them into a common format for a mailing. Merge/Purge detects duplicates.

Micro Micro-computer. Another name for a PC.

Migration The process of moving your database from one platform (such as an external service bureau) to another (such as your in-house mainframe). When you outsource, you should look ahead and be sure that you can migrate at some later date.

Mini Smaller than Mainframe computers. They may also need raised floors and air conditioning. They are less expensive than Mainframes, and generally do not have the power or input-output capability to manage a large marketing database.

MIPS Millions of Instructions Per Second. A measurement of the relative speed of a Mainframe computer.

MIS Management Information Systems. This term is used in many companies to refer to the data processing staff that runs the central company mainframe computer.

Modeling A statistical technique whereby you determine which pieces of data in your customer database explain the behavior of your customers. The output of a model is a series of weights which can be multiplied by customer data (income, age, length of residence) to create a score which predicts likelihood to respond to an offer.

Modem A device permitting a PC or terminal to send information over a telephone line. You have to have a modem at both ends. Modems are rated in Baud rate.

Mouse A small switch on a wheel used to control a PC.

MRI Mediamark Research, Inc. is a nationwide survey organization that distributes consumer purchase behavior data.

Multi-buyer A person who crops up on two or more independent rented lists. Multi-buyers usually respond better to a direct offer than other buyers.

Multiple Regression A statistical technique used in modeling whereby you develop a formula which explains the relationship between several variables in explaining behavior.

NCOA National Change of Address, a US Postal Service system under which about twenty service bureaus nationwide have exclusive use of the change of address forms filed by persons or businesses who are moving. These forms are keypunched, and can be used by the service bureau to update your tape of prospects to obtain their correct current address. A worthwhile service for mailers.

Net Names The actual names used in a mailing, after removing the duplicates and matches to your customer list. In some cases, you can rent names on a net-name basis.

Neural Network A type of modeling software on a PC which permits a marketer to determine the weights that should be applied to a large number of variables to predict the response or purchases by a target audience.

Niche Market A way of finding a special product that appealed to only one group, and selling that product very profitably only to that group, ignored by others.

Nixie A direct mail letter which has been returned to the sender because the address was wrong. Also, any undelivered piece of mail. Nixies are used to review what was delivered to the prospects.

Nth Name A software system whereby you can pick every 3rd or 4th or 250th name out of a file to use as a valid test of the file. To test a file of 400,000 with a test mailing of 40,000, you would pick every 10th name. If the test is successful, you mail next to every name except the 10th names.

Offer What you are offering in your direct mail: 10 for only $19.95.

Off-line An off-line database is kept on magnetic tape or cartridge. You cannot call up a record instantly from an off-line database.

On-line An on-line database is one in which all the customer records can be called up on your screen instantly when you want them. On-line databases are kept on disk. The opposite of on-line is off-line which usually means that the database is kept on magnetic tape.

On-Pack Offers Communications with customers by making an offer on the package that they purchase.

Outsourcing The process of having various database functions handled by external service bureaus. Typically, functions are outsourced to direct response agencies, computer service bureaus, data entry houses, mailshops, fulfillment houses, telemarketing companies.

Overlayed Data A process whereby a customer file has data appended to it (such as age, income, home value) from some external data file. See Enhancement.

Package The envelope or container or look of your outgoing direct mail piece.

PC Personal Computer. The versatile desktop workstation used for hundreds of applications. They can be used to access a marketing database resident on a mainframe.

Penetration Your customers as a percentage of the universe that defines your customer's type of household or business. "We had a penetration ratio in that zip code of 8 percent."

Personalization The process of including personal references in an outgoing mail piece such as "Thank you for your order of Feb. 23 for six boxes of hard candy, Mrs. Williams." With laser letters, personalization does not cost more than non-personalized letters.

POS Point of Sale. A cash register.

Postal Pre-Sort Sorting outgoing letters in a special way to take advantage of postal discounts.

Predictive Model A model which predicts the response to a promotion.

Present Discounted Value A financial process for calculating the present value of an amount of money to be received or paid in the future. The formula is $PDV = V / (1 + i)n$ where V = future value, i = market rate of interest, n = time in years.

Production A function in an advertising agency of producing letters and other direct mail pieces.

Profile A way of describing your typical customer. You create a profile by modeling your database. The profile could tell you that your typical customer was a woman of 35-54 with an income of $25-$50K.

Prospect A potential customer who you have targeted.

Prospecting Mailing or telemarketing to prospects who are not yet your customers.

Psychographics A way of grouping people by wealth, orientation, hobbies, and interests.

Pull The percent response to your offer by mail or phone.

Purge To eliminate undesirable names from a list.

Qualify In business-to-business, a process whereby respondents to an ad or a mailing are determined (usually by a telephone interview) to be worth a salesman's time and attention. In efficient operations, a telemarketer will qualify an incoming lead before the name is sent to a salesman for action.

Query A question designed to retrieve information from a database. The result can be a count, a cross tab, or a report.

Quintile One-fifth of a mailing, usually divided by percentage of response. "Our top quintile gave us 70 percent of our total revenue."

RAID Redundant Array of Inexpensive Disk, a new technique for storing records on PCs and Mainframes. Greatly reduces the cost of disk storage.

Random Access Modern computer disks can access database records in random fashion. The opposite is sequential access. Random access makes database marketing possible.

Reactivation A program which encourages lapsed customers to start buying again.

Recency A term for how recently a person has bought from your company. It is well established that people who have bought most recently are more likely to buy from you again on your next promotion than people who bought from you longer ago.

Record A collection of fields that describe all the information on a customer.

Referral Rate The percentage of new customers that begin buying this year as a result of encouragement from last year's customers. Expressed as a percentage of last year's customers. If we had 4,000 customers last year, and they recommended new customers to us, of whom 240 became customers, the referral rate would be 6 percent.

Reformatting Changing the format of a rented list to a new record format that matches a desired arrangement.

Regression Used in the phrase Multiple Regressions. It is a statistical technique, part of modeling, whereby you try to discover a mathematical formula which will explain trends in a set of data, and which variables determine response. A multiple regression might tell you that your best customers live in condominiums, have no children, and have income over $75K, for example.

Relational A relational database is what is needed for database marketing. Such a database is kept on disk and consists of related files (name and address, orders) which are related to each other by ID numbers and accessed by indexes.

Relationship Marketing The process of building a relationship with customers which results in the customers becoming more loyal, buying more, and staying as customers. Another word for Database Marketing.

Respondent   Someone who has answered a direct response letter or advertisement.

Response Device   On every outgoing direct mail piece, there is included a response device which usually shows up in the "window" in the envelope to provide the name and address. The response device is an order or donation form. It is important because it always contains the prospect number, and a source code that identifies the offer, package, list, segment, etc.

Response Rate   The percentage of people who responded to your offer. A typical direct mail response rate to prospects is 2 percent.

Retention   The tendency to keep customers buying. Success is measured by retention of customers.

Retention Budget   A budget for a program to keep customers from leaving.

Retention Rate   The percentage of last year's customers that are still buying this year.

Return on Investment (ROI)   A key measure of the success of any direct marketing activity. It is the total net profit from a direct marketing initiative, divided by the total cost of the entire operation. ROI from an initial offer is often negative. But when customer lifetime value is taken into account, it often becomes positive.

RFM   Stands for Recency, Frequency, Monetary. It is a method for segmenting or rating your customers. The best customers are those who have bought from you recently, buy many times, and in large amounts.

RFP   Request for Proposals; the document which is used to get external database service bureaus to bid on maintaining your marketing database.

Rollout   After a direct mail test of a few thousand letters, a rollout is the mailing to the rest of the names on the successful lists. It may be preceded by a second test or "continuation."

ROP Run of press, or Run of Paper. Advertising space purchased which the paper may insert wherever they see fit.

SAA System Application Architecture. An IBM term for a system whereby PCs can be connected to and used to run mainframes by co-operative processing.

Satisfaction Survey A survey of customers designed as much to learn something about customers for relationship building purposes as it is to learn about good and bad features of your servicing of the customers.

Saturated Market A situation in which everyone has the product, and the market is essentially a replacement market. For example, tires, batteries, room air conditioners, televisions.

SCF Sectional Center Facility. The first three digits of the Zip Code.

Seeds Names of yourself, friends, relatives, or employees inserted in a direct mail mailout to track delivery and quality, and to safeguard against unauthorized mailings. Also called Decoys.

Segmentation To divide outgoing direct mail into coded groups for testing or to improve response.

Sequential The way records are arranged on a tape. The opposite is random order, or a relational database.

SIC Code A coding system designed by the Department of Commerce for classifying the products and services produced by companies. It is a very inadequate system, but it is the only one around.

SKU Stock Keeping Unit A warehouse term for the products that a company produces. Each different product has its own SKU number.

Software Programs that run on computers. Programs tell the computer what to do in a step-by-step fashion.

Source Code A series of letters or numbers affixed to an outgoing advertisement or promotion that identifies the list, the offer, the package, and the segment (as well as the media) in which the promotion was made. Essential to testing the success of any direct marketing effort. The source code must appear on the response device (or in the case of telephone orders, must be asked for by the telemarketers).

SQL   A query language used with the IBM software DB2. Often pronounced "sequel."

SRI   Stanford Research Institute. A leading research institution which pioneered Psychographics.

Statement   An offer or newsletter included with a monthly Stuffer invoice or statement to a customer.

Storage   The capacity which a computer has for storing names, addresses, and other data. Storage is usually on magnetic disks, and is measured in megabytes (for a PC) or gigabytes (for a mainframe).

Stratification   Adding demographics to a name and address file.

Suppression   Using names on one tape (a customer file) to suppress or drop names from another tape (a prospect file).

Sweepstakes   An offer promising a randomly drawn prize to all respondents, regardless of whether they buy your product. Those who do not buy, but still respond to the sweepstakes, may be valuable names for rental or for other offers. In comparison to buyers, sweepstakes respondents are generally much less valuable.

System Integrator   Someone who can integrate the functions that have been outsourced to several different companies.

Tape   Magnetic tape is 1/2 inch wide, and holds about 300,000 customer records (depending on their size). Tape records are sequential (one after the other) whereas disk records can be in random order. Tape is the cheapest way to store information, but the data is hard to get at. Tape is used for backup and for sending information from one computer to another. Direct marketing tapes are 9 track, and 1600 or 6250 bytes per inch. They are ASCII or EBCDIC.

Target Marketing A marketing strategy aimed at a particular individual or group rather than to mass media.

Telemarketing Talking on the telephone to prospects or customers. Inbound telemarketing is usually customers or prospects calling your 800 number. Outbound telemarketing is when you place the call to a prospect or customer. Telemarketing can be done by your in-house staff or by an external telemarketing company.

Terminal A device that looks like a television screen with a keyboard which, when hooked up to a computer, enables you to enter data into the computer, and receive data from it which you see on the screen. The alternative to a terminal is a PC.

Test Database All marketing databases should have a companion test database which programmers use to write and test new software before it goes on the production database.

Third Class Over 85 percent of all mail carrying advertising or promotion is sent by third class. It is much less costly than first class. It usually requires postal pre-sort. Over 790,000 businesses and non-profits have third class mailing permits.

Tiger A census system for mapping the entire United States by Blocks, complete with roads and other landmarks. Customers and prospects can be shown on a map using geodemographic codes to represent where they are.

Update To modify a database record to insert new information into it, or to delete it. Updating is either done in batch mode (fast and cheap) or on-line (slow and costly).

Up Selling Prompting customers to buy upgraded products when they had intended to buy something of lower value.

UPS Uninterruptable Power Supply. A system of batteries that permits a mainframe to keep going even when the power fails. It is usually connected to a diesel generator that kicks in as soon as the batteries have begun to be needed.

WATS   Wide area telephone service. An 800 number whereby the call is free to the caller.

Weights   Numbers that are multiplied by database values to determine model or RFM scores.

White Mail   Mail received from a buyer or donor who has not included the response device, so you cannot determine the source code of the offer which promoted his purchase or gift.

Index

Also by Arthur Middleton Hughes

Strategic Database Marketing
Probus Publishing Company: 1994

The Complete Database Marketer
Probus Publishing Company: 1991

The American Economy
Norvec Publishing Company: 1968